DRAMA OF THE AGE

A DIVINE DRAMA IN SEVEN ACTS

An Exposition of the Book of Revelation

by

John Carroll Brown

Xulon
PRESS

KJV – King James Version
NKJV – New King James Version
NRSV – New Revised Standard Version
ASV – American Standard Version

ACKNOWLEDGEMENTS

I must acknowledge the invaluable help of my wife, Carldene Brown, in proof-reading the manuscript after I had done my best. She was able to find many errors that I had overlooked. She was also able to suggest rewordings that better expressed what I was trying to say. She also expressed great belief in this effort and gave strong encouragement. Thanks are due to my sons and daughters, as well as many other friends and students from whom I also received encouragement. I must also thank my son-in-law, Roland Bowen for the use of some of his electronic equipment and for some technical help along the way. Without the help of Rod Davis and a some of his friends I would not have been able to get this volume into print. I owe him much thanks, as well as some copies of this book.

TABLE OF CONTENTS

THINGS TO TAKE PLACE AFTER THIS
Part One: PREPARING FOR THE DRAMA

THINGS THAT ARE TO TAKE PLACE AFTER THIS
Part Two: THE DRAMA OF THE AGE IN SEVEN ACTS

APPENDICES

TABLES

PREFACE

A red dragon with seven heads; a seven-headed beast with ten horns that looks like a mixture of a leopard, lion, and bear; an idol that speaks; stars falling to earth; locusts with scorpion tails and hair like a woman's hair; winged creatures with faces like a lion, ox, eagle and man; a massive army of 200,000,000 soldiers on horses with lion heads and serpent tails—all this seems to come right out of the fantasies of science fiction, yet you find all this and lots more in the book of Revelation. This, however, is only part of the reason that interest in the book of Revelation is at an all time high.

Many have looked to the book of Revelation to find the meaning of current events that are taking place at a dizzying pace. Radio and Television evangelists fill the airwaves with attempts to connect the latest world events to the symbolism in the book of Revelation. Many books based on some aspect of Revelation have been published in recent decades to exploit this interest. Some writers have achieved fame and wealth from such works. I do not fault a person for receiving fame or fortune as a result of a sincere attempt to explain the message and meaning of the Revelation; however, those of us who write on this subject must make sure that this is not our motive. Such motivations are likely to tempt us to produce sensationalism in our writings at the expense of truth. I expect neither fame nor fortune from this work because the views expressed in it are not in line with the popular views, nor are they fully in harmony with the traditional ways of interpreting Revelation.

I believe that the book of Revelation has an extremely important message for our age. Its message is not limited to one generation or one age, but encourages, instructs, and gives insights to every generation involved in the fight against evil.

Since so many have already written on the book of Revelation how are we to justify another attempt at exposition? I don't believe that the last word has yet been written on the book of Revelation, nor will this present work exhaust its possibilities. There are many insights into its message and meaning yet to come. I am convinced that there are insights and explanations in this work that have not been found in other works—concepts that deserve to be published. This fact alone, if it is indeed a fact, justifies this work's publication.

But someone might say, "There are so many views of Revelation presented that the result is confusion. Why add to the confusion with yet another work?" This question implies that it is better to be content with existing misunderstandings, with any falsehoods or inaccuracies they may contain, than to risk the confusion that may result in any effort to correct those misunderstandings. This is a dangerous idea, for it locks in error and locks out all effort to correct the error. Hopefully, as understanding and insight progress there will be a lessening of confusion for the diligent seeker. My prayer is that this work will contribute to that end.

A word about the progression of this writer's study is in order here. I have been a student of the book of Revelation ever since I was called upon to teach a class on the subject at the ripe old age of twenty. With fear and trembling I approached the subject, determined to limit the study to general truths which could be plainly drawn from the book—principles which have significant application in our own Christian lives. The class turned out to be a profitable one, and I can recommend this approach for anyone. Often these principles are overlooked or buried in our search for the deeper meanings of the symbolism in the book of Revelation. By the study, however, my appetite for an understanding of the deeper meanings was whetted, and I decided to search them out as best I could. That search generally conformed to the following pattern:

1. I began my study by reading and rereading the book many times, until its message began to fall into some orderly pattern or outline in my

mind—a practice which I have continued to this day. I did not begin by searching out what others had said upon the subject, not because of any disdain for the intelligence of others, but because of a profound faith in the ability of the Bible to interpret itself. If I began by filling my mind with all the contradictory views of men, it would only have made my task harder. It is better to approach a study without preconceived ideas, since those very ideas sometimes serve as a roadblock to true understanding.

This does not mean that I despise efforts at exposition. After all, is not this book just such an effort? I did, in fact, begin to refer to commentaries and other reference works later in an effort to detect errors in my own thinking, and fine tune my own understanding. I especially sought to obtain from them important background information on history, culture, customs, and so forth. However, my textbook for the study of the book of Revelation throughout this effort has been, and still is, the Bible itself.

2. I began to search the text carefully for interpretations to its symbols that are given within the book of Revelation itself. I was surprised to find how often Revelation gives its own interpretation. Such interpretations are often passed over or greatly modified and expanded by some expositors. I became convinced that when an interpretation is given in the book of Revelation itself it should be taken at face value, and our interpretations should be kept within that framework. Any interpretation which disagrees with Revelation's own interpretation should be rejected.

3. I became aware that the Old Testament is the crucible from which the symbolism of Revelation is formed—i.e., that most of its symbols are drawn from Old Testament references. The need for a thorough familiarity with the Old Testament—its narratives, institutions, and prophecies—became obvious. Without such knowledge a full grasp of Revelation is impossible. Very many of its symbols are drawn from Old Testament events, institutions, prophesies, and symbolism. Some of these symbols, while not interpreted in Revelation, are interpreted for us elsewhere in the Bible. These interpretations are invaluable to our understanding of the Revelation. Care must be taken in applying Old Testament symbols however, for often it is only the general meaning and

not the specific Old Testament application that is to be applied to its use in the book of Revelation.

4. A fourth step in understanding is that the historical and cultural backgrounds of the nation of Israel, first century Christians, and the Roman Empire play an important role in the symbolism of Revelation. Histories, encyclopedias, Bible dictionaries, and commentaries are some of the works that are helpful for such studies.

5. As my skill in the use of the original language (*Koine* Greek) grew I began to search through the Greek text of Revelation to glean any grains of insight this might provide. This has been an invaluable tool, giving insights that are not apparent in the English translation, and sometimes are even covered up in the translating.

6. A technique I have employed is that of playing detective. This involves identifying all possible clues found in the text, and using both inductive and deductive reasoning to discover the facts. This demands that all clues be considered. To do this a certain amount of organizing, classifying and comparing is necessary. In the symbolism of Revelation as well as that of related prophets such as Daniel, there are many clues given. Ignoring these clues can lead to erroneous interpretations. On the other hand, if duly noted, they can result in the discovery of the truth pertaining to the passage being considered. It is my conviction that an interpretation must account for all the details. An interpretation has to be wrong if any bit of information does not fit.

This approach to the study of revelation is a study which has occupied my attention off and on for the past 50 plus years, resulting in this present work. The views presented here have been revised and refined over that period of time through teaching weekly Bible classes and seminars, including teaching the Revelation during eighteen years with the Bay Area School of Religion.

I have used the New King James Version throughout this book. When another version is quoted the fact is duly noted. Rather than quote all the Revelation passages being dealt with, I have merely given the reference, trusting that the reader will have his/her Bible open to the passages under discussion and will read them directly from the Bible. Comparison of various translations is encouraged. Wherever words or phrases within a scripture quotation are emphasized, the emphases are inserted by me. Notations inserted within brackets are mine.

Since I have attempted to write in a style that the average person can read with ease, I have tried to avoid using footnotes or endnotes except where it seemed necessary. When explanations are so lengthy that they interrupt the continuity of the text, I have placed them in appendices to which the reader is referred in the text.

Often the desire to publish was suppressed despite the urging of students, due to the realization that each time I study the book anew, invariably I make some adjustments in my views of its interpretation. However, I have come to realize that if I wait until I reach the point where no further adjustments will be made I will never get these insights into print.

It is with this humble realization that I submit this volume containing my present understanding (or misunderstanding as the case may be) of the interpretation of the book of Revelation. It is my prayer that all who read it may find help in understanding the message delivered by the Angel of the Lord to John on Patmos.

John Carroll Brown, June, 2005

INTRODUCTION

Before attempting an interpretation of the book of Revelation we need to answer some questions about the writing of the book. This will help us put the contents in their proper perspective. The things we need to consider are: 1. Who is the writer? 2. What is the date of the writing? 3. What are the various theories of interpretation men have used, and which, if any, is valid? 4. What are the principles of interpretation used in this volume? 5. How is the book of Revelation organized?

I. THE WRITER – JOHN THE APOSTLE

A. *JOHN WAS WELL KNOWN IN THE PROVINCE OF ASIA*

The Roman province of Asia was situated at the western end of Asia Minor. John came to this region after the destruction of Jerusalem in A.D. 70 or, at the earliest, shortly before this event. There is no compelling evidence that places him there earlier than approximately A.D. 68. He spent many years working among the churches there. Revelation is addressed to seven churches in Asia by the writer who simply calls himself *John*. Apparently he expected the churches to know him and recognize his authority. This would seem to indicate his importance among the churches there.

B. *A WITNESS OF CHRIST*

John identified himself at the outset as the one who "bore witness to the word of God, and to the testimony of Jesus Christ, to all things that he saw." John said that he **bore** witness, not that he is bearing witness or is about to bear witness; i.e., he is not speaking of what he is about to write in the book of Revelation but of some prior testimony. This testimony was about:

1

1. The Word of God. Perhaps we should capitalize *Word* since in John 1:1,14 the apostle uses this as a name for the Christ. This is its stated meaning in Rev. 19:13 and this is also its probable meaning in 1 John 1:1.

2. The Testimony of Christ. John bore witness to the words and teachings of Jesus—i.e., the things he had heard Jesus speak, especially as Jesus testified of heavenly things.

3. All That He Saw. John had witnessed the deeds of Christ as well as other marvels, such as His resurrection, which identified Him as the Son of God. He was a witness to the person, the words, and the works of Jesus Christ. In John 21:24 John said of himself: "This is the disciple who testifies of these things, and wrote these things, and we know that his testimony is true." In 1 John 1:1-3 he wrote:

> That which was from the beginning, which we have heard, which we have seen with our eyes, which we have looked upon, and our hands have handled, concerning the Word of life—the life was manifested, and **we have seen, and bear witness**, and declare to you the eternal life which was with the Father and was manifested to us—that which we have seen and heard, we declare to you....

Jesus appointed the apostles (including John) to be His witnesses. He said to them in John 15:27, "And you also will bear witness, because you have been with me from the beginning." Their task was to testify of what they had seen and heard concerning Jesus Christ. Just before His ascension Jesus said to them, "Thus it is written, and thus it was necessary for the Christ to suffer and to rise from the dead the third day.... And **you are witnesses of these things**." (Luke 24:46-48)

Jesus also said to His apostles, "But you shall receive power when the Holy Spirit has come upon you; and **you shall be witnesses** to Me in Jerusalem, and in all Judea and Samaria, and to the end of the earth." (Acts 1:8)

When the eleven remaining apostles met to determine who would take the place of Judas among them, they required that it be someone who had been with them from the beginning of the Lord's ministry until the day He ascended, so that he might "become **a witness with us** of His resurrection"

(Acts 1:21-22). On the day of Pentecost Peter stood up with the other eleven (2:14) and proclaimed, "This Jesus God has raised up, of which **we [the twelve] are all witnesses**" (2:32). In Acts 5:32, Peter and the other apostles answered the high priest and council concerning the things they were teaching with these words, "...and **we are His witnesses** to these things, and *so* also *is* the Holy Spirit whom God has given to those who obey Him."

All these considerations indicate a high degree of probability that the John who wrote the Revelation was the apostle John who wrote both the gospel of John and the letters of John, and that the witness which John bore at some time prior to Rev. 1:2 was the testimony which is recorded in the gospel of John.

C. JOHANNINE EXPRESSIONS IN REVELATION

Revelation contains many expressions which are strictly those of the gospel of John, the letters of John, and the Revelation, expressions which are not used by the other New Testament writers:

1. The Word. Only these writings use *the Word* as a name for Jesus, as in John 1:1, 14; 1 John 1:1; Rev. 19:13; and probably Rev. 1:2.

2. The Lamb. In the New Testament, only the writings of John use *The Lamb* as a title for Jesus. Others speak of His being **like** a lamb, but only John uses *The Lamb* as a name for the Christ (see John 1:29; Rev. 5:6,12; 6:1,16; etc.).

3. The Piercing of Jesus. The writings of John are the only New Testament writings which speak of Jesus' being pierced (see John 19:34,37; 1 John 5:6; Rev. 1:7).

4. The Water of Life. The writings of John are the only ones which speak of *the water of life* (See John 4:14; 7:38; Rev. 7:17; 21:6; 22:1,17).

5. Jesus As a Witness, and the Testimony of Jesus. These writings are the only ones which speak of Jesus as a witness, or of the testimony of Jesus (see John 8:18; Rev. 1:2,5; 3:14).

6. The Thought Patterns and Means of Expression. The thought patterns and expressions in Revelation are like those of John whose gospel abounds in figures. From a comparison of the expressions and terminology

3

used in the Revelation which are exclusive to the apostle John among New Testament writers, the probability of the writer's being that apostle is very great.

D. THE QUALITY OF THE GREEK COMPARED TO HIS OTHER WRITINGS

The quality of the Greek used in the Revelation has been represented as a definite proof that the apostle John did not in fact write the Revelation. This conclusion, I believe, is premature. Although the Greek of Revelation is less classical and deemed to be grammatically inferior to the gospel of John, the language is, after all, exactly what one would expect from John under the circumstances. Consider the following:

1. Different Subject Matter. First, the Revelation has a very different theme and emphasis than the gospel. It fulfills a different need and has a different purpose. The gospel of John focused upon the life and teachings of Christ and was written to engender faith in Jesus Christ in the hearts of the readers. John declares in John 20:31, ". . .these are written that you may believe that Jesus is the Christ, the Son of God, and that believing you may have life in His name."

Revelation, in contrast to this, focuses upon the victory of the saints in Jesus Christ; the sufferings they must go through on the way to victory; God's working in history to bring judgments upon those who oppress the saints; and ultimately, the triumph of the forces of right over the world and Satan. It was written to give assurance and consolation to those who suffer for the cause of Christ.

2. The Gospel Written Deliberately and Carefully. The gospel of John appealed to the philosophic mind, and dealt with various concepts of Greek philosophy and early Gnosticism. It was written to the unbeliever (particularly to the Greek) to convince him that Jesus is indeed the Son of God and the only Savior by which men may come to God. Jesus is presented as the Word, a concept first found in the early Greek philosophers as they pondered the ultimate cause and underlying reason behind all things. Jesus is set forth as that first cause and source of all things. This Word became flesh, thus refuting the teachings of the Gnostics who denied that God could or would come in the flesh. The gospel of John was a very scholarly and careful treatise or apology written for the Greek mind-set. We would expect the writer to take pains to use the best and most grammatically accurate Greek at his command.

3. Revelation Written Hastily. On the other hand, John wrote Revelation in the heat and excitement of the visions which He was seeing. Rev. 10.4 says, "Now when the seven thunders uttered their voices, **I was about to write**; but I heard a voice from heaven saying to me, 'Seal up the things which the seven thunders uttered, and do not write them.'" John was about to write what he had just seen; this indicates that he was writing down the visions as he saw them. The language which John uses expresses the nature and excitement of the Revelation.

Take any professional writer, place him in different circumstances, at widely different times in his life, let him write in a variety of literary styles, including dissertations for scholarly publication, novels, letters to close friends, news articles covering exciting events, etc. and you will certainly find that the style and quality of the language he or she uses will vary widely. There are no differences between the language and style of the gospel of John and Revelation which will not fit well within these boundaries, and which cannot be explained by this same logic.

4. The Need to Grasp the Precision of His Grammar. I believe that many of the so-called grammatical errors in Revelation are seen as errors because of a failure on the part of the critics to grasp the writer's intent and the significance of the seemingly aberrant uses of tense and case. Some notable examples are brought out in the exposition of the text in later chapters of this work. As a case in point, Rev. 1:5 speaks of the fact that Jesus "...loves [present tense] us and washed [aorist tense] us from our sins in his own blood...." (Most versions say *loosed us* or *freed us* instead of *washed us*.) Some translators want to render these as "loved" and "loosed" in order to correct the grammar and make the verbs agree in tense. To do so, however, misses the point. The love of Jesus is an ongoing love as expressed in the present tense while the loosing from sins is an accomplished fact of history, a completed work, finished at the cross, best expressed with the aorist tense. In other words, John said exactly what he meant, and the statement needs no correction to make it grammatical.

5. Ease of Translation. Add to the above considerations the fact that the gospel of John and Revelation share the distinction of being the easiest books in the New Testament for Greek students to translate and you will begin to understand that the Greek of Revelation is very much like that of the gospel of John. These considerations indicate that the differences need not be explained by assigning them to different authors. The same John could well have written all five of the New Testament books ascribed to him. The evidence, aside from the comparison of the Greek, favors strongly the view that they were all written by the apostle John.

E. The Testimony of Early Christian Writers

Christian writers before A.D. 265 are unanimous in assigning authorship of the Revelation to the apostle John. These writers include Justin Martyr, Irenaeus (whose teacher, Polycarp had been a disciple of John), Clement of Alexandria, Tertullian, Origen, and Hippolytus among others.

It is only with the increase of the time span following the writing of Revelation that some writers began to express doubts as to whether the apostle John wrote it. If indeed the apostle John did not write it then surely many of those closest to the time of its writings would have had at least an inkling that this was a different John. This, however, is not the case.

II: THE DATE – APPROXIMATELY A.D. 95

A. THE HISTORICAL SETTING

1. The Roman Empire... The empire was near its peak of greatness. It had built itself on conquest and trade. A great contrast existed between wealth and luxury on one hand, and dire poverty on the other. Moral conditions were about as low as they could go. Rome, as the headquarters of pagan religions, sent out representatives to various provinces to enforce emperor worship. Domitian was vigorously pursuing a policy of enforced emperor worship, and he had instigated the most widespread and vigorous persecution of Christians of the first century.

2. The Church. The church was undergoing its most trying period of persecution in the first two and one-half centuries of existence. Property was being confiscated, families broken up, Christians tortured, exiled and put to death. Earlier persecutions had been localized, while this persecution, although universal, was especially intense in the Roman province of Asia,

6

perhaps because of the great concentration of Christians there after the destruction of Jerusalem. Christians under such persecution were in danger of yielding to pressures to compromise with idolatry and to enjoy the security and luxury that could be theirs if they were willing to consort with the world. The church was also having its problems with false teachers such as Judaizers, Gnostics, Nicolaitans, Docetists, etc.

B. THE CONDITIONS MATCH

The conditions of the Roman Empire and of the church as set forth in Revelation fit the date A.D. 95 better than any other date suggested.

1. Universal Persecution of the Church. Prior to the destruction of Jerusalem (A.D. 70) there was no universal persecution of Christians by Rome. Domitian (A.D. 81 to 96) was the first emperor to instigate such widespread persecution. Even Nero's persecution in the 60's was limited to Rome, and it was only instigated because Nero needed someone to blame for the burning of Rome.

2. The Beast. Some expositors have attempted to identify Nero as the beast with the seven heads pictured in Rev. 13. Others have identified Domitian as the symbolic resurrection of Nero and his persecution, and thus the beast whose head received a death wound, but then revived. Both views are preterist views—i.e. those who view Revelation as having all been fulfilled in the first century, or at most in the first three centuries. In my opinion the beast is neither, and is not to be identified with a certain man, but with persecuting kingdoms that have usurped world dominion.

3. For All Christians. Some would point out that the Revelation was written to the seven churches of Asia (the province) and these were all situated within a very small portion of the eastern tip of Asia Minor (present day Turkey) and that a limited persecution like the one instigated by Nero would fill the bill. This ignores the fact that these seven churches were far away from Rome. The Aegean Sea, the Adriatic Sea, the Grecian peninsula and the bulk of the Italian land mass stood between them and Rome. A persecution taking place in the city of Rome could hardly be applicable to these churches.

Furthermore, these churches were representative. They stood in the place of the whole church the world over, throughout all time. "He who has an ear let him hear what the Spirit says to the churches." In the symbolic picture of the persecution and tribulation which the churches have to suffer, the persecution is far broader than just a limited area. It is a picture of universal persecution.

4. No Religious Toleration. Prior to the destruction of Jerusalem the Jews, as a conquered people, were generally granted religious toleration by the Roman Empire. Christians enjoyed protection under that same umbrella, since they were considered a sect of the Jews at that time. This restraint no longer applied after the elimination of the Jewish nation by Titus (Titian) when he led his troops in the destruction of Jerusalem. Christianity soon became recognized as a religion of its own. Since that religion was no longer associated with a particular conquered nation, but spread among all nationalities throughout the Roman world, it no longer enjoyed the protection of the government's policy of toleration; it was therefore denounced as an illegal religion.

There are a few notable exceptions to the tolerance of both Jews and Christians before Jerusalem's destruction—especially in the city of Rome itself. When Paul was occupied with his missionary journeys the emperor of Rome decided to drive out the Jews from that city. Priscilla and Aquila, who came to be Paul's associates in the gospel, were victims of that edict. Later Nero tried to divert the blame for the burning of Rome from himself by putting the blame on Christians, beginning a very severe persecution of the Christians in that city. These examples, however, were the exceptions, not the rule.

5. The Image of the Beast. Emperor worship began to be enforced on a widespread scale for the first time during the reign of Domitian. Images of the emperor were erected throughout the empire, and worship of these images became a test of loyalty to Rome. If Revelation was in fact written during this period, Christians everywhere would be familiar with the enforcement of emperor worship, and many would have already suffered because of it. Some of the symbolism in Revelation is drawn from this background. Because of the images of the emperors which were forced upon them, they could relate to "the image of the beast" as the symbol of something that was to take place in the future.

C. No Sound Basis for Early Date

The earlier date (prior to A.D. 70) for the writing of Revelation is almost exclusively held by those who advocate the *Preterist* view. This is usually based upon an interpretation of the reference to the temple and Jerusalem in chapter 11 as being the literal temple in literal Jerusalem. If the temple had still been standing then the writing would have to be before the destruction of Jerusalem since in A.D. 70 the temple was totally destroyed. The temple and the city are not literal but are used as symbols of the people of God, the church. Many symbols are drawn from the historical background of the destruction of Jerusalem—the three and one-half year siege, the conditions in the city, including the scarcity of wheat and barley during the siege—these are all used to tell the church of the persecution it would have to endure as the "Jerusalem which is from above," and as the "temple of God."

Many preterists see the Revelation fulfilled in the destruction of Jerusalem, that irs message was for Christians prior to A.D. 70, and that the bulk of its prophecies were fulfilled in the three and a half year siege ending in the city's destruction. If this is the case the book has little to offer any Christian who was not in the city of Jerusalem prior to its destruction. The destruction of Jerusalem was a judgment brought by God upon the nation of Israel. Most Christians living there escaped the siege as a result of Jesus' warning which is recorded in Matthew 24:15-21. Jerusalem's tribulation of can only apply to Christians in a symbolic sense, since it was directed against the Jews of Jerusalem not Christians. The church is the "heavenly Jerusalem," and its persecution is symbolized by the three and a half year period of suffering of the city of Jerusalem. Besides, Revelation was not addressed to Jerusalem but to Christians in the province of Asia?

If John is indeed the writer of the Revelation, then a pre-destruction date could not apply. John's relationship to the churches of Asia was not well established prior to A.D. 70. His exile on the isle of Patmos was not consistent with the practice of earlier emperors, but such exiles were commonplace in the reign of Domitian.

III. THEORIES OF INTERPRETATION

A. PRETERIST (PAST)—THE BOOK OF REVELATION LONG AGO FULFILLED

Some hold that Revelation was fulfilled during the first century A.D. Others hold that it was fulfilled within the first three centuries after it was written.

1. Modernists who hold the preterist view say that someone named John wrote the book in the second or later centuries about events that took place in the first century. These do not believe in predictive prophecy. Any prophecy which sets forth factual events of history had to be written after their fulfillment according to this view.

2. Some preterists accept the date of approx. A.D. 95 as the date when Revelation was written, but teach that its prophecies were fulfilled within the next few years, or within the first three hundred years.

3. Dating the book in the late 50's or in the 60's is almost exclusively done by preterists who hold that its prophecies were substantially fulfilled in the destruction of Jerusalem.

4. Most preterists are amillennialists—i.e., they teach that there is not to be a distinct period (millennium) of prosperity and favor to be enjoyed worldwide by the church. To some the millennium is the whole of the Christian age while others hold the view that the millennial reign is the reign of the souls of the martyred saints in heaven.

B. FUTURIST—REVELATION TO BE FULFILLED AT THE END OF THIS AGE

The futurist theory sees the fulfillment of Revelation in the events just preceding and just following the second coming of Christ.

1. These claim to be literalists. That is, they say that most of the events described in the book are to be taken literally.

2. Virtually all futurists are premilliennialists—i.e., they teach that Christ is coming back before (pre) the millennium of Rev. 20 to set up His kingdom and reign over the whole earth for a literal thousand years. All the righteous dead will be raised at his coming to reign with him. At the end of the thousand years, the wicked will be raised.

3. Dispensationalism is the most extreme form of premillennialism. It is the brand that is most popular today, having been popularized by many fundamentalist evangelists such as Hal Lindsay. This view says that history covers seven dispensations of a thousand years each. The seventh is the millennium, corresponding to the seventh day Sabbath. These see almost the entire book of Revelation fulfilled in a period of seven years during which the saints will be "raptured" or caught up with Christ in the air and the world will undergo "the great tribulation."

During this time the Jews, having returned to Palestine, will be converted and undergo three and a half years of severe persecution by the "Antichrist." At the end of the seven years Christ comes back with the saints to destroy the wicked regime, set up His kingdom and reign a thousand years on the throne of David in Jerusalem. After this the wicked and the saints who have died meanwhile are all raised, then comes the final judgment and the end of the world.

4. Historical premillennialists do not hold to the idea of the earth's history being divided into seven dispensations of a thousand years. They do not generally accept the idea of a seven year rapture. At the second coming Christ defeats His enemies and sets up His reign for a thousand years.

C. CONTINUOUS HISTORICAL—A DETAILED PLAN OF WORLD HISTORY

1. This theory teaches that the **prophetic scenes are simply history written in advance** in symbolism. In its truest form this view sees in Revelation a progress of history as it pertains to the church, beginning at chapter one and proceeding chronologically through chapter 22. Each new set of visions is simply another phase in that history.

2. According to this view **much has been fulfilled already, some is being fulfilled, and some is yet to be fulfilled.**

3. Many of those who hold the continuous historical view are **postmillennialists**—i.e., they teach that there is to be a period of prosperity for the church following a period of severe persecution. The millennium is an indefinite period of time in length, since a thousand is seen as a symbol for a long period of time rather than exactly one thousand years. The means by which the righteous hold sway is by the power of the word of God rather than by might of arms. The heads of governments and those in positions of authority are converted to Christ, and rule in righteousness. Persecution and the deceit of false religions virtually cease. After (post) this millennium of indefinite length, Christ appears in his second coming, all the dead, both good and bad, are raised, judged, assigned their eternal destinies, and the world is brought to its end.

D. *PHILOSOPHY OF HISTORY—PRINCIPLES OPERATING IN HISTORY*

This theory interprets the visions of Revelation as **principles** which are in operation throughout the Christian era. These principles, (persecution, deceit, enticements, righteousness, perseverance, judgments of God, victory), explain the happenings of this whole age as being under the guidance and providence of God who reigns and will triumph over evil. The conflicts in Revelation are seen on a spiritual plane.

Adherents of this view can be found holding to premillennialism, post-millennialism, or amillennialism. Most however, hold the amillennial view, seeing the millennium of Rev. 20 as a picture of the reign of the saints in heaven during the whole of the Christian age. They, through death in Christ's service, are raised to thrones where they reign with Christ, while the saints on earth are still downtrodden and persecuted. Amillennialists do not look for the victory of conquest on this earth, but believe that they are destined to continue as a minority and be persecuted as long as the earth lasts. The victory is seen as the conquest of the forces of evil that will occur at the second coming of Christ and the end of the world.

1. According to this view **no specific events are foretold** except the second coming, final judgment, and the final rewards of the saints.

2. Many of those who hold this view see **each series of symbols as parallel to the others in that they each cover the whole of the Christian age.** Sometimes this view is combined with the historical to give, in each series of symbols, a broad outline of the history of the whole Christian age, without dealing with detailed events.

E. *LET THE REVELATION INTERPRET ITSELF*

1. Why must we pick out one theory to follow? In revealing the book the Holy Spirit was not limited to men's systems and categories. Actually some elements of all of these theories are found in Revelation.

—From Rev 1:1, 19; 4:1; and chapters 20 – 22, we learn that Revelation covers the whole of the Christian era.

—From Rev. 1:1, 19; and 4:1, we learn that Revelation was to be about things that were to occur in the future from John's time.

—From Rev. 2:7; 22:18-19, we learn that there are truths or principles to be applied in all ages, whenever and wherever a person has ears to hear.

2. We should **let the meanings fall as naturally as possible** without trying to force them into one theory or another.

IV. PRINCIPLES OF INTERPRETATION

A. *SEARCH OUT ANY INTERPRETATION THAT THE BOOK OF REVELATION ITSELF GIVES*

It is surprising how much of the book is self-interpreting, (e.g., Rev. 1:20; 17:18).

B. *SEEK FOR EXPLANATIONS GIVEN ELSEWHERE IN THE BIBLE*

1. Much **Old Testament symbolism** is adopted and adapted for use in Revelation, (e.g., Ezek. 1; Dan. 7; Ezek. 9:3-8; etc.)

2. Old Testament events and institutions often serve as the source of Revelation's symbolism (e. g., the plagues of Egypt [Exod. 7 – 11]; the tabernacle/temple and its furniture [Exod. 25 – 30], etc.). Many of those things are foreshadows explained elsewhere in the New Testament. For example, the symbolism of the temple is explained in Heb. 8 – 10.

C. *SEEK FOR CLUES IN THE HISTORICAL BACKGROUND OF REVELATION*

Examples of this are the destruction of Jerusalem, and the enforced worship of the image of the emperor.

D. SEARCH OUT CLUES FROM THE TRADITIONS OF JOHN'S ERA

The white horse of victory and the white stone of approval are examples of this.

E. READ AND REREAD, STUDY AND RESTUDY

Do this until you have a thorough grasp of the contents of the book. An attempt to interpret its parts separately will result in confusion. Its parts must fit the whole picture. One must have a thorough grasp of the overall outline of Revelation to see how its parts fit in. For instance, Rev. 20 cannot be interpreted properly without seeing how it fits into the overall plan of the drama given in chapters 12 – 22.

F. TAKE INTO CONSIDERATION ALL THE FACTS

Consider the facts both in the text under consideration and in other passages of Revelation, or elsewhere in the Bible, that address the same subject.

Much interpretation falls apart at this point. No interpretation can be right if it is out of harmony with any of the facts given in Revelation or elsewhere in scripture. For example, the interpretation of the beast of Rev. 13 must be done in the light of all the information given there, plus the information in Rev. 17, plus the information in Dan. 7.

G. MUST HARMONIZE WITH PLAIN STATEMENTS OF SCRIPTURE

For example, how does Rev. 20.6 harmonize with John 5:28-29?

1. Always interpret the ambiguous, the symbolic, and the unclear in the light of the plain, never the other way around.

2. Never ignore clear statements or attempt to force them into fitting a preconceived interpretation of the figures in Revelation.

H. ARE THE DETAILS BEST UNDERSTOOD AS AN EVENT OR AS A PRINCIPLE?

1. Sometimes the language implies a time frame, thus indicating an event, or group of events (e. g., Rev. 17:10, 8, 17; etc.).

2. Sometimes only a generic picture is presented, indicating a general truth (e. g., Rev. 6:1-2).

I. CONSIDER THE POSSIBILITY OF DOUBLE MEANINGS

Often prophecies were given in such a way as to be meaningful for the day in which they were written as well as for a day in the distant future.

Some things are applicable in the days of the writer. 2 Sam. 7:12-17 was fulfilled when Solomon, David's son ascended the throne and built the temple in Jerusalem. Some things, however, do not fit Solomon; i.e., his kingdom did not last forever.

Some things are applicable in a broader, more far-reaching and remote sense. E.g., this same prophecy was fulfilled centuries later by Christ ascending to the throne of God (Acts 2:29-36), and building his church (Matt. 16:18; 1 Tim. 3:15).

Perhaps some of the prophecies of Revelation have both a near and far fulfillment. For example, consider Rev. 13:14-15, 17-18 in this light.

V. ORGANIZATION AND CONTENT OF REVELATION

In order to understand the book of Revelation it is necessary to see the way the book is put together—its organization and content. That is our objective in this overview.

A. PRELUDE (1:1-8)

First John gives information about how the message came to him. He also provides some information about himself so we will know who he is—i.e., the John who bore witness to Christ. He tells us the source of the message (the three in the Godhead), and of its dedication to Christ our Savior.

After the introductory matter John is instructed to write Revelation in three divisions (1:19): 1) the things John had seen—i.e., the vision John saw in chapter 1; 2) the things which are; found in the letters of chapters 2 and 3; and 3) the things that will take place hereafter, including the rest of the book, including chapters 4 - 22. Obviously, the third division is the larger part of the book, dealing with future events from John's day. The closing remarks, or postlude, are found in Rev. 22:6-21.

B. *THINGS JOHN SAW (Rev. 1:9-20)*

These things include the vision of One like the Son of Man in the midst of seven lampstands which are the seven churches, holding seven stars in His right hand which are the angels (messengers) of the churches. Also included are the words of the voice that spoke to John and the assignment given to him by Christ—i.e., writing these things in a book and sending them to the seven churches.

C. *THINGS THAT ARE (Rev. 2 and 3)*

Seven churches in the Roman province of Asia are singled out as representative of the whole church, then and now. These churches are: 1) Ephesus; 2) Smyrna; 3) Pergamum; 4) Thyatira; 5) Sardis; 6) Philadelphia; and 7) Laodicea. The details given in the letters to these churches in chapters 2 and 3 can be found in congregations throughout the Christian age. The problems that were found in Ephesus can be found in congregations today.

The problems of Thyatira, Sardis and of Laodicea—in fact all seven—are typical of problems in churches today. Any congregation can see itself in one or more of these letters. The fact that Jesus says, "whoever has an ear, let him hear," is an indication of this.

In the seven letters we see a pattern that is found in the rest of the book. The churches were suffering temptations in three ways, just as we all do. 1) They were being deceived by false teachers; 2) they were being enticed by the things of the world; and 3) they were being persecuted and killed because of their faith and testimony. These are the only three ways that Satan has of subverting men. These are the trials that Christ Himself had to undergo. They are trials which Christians throughout the age must undergo.

D. *THINGS TO TAKE PLACE—PREPARATION FOR THE DRAMA (Rev. 4 – 11)*

In Rev. 4:1 – 22:5 we are given what John saw concerning the things that were to take place in the future. According to Rev. 1:1 these are things which were to begin to take place shortly. These things are divided into two parts.

16

The first is preparation for the action of the divine drama. The second is the playing out of the drama.

1. The Theater Where John Views the Visions of the Future. John is caught up to heaven where he sees the temple in heaven and the throne of God, with the glory of God on the throne. The things he sees in the temple correspond to the items found in the Old Testament tabernacle and temple. There are 18 items which can be identified, fifteen of which are found in chapters 4 and 5. The other three are seen in subsequent returns to the temple scene in chapters 6, 8, and 11. If we think of the visions of future events as a drama, then the temple in heaven is both the control room and the theater in which John views the drama.

2. Producer, Director, and Script. We have seen the theater, but who are the producer and director of the drama? Where is the script? What are the themes it presents? What is the plot? Who are the stars and other actors?

The script is seen in chapter 5 where the Lamb (Christ) receives the book from the hand of God. There are seven seals securing the book. The Lamb first must remove the seals before the script can be read. Obviously, God is both the author and producer of the drama. Since the script is given to the Lamb, then He is the director, the one placed in charge. We will also see that He is the star of the show, along with His people, the servants of God. In the language of drama He is called the *protagonist*, while later we see Satan, the Dragon, as the *antagonist* or in common terms, *the bad guy*.

3. Through Persecution to Vindication and Victory. In Rev. 6, as the Lamb removes each seal, John sees a vision revealing a portion of the theme of the drama. The foremost item in this theme is the ultimate victory of the saints. Meanwhile they must undergo bloodshed, economic oppression, and death because of their faith and testimony. The persecuted church cries out for vindication and justice (fifth seal), and God's answer is His wrath in judgment upon the world system which has persecuted and downtrodden the saints (sixth seal).

4. Protection Now, Glorification Then. In Rev. 7 time out is taken before the removal of the seventh seal to see the marking of the servants of God to protect them during His judgments upon the world. Also seen are the saints, redeemed and victorious, before the throne of God. When the seventh

17

seal is opened, the peace and rest of the saints in eternity is signified by silence (8:1).

5. Predominance of the Theme of Judgment. Special emphasis is placed upon the theme of God's judgments on the world, punishing the evildoers and vindicating the saints. Much of the book presents various pictures of the outpouring of God's wrath. Such judgments are seen as part of the vindication and victory of the saints in answer to their prayers. In chapters 8 and 9 the theme of judgment is expanded by showing the various ways in which God's judgments may be seen in this world.

Before the blowing of the last (seventh) trumpet which announces the final judgment and end of the world, there are six trumpets announcing warning judgments which are partial and not complete. The first four areas of judgment are parts of man's habitat—i.e., earth, sea, fresh water sources, and the heavens. Two judgments are directly against the persons of those who belong to the world. These are the mental torture of the sting of sin, and the physical destruction of life through warfare.

6. The Open Book. In the opening of the seals we have seen the themes which will be followed in the drama. Chapter 10 shows the book with its seals removed, lying open in the hand of the giant Angel of the Lord. The Angel gives it to John who is told to devour the book. His job is to reveal its contents to the nations. There is yet one more trumpet of judgment to blow. The last trump will announce the final judgment in which the plan of God for mankind on this earth will be finished. Before that trumpet is blown the plot of the drama is revealed to John in symbols representing a broad outline of events to take place.

7. The struggle between the forces of evil and good. In Chapter 11 the plot of the drama is presented. It gives two pictures of a period of persecution of the saints: 1) The holy city is trodden under the feet of the gentiles for 42 months; and 2) two witnesses, called two lampstands and two olive trees, prophesy in sackcloth for 1260 days (both time periods are the same). At the conclusion of the period of persecution is the apparent victory of evil over the servants of God. The two witnesses are killed by the beast which arises from the abyss. At the apparent defeat of the servants of God the world rejoices, but the rejoicing is short-lived. After a very brief time the witnesses come to life, ascend up into the clouds, and they are seen by all men men who are terrified by this event. There is a reversal of fortunes. One-tenth of the city of the world is destroyed, 7000 men are killed, and the rest give glory to God.

The meaning of this last event is revealed when the seventh trumpet is blown. The kingdom of the world has become the kingdom of the Lord, and of His Christ. God has taken His great power and has begun His reign, a reign which will extend through eternity. Three things take place in this order: 1) the Lord's reign over the kingdom of the world is established, 2) after this the nations rebel in rage against Christ, and 3) the time of judgment comes when God rewards the saints and prophets and destroys the destroyers of earth. The last trumpet announces the final judgment and end of the world, as may be seen elsewhere in the New Testament.

Now the temple in heaven is opened and the ark of God's covenant is visible. This as like the opening of the curtain to begin the play.

E. THINGS TO TAKE PLACE—THE DRAMA IN SEVEN ACTS (Rev. 12:1 – 22:5)

The division of this divine drama into acts is, of course, arbitrary. I have chosen seven divisions as the most natural without making any act too long. These are:

Act 1—Rev. 12;

Act 2—Rev. 13:1-14:5;

Act 3—Rev. 14:6 – 16:17;

Act 4—Rev. 16:18 – 19:10;

Act 5—Rev. 19:11-21;

Act 6—Rev. 20; and

Act 7—Rev. 21:1-22:5.

Rev. 12 and 13 deal with the conflict between the forces of good and of evil. Rev. 14-20 deal mostly with the wrath of God which is to be poured out on the forces of evil. Since God's judgment is presented from several different perspectives, and different pictures are given of the same event, it is a mistake to try to interpret everything chronologically.

Act 1. THE CONFLICT IN HEAVEN (Rev. 12)

The first act, Rev. 12, shows the basis of our spiritual warfare, the efforts of Satan to overthrow the plan of God. His target is first the Man-child (Christ), second the Woman (the body of God's people), and third the witnesses (individual followers of Christ). Israel (God's people prior to the cross) brings the Man-child into the world, but the Dragon (Satan) is waiting to devour Him. The Man-child, however, is caught up to God and His throne, out of the reach of the Dragon. Not seen in the act is the fact that as this scene is being played out in heaven, a young virgin on earth brings forth a Son who is to save His people from their sins. All the attempts of Satan to destroy Him are for naught. His final attempt was to crucify Christ, but even that failed to destroy Him. He broke the bonds of death, was raised to life, and a few days later was caught up to the throne of God where He reigns at God's right hand.

The death and resurrection of Christ, together with the preaching of God's eternal plan, is the occasion of the warfare in heaven pictured in chapter 12. Satan is defeated and cast down to earth by **the blood of the Lamb** and **the word of the testimony** of the brethren.

Now the Dragon's attention is turned to the woman with the crown of twelve stars. However, she escapes by the help of God to a place in the wilderness where she is nurtured from the presence of the Dragon for 1260 days (three and a half years). During this time the woman (God's people, the church) is safe from destruction.

Since the Dragon failed to destroy Christ, and the church is out of His reach, he turns his attention to the individual Christians, the children of the woman, who bear testimony to Christ.

Act 2. THE CONFLICT ON EARTH (Rev. 13:1 – 14:5)

The Beast—the Persecutor. In Act 2 the resulting conflict is seen on earth. Satan calls forth an agent from the sea, **persecution**, personified as the Beast with seven heads and ten horns. This conflict is for the same period that the woman is in the wilderness. It is expressed this time as 42 months, during which the Beast is given the task of making war on the saints.

Although the church is out of his reach, Satan can still persecute and kill individual Christians.

The False Prophet—the Deceiver. A second agent of Satan is called forth from the earth, the personification of **deceit and false teaching**. He is pictured as a beast with two horns and is later called *the False Prophet*. His task is to deceive the nations. He is given the authority of the first Beast which he exercises in the presence of the Beast, directing the operations of the Beast. The False Prophet is embodied in the false religions which are established through his false teachings. He, through them, deceives the nations so that they worship the Beast and make war on the saints. The Beast is embodied in governments that serve Satan in persecuting the saints.

The Victory of the Saints. The victory of the saints is seen in Rev. 14:1-5 as they stand on Mt. Zion before the throne of God with the Lamb. There they praise God and sing a song of exultation.

Act 3. SCENES OF GOD'S WRATH (14:6 – 16:21)

Judgment Announced (14:6-13). Three angels fly through the heaven announcing the time of God's final judgment, the day of wrath. The first is a general announcement, the second announces the destruction of Babylon the Harlot, and the third announces God's wrath on those who worship the Beast.

Reaping the Harvests (14:14-20). Judgment is presented as the reaping of two harvests—the harvest of the grain (righteous) and the harvest of the grapes (wicked). Christ himself harvests the grain when an angel from the temple announces the time. An angel reaps the grapes and throws them into the winepress of God's wrath at the instruction of an angel from the altar. There they are trodden and a great amount of blood comes out of the wine press.

Seven Bowls of Wrath (15 – 16). In another group of symbols God's judgment is pictured in terms of plagues poured out upon mankind. Four bowls of wrath are poured out on earth, the sea, the fresh water sources, and the sun. Unlike the trumpet judgments, the bowls bring total destruction to man's habitat. The symbolism is drawn from the plagues of Egypt, as were the seven trumpet judgments.

The dust of the earth produces boils or sores upon men, the sea and fresh water sources are turned to blood. Every living thing in and on the sea dies, and men have nothing to drink but blood. The sun becomes so hot it scorches men. The fifth bowl produces great pain and men curse God because of the sores and pain. When the sixth bowl is poured out the Dragon, Beast, and False Prophet gather the nations at Armageddon in preparation for the final battle. The end comes with the outpouring of the last bowl. "It is done." What we see in the first six bowls is a symbolic picture of events immediately preceding the final judgment.

Act 4. BABYLON THE HARLOT (17:1 – 19:10)

Babylon and the Beast Explained (17). Act 4 focuses upon the judgment of Babylon the Harlot. She is referred to for the first time in the announcement of her fall in chapter 14. Her destruction is announced again at the end of chapter 16 in preparation for the description of her judgment. Chapter 17 takes time out to explain both the Harlot and the Beast. The Harlot is **a third agent of Satan**, the counterpart of the woman with the crown of 12 stars in chapter 12.

There are two realms or systems represented by these two women. The woman with the crown of stars is the body of Christ consisting of the saints of God. She is also represented as the holy city New Jerusalem and the pure bride of Christ. The Harlot, robed in purple and Scarlet is the world system, and incorporates the people of the world. She is called *Sodom and Egypt* in chapter 11. Here she is called *Babylon*, and is portrayed as the ruling city, Rome, in the days of John. She is the farthest thing from a pure virgin for she is a harlot, and her purpose is to entice the nations and peoples of the world into indulging the lust of the flesh, the lust of the eye, and the pride of life. Worldliness and materialism are her stock in trade.

She sits astride the heads of the beast, indicating that she exercises a controlling influence over the governments. She holds out her cup of abominations to them. She also sits on the many waters, indicating her influence on the peoples and nations of the world.

Destruction of Babylon the Harlot. In Rev. 18 her destruction is announced again, and the chapter proceeds to describe her judgment in symbols drawn from the Old Testament prophets. In the first part of Rev. 19

the rejoicing of the saints over her destruction ends with the celebration of the marriage of the Lamb to His bride, the saints of God. His bride is clothed in fine linen pure and white, representing the righteous deeds of the saints. The contrast to the Harlot is striking. She who is impure represents the allurements of the world, is made up of "those who dwell on earth," and is destined for utter destruction—to be burned with fire. She who is pure represents the people of God and is destined to be joined with Christ, to live with Him through eternity.

Act 5. DESTRUCTION OF THE BEAST AND FALSE PROPHET (19:11-21)

The Triumvirate. The three weapons that Satan uses to subvert the souls of men are the allurements of the world (the Harlot), the deceit of false religions, philosophies, and science (the False Prophet), and the coercion of persecution, torture, and death (the Beast). We have just seen the destruction of the Harlot. Now in Act 5 we see the destruction of the Beast and False Prophet.

The Second Coming. Christ comes from heaven with His holy angels, all riding on white horses. This is the second coming.

The Destruction of the Beast and False Prophet. The Beast and False Prophet have gathered the nations for the final battle. The Beast and the False Prophet are taken and thrown into the lake of fire (hell).

All Who Are Of the World Are Slain. The people of the nations who are gathered against Christ are killed with the sword (word of God) from the mouth of Christ, and the birds feast upon the dead bodies. Once more we come to the end. The details of the resurrection and final judgment are seen in Rev. 20:11-15.

Act 6. THE MILLENNIUM AND DESTRUCTION OF SATAN (Rev. 20)

The 1000 Year Reign (20:1-6). Time out is taken from the pictures of judgment to go back 1000 years and give some details of the victory of the saints on earth. There has been a previous reference to this reign in 11:11-17. The time of the reign of the saints on earth is given as 1000 years. Before that can take place Satan must be banished from the earth so that he can no longer deceive the nations and rouse them to make war on the saints. He is chained and cast into the lowest region of Hades, called *the bottomless pit,* or *the abyss,* for 1000 years. The persecuted church, formerly seen as the souls of the witnesses under the altar, is now seen as souls raised to thrones. Judgment is given on their behalf, and they who have lived with Christ through times of tribulation now reign with Him for 1000 years. Satan is released from his prison only after the 1000 years is completed.

The Judgment of the Dragon—Satan (20:7-10). Now we return to the scenes of Judgment. This time it is pictured as the judgment of Satan himself. Satan, released from the abyss, deceives the nations again (the work of the False Prophet), and enlists them to make war on the saints (the work of the Beast). We see another picture of the gathering of the nations for the final battle. Once more we see an immediate defeat of the forces of evil. Fire comes down from heaven and destroys the nations arrayed against the saints. Satan is taken and cast into the lake of fire (hell), just as the Beast and False Prophet had been in the previous scene of judgment. The two scenes of 19:19-21 and 20:7-10 are not separate judgments, but two pictures of the same judgment, one from the perspective of the Beast and False Prophet, and one from the perspective of the Dragon.

The Wicked Dead. In both judgment scenes all those who are on Satan's side as part of the world system are killed. This is one of the ways that we know that they are two pictures of the same judgment scene. In Rev. 19:11-21 they are killed by the sword (word of God) proceeding from Christ's mouth. In Rev. 20:7-10 they are killed by fire from heaven. These are two different ways of picturing the same judgment. While those in the camp of the saints are still alive, all the wicked have been killed and are awaiting the resurrection.

The Final Judgment (20:11-15). The judgments we have seen thus far have all been about the destruction of the spiritual forces of Satan, and of Satan himself. They all come immediately before the resurrection of the dead and the great white throne judgment. The lake of fire is prepared for the Devil and his angels. They are the first ones to occupy it. Now there is a general resurrection of all the dead, including those most recently killed by the word of Christ, the fire from heaven. All men stand before the throne to be judged out of the books according to their deeds. The living in Christ have no advantage over the dead in Christ according to 1 Thess. 4:15-17. First the dead in Christ are raised incorruptible, then those who are still living are changed to be like them.

All whose names are not recorded in the Book of Life are thrown into the lake of fire where Satan has already been thrown. Death and Hades are also said to be thrown into the lake of fire where the Beast and False Prophet have already been thrown. These four are personifications, so they cannot literally be thrown into the fire. This is a figurative way of saying that Death, Hades, Persecution, and Deceit are utterly destroyed and will afflict the saints no longer. There is no release from the lake of fire. It is called *the second death*, and is said to be an eternal punishment (Matt. 25:41, 46). The righteous will live eternally with God and the Lamb in the new heaven and earth.

Act 7. THE FINAL DWELLING PLACE OF THE RIGHTEOUS (21:1 – 22:5)

The New Heaven and Earth. The redeemed saints (the bride of Christ) are pictured as a beautiful city, New Jerusalem, coming down from heaven to the new heaven and earth. The first heaven and earth have passed away. They fled away before the face of the one on the judgment throne, and no more place was found for them. According to 2 Pet. 3:10-13 they are dissolved in fervent heat. The place Jesus has gone to prepare for us is a new heaven and earth wherein dwells righteousness.

God Dwells with Men. God has brought His own throne to the new earth in order to make His dwelling with the redeemed saints in the new heaven and earth. There is one eternal day there. We will drink of the river of the water of life, and eat of the fruit of the tree of life, and live forever in eternal bliss, with no more pain, sorrow, crying, or death.

F. THE POSTLUDE (22:6-21)

Revelation ends with some final admonitions and warnings given to John, and through him to us. "He who testifies to these things says, 'Surely I am coming quickly.' Amen. Even so, come, Lord Jesus! The grace of our Lord Jesus Christ *be* with you all. Amen."

THE THINGS JOHN SAW
AND THE THINGS THAT ARE

Rev. Chapters 1 – 3

Chapter 1

PRELUDE AND JOHN'S FIRST VISION
Rev. Chapter 1

As we begin the study of the book of Revelation you should read *V. Organization and Contents of Revelation* in the Introduction before proceeding with the rest of the book. You should also have your Bible open to the chapter under consideration so you can read the references from the Bible before reading the commentary on those passages. You will need to refer back to these references from time to time.

I. INTRODUCTORY INFORMATION

The apostle John was condemned by the Roman Emperor Domitian to a life of exile on the Isle of Patmos in the Aegean Sea (Rev. 1:9). The record says that he was "in the spirit on the Lord's Day" (Rev. 1:10). I picture him on a day in A.D. 95, a day which he calls *the Lord's Day*, poring over his parchment scrolls, perhaps getting ready to write to the Christians in Asia. This is the Roman province of Asia, on the western tip of Asia Minor, in modern Turkey. He labored so diligently with these Christians in the years following the destruction of Jerusalem in A.D. 70. The parchments, no doubt, included his personal copies of the letters and books written by his fellow apostles such as Matthew, Paul, and Peter, and other prophets such as Mark and Luke, documents which later came to be called *The New Testament*. There were twenty-six of these documents in existence. John himself had written four of them, and he would shortly learn that there was yet one more to be added to the collection to complete it. He was about to be called by the Lord to write the work we call *The Book of Revelation*.

29

The Things John Saw

I imagine I see John on his knees, praying diligently to God for the believers on the mainland who had begun to suffer severe persecution at the hands of their enemies. While he is in a state of intense spiritual communion with his Lord, the Angel of the Lord is dispatched from the throne of God in heaven; His mission—to deliver to John the Revelation sent by Jesus for His people. The Father wanted to close the volume of inspired writings with a prophetic unveiling. This was to be a fuller account of the future sufferings and victory of the people of God and of His judgment upon the forces of evil than had ever before been given. This account would bring comfort and patience to those who were under persecution, giving them assurance that through their sufferings they would be vindicated and emerge as victors, for the war was already won (Rev. 12:10-11).

Revelation would bring comfort and hope to millions throughout the centuries, down to this present time and beyond. Many scratch their heads over its puzzling message, but in spite of the confusing scenes presented there, one truth shines forth for all to see, i.e., the battle belongs to the Lord! Although it may seem at times that the forces of evil are winning, in the end it is the saints who are given the victory and who possess the kingdom (11:15).

The message of Revelation was not for everyone, but for the followers of Christ. If the Roman rulers could readily understand its deeper message the persecution of Christians would be further intensified because of its anti-Rome message. It is written in such a way that only the mind steeped in the Old Testament scriptures could, with diligence and the help of the Holy Spirit, come to grasp its meaning. Christians were schooled in the Old Testament, not only because many of them were Jews, but because it was the only Bible the early church knew for much of the first century.

The Lord's Angel arrives at Patmos while John is still communing in his spirit with the Spirit of God. Immediately John hears a loud voice, like a trumpet, charging him to write what he sees and to send it to the seven churches of Asia. Turning to see who was speaking, John sees the vision of one like a Son of Man who says in Rev.1:11, 19:

> I am the Alpha and the Omega, the First and the Last....
> What you see, write in a book and send *it* to the seven
> churches which are in Asia: to Ephesus, to Smyrna, to

30

Pergamos, to Thyatira, to Sardis, to Philadelphia, and to Laodicea.

Write the things which you have seen, and the things which are, and the things which will take place after this.

II. THE PRELUDE (Read Rev. 1:1-9)

Remember to read from your Bible the verses given before proceeding to read the following commentary. In this way you will be better able to make the connections and understand what is being discussed. Continue this practice throughout the reading of this book for the best results. It will also help to refer back to the passage from time to time as indicated by the references.

A. HOW JOHN RECEIVED THE VISIONS OF REVELATION

In my mind I see John, when he had gotten over his alarm at hearing his Master's voice (Rev. 1:17-18), hurrying to the crude table where he does his reading and writing, there retrieving blank pieces of parchment or velum, or possibly the less expensive papyrus. He sits down, picks up his quill, sharpens its nub, dips it in ink, and begins to write, explaining what has just happened, and how he has received this vision. He begins with the introductory words of Rev. 1:1-3:

> The Revelation of Jesus Christ, which God gave Him to show His servants—things which must shortly take place. And He sent and signified *it* by His angel to His servant John, who bore witness to the word of God, and to the testimony of Jesus Christ, to all things that he saw. Blessed *is* he who reads and those who hear the words of this prophecy, and keep those things which are written in it; for the time *is* near.

John is saying that this message came from God the Father Himself, Who gave it to His Son Jesus Christ; then Christ relayed it by His Angel to His servant John. This message is not just for John, but for "His servants," the saints of God. (Remember this term *His Servants*, for we will see it often in this book.) John had an awesome task—to write it all down and send it to the

31

churches. He also tells us that the main thrust of the message is things which must shortly (speedily) begin to take place.[1]

John lets us know the method by which the message is given: "He sent and signified it by His angel to his servant John." He SIGN-ified it[2] or gave it in signs. A sign is something that points to something else, just as a road sign is used to direct one to a certain city, or a dot on a map represents a certain city. When we say that the dot is Dallas, we mean that it represents Dallas. It signifies or symbolizes something.[3] So right at the beginning John identifies the book as one written largely in symbols or figures. Of course, not everything in the book is symbolic; some things, of necessity are literal. This is true of most of the explanations of the symbols given in the book.

B. WHO IS THIS JOHN?

John identifies himself as the one who "bore witness . . ." (Rev. 1:2, past tense). He bore witness to **the Word of God**—i.e., Jesus Christ. He bore witness to **the testimony of Christ**—i.e., to the words or teachings of Jesus, and to **all that he saw** (also past tense), meaning the life and deeds of Christ that John had seen. A person bears witness by telling what he has seen and knows of his own knowledge. John had been with Jesus from the beginning of His ministry, and had seen His works and heard His teachings. At the end of his account of the life of Jesus the apostle John wrote in John 21:24-25:

> This is **the disciple who testifies of these things**, and wrote these things, and we know that his testimony is true. And

---

[1]*Take place* (γενέσθαι – *genesthai)* is a 2nd aorist (simple tense) infinitive. The aorist is the tense of punctiliar (point) action. Since it is speaking of future events rather than past, it is to be understood as inceptive aorist, the point of the beginning of the action—thus *begin to take place.*

[2]In the Greek it is the word σημαίνω *(semaino* –pronounced *say-my-no)*—to indicate by signs or symbols. *Thayer's Greek Lexicon* defines it as: *1) to give a sign, to signify, indicate, and 2) to make known.* This word is used five times in the New Testament, including Revelation 1:1. The other uses of *semaino,* here translated *signify* in the NKJV, are found in John 12:33; 18:32; 21:19; Acts 25:27.

[3]The Greek for sign is νσημεῖον *(semeion),* the noun form of σημαίνω *(semaino). Thayer's Greek Definitions* gives the meaning as: *an indication, especially ceremonially or supernaturally:--miracle, sign, token, wonder.*

there are also many other things that Jesus did, which if they were written one by one, I suppose that even the world itself could not contain the books that would be written. Amen.

John also wrote concerning these things in 1 John 1:1-2:

That which was from the beginning, which we have heard, which we have seen with our eyes, which we have looked upon, and our hands have handled, concerning the Word of life—the life was manifested, and **we have seen, and bear witness**, and declare to you that eternal life which was with the Father and was manifested to us....

Compare these verses from John and 1 John to what is written in Rev. 1:2. Apparently he wants us to understand that he is the same John who wrote the gospel. In this way he identifies himself as the apostle John. For further indications that the writer is the apostle John you may go to *I. The Writer – John the Apostle* in the Introduction.

C. BLESSINGS PRONOUNCED ON THE READER, HEARERS, AND DOERS

In verse 3 John pronounces blessings on three groups of people. These are: 1) The one who reads the book (to the assemblies)—perhaps the one later called the angel or messenger of the church; 2) those who heed its message—those who not only listen, but obey its message; and 3) those who keep the things it says, who guard and keep its message. Then John delivers a message of greeting from the source of the message.

D. THE GREETING FROM THE THREE IN THE GODHEAD *(1:4-5a)*

In verses 4 and 5 there are three who send greeting: 1) "Him who is and who was and who is to come," i.e., God the Father; 2) "the seven Spirits who are before His throne," a figurative way of saying the Holy Spirit; and 3) "Jesus Christ, the faithful witness, the firstborn from the dead, and the ruler over the kings of the earth." These greet the reader with grace and peace. These three are often mentioned together, but usually Jesus is mentioned second instead of last—i.e., Father, Son and Holy Spirit. Possibly He is mentioned last as a transition to the subject of the book. The message is about Jesus. He is the star of the show. In verse 1 the book is called, "the revelation of Jesus Christ," not "the revelation of the Father," or "the revelation of the Holy Spirit." It is Jesus, His person, and His works that are being revealed to the saints in this book.

In the New Testament these three are the three manifestations or personalities of the one God. The titles that are ascribed to God are also the titles of Christ. He is the first, and the last, and the living one; the alpha and omega; the beginning and the end; the one who is and who was and who is to come; the Mighty God and Everlasting Father (Isa. 9:6); the creator (John 1:1-2); God (Heb. 1:8); and Lord (YHWH, Rom. 10:13).

E. WHY THE SEVEN SPIRITS OF GOD?

Why is the Holy Spirit referred to as *the seven Spirits before the throne of God*? This is a strange way of speaking about the Holy Spirit. An interesting passage is found in Isa. 11:2 which might help us understand. He speaks of the Holy Spirit of God as seven Spirits. They are: 1) the Spirit of the Lord; 2) the Spirit of Wisdom; 3) the Spirit of Understanding; 4) the Spirit of Counsel; 5) the Spirit of Might; 6) the Spirit of Knowledge; and 7) the Spirit of Fear of the Lord. Seven Spirits are named, but obviously they are all intended to refer to the characteristics of the one Spirit of God.

The number *seven* is a symbolic number that represents fullness, completeness or wholeness. It represents the totality of a thing, just as seven days make up one full week. God rested on the seventh day of creation week, indicating that the work of creation was complete (Gen. 2:1-2). Seven is a number much used throughout the Bible as well as in the book of Revelation. Here it refers to the fullness of the Holy Spirit in all His working and characteristics. We will run into *the seven Spirits of God* several more times in our reading of Revelation. In addition we will find many other uses of the number *seven* in which the symbolic meaning of completeness applies.

F. THE DESCRIPTION OF JESUS AND HIS WORK (1:5b-7)

1. The Redemptive Work of Jesus. Now let us look at the rest of what the angel says about Jesus. He says that this message is dedicated to Jesus who loves us and washed (or loosed) us from our sins.[4] The King James and

---

[4]*The Majority Text uses λούσαντι (lousanti), a form of λούω (louo), to wash, whereas the*

New King James versions put *loved* in the past tense while most other translations use *loves* in the present tense. The bulk of the Greek manuscripts use the present tense.[5] Jesus still loves us; he keeps on loving us. On the other hand, the sacrifice of Christ by which he washed or freed us from our sins is a past act—a done deal. John uses the aorist tense of point action in the past.

Some liberal scholars point to the lack of agreement in tense as poor grammar on John's part, using this to deny that the writer was the apostle John because of the superior grammar he used in writing his gospel, but John said exactly what he wanted to say. It was the continuing love that God has for us that caused Him to send Jesus to die for us. It was the love that Jesus continues to have for us that caused Him to give His life's blood almost 2000 years ago to redeem us, free us, and wash us pure from sin. Praise God for His unspeakable love!

2. He Made Us a Kingdom of Priests. Jesus is the one who has made us a kingdom of priests before the throne of God. The KJV and the NKJV translate this *kings and priests,* but most other versions use *a kingdom of priests.*[6] Jesus came to establish His kingdom, His nation of people. Although the word *kingdom* can have a broader meaning than just a nation, i.e., the dominion that Christ will ultimately exercise over all the earth, here he is talking about His people who have been redeemed out of every nation and people and tribe and tongue. This kingdom is already present. He has made us a kingdom (past tense). His kingdom includes all those who have submitted to His Lordship.

Nestle/UBS text uses λύσαντι *(lusanti),* a form of λύω *(luo),* **to loose** or **release.** While the majority of manuscripts have *lousanti,* a significant minority of manuscripts uses *lusanti.*

[5]The *Nestle/UBS* text uses the present participle ἀγαπῶντι *(agaponti),* a form of ἀγαπάω *(agapao)* for *loves,* as does *The Majority Text. The Textus Receptus,* from which the *King James* and the *New King James* are translated, uses the aorist singular participle ἀγαπήσαντι *(agapesanti),* as do a significant number of other Greek manuscripts. The preponderance of the evidence seems to be on the side of the present *loves,* rather that the aorist (past) loved.

[6]*The Majority Text* as well as the *Nestle/UBS* text uses βασιλεία *(basileia, kingdom). The Textus Receptus,* from which the *KJV* and *NKJV* were translated uses βασιλείς *(basileis, kings),* a plural form of βασιλεύς *(basileus), king.* The preponderance of textual evidence favors *a kingdom* rather than *kings.*

This kingdom is made up exclusively of priests. As Exod. 19:6 puts it to Israel, "And you shall be to Me a kingdom of priests and a holy nation." Peter wrote in 1 Pet. 2:9:

> But you are a chosen generation, a royal priesthood, a holy nation, His own special people, that you may proclaim the praises of Him who called you out of darkness into His marvelous light.

Every citizen of His kingdom, has the right and responsibility as a priest to intercede for all men, to minister the gospel to them, to offer up the spiritual sacrifices of praise and service, and to offer himself as a living sacrifice to God (see 1 Pet. 2:5; Heb.13:15-16; Rom.12:1).

3. He Will Come in the Clouds. The last thing the angel says of Jesus in verse 7 is that He is coming in the clouds, just like He went (see Acts 1:10-11). When that happens every eye will see Him, including those who pierced Him. That means the eyes of all who are in the graves as well as those who are living. Even the soldiers who pierced Jesus' brow, hands, feet, and side will see him. How is that possible? John 5:28-29 says:

> ...the hour is coming in which all who are in the graves will hear His voice and come forth—those who have done good, to the resurrection of life, and those who have done evil, to the resurrection of condemnation.

All will be raised at His coming. The chief priests who took Jesus before the authorities, Pilate who sentenced Him to the cross, the Jews who yelled, "Crucify Him, crucify Him," and the soldiers who mocked Him, spat on Him, placed the thorns on His brow, nailed Him to the cross, and pierced His side will all see Him coming with the clouds. This includes all of us, because we are all guilty of piercing Him by our sins which put Him on the cross. They, and all those who reject Him and rebel against His authority, will have cause to mourn when they see Him because they will be subject to His great wrath. On the other hand, those who have been waiting and longing for His coming will rejoice because of His coming, for He is bringing their reward with Him.

G. *GOD, THE ALPHA AND OMEGA, THE BEGINNING AND THE END (1:8)*

"'I am the Alpha and the Omega,' says the Lord,[7] 'who is and who was and who is to come, the Almighty.'" (RSV) With this statement the greeting from the Godhead is completed. Here God the Almighty claims to be the Alpha (A – beginning) and the Omega (Ω – end). Alpha is the first letter of the Greek Alphabet, and Omega is the last. He has always existed and will always exist. He is the beginning of all things. He is the A to Z of creation. He spoke all creation into existence, and He also will speak the end of this creation just before introducing His saints to the new heaven and earth. Just three verses later, in verse 11, Jesus uses the same wording with reference to Himself. He is the Alpha and Omega, the First and the Last. Do you suppose that this means that the Father and the Son are one? I believe it does.

H. *John's Kinship with the Churches (1:9)*

John claims kinship with the servants of God to whom this Revelation is addressed. He calls himself their brother. He shares with them in **the tribulation, the kingdom,** and **the patience** of Jesus Christ. All three of these terms have special meaning in the Revelation. The first of these terms, *tribulation,* is found in various places in the New Testament. Notable are the statements of Jesus in Matt. 24.

1. A Brother in the Tribulation. Jesus told His disciples in Matt. 24:1-22 that the temple they had just visited would be destroyed. Not one stone would be left resting on top of another. This was a startling statement to a devout Jew. The temple was the very heart of his religion and devotions. This was where God's glory rested between the cherubim on the mercy seat. God's promise to be with His people Israel was tied to the temple. To destroy the temple was, to them, to destroy their tie with God. The temple is where He promised to dwell among them.

The disciples asked two questions: first, they wanted to know when the temple was going to be destroyed; and second, what sign would be given to signal Christ's return and the end of the age. They probably thought the temple would be destroyed at the end when Christ returned. As a result, they tie these questions together. History informs us that the temple was destroyed

---

[7]*The Majority Text* adds *God.*

in A.D. 70 by the Roman army. These questions gave Jesus an opportunity to teach both about the destruction of the temple and the end of the age.

John was a partaker with his brethren in the tribulation. Jesus gave a general statement about the tribulation and persecution that was to come upon the followers of Christ (Matt. 24:4-14). He told them that people would rise up claiming to be the Christ. In my own lifetime there have been several men who claimed that they were Jesus Christ. This has gone on ever since the first century A.D. There would be wars and much war talk, with nations going to war against one another. Today there continues to be wars and war talk. This also has gone on since the first century. There would be famines, disease, and earthquakes. None of these things are themselves a sign that the end is near. These have all occurred in every century since Christ. He told them this was only the beginning of troubles.

In Matt. 24:9 Jesus says, "Then they will deliver you up to tribulation and kill you, and you will be hated by all nations for My name's sake."[8] This started with the persecution of the apostles in the first century. Tradition has it that all the apostles with the exception of John were put to death because of the gospel they preached. Not only would disciples have to suffer the wars, famines, and diseases of this world, but the people of the world would persecute them. To make matters worse Christians would turn on Christians and they would hate one another. Times would get so bad that lawlessness (crime and criminal activity) would be everywhere, and hearts would grow cold and loveless. This sounds familiar, doesn't it? Have you checked the news lately?

I was shocked to learn that more Christians have been killed in the twentieth century because of their faith than in all the rest of the time since Christ. The number continues to increase in the twenty-first century. This increase of persecution also has been going on ever since the first century. Matt. 24:13 says that if you would be saved you must endure until the end.

What is Jesus saying? Christians are going to have suffering, persecution, i.e., tribulation, in this world, and more as time goes on. Paul is talking about

---

[8]The Greek word for *tribulation* here is θλίψις *(thipsis)*. According to the Greek lexicons this word literally means *pressure*. It is used to mean *affliction, anguish, persecution, tribulation, trouble*. It is not a code word for some special period of affliction.

the same thing when he writes in 2 Tim. 3:12-13, "Yes, and all who desire to live godly in Christ Jesus will suffer persecution. But evil men and impostors will grow worse and worse, deceiving and being deceived." Tribulation is used in the context of Matt. 24 concerning the suffering brought against Christians throughout the age. Tribulation is not the sign of His coming and of the end of the world. There is something else that must take place first.

The Gospel to Be Preached in All the World Before the End. Matt. 24:14 says, "And this gospel of the kingdom will be preached in all the world as a witness to all the nations, and then the end will come." In Matt. 4:23 and 9:35 as well as Mark 1:14 (*KJV* and *NKJV*) the message that Jesus preached is called "the gospel of the kingdom." Everywhere else it is simply called, "the gospel." The gospel of the kingdom is the gospel that belongs to, is received by, and is preached by those who enter the kingdom. It is the gospel of salvation which people must hear, believe, and obey in order to become a part of the kingdom, the holy nation of priests.

The Destruction of the Temple and the City. In Matt. 24:15-22 Jesus answers the first question about the destruction of Jerusalem. The indication of it would be the *abomination of desolation* in the holy place (the temple). This is talking about the defilement of the temple by the gentiles—in this case, the Roman soldiers who set up the standard of the Roman legions in the temple. Jesus warns the disciples to flee when they see this taking place. The mountains around Jerusalem would be preferable to remaining in the city. According to church historians these instructions given by Jesus enabled many Christians to escape the tribulation which Jesus said would occur in the city as a result of the siege of Jerusalem.

The Specific Tribulation for Those in Jerusalem. The terrible severity of the tribulation upon the city of Jerusalem during the three and one-half year siege by the Roman soldiers under Titus (Titian) is described by Josephus,[9] a Jewish historian who lived through that siege. This tribulation was not directed specifically against Christians, but against the Jews in the city of Jerusalem. The temple plays a large part in the imagery of Revelation. In Rev. 11:1-2 Jerusalem and the temple are used as figures of the

---

[9] *Josephus—The Complete Works*, Tr. by William Whiston, A.M., Thomas Nelson Publishers, Nashville, 1998. *The Wars of the Jews*, Books 5, 6 and 7, pp. 835-925.

persecution of the Christians for a period represented as forty-two months (three and one-half years). This is the period of time which many Christians, especially those who believe in the dispensational pre-millennial theory, refer to as *the great tribulation*. We will deal with this more fully when we come to it.

False Christs and False Prophets. Following these verses Jesus returns to the subject of the tribulation that Christians are to suffer. False prophets and false Christs would come (Matt. 24:23-26). Some of them would be so convincing, working apparent signs and wonders, that even the chosen of God could be deceived by them. Jesus warns them not to believe these false teachers and false Christs. But there would be a price to pay in terms of tribulation. So after the destruction of Jerusalem, Christians had more tribulation coming to them. Jesus warns them not to believe the claims of the false Christs because when the true Christ returns every eye will see him, like the lightning is seen from the east to the west. This is certainly not the case for any of those who have arisen claiming to be Christ, nor will it be true of any future false Christ.

The Coming of Christ and the End of the Age. Finally Jesus answers the second question about the return of Christ and the end of the world (Matt. 24:26-31). It would be at the end of the tribulation. The sign is a simple one.

Matt. 24:30 says,

> Then the sign of the Son of Man will appear in heaven, and then all the tribes of the earth will mourn, and they will see the Son of Man coming on the clouds of heaven with power and great glory.

This sounds like what we read in Rev. 1:7 doesn't it? The tribulation Jesus described, as well as that referred to by various New Testament writers, is the persecution and suffering that all Christians are subject to in this life. John told the Christians in Smyrna who were to undergo severe persecution (Rev. 2:10) to be faithful even unto death so that they would receive a crown of life. John was the brother of every other Christian and shared in the tribulation that all Christians suffer. It will help to read the whole of Matt. 24 to better understand some of the things we will be dealing with in the Revelation.

2. A Brother in the Kingdom. John is our brother in the kingdom. Yes, there is a sense in which the kingdom is yet to come. That sense is in the coming of the dominion of Christ over all the earth. Satan offered Jesus all the kingdoms of the world but Jesus would not receive them as a gift from Satan. They were His by right, and through the might of His word He will take dominion in God's own timing. But the kingdom of Christ is here now. We are His holy nation, a people for his own possession—a kingdom of priests (1 Pet. 2:5,9). This is the kingdom that John shared with all his brothers and sisters in Christ.

When did this kingdom come? In Rev. 12:10 John writes, "Then I heard a loud voice saying in heaven, 'Now salvation, and strength, and the kingdom of our God, and the power of His Christ have come.'" This occurred when Satan and his angels were defeated by the blood of the Lamb, and by the proclamation of the testimony of the brethren, i.e., by the preaching of the gospel. That kingdom had its beginning when Jesus was crucified at Calvary on the day of the sacrifice of the Passover lamb, and when the gospel was first proclaimed after the Holy Spirit was poured out and became available for all men on the day of Pentecost. These two events are tied together. The first event enabled the second; the outpouring of Christ's blood paved the way for the outpouring of the Spirit. In this way salvation came, the kingdom of Christ had its beginning, and Jesus took His position of power as Lord of all.

There is to come a time when the kingdom (dominion) of this world becomes the kingdom (dominion) of our Lord (11:15), but until that time the kingdom (nation) of God is here, and it is made up of people out of every nation, tribe, and tongue who come to Jesus in faith. This kingdom had already come into existence in John's day. The apostles were told that they would not taste of death until they see the kingdom of God come with power (Mark 9:1). John saw the coming of the kingdom, and being a part of it he could say that he was our brother in the kingdom.

3. A Brother in the Patience. Patience in suffering is something John shared with the saints. In several places in Revelation, after assuring the suffering saints of the ultimate downfall of the forces of evil, John says that this assurance is "the patience and faith of the saints." We will take note of these passages when we get to them. In Rom. 8:25 (NRSV) Paul wrote, "But if we hope for what we do not see, we wait for it with patience."

III. CHRIST AMONG THE SEVEN LAMPSTANDS (Read 1:10-20)

A. JOHN IS TOLD TO WRITE HIS VISIONS (1:10-11). John tells us what he was doing when the Angel delivered the Revelation from God. He was in deep spiritual communion with the Spirit of God—probably in earnest and agonizing prayer for the saints in the province of Asia. He heard a loud voice like a trumpet (1:10), which said, "I am the Alpha and the Omega, the First and the Last" (1:11), then the voice gave John a commission: "What you see, write in a book and send it to the seven churches which are in Asia." The Voice proceeded to name the cities where these churches were located..

Strange! The voice, which is understood to be the voice of the glorified Christ, claims the same things for Himself that are claimed for God. He is the Alpha (the first Greek letter) and the Omega (the last Greek letter). It is like saying "I am A and Z." He is the beginning and the end. This could be said of any of the three personalities who make up the one God. It not only speaks of the eternal existence of the Christ, but ascribes to Him both the beginning and the end of all things.

Verse 1 tells us that Jesus Christ sent and signified the Revelation to John by His angel. To say "His Angel" is the same as saying "the Angel of the Lord" since Jesus is the Lord. The Angel of the Lord was the appearance of God Himself in the form of a man. When the Angel of the Lord appeared in the Old Testament He accepted the worship offered Him. On the other hand, in Rev. 22:8-9 John offered worship to the angel who spoke to him there (one of the seven with the bowls of wrath), but the angel refused the worship, and told John not to do it. Instead he told John to worship God.

The Angel of the Lord is thought by many to be the pre-incarnate Christ. I am inclined to agree with this. The angel who appeared in chapter ten and gave John the open scroll containing the Revelation is described in terms that indicate deity, much as Jesus is here described. Probably this, also, is the Angel of the Lord. Jesus sent His Angel and the Angel appeared in the vision as the glorified Christ and gave John his assignment.

B. *JOHN'S VISION OF THE GLORIFIED CHRIST (1:12-18)*

John describes the vision he saw when he turned to look at the One who spoke to him in Rev. 1:12-18. Verse 12 says, "Then I turned to see the voice that spoke with me. And having turned I saw seven golden lampstands, and in the midst of the seven lampstands *One* like the [a] Son of Man...."

1. Jesus in the Midst of Seven Golden Lampstands. The first things John saw when he turned around were seven gold lampstands. I told you we would run into that number *seven* again. What are these lampstands? John explains later on. I'll give you a hint. They are not literal lampstands, but are symbols representing something else. When he sees the lampstands, John's eyes are riveted on a frightful figure standing among the lampstands. This figure is so awesome that John falls down at His feet in apoplexy. This happened with several Old Testament characters when an angel appeared to them. Consider Daniel's reaction to the appearance of the Angel of the Lord in Dan. 10:4-12. Who is this figure John sees? First he describes Him as one who looks like a Son of Man (the definite article *the* is not in the original). This was a common way among those who spoke Aramaic (or Chaldean) of referring to a person as a human being. Frequently it is used in the Aramaic portions of the Old Testament, but Ezekiel uses it more than all the other books put together. God addresses Ezekiel as "son of man," thus reminding him that he is only human.

2. The Son of Man. Jesus took for himself the title "Son of Man" to emphasize that He had become a human. This was part of the plan God had for redeeming mankind. Jesus took upon himself humanity so that He could be offered as a sacrifice for sins, to die to pay the price for our wickedness. When He became a man He did so for all eternity. He died as a man, was resurrected as a man, ascended to heaven as a man, and as a man he will come back to judge the living and the dead.

Acts 17:31 says, "...because He has appointed a day on which He will judge the world in righteousness by the Man whom He has ordained. He has given assurance of this to all by raising Him from the dead." As a man he will share the throne of God throughout eternity. Rev. 22:3 proclaims of the new heaven and earth, "And there shall be no more curse, but the throne of God and of the Lamb shall be in it, and His servants shall serve Him." This one like a son of man is indeed **the** Son of Man, who is also the Son of God, Jesus the Anointed of God.

He is described by John as wearing a robe down to His feet, and a golden band around His chest. The pure linen garment signifies righteousness (Rev. 19:8). Such robes are to be given to the saints of God who are His priests (see Rev. 3:5; 4:4; 7:9, 13-15). Jesus wears the priestly robe because He is the great High Priest.

Jesus' hair is described as white like wool and snow. This is a description of someone who is old and white-headed. It is the description of God in Dan. 7:9 where He is called "The Ancient of Days." Jesus was older than the thirty-three years He spent on earth. In John 8:58 Jesus said, "Most assuredly, I say to you, before Abraham was, I AM." He is from everlasting to everlasting. He was in the beginning with God and was God (John 1:1-3). Through Him all things were created. We can truly call Him *the Ancient of Days.*

His eyes are described as being like a flame of fire. This speaks of His ability to see and know. His gaze is piercing, and He sees into the hearts of men. Nothing is hidden from His gaze. His feet are highly polished bronze, glowing and reflecting the sun's rays with their mirror finish. Feet are used to describe beauty or splendor (Rom. 10:15). This is a picture of the splendor and glory of Christ, the Son of Man. His voice sounded like the roar of Niagara Falls or the roar of the ocean surf as it breaks on shore. When I took my wife to Yosemite National Park on our honeymoon in June 1953, we walked up to lower Yosemite Falls. As we approached the falls she was overwhelmed with the power and awesome sound of the falls. The voice of many waters is a suitable figure to describe the compelling nature of the voice of the one who spoke the worlds into existence.

3. The Seven Stars. In His right hand Jesus held seven stars. Here is that number *seven* again. What are the seven stars? Just wait. John is going to explain shortly. Many of the symbols in revelation are explained for us so that we don't have to guess their meaning.

4. The Sword of His Mouth. The Son of Man also had a sharp two-edged sword proceeding out of His mouth. If you are acquainted with Eph. 6:17 and Heb. 4:12 you know what that sword is. This is the word of God which comes out of His mouth. When I was a "preacher student" with others who were like minded, each of us referred to his Bible as *the sword.* In retrospect, some of us did not wield that sword too effectively. Hopefully for most of us that improved with time and experience.

The word of God, like a sword, pierces the very heart of man. That word is living and powerful. God spoke and the worlds came into being. With His word the worlds that now are will be destroyed with fervent heat. Heaven and earth will pass away, but His word will not pass away. We had better pay attention to His word. It is an all-powerful weapon with which no nuclear bomb, nor any other force of man or nature can compare. With it He will smite the nations (Rev. 19:15).

5. The Glory of His Face. His face was radiant like the sun. When Jesus went up to the mountain with Peter, James, and John, He was changed before them so that His face shone like the sun (Matt. 17:1-3). One day we will be like that. 1 John 3:2 says that we don't know exactly what we will be like, but when we see Him, we will be like Him. We will share His glory. The vision John saw revealed the glory of Christ. If I were to see a vision like this one that John saw, I think I would fall on my face like a dead person, just as he did. Wouldn't you?

C. WHAT JESUS SAID TO JOHN (Rev. 1:18-20)

The last part of the vision has to do with what Jesus said. In 1:18-20 Jesus reveals these things; "I *am* He who lives, and was dead, and behold, I am alive forevermore. Amen. And I have the keys of Hades and of Death."

1. He Has the Keys of Death and Hades. Christ has revealed Himself as the first and the last, and the one who is alive although He was dead. He has the keys with which to unlock death and hades.[10] He Himself came forth from the grave; life returned to His body, and his soul returned from hades, the abode of the dead (Acts 2:31). Body and soul were reunited, and He is

---

[10] ᾅδης *(hades)*—pronounced *hah'-days. Strong's Greek Dictionary* defines this word as: "properly unseen, that is, 'Hades' or the place (state) of departed souls:--grave, hell." Although *hell* was used by the *KJV* to translate both *hades* and *gehenna,* later translators, including *NKJV,* have almost unanimously made the distinction, using *hades* to refer to the state of the dead and *hell (gehenna)* for the lake of fire, the fate of the wicked after judgment. For a more complete study of hades go to *Appendix A* at the end of the book.

alive forevermore. The fact that He holds the keys of death is the guarantee that He can keep His word. At His coming He will unlock the graves for all of us, and those who belong to Him will come forth to live forevermore.

Figuratively both death and hades are given personality, i.e., *personification*—as in Rev. 6:8 where the rider on the pale horse is "Death," and he is followed by "Hades." As Death claims the body, Hades claims the soul. In Rev. 20:14 both Death and Hades are said to be cast into the lake of fire (hell) at the end of time. The reason is that there will be no more Death, and so, no more need for Hades. Death and Hades are both states of being, and not objects or persons that can be literally cast into hell. Because Jesus has the keys of death and hades we can look forward with hope to His coming. He is going to use the keys to unlock both death and hades so that the souls can come out of hades and the bodies out of their grave. Body and soul will be united just as His body and soul were reunited in His resurrection. This is a blessed hope and comfort to believers who look forward to the return of Christ and the resurrection. What a glorious hope! (For further study on hades go to *Appendix A - Hades and Hell*.)

2. Jesus Gives John His Assignment (1:19). After this Jesus gives John an awesome assignment in verse 19. This consisted of three things:

"Write what you have seen." John wrote down the vision he had just seen. This is the vision of chapter one.

"Write what exists." This is the next thing that he does. Chapters 2 and 3 are all about the things that exist in the congregations of God's people. The seven letters that Jesus dictates to John deal with the way things were in his day as well as the way they are in our own day.

"Write what will take place in the future." That part begins in chapter four and takes up the rest of the book. In it Jesus reveals more about the fortunes of Christians in the hundreds and thousands of years that would follow than had ever been revealed before.

3. Jesus Explains The Seven Stars and Seven Lampstands (1:20)

> The mystery of the seven stars which you saw in My right hand, and the seven golden lampstands: The seven stars are the angels of the seven churches, and the seven lampstands which you saw are the seven churches.

What are those lampstands and stars? Jesus doesn't leave us to guess or wonder. We don't have to resort to our great spiritual insight to know the meaning. He tells John that the seven lampstands are the seven churches, and the seven stars are the seven angels (messengers) of the churches. We can see why the messengers might be likened to stars. We use the same word today when we are talking about people who shine, whether they are stars of stage and screen, or the athletic arena, or leaders among people. Heavenly angels are often referred to as stars. Those who lead churches are also portrayed as stars.

How are the churches lampstands? A lampstand has a purpose, i.e., to hold up the light. A lampstand (*candlestick* in the *KJV*)[11] does not produce any light by itself. It is intended to hold a lamp. It is only in this way that churches can bear light to the world. They are not themselves light, but they are to bear the light which comes from the Holy Spirit of God. They bear the light in their lives and conduct by proclaiming the word of God which was given by the Holy Spirit.

In Rev. 4 the seven lamps of fire are the seven Spirits of God. The lampstands are individual congregations, but these seven churches represent the whole church and are each part of the whole, just as the seven Spirits of God are essentially One Spirit. In the tabernacle in the wilderness, and later in the temple in Jerusalem, the seven lampstands were all joined on a common base. They were one lampstand with seven branches. These stood in the Holy Place to give light. They held up the lamps which were the source of the light. This explains the symbolism in Rev. 1. The churches stand as lamp-bearers to spread the light of revelation and knowledge given by the lamps which are the seven Spirits of God.

Once again we see the significance of the number seven. The seven churches of Asia are named, but the number seven symbolically indicates that they are representative of the whole church. This figure is intended to include churches today as well as those at the end of the first century. We can look at the seven churches named and see in them the conditions that exist in our own churches. The letters are all ended in such a way as to let us know that

---

[11]The Greek text uses the word λυχνία *(luchia)*. *Strong's Greek Dictionary* defines this word as "a *lamp stand (literally or figuratively):—candlestick.*" Since candlesticks as we know them were unknown in this historical context, the better translation is *lampstands.*

they are intended for us all and not just for them. "Whoever has an ear, let him hear what the Spirit says to the churches." These are "the things that are." They not only refer to existing situations in the first century churches, but they also apply to the things that exist in the churches at whatever time these messages are being read. They are the things that are in the first century, and the things that are in the twenty-first century.

In like manner, the seven angels stand for all those who proclaim the word of God to the church. Christ holds them all in His hand and is in control of the messenger as well as the message. These have the responsibility of delivering the words of Christ, His encouragements and commendations, His warnings and admonitions, His words of instructions to the congregations. He will be with them if they are faithful in their charge, and enable them to accomplish what He wills.

Jesus is in the midst of the churches, not off somewhere in heaven away from them. He cares for them and wants to help them to become what He wants them to be. He is at work today among the churches. Jesus told His disciples in Matt. 28:20, "...l am with you always, *even* to the end of the age."

Chapter 2

LETTERS TO THE SEVEN CHURCHES
Rev. Chapter 2 – THE FIRST FOUR LETTERS

I. THE THINGS THAT ARE

A. THE LETTERS ADDRESSED TO THE SEVEN ANGELS

Jesus dictated seven letters to John, and addressed them to the angels (messengers)[1] of the seven churches in the Roman province of Asia; this is not the continent of Asia where China is, but a small part of Asia Minor, on the west coast of modern Turkey, across the Aegean Sea from Greece. The angel (messenger) of each church is the person who delivers the word of God to the congregation.

B. TO THE CHURCHES, NOT JUST TO THE MESSENGERS

The letters were probably addressed to the messengers because the churches had no address. Churches did not own property and buildings as they do today. They met in homes, or in rented buildings, or in the synagogues if the Jewish rulers would allow. When they were under persecution they met in secret, in caves or underground passages such as the catacombs of Rome. Any message sent to a church had to be addressed to

---

[1]The Greek word for *angel* is ἄγγελος *(aggelos* pronounced *ang'-gel-os). Strong's Greek Dictionary* defines this word to mean **"a *messenger;* especially an *'angel';* by implication a pastor:—angel, messenger."** Thayer's lexicon defines the word as follows: **"a messenger, envoy, one who is sent, an angel, a messenger from God."** Thus the term can refer to a heavenly being who brings a message, commonly called an angel, or to a human who has been given a message to deliver, such as an elder or preacher.

49

one of its members. The logical one was whoever most often spoke to the congregation.

C. HOW DELIVERED

When I began writing about these letters, my eldest son asked me, "Did the seven messengers come to Patmos to pick up their letters, or did John mail them?" I don't know the answer for sure, but I had always pictured John putting the letters in the hands of someone like Timothy, or Titus, or Silas, or Luke, or perhaps John Mark, on board a ship headed for the coast of the province of Asia. Then that person, whoever he was, would deliver the letters to the different messengers in each of the cities—John's own private postal service. But, of course, there are other possibilities.

Since the whole book of Revelation was addressed to all seven churches (1:11) it is likely that the whole book was sent at once, and then passed around from church to church. They would surely copy it so that each church would have its own copy. This was a common practice when a congregation received a letter from one of the apostles. Each congregation would have its own letter, as well as being able to read the other six letters as well, just as we are doing. Talk about snooping in other people's mail!

D. FOR THE WHOLE CHURCH

Jesus wanted all seven churches (and us) to read all the letters because in each letter the Spirit was speaking to the churches (plural). "He who has an ear, let him hear what the Spirit says to the churches" (Rev. 2:7,11,17,29; 3:6,13,22). A close inspection of the letters lets us know that they are intended for the whole church, not just the literal seven congregations. Each letter ends by urging everyone who has an ear to pay attention to what is said. These seven churches with their problems represent the whole church.

Seven is a symbol for fullness, completeness, or wholeness. The Lord chose seven congregations with their problems to represent the whole. The problems in these seven churches are the same problems that have plagued the church in every generation. All these problems in one form or another are found in the churches of our day. John was writing *the things that are* in our own generation as well as theirs.

E. *EACH LETTER RELATED TO DESCRIPTIONS OF JESUS IN CHAPTER ONE*

In each of the seven letters in Rev. 2 and 3 Jesus refers to one or more of the descriptions given of Jesus in the vision of 1:9-20.

2:1—He holds the stars (messengers) in His right hand, and walks in the midst of the lampstands (churches).

2:8—He is the First and the Last; the one who was dead but came back to life, and now lives forever.

2:12—He is the one who has the two-edged sword (His word) coming out of His mouth.

2:18—He is the one whose eyes burn like fire and His feet are highly polished bronze, brilliant and glorious.

3:1—He is the one who has the seven-fold Spirit of God.

3:7—He is the one who is trustworthy, faithful and true. He holds the keys of death and Hades, and the key (authority) of the king.

3:14—He is the Amen (the one who makes it so), the faithful and true witness.

All these things are related to the messages that are found in the letters. As you read the letters, you can see how they apply to each church.

II. LETTER ONE: TO THE CHURCH AT EPHESUS (Rev. 2:1-7)

The first letter is addressed to the messenger of the church in Ephesus. In verse one Jesus refers to Himself as the one who holds the seven stars and walks among the seven lampstands. Remember that the stars have been identified as the messengers. Christ holds His messengers in His right hand. They belong to Him; He controls them and protects them; He gives them the messages to deliver as well as the power and ability to deliver them effectively. The lampstands represent the churches. Jesus is not far off from them but walks among them, is present with them, and is active among them. He is in control, directing them. He knows them and cares for them. He sees their needs and their shortcomings, and wants to guide, correct and discipline them. In extreme cases He can even remove their lampstand—that is, He can remove a church from His favor, or even from existence as a congregation of the Lord's people.

A. What Jesus Says about Ephesus

Take a look at this church's description in verses 2 and 3, and also verse 6. How about that Ephesian church! WOW! What a congregation.

1. They were hard workers.

2. They did not put up with evil practices or evil people. No immorality or false teaching was tolerated there!

3. They checked out those who claimed to be apostles of Christ, and rejected those who were fakes.

4. They did not give up, but kept on persevering. They practiced being patient and did not tire of doing their work.

5. They hated the things the Nicolaitans did and taught. They stood firmly against these practices.

The Nicolaitans were people who insisted that it was acceptable to be sexually immoral and to worship idols by eating the sacrifices. These were the practices that the people in the city accepted and did. Ephesus was a pagan city with pagan temples where these things were done as acts of worship to their gods. "Hey. We've got to get along with our neighbors, don't we? Shouldn't offend them, you know." The church in Ephesus didn't buy that, and refused to make such excuses or try to justify such immoral and ungodly actions.

B. *PRAISE FROM JESUS CHRIST HIMSELF*

Again, WOW! Could you think of a better recommendation? Christ Himself was commending them for these things. Many would point to such a church today and say, "Now here's an example of what a church should be like. We ought to try to be like this church." But wait! Something was very wrong—just one thing, according to verse 4. It says they had quit loving like they did at first. "Well, no problem—right? After all, they got all of the rest right, didn't they?" Could love be so important? Yes it could, according to the apostle Paul. In 1 Cor. 13:1-3 he said that it doesn't matter how good work you do; if it is not done in love it is worthless.

C. JUDGED FROM THE HUMAN POINT-OF-VIEW

Many would judge the congregation in Ephesus to be just about perfect. But this was not what Christ thought. When we lose our love, we often turn to law-keeping and accomplishment to justify ourselves. Perhaps the church in Ephesus did this. One thing we know; since they had left their first love they were doing all the right things for the wrong reasons. Perhaps they thought they had to do those things in order to be good enough to be saved. In Gal. 5:4 Paul says that when you try to be justified by law you have fallen from grace, and are estranged (separated) from Christ. Christ said to the church in Ephesus in Rev. 2:5: "Remember therefore from where you have fallen." They had fallen, and were in danger of being separated from Christ, not just as individuals, but as a church.

D. LOVE BETTER THAN LAW

When it comes to motivating us to do good works, love is much more effective than law. Love goes the second mile. Love was the reason God sent Jesus to save us (John 3:16-17). Love is what motivated Jesus to die for us (Rom. 5:8). Love is the very nature of God Himself (1 John 4:8, 16). Jesus said that love for God and love for our fellow man were the two most important commands (Matt. 22:36-40). They are at the top of the list; nothing else can take their place. Love fulfills all the law, but none of the law can substitute for love. The one new command that Jesus gave was to love as He Himself had loved (John 13:34; 1 John 4:21).

1. To Fall Away from Love Is to Fall Away from God. Since God is love, to fall away from love means to fall away from God. The person who follows law without love has a tendency to be arrogant. He has been known to say, "I'm right and you're wrong, and you're going to hell if you don't get it right like me," or words to that effect. In an illustration I once heard (I don't remember when or where) a person had been attending church for several months, but resisted accepting Christ. When a new preacher came, it wasn't long until the man responded and accepted Christ. Someone asked him why he hadn't responded before this. What made the difference? He

preached the same thing; they both told me that without
to hell. The difference is that the first preacher seemed to
eemed to break the heart of the new preacher to think that

_____ ntial to the Life of a Christian or a Congregation.** To
fall away from love surely calls for drastic measures. Ephesus was warned of
the results in verse 5: "I will come to you quickly and remove your
lampstand from its place—unless you repent." In other words, "You will no
longer be My church." Drastic measures? Yes indeed. But the hope is that
the church in Ephesus would repent and return to the love which formerly
motivated their works before their lampstand (congregation) was finally
removed.

E. REQUIRED ACTION

1. Remember. "Remember therefore from where you have fallen...."
What does that mean? They had to remember what it was like—that sweet
fellowship with one another and with God in the bond of love—and return to
the love that they had at the beginning. They had to begin again to look at
people with concern. They had to see them as objects of God's love, and love
them too. They had to see one another as brothers and sisters, children of the
same Father God, and begin to be more tolerant and helpful, instead of
judgmental and condemning. They had to quit putting God's erring children
out of the church with harshness and begin to try to reclaim them with the
discipline of love.

2. Repent. "...repent and do the first works." Real repentance would put
the works they were doing back on track in the context of love. The first
works were works of love. The result of overcoming their problem (verse 7)
would be that they would be accepted and included rather than removed from
God's fellowship. The result would be eternal life in God's paradise. They
could not function properly under their own power. They had to remember
that Jesus is the one who holds not only the messengers in His hand, but all
the members as well. They had to remember that He walks among them and
knows the inmost secrets of their hearts. Their love had to be genuine; they
could not fake it.

F. THESE ADMONITIONS MEANT FOR US

Please notice that verse 7 says these admonitions are meant for "whoever has an ear." Since I have an ear, I guess that means me. What about you? It also says the Spirit is speaking to the churches (plural). This is not just for the church in Ephesus. That means if you as an individual, or your church, find yourselves pictured in this letter, then you too need to "repent and do the first works," or else the Lord may remove you like He did the church in Ephesus.

The apostle Paul spent three and one-half years preaching and teaching in Ephesus. He had poured himself into that church. But now it is all gone. History shows that the lampstand at Ephesus has been removed. It no longer exists. I wonder how that makes Paul feel, looking down from above, to see his work of love and this church which he loved go down the drain. It reminds me of something Paul wrote in 1 Cor. 3:12-15:

> Now if anyone builds on this foundation *with* gold, silver, precious stones, wood, hay, straw, each one's work will become clear; for the Day will declare it, because it will be revealed by fire; and the fire will test each one's work, of what sort it is. If anyone's work which he has built on *it* endures, he will receive a reward. If anyone's work is burned, he will suffer loss; but he himself will be saved, yet so as through fire.

III. LETTER TWO: TO THE CHURCH AT SMYRNA (2:8-11)

When John finishes writing the letter to Ephesus, he has another one to write. Jesus continues to dictate His letters; the second one is to the church in Smyrna. This is a short letter because Jesus doesn't find anything to criticize in the church at Smyrna. There are some things I seem to remember about this church.

A. POLYCARP AN EXAMPLE OF THOSE KILLED UNDER THE PERSECUTION

In Smyrna Polycarp served as an overseer of the church (bishop, elder, pastor, take your pick since these names all refer to the same position of

55

leadership in the Bible). Polycarp is famous as an early church father. He was one of those who were called *Apostolic Fathers*—i.e., Christian writers who had been associated with one or more of the apostles. He wrote several letters, but only one is available today. He was a student of the apostle John who wrote the book of Revelation. Who knows? Polycarp may have been the angel (messenger) of the church in Smyrna. If so, I imagine that when he received this letter he was glad to hear from John, and from Jesus through him; but he must have been troubled at the same time, because the letter told of troubles the church there was going to have. The message in the letter would relate especially to him because he was one of those who was persecuted and killed as a martyr in the persecution that came to Smyrna.

B. SMYRNA IS COMMENDED BY JESUS

Verse 9 tells us that this church was a working church, but also a very poor church in material things; however, they were very rich in the things that count—in the things of the spirit. This verse also says they were undergoing tribulation (persecution) and suffering. Many in this church were going to be put in prison or killed for their faith in Christ.

In life or death, Jesus would always be with them. Jesus prepares them for suffering by letting them know that He is the First and the Last. He was already here in the beginning, and He will be around when the world is gone. He is the eternal one; but He became a man so that He could die for us.

C. JESUS IS OUR EXAMPLE OF SUFFERING

A body was prepared for Jesus in the womb of Mary so that He could give the life of His body as a sacrifice for sin (Heb. 10:5, 10). He was killed, but He didn't remain dead. He came back to life, and He is alive forevermore. Praise God! He lets them know that death is not the end. According to 1 Cor. 15:22-23 Jesus was the first to rise from the dead never to die again.[2] When

---

[2]There were some who had been restored to this life, such as the widow of Zarephath's son, the widow of Nain's son, the nobleman's son, Jairus the ruler's daughter, Lazarus, etc., but Jesus was the first to rise from the dead into a new life, never to die again. His body had undergone a metamorphosis so that He was not subject to death or pain. It is amazing to me that His risen body bore the marks of His crucifixion. I think this will be a reminder through eternity of the love and grace of God in His sacrifice for us. When we see Him there, we will

He comes back from heaven, those who belong to Him will also come back to life and go to live forever with Him. Jesus tells them not to be afraid. Must they suffer prison and death? That is no problem. He has been there and done that. Of course it would involve suffering on their part, but in the end it will be worth it (Rom. 8:18).

D. DEATH NOT TO BE FEARED

Jesus did not want the Christians of Smyrna to fear death. He said in Matt. 10:28 that we should not fear those who only can kill the body. The one we should really fear is Him who is able to kill both body and soul in hell. In Rev. 20:14 and 21:8 this is called "the second death." This is the death we want to avoid. In verse 11 he assures the church in Smyrna that if they overcome they will not have to worry about the second death, since it will not touch them. In this case *to overcome* means to be faithful during the persecution, even to the point of death. Don't be afraid of what they can do to you (verse 10). This suffering was to be a test of their faith. Jesus admonishes them to be faithful unto death[3] and He will give them the crown of life. He is asking them to be faithful even if it costs them their life.

Jesus told the church that they would have tribulation ten days (verse 10). This would mean imprisonment and death for many, but for those who were faithful it would result in eternal life. The real source of this persecution is the Devil (Satan) just as it was really the Devil who caused all of Job's suffering (see Job 1 – 2). Satan is the one who directs the rulers of the nations and the people of the world to persecute Christians.

Just what does Jesus mean by *ten days*? If He means ten literal days, it would be an extremely short persecution. Ten years would be more like it. Since Revelation was signified (given in symbols) to John, perhaps this has a symbolic meaning. The number *ten* is often used to signify a small amount or

---

know that because of the nail scars and the wound in his side we were given admittance into the eternal kingdom.

[3]Some versions translate this to mean *until death*. Although this is a possible meaning of the words ἄχρι θανάτου (achri thanatou), the basic idea is *even to the point of death*. *Unto* is a better translation because it better expresses what Jesus is saying. He is not just saying, "be faithful as long as you live," but "be faithful even if it costs your life."

short period of time, but there are several instances in the Old Testament where a day is used to mean a year (see *Appendix B*). Maybe Jesus means a period of approximately ten years. Church history tells us that there was just such a period of persecution in that region soon after John wrote this.

While John was writing the Revelation Pliny the Younger was a senator of Rome under Emperor Domitian. In the early second century the Roman Emperor Trajan put Pliny the Younger in charge of enforcing emperor worship in portions of Asia Minor. Trajan and Pliny wrote many letters to each other which have been preserved and translated into English. Pliny felt that the Christians were harmless, and tried to get Trajan to go easy on them. In response Trajan wrote that Pliny should not go looking for Christians to persecute, but if any were brought to his attention, he was to ask them to prove their loyalty to Trajan by sprinkling incense on the altar fire in worship to the emperor's image. If they would do this they could go free. If they refused, they would be imprisoned or killed, and their property confiscated, leaving their families destitute. Pliny did his job, and the families of many Christians lost their fathers and husbands, as well as their property and means of making a living. This persecution went on for approximately ten years in that region.

E. FALSE JEWS LEAD THE PERSECUTION

The false Jews of Smyrna led in the persecution. I doubt that the church in Smyrna met in the Jewish synagogue, since the Jews there hated them. In fact, they were stirring up persecution against the Christians. Verse 9 calls them false Jews. Paul wrote that a real Jew is a person whose heart is right with God, and real circumcision takes place in the heart (Rom. 2:28-29; Col. 2:11). In the persecution which the Romans brought against this region, the Jews were the ones who rushed to gather the wood used for burning Christian leaders at the stake. According to *Fox's Book of Martyrs,* this is how Polycarp died.

F. APPLICABLE TODAY

What does this letter have to do with me? It was written over 1900 years ago to a church far off in what is now Turkey. What can it possibly say to me in the 21st century? As a matter of fact, there were more Christians killed for their faith in the 20th century than in all the centuries before this put together. Amazing but true! Jesus says in verse 13 that if we have an ear we should listen to what He says to Smyrna. Persecution is still going on today, in the beginning of the 21st century, even as I write this.

Not many years ago the government of Uganda was targeting Christians, and killing Christian ministers. By the grace of God that country now respects Christianity, and many Christians are in positions of influence in the different levels of government. A missionary friend in Uganda lives under constant threat of death, because the godless guerillas from across the border in the Congo have put out a "contract" on his life. Thank God that He has seen fit to protect him so far. There is a very real possibility that we may be called on to suffer persecution and death because of our faith in Christ. What should we do? The assurance and admonition given to Smyrna is for us also. If we want that crown of eternal life we must be faithful even if it costs our lives. I want it! Don't you?

IV. LETTER THREE: TO THE CHURCH AT PERGAMUM (2:12-17)

In this letter Jesus pictures Himself as the one who has the sharp two-edged sword (verse 12). He is referring back to the vision in chapter one where He is pictured as having a sword coming out of His mouth (1:16). We'll soon see how this has an application to the church in Pergamum.

One thing Jesus says in all seven letters, (and that means to all congregations) is, "**I know your works**" (verse 13). He can say this because He walks among the churches. He knows them intimately. Pergamum is no exception, and neither is your congregation or mine.

Jesus knew that the church in Pergamum held on to His name and wouldn't let go of their faith in Christ. He knew that one of their members, a man named Antipas was a faithful witness,[4] i.e., he faithfully told others about his faith, and Jesus knew that he had lost his life because of it. But

---

[4]The word *martyr* in this verse, translated from the Greek μάρτυς *(martus)*, is defined as *witness,* and is so translated in some Bible versions. It came to mean *martyr* by analogy, since, as in the case of Antipas, those who bore witness of their faith in Christ were often killed.

Jesus also knew some things about them that were not so good—things like fornication and idol worship (verse 14).

A. The Wickedness of Pergamos

The city of Pergamum was so wicked that Jesus said Satan's throne was there and that he made it his home (verse 13).[5]   Satan rules and lives wherever people will let him. When God created man He gave this world to him to have dominion over it, but because Adam and Eve gave in to Satan's lies and obeyed Satan instead of God, man forfeited his dominion to Satan. Now, as a result, this earth is the domain of Satan. He lives and rules here. He is called *the god of this age* (2 Cor. 4:4), *the ruler of this world* (John 12:31), and *the prince of the power of the air* (Eph. 2:2). This rule of Satan is manifest on a smaller scale in Pergamum.

1. A Center of Idolatrous Practices. This city was a center for the worship of pagan gods, and all the wickedness that went along with that. Men and women would worship in their temples by having sexual intercourse with the male and female prostitutes who were called *priests* and *priestesses.* They would also partake in the animal sacrifices that were given. The meat was usually sold in the temple meat market, and people would buy this meat to eat. Paul tells us there is nothing wrong with the meat itself but to partake involved too many problems (1 Cor. 8:4-10; 10:18-21, 27-29). Those who came out of idolatry found it difficult to eat of this meat without defiling their conscience. But some in the church in Pergamum were openly going to the temple not only to eat of the sacrifices, but to partake in the sexual immorality that was part of the pagan worship.

To worship idols is to worship demons according to both Old and New Testaments (1 Cor. 10:19-20). The images themselves are nothing but wood or stone, or metal such as gold, silver or bronze, but in fact there are evil spirits under Satan's control, called *demons* or *devils,* who are behind these idols and influence those who worship them. These demons are fallen angels like Satan (2 Pet. 2:4). They are called *angels of the Devil* (Rev. 12:7-9).

---

[5]For insights into archeological finds concerning geological and historical conditions in Ephesus, Pergamum, Sardis, and Laodicea I am much indebted to Ray Vander Laan's video series *That the World May Know,* Volume Five, *Faith Lessons on the Early Church,* published by Focus on the Family, 1999.

Idolatry is a work of the Devil. Except for the Christians in Pergamum, the city was totally under the influence of the Devil.

2. False Teachings. Some in the church espoused the teachings of the Nicolaitans. In Acts 20:28-31 Paul warned the elders of the church in Ephesus against false teachers who were coming soon. Some would sneak into the church from outside while others would come from among the leaders in the church. One of these false teachers was a man called Nicolaius. His followers were known as Nicolaitans. He taught that it was permissible to commit fornication and worship idols. This is also called *the doctrine of Balaam.* Balaam was a Gentile prophet of God who went wrong because he loved money too much. He tried to curse the Israelites in the wilderness because Balak, king of Moab, offered him money.

The teaching of Balaam caused Israel to sin and incur God's wrath. The Israelites were traveling in the wilderness, and wanted to go through Moab to get to the promised land. Balak was afraid of the Israelites and wanted them stopped. You can read the whole story in Num. 22 - 25. When God would not allow Balaam to curse Israel, he quit trying, but he still coveted the money, so he taught Balak how he could get the Israelites to curse themselves. Balak could send in Moabite women to seduce them to have sex, and to worship their idols. This would make God angry, and He would punish them.

The plan worked; God became angry with His people (Num. 25:1-3 and 31:16). As a result, those who practice the things done by some in the church in Pergamum are said to be following after the teaching of Balaam (read 2 Pet. 2:15 and Jude 1:11). Not all the members of the church in Pergamum were faithful, for some were following this false doctrine. What was going to happen to them?

B. THE TWO-EDGED SWORD

1. The Power of the Sword. Here is where the two-edged sword of verse 16 comes in. Pergamum was the capital of the province of Asia, and the governor of Pergamum was the only one in all Asia who held "the power of the sword." This means that he had the power to decide whether men lived or died. But it is Jesus who holds the two-edged sword. He is the one who has the power to give life as well as to take it, and the life that He gives is eternal life.

The temple of Dionysus was in this city. This god was able, supposedly, to give eternal life. This could be attained (again supposedly) by the worshipers eating of the raw meat of the sacrificed animals, and by becoming drunk. In this drunken state one was supposed to be united with Dionysus. Jesus wants the Christians in Pergamum to know that only He has the power to give eternal life.

2. The Church in Pergamum to be Pruned. In effect Jesus says "knock it off or be cut off!" Repent! In other words, stop doing these things and start living lives that are pure and righteous. If you don't, then the sword of His mouth will cut you off. To be cut off from the church and from Christ, means to be cut off from eternal life.

This sword, in fact, is the word of God (see Eph. 6:17 and Heb. 4:12). God can do powerful things by just speaking since He has all power. He said, "Let there be light," and it happened. He spoke and the worlds sprang into existence. Just let the governor of Pergamum try doing that with his sword! Jesus spoke and demons came out of people. Evil spirits tremble at His word. When Peter spoke the word of God, Ananias, the liar, fell down dead. When Jesus returns, His word will call down judgment and destruction on all the forces of evil (see Rev. 19:11-21, especially verse 15). If I were doing the things some in the church in Pergamum were doing, I would be afraid of the sword of His mouth.

C. REWARDS FOR REPENTANCE AND FAITHFULNESS

1. Jesus to Feed Them with Hidden Manna. This is the spiritual food that gives life to the soul. One of the temples in this important city was that of Demeter, the goddess of grain. She was supposed to be the source of bread and other food. Christ wants the church there to know that He is the source of the food for the spirit, here called manna, a figure taken from the manna that was given by God to the Israelites to eat in the wilderness. God, not Demeter, is the real provider of grain, but God can also provide us with the bread of life. That bread is Jesus Himself (John 6:27-35).

2. A White Stone. A white stone is a symbol of acceptance and approval. When a person applied for membership in some important group, or when he was on trial, the ones doing the judging would place stones in a container or in the hand of the one being judged. A black stone meant rejection or a verdict of guilty. A white stone meant acquittal or acceptance. Jesus draws on this custom by using the white stone as a symbol of His approval.

There may be another meaning to the white stone in this letter. Another temple in Pergamum was the temple of Aesculapius, the god of healing. He is the one who is associated with medical doctors.[6] When this temple was uncovered by archaeologists, in front of the temple were many large blocks of white stone upon which those who believed themselves healed by Aesculapius had carved their names and listed the nature of their healing. Jesus may have been saying, "I am going to give you a similar stone and write on it your new name." He wanted them to know that He is the source of healing, not the pagan god Aesculapius. They alone would know the name Jesus would give them. This stone is the symbol of their testimony to the fact that they have become a new creature in Christ. He has not only given them healing, He has given them a new name and life everlasting.

D. APPLICABLE TO US ALSO

"He who has an ear, let him hear." Do I need to explain how this letter could apply to all of us? Just put yourself in the place of the members of this church. Are you one who is faithful, like Antipas? Or are you one who yields to the pressures of society around you to conform to its ways? Idolatry is more than just bowing to images made of wood, stone or metal. Paul says that covetousness (lusting after money or things) is idolatry (Col. 3:5). We are guilty of idolatry when we put anything or anyone ahead of God. Immoral sexual acts are as wrong today as they were then. Society says they are all right, but God does not bend to the whims of society. Destruction came upon the Israelites in the wilderness when they yielded to the Moabite women (1 Cor. 10:6-11). Paul said what happened to them are examples for

---

[6]The symbol displayed in the medical profession is a staff with a snake coiled around it. The snake is the sign of Aesculapius, the god of healing, also called *the snake god.*

us. The sword from the mouth of Christ is just as sharp and effective today as it was then.

V. LETTER FOUR: TO THE CHURCH AT THYATIRA (2:18-29)

A. PRAISED FOR ITS WORKS, LOVE, SERVICE, FAITH, AND PATIENCE

Praise for the church in Thyatira, coming from the mouth of Jesus, is no small thing; however there were some things that were displeasing to Him. The church, especially its leadership, had not been as diligent as it should have been in protecting the flock from hurtful and dangerous doctrines and practices. In particular, He talks about the same false teachings and practices we saw in Pergamum, the same things that were strongly opposed by the church in Ephesus.

B. THE TEACHING AND PRACTICE OF JEZEBEL

1. The Persistent Teaching of Balaam. Someone in this church was teaching the doctrine of the Nicolaitans, the doctrine of Balaam. Jesus does not name this doctrine here, but He does describe the contents of that teaching. It is the same old problem that invaded so many churches in the idolatrous province of Asia, It involved committing fornication and worshiping idols. One big difference here is that the one who was teaching this to the Christians was herself a member of the church, or at least she was allowed to come into the church to teach her abominable practices. Was she given an active role in the church? Was she a Bible class teacher? Was she recognized by the church as prophetess? I don't know, but I doubt that she was any of these things. The letter says that she called herself a prophetess. This seems to indicate that she was not officially recognized as a prophetess by the church. I have known women like that, self styled prophetesses who stirred up trouble in the congregation.

2. The Woman in Thyatira Called Jezebel. This self-styled prophetess was called *Jezebel.* I doubt that this was her real name. It is used in much the same way that we use it today. People often call a woman a Jezebel who makes a practice of seducing men, especially the husbands of other women. That is what this woman did in Thyatira. She seduced the men in that congregation to commit fornication with her, and to eat the sacrifices made to idols. She may have been one of the priestesses or temple prostitutes at one of the local idolatrous temples. In any case, she was a tool of Satan to corrupt the church in Thyatira.

The original Jezebel was the queen of the northern kingdom of Israel, the wife of King Ahab. This kingdom had worshiped idols from its beginning. Jezebel, being a high priestess of Baal, was the main influence in idol worship in the days of King Ahab. She seduced people to commit fornication and worship idols. Read the story of Ahab and Jezebel in 1 and 2 Kings. Jezebel was an appropriate name to call this woman in Thyatira.

C. APPLICATION OF THE DESCRIPTION OF JESUS TO THIS CHURCH

1. The Flaming Eyes of Jesus. Jesus ties the letter to the description of the vision of Christ in the first chapter. He begins this letter by saying, "These things says the Son of God, who has eyes like a flame of fire, and His feet like fine brass." Why does he refer to these characteristics? Because they needed to know of His ability to see into their hearts and know its condition. He has eyes that can pierce into the very secret places and know the intents and motivations of each person's heart.

Jesus wants all the churches to know that He is the one who searches the minds and hearts. He is able to give to each one punishments or rewards according to the works of each. There is no miscarriage of justice with Him because He knows exactly what is what. In chapter 5 Jesus is pictured as a Lamb with seven eyes. The seven eyes stand for perfect sight or perfect knowledge and understanding. There is nothing He does not see or know.

2. The Gleaming Feet of Jesus. Secondly, He refers to His feet which are like highly polished bronze, the symbol of His beauty and glory. He **will** be glorified in His church, either through the righteous deeds of the saints, or else through His righteous judgments upon them.

D. THE JUDGMENT OF JEZEBEL AND HER CONSORTS

Notice the righteous judgments of Christ upon Jezebel and upon those she has seduced. The God of all mercy even gave the woman called Jezebel time to repent, but she refused.

1. Jezebel to be Cast into a Sickbed. This is a play upon the fact that the tool of a prostitute is a bed. Her bed was to be turned against her. It was to become a bed of sickness and suffering for her.

2. Her Children to be Killed with Death. *Death* is probably a reference to pestilence, such as *the black death* or *bubonic plague*. This term (*death*) was often used to indicate death-dealing pestilence. The children of Jezebel, possibly the offspring of her abominable practices, would suffer death, perhaps from the same sickness that was to afflict the woman herself.

3. Great Tribulation and Suffering upon Her Consorts. Those who participated with her were to suffer tribulation unless they repented. What was the tribulation? I don't know. Maybe they would suffer from some dreadful venereal disease which they caught from the woman. Whatever it was, it was a just judgment.

4. Destruction from God's Presence (2 Thess. 1:8-9). There would also be eternal consequences—eternal destruction and exclusion from the presence of God. There was only one way for them to escape these consequences. That is through genuine repentance. This is something often accompanied by weeping and loud cries of pleading. It takes a strong emotional upheaval to affect a true change of life. God loves a broken and contrite heart. He is always willing to hear and have mercy on the truly penitent. There is forgiveness in abundance because of the blood shed by Christ on the cross, but, "except you repent you will perish" (Luke 13:3, 5).

E. REWARDS OF THE FAITHFUL

1. Not Everyone in this Church under Condemnation. Like Pergamum, the majority of the church was not involved with this practice; many were faithful—so faithful, in fact, that Jesus commended them for their works, love, faith, service and patience. Not only that, but their works were increasing. The latter were more than the former. The works here were not a mere formality, the result of legalistic duty. Their works were the service of love. Service is another term related to works. I think it is interesting that Jesus refers to their works in these three ways—works, service, and more or greater works.

2. Admonition to the Faithful. Jesus has words of admonition for these faithful also. They are the ones who were not drawn into this doctrine of Balaam. They had not participated in the fornication or idol worship. They had not even tacitly approved of it. They were the ones who haven't become acquainted with the depths of such Satanic evil, but had kept themselves separate from such things. These were the ones holding fast to Christ and His work until He returns. He would not put any greater burdens upon them than what they were already bearing. Instead they would share in the rewards of faithfulness. Two things are mentioned as rewards for the faithful:

First, they will receive great power to rule over nations. The passage does not say exactly how this will play out. There are many ideas that people have about this. I have my own, but that remains for the examination of later passages.

Second, they will be given the Morning Star. I have capitalized Morning Star, because in Rev. 22:16 Jesus calls Himself *the Bright and Morning Star.* What greater reward could a lover of Jesus have than to possess Him as an ever present friend and companion, to be able to look upon and embrace Him who loves us and redeemed us with His own precious blood?

F. WORDS FOR YOU AND ME

In this letter, Jesus addresses you and me, i.e., whoever has an ear to hear. Do you see how you and your church might fit into this picture? Is Jesus addressing "the things that exist" in your church? Are there idolatrous practices among the members, such as covetousness and materialism? Are there sexually immoral practices? There are churches which condone or put up with such things in our day. Is yours one of them? For many of us there is a lot to think about and to repent of. There are three more letters written to the churches, including yours. Will they help us to realize a greater burden of repentance? We will see as we read chapter 3.

Chapter 3

LETTERS TO THE SEVEN CHURCHES
Rev. Chapter 3 – LETTERS FIVE, SIX, AND SEVEN

I. THE THEME OF REVELATION IN THE LETTERS

The seven letters are connected to the overall theme of the book of Revelation—i.e., **through persecution and tribulation to victory**. "But thanks *be* to God, who gives us the victory through our Lord Jesus Christ" (1 Cor. 15:57). "Now thanks *be* to God who always leads us in triumph in Christ" (2 *Cor.* 2:14). The letters are calling His church to repentance, to remembrance, to purity, and to perseverance. The victory is Christ's, but those who participate in that victory must persevere in their Faithfulness to Him and not give in to the pressures of the world or to the trials of Satan who wants to turn us aside from the faith and cause us to be lost. The Devil himself has no power to make us fall. He can only tempt us. If we fall it will be because we choose to yield to those temptations.

A. THREE KINDS OF TEMPTATION

In these letters we can see three ways Satan tempts us:

1. The Appeal of the World to Entice us. Satan uses the lust of the flesh, the lust of the eye, and the pride of life to lure us into his kingdom.

2. The Pressures of Persecution. He uses persecution to try to force us into yielding to him.

3. The Deceit of False Teachings. He sends false teachers who teach the doctrines and philosophies of men (really the doctrines of demons) to delude us and cause us to believe and practice lies. These three weapons of

Satan are seen in the seven letters, and are represented in the drama of the things that are to take place after this.

B. THE PREVALENCE OF TEMPTATIONS

These temptations are still much in evidence today. Peter wrote in 1 Pet. 5:8-9:

> Be sober, be vigilant; because your adversary the devil walks about like a roaring lion, seeking whom he may devour. Resist him, steadfast in the faith, knowing that the same sufferings are experienced by your brotherhood in the world.

1. Allurements of the World Everywhere. In our own day the senses are bombarded with images on radio, TV and the movies that lure us into impure thoughts and immoral practices. Billboards, magazines, and even store window displays, etc., also add to this temptation.

2. Persecution in Many Forms. In the work place and in school those who are considered religious fanatics because they believe in Christ and His way of living are often ignored, or laughed at, ridiculed, and shunned while in parts of the world believers suffer the worst kinds of persecutions, torture and death.

3. False Teachings Rampant. Television, radio, books, magazines, schools and other public forums, and even pulpits are busy spewing out all kinds of doctrines and philosophies that turn the minds of people to every conceivable belief system, from eastern mysticism to spiritism, new age religions and philosophies, animism, pantheism, atheism, etc. People don't know what to believe. Even the saints are not immune to the influence of such teachings, especially when they come in the guise of science and scholarship. Paul said that false teachers would show lying signs and wonders so as to deceive even the elect (2 Thess. 2:9-10; Acts 20:29-30; Mark 13:22). These letters warn us to be watchful so as to avoid such deception. They also admonish us to stand firm in the face of persecution and enticements.

II. LETTER FIVE: TO THE CHURCH AT SARDIS (3:1-6)

A. REPRESENTATIONS OF JESUS

1. The Seven Spirits and the Seven Stars (See 1:4, 16). Remember that in each letter Jesus introduces himself by one or two of the features of the vision that John saw in Rev. 1. If the reader's memory is a bit hazy about this description, he/she should go back to chapter one of this book and review the information about the vision. The fact that Jesus is the one who has the seven Spirits of God and the seven stars is going to be important to the church at Sardis.

2. The Holy Spirit Represented as the Seven Spirits. The Spirit raised Jesus to life after His crucifixion, and He is going to give life to our mortal bodies also (Rom. 8:11; 1 Cor. 15:53-54). This same Spirit first breathed life into the church at Jerusalem on the day of Pentecost just days after Christ arose from the dead. If a church is dead it means they have quenched the Spirit which gives life. Jesus is the one who has the Spirit who can give life to a congregation. Sardis needed this, because Jesus said they were dead even though they had a reputation for being a living, vital congregation.

3. Leaders of the Church Represented as Seven Stars. Jesus wanted them to know that He holds the messengers in His hand. He is the one who loves and cares for them, and will be with them always provided they remain faithful to Him. This posed a problem in Sardis because the leaders had not been very effective or faithful. The church needs to heed the star of this congregation who presents this message to them so they will repent and get back on track.

B. THE CONDITION OF THE CONGREGATION

1. Defiled Garments. Most, but not all, had gotten their robes of righteousness all dirty. We read about these garments of linen several times in the book of Revelation (3:5,18; 4:4; 7:9; etc.). In 19:8 the church (the bride of Christ) is clothed in fine linen, pure and bright, which are the righteous deeds of the saints. These garments are given to us because we are unable to clothe ourselves with righteousness. Paul wrote in Phil. 3:9; "...not having my own righteousness, which *is* from the law, but that which *is* through faith in Christ, the righteousness which is from God by faith."

In speaking of this righteousness Paul said in Rom. 4:24, "...It shall be imputed[1] to us who believe...." Our white garments are a gift from God. When we strive to walk in His light, the sins we commit are automatically erased (1 John 1:7-10). When we start substituting our own righteousness for the righteousness of Christ, we defile our garments. When we use the grace of God as a license for sin, we defile our garments.

2. Spiritually Dead. The seven Spirits of God are the source both of our power of service in Christ and of purity and sanctification of life. When the Holy Spirit is in control we are really alive. When the Spirit is resisted and quenched we are surely dead. Since the seven Spirits are lamps of fire, then to quench the Spirit is to put out the light.

3. The Meaning of Spiritual Death. What does Jesus mean when He says that the church in Sardis is dead? He did not necessarily mean that the congregation had only a few members. I think there are many churches today that seem to be vital and growing, but they are dead spiritually because they are operating under their own power instead of under the power of the Holy Spirit. Perhaps the Christians in Sardis were depending upon themselves, their own plans, their own efforts, their own righteousness.

Churches can be "gung-ho" and grow in numbers by leaps and bounds through the efforts of "charismatic" leaders. They are able to sway multitudes by their speaking abilities and by the theatrics they use so that people flock to them. They plan great programs, and because they have abundant funds they are able to hire "ministers" to run these programs. But unless the Spirit of God is in it, that church only has a reputation for being alive. Their works are imperfect before the Lord.

I have known of congregations that were powerful in the Lord for awhile, but, after they had accomplished great things for the Lord by the help of God's Spirit, they were enticed into taking pride in what had been accomplished. They stopped working and just settled into a pattern of house-keeping while taking satisfaction in past glories. Such a congregation also

---

[1]The word in the Greek is λογίζομαι (logizomai—pronounced log-ee´-dzo-my). it is a term sometimes used in accounting. A sum of money may be set down, counted, reckoned to a particular account. In this case it is righteousness that is set down to one's credit in God's reckoning, not by merit on our part but by substituting Christ's righteousness for our own (See Rom. 5:5-6). A deposit of Christ's righteousness is made to our account.

may have a reputation for being alive while being dead. They are coasting on their past reputation. The works of such a congregation are not perfect before the Lord. Perhaps Sardis was a church like this.

4. Compromise with Culture. Archaeological finds in Sardis show both Jewish and Christian shops with their respective symbols existing side by side with the shops of the idol worshipers. The Christian shops displayed the sign of the fish and/or a cross. This indicates that Christians, even in the shadow of pagan idolatry, were taking a stand and bearing testimony to the true God and Savior. Also found in the Christian shops were defaced symbols of pagan gods. There was the lion that carried Cybele with the figure of Cybele broken off. They were trying to show that the true Lion is Christ. Some pagan artifacts had the inscriptions scratched off and replaced with Christian symbols.[2]

There was a Christian meeting place built right in a corner of the temple of Artemis. Was this intended to be a testimony to the pagans of the one true God? Probably they hoped to influence the pagan society by worshiping Yahweh and Jesus in the midst of their pagan idolatry. Yet there is indication that they began to compromise with the pagan society, and their testimony was compromised as a result. They had started out with great fervor and zeal, but they quit before their work was completed. So Jesus told them, "I have not found your works complete." They did not finish what they started.

C. THE REMEDY

What is the Lord's prescribed remedy for this situation? It is found in verses 2 and 3:

> Be watchful and strengthen the things which remain, that are ready to die, for I have not found your works perfect before God. Remember therefore how you have received and heard; hold fast and repent.

1. Be Watchful. In verse three He says that if they don't watch, He will come upon them like a thief in the night. The most popular king of Sardis was the legendary King Croesus, noted for his great wealth. He reigned in

---

[2]Ray Vander Laan's video series *That the World May Know,* Volume Five, *Faith Lessons on the Early Church,* published by Focus on the Family, 1999.

Sardis until approximately 550 B.C. At that time King Cyrus of Persia found a way to enter the city by stealth at night. Destruction came upon Sardis like a thief in the night. The citizens of Sardis were no doubt aware of this history and could appreciate Jesus' reference to His coming upon them like a thief.

We must be prepared for the Lord's coming by being watchful.[3] We are admonished to "watch and pray" (Matt. 12:13). If we are watching for His coming we will not be taken by surprise, as if by a thief in the night. Jesus has not published His time-table. We don't know when He will come again. We should live each day as if it were the last—the day of the return of our Lord. If we do this, we will not be caught unprepared.

2. Strengthen What Remains. They were just about to die. If that happens this church would cease to exist. Jesus told the church in Ephesus that He would remove their lampstand if they didn't repent. In the case of the church at Sardis the lamp would simply have gone out. But there was still hope. The lamp was still smoldering. Their hope rested in deliberately focusing on the things that remained—that is, upon the little faith that still remained, upon the few that had not defiled their garments, upon the righteousness which comes from God rather than from men, and upon the light of the Holy Spirit which had just about gone out on their lampstands. In Rev. 4:5 the seven lamps of fire before the throne of God are the seven Spirits of God. The seven lampstands (churches) are for holding up the seven lamps of fire. Here is the importance, then, of Jesus telling them that He has the seven Spirits. He can help them fan into flame the fire on their lampstand.

To strengthen[4] what remains they would have to fan the flame diligently so that the Spirit would burn brightly again in their lives and hearts. If they were practicing immorality, they would need to submit their lives to the Holy Spirit's sanctifying power, so that He could develop in them purity of life. If

---

[3]Translated from γρηγορῶν (gregoron) from γρηγορέω – *Strong's Greek Dictionary* defines this as, "to *keep awake,* that is, *watch* (literally or figuratively):—be vigilant, awake, (be) watch (-ful)." Thayer's definition is, "1) to watch, 2) metaphorically give strict attention to, be cautious, active, 2a) to take heed lest through remission and indolence some destructive calamity suddenly overtake one."

[4]From στηρίζω (*sterizo*—pronounced *stay-ree'-dzo*) – *Strong's* definition is, to set fast, that is, (literally) to *turn* resolutely in a certain direction, or (figuratively) to *confirm:*—fix, establish, steadfastly set, strengthen.

they were following their own plans and agendas and depending upon their own strength, they would have to submit to the Spirit's guidance and power to accomplish through Him what God wanted to accomplish. If they were resting on their laurels, they would have to forget what is behind and press forward to what is ahead, rekindling the flame of the Spirit of God, of wisdom and understanding, of counsel and might, of knowledge and the fear of the Lord.

They would need to fan this flame into burning zeal for the Lord. They would have to get down on their knees in prayer and tears of in repentance, and seek revival and the guidance from the Lord, and the power to accomplish whatever it is that God wanted to accomplish through them.

3. Remember. Remember how you have received and heard. This is where the seven stars come into play. Jesus holds the angels (messengers) in His hand. That means He is in control both of the messenger and the message. That may be why these letters are addressed to the messengers. Faithful ministers will deliver the message the Lord gives them. So Jesus tells the church at Sardis to remember how they first received and heard the word. Remember the gospel message faithfully delivered by Christ's ministers.

Just as Ephesus was told to return to their first love, so Sardis is being admonished to return to what they had heard and received. Churches that have drifted into doctrines and commandments of men need to remember. Churches that have adopted a social gospel or a "Reader's Digest" gospel mentality need to remember. Churches that have been lured into liberalizing the Word of God need to remember.

4. Hold Fast to What Remains. "Hold fast the word which was preached to you, the pattern of sound words which you heard and received" (1 Cor. 15:2; 2 Tim. 1:13). "Test all things; hold fast what is good" (1 Thess. 5:21). ". . .hold fast the confidence and the rejoicing of the hope firm to the end" (Heb. 3:6). "Let us hold fast the confession of *our* hope without wavering" (Heb. 10:23; see also 4:14). "Therefore, my beloved brethren, be steadfast, immovable, always abounding in the work of the Lord, knowing that your labor is not in vain in the Lord" (1 Cor. 15:58).

5. Repent. Repentance is a change of heart that results in a change of life. There was much for which the church of Sardis needed to repent. The few who had not defiled their garments should be looked to as the example. Where they were largely ignored before, these are the ones who should be heeded and followed. They are the kind of leaders the Lord wants in a congregation. Too often a church that is worldly-wise will ignore such people, considering them to be an embarrassment and a hindrance to their plans. But these are the ones who know the score, who sense the need, and who weep for the condition of their church.

I have known of congregations who have put "those who have not defiled their garments" out of the church. They were a grievous sore upon those congregations, reminding them of things they didn't want to remember. Repentance, then, means that where the leaders ignored and put down those who were truly spiritual they will seek out and pay heed to their counsel.

Repentance means that those congregations which are operating under their own power will begin to operate under the power of the Holy Spirit. Repentance means that those who have quit ministering and are resting on past glories will once again fan the flame into the fire of zealous ministry. Repentance means that those who have adopted immoral lifestyles will quit, and begin to live under the power and direction and sanctification of the Holy Spirit. Repentance means that those who have depended upon their own righteousness will acknowledge their own filthiness and let Christ clothe them with His righteousness. Repentance can bring this church to life again, because it will allow the life-giving Spirit of God to resume His work in them.

D. THE REWARDS

What are the rewards for the faithful and for those who repent? Those who have not dirtied their white garments will hear Jesus say, "Come and walk with Me in your clothes of righteousness. You are worthy, because I have made you worthy. Come share My glory." Those who overcome by repenting and holding fast will hear Him say, "Here are some clean clothes for you to wear, made clean and white in My blood. Come walk with me in these clothes of righteousness." Then Jesus will look at His book of life and think, *Their names are here. They have overcome, so I will not erase their names from my book.* Then He will take them, the ones who have not soiled their garments and those who have overcome their past sorry state, and will lead them to the throne and say, "Father, here are Your children. I'm not ashamed to acknowledge them as Mine because they are sinless since they are clothed in My righteousness. My blood has erased their former sinfulness."

E. THE MESSAGE FOR US ALSO

Finally, this letter says the same thing they have all said. **"He who has an ear, let him hear what the Spirit says to the churches."** Do you have an ear? Then this letter is for you as well as for Sardis. What kind of church are you in? How many of its members have not defiled their garments? Does your church have a reputation for being alive and growing? Is the reputation true or is the congregation following its own agenda? Is it operating under its own steam, where its growth is due to the magnetism of some "charismatic" leader? Is the church's reputation based upon past successes in ministry? Has it begun to look back and glory in those successes, thinking that it has already made its mark and can coast along? Is your church one which has snuffed out the light of the Spirit through false teaching or immorality?

In other words, is your church a dead church? If it is, it needs to heed the admonitions given to Sardis. If you are one who has gone along with such a church, you are one who has defiled your garment of righteousness. You need to watch, to strengthen what remains, to remember, to hold fast, and to repent.

If you will heed these warnings and repent, Christ will give you a white garment so you can walk with Him up to the Father, before His angels, and hear Him say that you are His. He will conduct you to your mansion of glory where you will live forever in His presence. Praise be to the Lamb Whose blood cleanses us and makes us perfect in His sight.

III. LETTER SIX: TO THE CHURCH AT PHILADELPHIA (3:7-13)

The name *Philadelphia* comes from a combination of two Greek words which mean *to love*, and *a brother*.[5] This is why some call Philadelphia, PA *the city of brotherly love*.

A. PHILADELPHIA'S CONDITION

Like the letter to the church in Smyrna, this letter says nothing bad about the church in Philadelphia, unless you think Jesus said something bad when he pointed out that they have only "a little strength." However, this statement is included with a list of virtues. Contrast the strength of the church at Philadelphia with that of Sardis or some of the others. Sardis was dead—no strength at all. Ephesus was about to die out completely unless they repented. Pergamos and Thyatira were putting up with false doctrine and immorality. Laodicea had become lukewarm and materialistic. Philadelphia comes out smelling like a rose compared to all of these.

The churches of Smyrna and Philadelphia are the shining stars among these seven. They are the only two that were not commanded to repent of anything. There was no word of censure to either congregation. Apparently they had nothing for which they, as congregations, needed to repent.

B. CHARACTERISTICS OF JESUS THAT PERTAIN TO PHILADELPHIA

1. Holy and True. Jesus identifies himself as the one who is holy and true. In Rev. 1:5 He is described as "the faithful witness." The church needs to know that what Jesus says is true. He is faithful to His promises. Their continuing faithfulness will not be ignored or in vain. They can depend on Jesus. He says that He is the one "who has the key of David, He who opens and no one shuts, and shuts and no one opens." In Rev. 1:18 Jesus says that He was dead but is now alive. The reason He is alive is that He has the keys of Hades and Death. Hades is the unseen state of those who are dead as they await the resurrection (see *Appendix A*). This is the ultimate example of His

---

[5] φιλέω *(phileo, pronounced fee-lay'-o – to love, have affection for)*, φιλία *(philia, pronounced fee-lee'-ah – affection, fondness, love)*; and ἀδελφός, *(adelphos, pronounced ah-del-fos' – a brother, a relative).*

having the power to open doors. He opened the doors of Death and Hades and came forth from the grave alive after His death.

2. The Possessor of the Keys. Jesus has the keys. Keys are used to open and shut, to lock and unlock. The keys described in chapter 1 are to be used to open Death and Hades. Another key that He possesses is called the "key of David"; that is, the authority of the King of Israel to open and shut: "He who opens and no one shuts, and shuts and no one opens." Acts 2:30 tells us that Christ was raised to sit on David's throne. This He did when He ascended to heaven. He Himself is the David[6] prophesied in the Old Testament prophets. The next verse shows us how he uses the statement about the key in this letter.

C. *JESUS PROVIDES FOR PHILADELPHIA*

1. Jesus Knows Their Works. This is the same thing He said to all seven churches. There is no hiding from His eyes. Then He said, "I have set before you an open door; and no one can shut it." Jesus used "the key of David" to open a door for them because they had a little strength, had kept His word, and had not denied His name.

2. A Door of Opportunity. Jesus opened a door of opportunity to influence the false Jews. They were pronounced false not because they were not born of the proper Jewish parents, or because they had not been circumcised in their flesh, but because they had rejected Christ. In verse 9 Jesus says, "Indeed I will make *those* of the synagogue of Satan, who say they are Jews and are not, but lie—indeed I will make them come and worship before your feet, and to know that I have loved you." How far did this door of opportunity reach? These Jews were to come and worship before the feet of the Christians and would understand that the Son of God loved these Christians whom they had previously despised and persecuted. That is, they would worship God in the presence of the Christians. Jesus would hardly cause the Jews to worship the Christians. The expression *before the feet of* often referred to the position of a disciple or student before his teacher.

---

[6]Centuries after David died and was buried Ezekiel prophesied that David would reign as king forever and would be our shepherd (Ezek. 34:23-24; 37:24-25). This was a prophecy of the Christ.

When one is instructed or led by another, it is said that the he sat at the feet of the teacher or leader.

Jesus also called the Jews in Smyrna false Jews in Rev. 2:9: "*I know* the blasphemy of those who say they are Jews and are not; but *are* a synagogue of Satan." There is no indication that these Jews in Smyrna were to be influenced for good as they were in Philadelphia. In both places they are called a synagogue of Satan. Because they rejected Christ and persecuted His church they were worshiping Satan and doing His work. Christ denied they were Jews. In Rom. 2:28-29 Paul wrote this:

> For he is not a Jew who *is one* outwardly nor *is* circumcision that which *is* outward in the flesh; but *he is* a Jew who *is one* inwardly; and circumcision *is that* of the heart, in the Spirit, not in the letter; whose praise *is* not from men but from God.

The test of being a true Jew was circumcision of the heart, in the Spirit, not literally circumcision in the flesh. The Jews, both in Smyrna and Philadelphia, had failed this test. In Rom. 11:1-5 Paul speaks of a remnant of the Jews who had not been cast off. These are the ones who, like Paul, had believed in the Son of God and had accepted Him as Lord, being justified by faith. Paul goes on in verses 16-24 to liken Israel to a tame olive tree. The Jews are the branches. The unbelieving Jews are cut off of the tree and are replaced by believing Gentiles, the branches from the wild olive tree that are grafted in. So Gentiles who had not been circumcised in the flesh, but were circumcised in the heart, became a part of Israel as God had intended it. Paul writes in Col. 2:11-12:

> In Him you were also circumcised with the circumcision made without hands by putting off the body of the sins of the flesh, by the circumcision of Christ, buried with Him in baptism, in which you also were raised with *Him* through faith in the working of God, who raised Him from the dead.

Those who were broken off the tree of Israel were no longer Jews in God's sight, while He sees all true Christians, both Jew and Gentile, as true Jews—a part of His true Israel. This is why Jesus could say that those in the Jewish synagogue in these two cities lied when they said they were Jews. But here is a note of hope in Philadelphia. These Jews were to be brought to worship God and understand that the Christians are God's people. Did some

79

or all of them become Christians? Let us hope so. After all, Paul did say in Rom. 11:23, "And they also, if they do not continue in unbelief, will be grafted in, for God is able to graft them in again." (For a fuller study of God's Israel, go to *Appendix D*.)

3. Kept from Persecution. Christians in Philadelphia were to be kept from the severe persecution that was coming upon the church throughout the world. Jesus tells them, "Because you have kept My command to persevere, I also will keep you from the hour of trial which shall come upon the whole world, to test those who dwell on the earth." The church in Smyrna was not kept from that tribulation. *Fox's Book of Martyrs* tells us that it was the Jews in Smyrna who accused Christians to the Roman inquisitors, and helped in burning them at the stake. Perhaps, then, the change of heart of the Jews in Philadelphia helped to ward off the persecution. For whatever reason, the persecution did not come upon them. Why? Jesus said it was because they had kept His command to remain faithful. They kept on persevering in their faith and in their service to the Lord Jesus.

It may be that Jesus wanted to spare them further suffering because they only had a little strength. Perhaps it would have been more than the church there could bear. Maybe they would have gone out of existence. Jesus did not want their lampstand to be removed. He is able to preserve His own people. He is able to protect the weak. He is faithful and true, and can be trusted to keep His word. Some strong churches, like the church at Smyrna, could be a powerful testimony to the people of that city by undergoing persecution and death while remaining faithful to Christ. This, apparently, was not the case in Philadelphia. As a result they were not called to suffer the severity of the persecution.

The persecution was to test or try the saints of God. Smyrna was told they would he tried or tested. Perhaps Philadelphia had already proved itself and didn't need to be tested further. They had kept Jesus' command to persevere. They had continued faithfully through the taunts, opposition, and resistance of the Jews. They had remained faithful through whatever persecution had already come upon them. Maybe this is why they were left with only a little strength. Jesus honored their perseverance and faith, and promised to keep them from further trials.

4. Jesus is Coming. Jesus said, "Behold, 1 am coming quickly! Hold fast what you have, that no one may take your crown." He wanted them to know that they would not have to struggle forever. He was going to come soon. Of course, that was 2000 years ago and He still has not come. Maybe we should look at it from God's eyes. In 2 Pet. 3:8 Peter said, "...with the Lord one day *is* as a thousand years, and a thousand years as one day." So from that perspective it has only been a couple of days since Jesus told the Philadelphians that He was corning quickly. The point is, He wants them to keep on holding fast so that nobody will take away their crown of life.

2 John 1:8 says, "Look to yourselves, that we do not lose those things we have worked for, but *that* we may receive a full reward." 2 Pet. 1:10-11 puts it this way:

> Therefore, brethren, be even more diligent to make your call and election sure, for if you do these things you will never stumble; for so an entrance will be supplied to you abundantly into the everlasting kingdom of our Lord and Savior Jesus Christ.

Also in Gal. 6:9 Paul says, "And let us not grow weary while doing good, for in due season we shall reap if we do not lose heart."

Christ did not want them to lose their inheritance after having held on so far. He did not want them to lose heart and give up. He had opened the door for them, and no one could close it. He did not want them to miss out on anything that God had in store for them. For them, overcoming means holding fast until He comes.

D. REWARDS FOR THOSE WHO OVERCOME

1. A Pillar in God's Temple. For the one who overcomes he has some exciting rewards. First, Jesus will make him a pillar in the temple of God. The temple is a figure of the church according to Eph. 2:19-22 and 1 Cor. 3:16-17.[7] Peter says Christians are living stones built into this house of God

---

[7]The temple in 1 Cor. 3:16-17 has been interpreted by some as referring to the physical body of individual Christians. However, the 2nd person pronoun, ὑμῖν, is plural rather than singular. In the *KJV* the pronoun is translated *ye*, the nominative plural form of the pronoun *you* in Elizabethan English. This conforms to the Greek in the text. Paul is speaking in this

(1 Pet. 2:5). A pillar in the temple in Jerusalem was a thing of beauty, as well as a means of supporting the temple. In Gal. 2:9 Paul refers to James, Cephas (Peter) and John as pillars. He was referring to their important position in the church in Jerusalem. It would be quite an honor to be made a pillar in God's heavenly temple. There will never be any danger of being cast out of that place of safety and security. They will never have to go out any more.

2. Three Names Written on Them. Jesus is going to write three names on the one who overcomes: 1) the name of God; 2) the name of God's city, the New Jerusalem; and 3) Jesus' own new name. What is Jesus' new name? I don't know what that name is, and neither does anyone else except Jesus and the Father. His own new name written on those who overcome indicates that they will be His own people throughout eternity.

The name of God's city is written on those who overcome. This is the New Jerusalem which comes down from heaven to the new heaven and new earth in Rev. 21:2. In Heb. 12:22-24 this city is called *Mount Zion* (the site of Jerusalem), and *the heavenly Jerusalem*. It is composed of a multitude of angels as well as the church of the firstborn ones who are enrolled in heaven. Jesus and His redeeming blood are there also. In an allegory which Paul gives in Gal. 4:26 He tells us that, "...the Jerusalem above is free, which is the mother of us all." This city in the new heaven and new earth not only belongs to the redeemed, it is composed of the redeemed. It is a figure of God's people, His redeemed church. They will live with God, Christ, and His holy angels in this new heaven and new earth throughout eternity. Most cities have their own name written on them somewhere, if only on the city limits sign. God will write on the saints the name of the New Jerusalem because they are that holy city.

The name of God, written on those who overcome, indicates that they belong to God. What is that name? God has many names, but there is one in particular by which He wants to be known. It is the name He revealed to Moses at the burning bush. It is *Yahweh—the self-existing and eternally existing one.* He is the one true and living God.

When David thought of the overwhelming greatness of God, he said in Psalm 8:4, "What is man that You are mindful of him, And the son of man

---

verse of the Christians collectively. They, as a body, are God's temple.

that You visit him?" It is an overwhelming thing to consider that we, the creatures of God, can be adopted into the family of God, be sons of God, brothers of His only begotten Son, joint heirs with Him. This is what it will mean to have the name of God written on those who overcome.

E. THIS LETTER WRITTEN TO YOU ALSO

Jesus concludes the letter in the same way He ends all the others. "He who has an ear, let him hear what the Spirit says to the churches." I would count it an honor to be a member of a church like the one in Philadelphia. Maybe you are a member of a church like this. If so, this letter is for you. You need to listen to the advice to hold fast what you have so that you will not lose your crown. Then you can look forward to all the wonderful things promised to the Philadelphians. In this life you will have an open door of influence to others in your community, even those who resist and oppose the church. You will receive the providential care and protection of Christ from the tribulation that comes upon Christians. In the life to come you will be an important pillar in God's temple and have God's name, the name of the Heavenly City, and the new name of Jesus written on you. Then you will know the importance of that name and understand its meaning. You will be safe and protected, never again to be subjected to the trials of this life. What a glorious future! May it be so for all those who belong to Him. Amen.

IV. LETTER SEVEN: TO THE CHURCH AT LAODICEA (3:14-22)

John has finished six letters so far. Only this one is left. Before he can rest he must finish this, the seventh letter. It is to a very important city in the ancient province of Asia.

A. WHAT LAODICEA WAS LIKE

Laodicea, in the Roman province of Asia, was located east of Ephesus. It was an important city, very rich in natural resources and industry.

1. Laodicea was a Banking Center Where Gold Was Traded. The Pactolus River ran near that city from whose banks much gold was mined. Fortunes were made through various enterprises and the city was a center of financing.

2. It Was the Center of Healing Industries. There was an important medical school there. It was also a place where pharmaceuticals were manufactured. One of these was a powder that was used to make a salve for anointing eyes.

3. Black Sheep Were Raised in the Fields. The wool from the black sheep of that region was woven into cloth which was desired far and wide for its fine soft texture, and it brought a high price.

4. The Madder Root Was Grown in the Fields. This was a source of an expensive purple dye which was used to dye threads which were woven into fine purple cloth. Lydia, whom Paul met and led to Christ in Philippi, was a business woman from Laodicea who sold this purple dye, or perhaps the cloth which was dyed purple.

5. Hot Mineral Springs Existed to the East at Hieropolis. To these springs people came from great distances because bathing in the waters was thought to produce beneficial results due to their soothing and healing properties.

6. Cold, Delicious Water for Drinking flowed to the North-east at Colosse. This was refreshing and reviving water, the best anywhere in Asia.

7. The Water at Laodicea Was Putrid. Hieropolis and Colosse were noted far and wide for their good water, one for drinking, another for bathing; but Laodicea had a reputation for having the worst water in Asia. The waters from the cold springs and the hot springs flowed together before reaching Laodicea. This made it tepid and full of minerals. It was nauseating and virtually impossible to drink. The water which reached Laodicea was lukewarm and smelly with mineral deposits. Jesus knew all these things, and He used them to make His points in the letter to the church in Laodicea.

B. *CHARACTERISTICS OF JESUS*

1. The Amen, the Faithful and True Witness. Jesus identifies Himself as *the Amen, the Faithful and True Witness,* and *the Beginning of the creation of God.* These descriptions also come from the way He is described in the vision of chapter one. In Rev. 1:5 Jesus is called *the faithful witness.* In the letter to Philadelphia, in Rev. 3:7 Jesus is described as *He who is true.* Here He is called *the Faithful and True Witness,* combining both these terms. The terms are similar in meaning, because if a witness is faithful, his testimony is true.

You can depend upon the word of Jesus. His promises are true and His blessings are real. You can trust Him completely because He has every intention of doing what He says, and whatever He promises He will provide. Since He has all power and all knowledge there is nothing to keep Him from fulfilling His intentions. Sometimes humans make promises they cannot keep. This is never true of God. Any promise He makes He will keep. The Laodicean church needed to know these things.

Jesus is the Amen.[8] This word means *certain, sure, trustworthy* or *firm; that which is established.* It may be translated, *so be it* or *It is true.* He is the one Who makes it happen. By His word He sets it firmly and makes it certain. The reason He can do this is that He Himself is the one Who created all things (John 1:2-3; Col. 1:16; Heb. 1:2, 8-10).

2. The Beginning of Creation

He is *the Beginning of the creation of God.* In Rev. 1:8 the Almighty says, "'I am the Alpha and the Omega, *the* Beginning and *the* End,' says the Lord, 'who is and who was and who is to come, the Almighty.'" Jesus says the same thing about Himself in 1:11. "I am the Alpha and the Omega, the First and the Last," and in 1:17b, "Do not be afraid; I am the First and the Last." He is the First and the Last, the Beginning and the End, the Alpha and the Omega. He was in the beginning with God. He was before all things.

When He says that He is the beginning of the creation of God, He does not mean that He was the first thing created as some teach, but that He was the source of all things that were created. "In the beginning God [the Word of God, later called the Son of God], created the heavens and the earth" (Gen. 1:1; John 1:1-2, 14). He is, therefore, both the beginning and the end of all things. As the creator He has the power and ability to carry out His word. His word is powerful. Whatever He speaks comes to pass.

---

[8] 'Ἀμήν – *Amēn'* pronounced *ah-main'* – *Strong's Greek Dictionary* defines this word thus: "...of Hebrew origin; properly *firm*, that is, (figuratively) *trustworthy*; adverbially *surely* (often as interjection *so be it*) – amen, verily." The Hebrew word אָמֵן is pronounced the same. *Strong's Hebrew Dictionary* gives this definition: "...*are; abstractly faithfulness; adverbially truly:* – Amen, so be it, truth."

Now the things we have learned about Laodicea are used to teach some valuable lessons. In verses 15 and 16 Jesus says:

> I know your works, that you are neither cold nor hot. I could wish you were cold or hot. So then, because you are lukewarm, and neither cold nor hot, I will vomit you out of My mouth.

Both the cold water to the north-east of Laodicea and the hot water to the east were good. The lukewarm water of Laodicea was nauseating.

C. THE NEEDS OF LAODICEA

1. To Be Hot or Cold. Jesus wants His people to be soothing, healing hot water, or else refreshing, enlivening cold water. But the Laodicean Christians were nauseating to Him. He said, "I will [not *might*] vomit you out." If they remained like the tepid water, they were destined to be expelled by Christ. What made them like the nauseating water of Laodicea? The water was not only lukewarm in temperature, but it was contaminated with bitter, foul-smelling minerals. The church in Laodicea was contaminated with some things that were terribly distasteful to Christ. Most important, they had become self-important and self-sufficient. Verse 17 show this: "Because you say, 'I am rich, have become wealthy and have need of nothing'...."

2. To Depend on God. They were saying, "No help wanted. I can do this job all by myself." They had absorbed this independent attitude from the city in which they lived. Laodicea had been destroyed by an earthquake in 17 A.D. and again in 60 A.D. The Roman emperor, in each case, offered to help this important city rebuild, but the Laodiceans, in their pride, said, "No thanks. We are rich and need no help." The church there echoed this pride. No doubt they shared in the prosperity of the city. Could it be that they had accomplished this by compromising with the paganism and immorality in this city?

Christians in the province were unpopular with the pagans because they did not worship their pagan gods. As a result faithful Christians did not have much opportunity to share in the economic prosperity of a city. The fact that the Laodicean Christians did share in this prosperity is an indication that they probably compromised with the culture. There is not much indication from archaeological digs that this rich and powerful church ever existed there. Apparently they did not heed the advice Jesus gave, and they had been vomited out—a forceful way of saying their lampstand was removed.

3. To Obtain True Riches. The Laodiceans thought they were rich because of their material possessions, but were, in fact, "wretched, miserable, poor, blind, and naked." They had plenty of material possessions, but few of the things that really count. Jesus gives them some good counsel. He tells them to buy from Him "gold refined by fire, that you may be rich." True wealth is found in a different kind of gold than that found in the banks in the financial district of Laodicea, or on the banks of the Pactolus River. The gold that counts is the gold of Christian faith and character, smelted and refined in the fires of trial and persecution.

4. To Put on Spiritual Clothing. The clothing that counts is not the garments of black wool or the rich purple robes colored with dyes made from the madder root, but the white garments of righteousness which Jesus gives to those who are redeemed and sanctified. Without these garments a person is spiritually naked before the eyes of Christ.

5. To See with Spiritual Eyes. They thought they could see but they were blind. They were only looking with the physical eye. The things they thought were important were their material possessions. Their kind of blindness could not be helped by the Laodicean eye salves. They needed the salve that only Christ could provide. They needed to have Jesus open their eyes to the realm of the Spirit so they could see what was of true importance and value. They did not see. They did not know. They were deluding themselves as to their real condition.

6. To Repent. Jesus was telling them these things because He loved them and wanted to correct them for their own well-being. "As many as I love, I rebuke and chasten. Therefore be zealous and repent." His words of rebuke, this verbal spanking, was not out of a fit of rage, but out of love for their souls. He is not willing that any should perish, but wants all men to come to repentance (2 Pet. 3:9).

Of the seven letters, this is the only letter which has no word of commendation or approval. Apparently Christ saw nothing to commend, or else he would have done so. They needed to make a 180 degree turn-around.

That is what it means to repent. They had worked for the material possessions of this world when they should have been laying up treasures in heaven. They needed to repent of their wrong-headed value system. They had placed their trust in their own abilities, their own wealth and possessions. They needed to repent and realize that no man is sufficient of himself. They simply cannot do it on their own. Everyone needs the help of Christ and His Holy Spirit.

Lukewarmness is also a term which means complacency. A feeling of being satisfied with the *status quo*. They needed to repent of complacency and become zealous for Christ, the gospel and righteous living. They needed to quit all those things which had contaminated their lives and polluted their testimony, and be zealous.

7. To Open Their Heart to Jesus. In verse 20 Jesus gives a very moving invitation. "Behold, I stand at the door and knock. If anyone hears My voice and opens the door, I will come in to him and dine with him, and he with Me." Jesus is the one who opens doors of opportunity, as in Philadelphia. He even opens the doors of death and hades. But He will not open the door to your heart. You have to do that yourself. Jesus will not force His way in.

I think it is significant that Jesus is begging entrance into the hearts of those who were already Christians. Generally we think of Him as seeking entrance into the hearts of the unbelievers. But in this case, He had been shut out of the lives of the Laodicean Christians. They didn't look to Him for help. They didn't think they needed anything. They did not operate under the direction of the Holy Spirit. They felt they could take care of any problem themselves.

The power of Christ and the work of the Holy Spirit had no part in their lives. At one time they had accepted Christ and had been baptized. Now they felt they had it made. They could live their lives as they pleased, do what they wanted to, live like they wanted to, pursue their own wealth and pleasure, and get into heaven on the strength of their initial response to Christ. It just doesn't work that way. Christ was not in their hearts. All they had to do was let Him in and He would have sweet fellowship with them; but they must hear His voice in order to do that.

I once heard an anecdote that made an impression on me. I don't know who first told it. It goes like this: A poor, ragged man lived in a neighborhood where there was a rich and popular highbrow church. This church catered to the "important" people, to the rich and famous, to the well-dressed, sophisticated sort. To this church the poor man came every Sunday, and every Sunday he was turned away by the usher because of his poor clothes and shabby appearance. He did not have on the right clothes, or the right haircut and cologne, and he did not put on the required airs. Finally, after being turned away once more, he knelt down on the sidewalk and prayed, "Lord, I have tried many times to get into this church, but they just won't let me in." A voice from heaven came to him that said, "That's alright son. I've been trying for years to get into this church, and they won't let Me in either."

That sounds like the church in Laodicea, doesn't it? Do you know any churches like this? I have known churches where the members would be very uncomfortable if people came in who didn't have on the right clothes, or the right haircut, or the right accent, or the right color of skin. I wonder if Christ was there? I doubt it.

D. THOSE WHO REPENT WOULD REIGN WITH CHRIST

The church in Laodicea had some wonderful things in store for them if they would only change their ways and follow the advice given by Jesus. Verse 21 says, "To him who overcomes I will grant to sit with Me on My throne, as I also overcame and sat down with My father on His throne." The Laodicean Christians were trying to be in charge of their own lives—to be their own king, their own god. "I am the master of my own fate; I am the captain of my own soul," is a policy a lot of people try to live by. It can't be done.

If those in Laodicea would only follow the counsel Christ gave them and overcome their wretchedness, spiritual poverty, and blindness, they could really become important. They could reign with Christ on His throne. So can you if you overcome (see Eph. 1:19-21; 2:4-6).

E. IS THIS MESSAGE FOR YOU?

Do you know any church like Laodicea? Perhaps you are a member of one. Do you see any of the attitudes of the Laodiceans in your own heart?

The Things That Are

What is the source of your wealth? Where have you placed your values? Has your life become polluted with the contaminants that make it bitter and nauseating to the Lord? Or is there a fountain flowing out of your inner being which is cool and refreshing to the thirsty souls of others? Is your life like the hot springs, giving comfort and healing to others? Does it project the character of Jesus Christ?

Is the Spirit of God working through you to provide rest to the weary, solace to the troubled, and healing to the sick of heart and soul? Do you place more emphasis on the stylish clothing on your body while going naked spiritually, or are you clothed with the garments of righteousness? Do you see like those of the world see, or do you have the spiritual insight that God's world-view provides? Remember that this letter is for you also. "Whoever has an ear, let him hear what the Spirit says to [all] the churches." Maybe you need to heed Christ's admonition to be zealous and repent.

So much for the things that are. With chapter 4 we begin the preparations for the Divine Drama of the Age which presents the things that will take place in the years to follow. These things were to begin shortly after John's visions on the Isle of Patmos.

THINGS TO TAKE PLACE AFTER THIS

Part One: PREPARING FOR THE DRAMA

Rev. Chapters 4 - 11

Chapter 4

GOD'S TEMPLE—THE THEATER
Rev. Chapter 4

We come now to the third part of John's assignment—to write the things which would begin to happen shortly. Beginning in 4:1 and continuing through 22:5 John writes about the things that were to take place in the future.

Revelation is presented in a manner that can be likened to a drama. Chapters 4 - 11 reveal the preparation for the drama, including the theater where it is to be viewed, the producer, the director, the script, the theme, and the plot of the drama.

I. JOHN CALLED INTO THE THRONE ROOM IN HEAVEN

In Rev. 4:1 John is called up into the theater from which he is to view the drama that will reveal future events. Verse 1 says:

> After these things I looked, and behold, a door *standing* open in heaven. And the first voice which I heard *was* like a trumpet speaking with me, saying, "Come up here, and I will show you things which must take place after this."

John sees a door in heaven standing open, and he hears a voice like a trumpet telling him, "Come up here...." The first voice John heard was the trumpet-like voice in Rev. 1:10-11. It was the voice of Christ who identified himself as "the Alpha and Omega, the First and the Last, the Beginning and

93

the End." This same voice now calls John to enter through the open door into heaven itself.

Christ was going to show him those things which were going to happen in the future. Where would he see these things? The voice said, "Come up here, and I will show you things which must take place after this." The temple in heaven, then, was to serve as the theater where John would see these events played out in his visions, as if on a stage or, in our day, on a movie screen.

"Immediately I was in the Spirit; and behold, a throne set in heaven, and *One* sat on the throne" (Rev. 4:2). What did John mean when he said he *was in the Spirit*? Some think he meant that he was in a state of ecstasy—a trance in which he was unaware of his surroundings or even his body—kind of a disembodied state. Was he having an out of body experience? I doubt it. Paul speaks in 2 Cor.12:2-4 of a similar experience, of knowing a man who was caught up to the third heaven:

> I know a man in Christ who fourteen years ago—whether in the body I do not know, or whether out of the body I do not know, God knows—such a one was caught up to the third heaven. And I know such a man—whether in the body or out of the body I do not know, God knows—how he was caught up into Paradise and heard inexpressible words, which it is not lawful for a man to utter.

Although it is not certain that Paul was speaking of himself, interpreters almost unanimously believe so. Paul was not even certain as to whether it was an out of body experience or not. There is one big difference between Paul's experience and John's. Paul was speaking of a literal visit to heaven, whether in the body or out of it. John's visit to heaven was part of his vision rather than literal.

Being in the spirit, as John was, involves close communion with the Holy Spirit. This includes prayer, and listening for the impressions or instruction the Holy Spirit may place upon your heart. I believe that John was saying that he was immediately in a state of intense communion between his spirit and the Spirit of God. He said something similar, "I was in the Spirit on the Lord's Day," in Rev. 1:10 when he received the initial vision from the Angel sent to him. John was communing with God in spirit when God chose to

94

send to him the visions of the truths God wanted to reveal; yet John was aware of what was going on because God expected him to write what he saw and heard.

In Rev. chapters 2 - 3 John wrote down the things Jesus was dictating to him. In chapter 4 onward, apparently John was writing the things he saw and heard as they were revealed. An event in Rev. 10:3-4 indicates that this was the case. John heard the seven thunders and as he started to write what he heard he was forbidden to write what the thunders said. This also means that he was aware of what was going on during the visions and could function normally.

II. THE SOURCE OF THE SYMBOLISM IN THE THRONE ROOM

John begins to describe the things he saw in the throne room of God. A familiar pattern emerges as he is describing the scene. Those who are students of the Old Testament have read of these things before. Although the details are not precisely the same as the description of the temple in Jerusalem, never-the-less he is describing a similar temple scene.

A. THE OLD TESTAMENT TABERNACLE/TEMPLE

The Tabernacle was a portable temple that was constructed for use during the wilderness wanderings of the Israelites.[1] A larger, more elaborate, permanent temple was built later in Jerusalem.[2] Both were built on a similar pattern. Moses was told in Exod. 25:40 to build everything according to the blueprint or pattern which God had given him in the mount. The reason for this was because every part of the essential pattern was symbolic of a greater reality. Heb. 8:1-2 speaks of the sanctuary and true tabernacle which God erected and not man. Then in verses 4 and 5 the priests of the Old Testament tabernacle are said to serve the copy and shadow of the heavenly things. For this reason Moses was instructed to be sure to follow the pattern God gave him. What was that pattern? The most important parts of the pattern are

---

[1] Read Exodus chapters 25 through 30 for a full description of the tabernacle, furnishings, and priesthood.

[2] 1 King 7 gives a description of the building of the temple in Jerusalem.

shown in the summary below. Meanwhile, for a more detailed study of that pattern go to *Appendix C* on *The Temple of God.*

B. *A List of Things in the Old Testament Tabernacle/Temple*

The following items are found in the pattern of the tabernacle/temple in the Old Testament. Included in this list are the items foreshadowed or symbolized by these things.

1. The Holy of Holies—God's throne room, His sanctuary in heaven.

2. The mercy seat—God's throne.

3. The visible glory of God—the brilliance of His presence, called the *shekina* in the Hebrew.

4. The golden cherubim—angels of a high order chosen to wait upon God's throne. They are represented in Revelation as *living creatures.*

5. The ark of the covenant—an obvious representation of God's covenant with His people.

6. The Holy Place—the church, God's house (1 Tim. 3:15) both on earth and in heaven.

7. The altar of incense—the offering up of the prayers of the saints.

8. Golden bowls—used by the priests to offer up the incense.

9. The incense—the prayers of the saints.

10. The seven lamps of fire—the Holy Spirit who gives the light of revelation.

11. The seven branched lampstand—the significance of these branches has already been shown in chapters 1 - 3. The church together with the written word are the lampstands which hold up the light.

12. The table of the bread of the presence—not clearly represented in Revelation.

13. The bread of the presence (show bread)—Christ is the bread of life—the presence represented by the bread on the table.

14. The outer court—the world.

15. The altar of burnt offering—offering up of sacrifices both by the High Priest (Christ), and by the priests (Christians). These offerings are in the outer court (the world).

16. The blood sacrifices—the blood of the Lamb of God that takes away the sins of the world, and the souls (lives) of the martyrs who give their lives because of their testimony for Christ.

17. The sea (*laver* in the tabernacle)—the cleansing of the priests (Christians) in the blood of the Lamb..

18. The priests—Christians who offer up spiritual sacrifices.

19. The high priest—the Great High Priest, Jesus Christ.

Eighteen of these nineteen items from the Old Testament tabernacle or temple are all found in the temple scene in heaven. The outer court is where the altar of burnt offering and the sea are located. The outer court represents the world where most of the action of the drama in Rev. 6 - 20 takes place. Not all items of the temple or tabernacle appear in chapters 4 and 5, but there is a return to the temple scene elsewhere in Revelation. The altar of burnt offering is found in Rev. 6:9. The altar of incense is seen in 8:3-4. The ark of the covenant is in the temple in 11:19. There the heavenly scene is called the Temple of God, as it is also the case in 15:5-8.

C. THINGS FROM THE ABOVE LIST IN THIS CHAPTER—(Look for these)

1. The Holy of Holies—**the throne room in heaven;**

2. The Holy Place where the priests do their service—**the people (church) of God**, seen as the temple in 11:1;

3. The mercy seat—**God's throne;**

4. The shekina, the glory of the presence of God resting on His throne (the mercy seat)—**the radiance like jasper, sardius and emerald;**

5. The cherubim whose wings overshadow the throne—**the living creatures;**

6. The priests who do service in the temple—**the 24 elders;**

7. The sea in which the priests cleanse themselves, crystal rather than bronze—cleansing **through the blood of Christ**;

8. The seven lamps of fire—**the seven Spirits of God**—the Holy Spirit;

9. The golden lampstand(s) (from chapter 1)—**the church** which holds up the light of the Spirit.

10. The outer court—**the world**—is where the crystal sea is located (as well as the altar of burnt offering which is seen later.)

These 10 of the 19 items are found in this chapter. We will see five more in chapter 5 where the temple scene continues. The two altars and the ark of the covenant do not appear in chapters 4 and 5, but they show up when we return to the temple scene in chapters 6, 8 and 11. One item does not appear in the temple scene in Revelation—the table of the bread of the presence (table of show bread). There is no need for the table since the true bread, Jesus the Lamb, is present in person, and needs no table to rest upon.

With these facts we are in a better position to interpret the meaning of the things seen in John's vision of the throne room.

III. What John Saw In the Throne Room (Read 4:2b-5)

A. The Glory of God on the Mercy Seat

In verse 2 John describes one who is sitting on the throne. Whether he saw the form of God is uncertain, although in chapter five he sees the right hand of God holding a scroll. In verse 3 there was a shining forth from the throne—a brilliance like that of Jasper and Sardius stones. This is the representation of the glory of God. Just as in the tabernacle and temple in the Old Testament, the glory of God rested upon the mercy seat. After the Lord had descended upon the mercy seat in the newly dedicated temple in Jerusalem, 2 Chron. 5:14 declares, "...the priests could not continue ministering because of the cloud; for the glory of the LORD filled the house of God."

Around the throne was a brilliance like an emerald which John describes as a *rainbow*. This was part of the radiance of God's glory. It was no accident that it was called *a rainbow*. It is a symbol indicating that God is the God of covenants. It came to have this meaning because God gave the rainbow in the cloud as the sign of the covenant He made with mankind in Gen. 9:8-17.

Rev. 4:5 says, "And from the throne proceeded lightnings, thunderings, and voices." When Moses brought the Israelites to Sinai they were startled and frightened by the trembling of the mountain and the lightning, smoke and fire, the trumpet blast and the voices (Exod. 20:18; Heb. 12:18-21). These all indicated the awesomeness of the presence of God on the mountain, and were calculated to instill the fear of God in the hearts of the people. In this scene also, from the throne come lightnings and thunderings and voices. These are probably intended to impress upon our hearts the awesomeness of the presence of God on His throne. Such things also have another purpose in much of the book of Revelation. Several times through the book they serve as portents to introduce earthshaking events which are about to take place. It is an indication that the hand of God is directing these events (6:12; 8:5; 11:19; 16:18).

B. THE 24 ELDERS

Around the throne were 24 thrones (seats) upon which sat 24 elders. These were clothed in white robes, and on their heads were crowns of gold. Who are these elders? Why are there 24? What are the crowns of gold? What are the white robes they are wearing? Let's answer the questions in reverse order.

1. The White Robes. The white robes appear many times in Revelation as a symbol of righteousness and purity. In Rev. 6:11 the martyred saints under the altar are given white robes. They did not buy the robes or make them. They were a gift of God's grace. In Rev. 7:9 the redeemed saints around the throne have white robes. In verse 14 these robes were washed and made white in the blood of the Lamb. In Rev. 19:8 the robe worn by the bride of Christ is called *fine linen*, clean and bright, said to be *the righteous deeds of the saints*. Rev. 3:5 says, "He who overcomes shall be clothed in white garments."

These are priestly garments. Psalm 32:9 says, "Let your priests be clothed in righteousness...." The white robes are robes of righteousness—a righteousness not their own, but the righteousness of Christ, imputed to them, set down to their account as though the righteousness were their own. These robes are a gift from God.

2. The Victory Crowns. What are the crowns of gold? The word *crown* here is not the royal crown (*diademos*) of rulership, but the laurel wreath of victory (*stephanos*).[3] This wreath was worn by victors in the games or in wars. The winner in the contest would come before the presiding ruler of the games, who would then place a laurel wreath upon the victor's head as a symbol of his victory. Often Caesar, who led his victorious army in battle, would wear such a crown.

These elders are those who have become triumphant. 1 Cor. 15:57 states, "But thanks *be* to God, who gives us the victory through our Lord Jesus Christ." The victory is not our own doing, but it is given to us by God. By His grace we will wear a crown of victory. 2 Cor. 2:14 has a similar passage, "Now thanks *be* to God who always leads us in triumph in Christ...."

In 2 Tim. 4:8 Paul speaks of a crown of righteousness which was laid up for him. This is the *stephanos*, the crown of victory. In verse seven Paul says that he has fought the good fight. It doesn't say he won the good fight. The victory is something which was given to him. He was triumphant because of the grace of God. This is the crown of life that will be given to those who are faithful even to death, according to Rev. 2:10. These 24 elders, like faithful Christians everywhere, have been given the victory, and thus they wear golden victory crowns. They are seen not only as righteous (the white robes), but as victorious (the victory crown).

3. The Significance of the number 24. Why are there 24 elders? Why not more, or less? The source of this symbol goes back to the provision made for the service in the temple in Jerusalem. This account is found in 1 Chron. 24. The priests were divided into 24 divisions. These were assigned service in the temple according to a schedule determined by casting lots (like casting dice or drawing straws.) This does not always mean that it was left to chance. Remember that the 11 apostles who were left after the death of Judas Iscariot chose a twelfth to take his place by casting lots (Acts 1:23-26). This was

---

[3]The word here is στέφανος (*stephanos*). It is the laurel wreath that is used to crown the victors in the games. It is the symbol of victory. The royal crown of kingship is διάδεμος (*diademos*).

their way of leaving the final decision up to God. They asked God to enter into the process and choose the one He wanted. In like manner the choice of the order of service of the priests was left to God.

Aaron had four sons, but Nadab and Abihu died before their father Aaron. Eleazar and Ithamar were left to inherit the priesthood from their father. Eleazar had sixteen sons while Ithamar had eight. There were a total of 24 grandsons of Aaron. These and their descendants were the basis for the 24 divisions (see 1 Chron. 24:1-19). Their names are as follows:

1) Jehoiarib, 2) Jedaiah, 3) Harim, 4) Seorim, 5) Malchijah, 6) Mijamin, 7) Hakkoz, 8) Abijah, 9) Jeshua, 10) Shecaniah, 11) Eliashib, 12) Jakim, 13) Huppah, 14) Jeshebeab, 15) Bilgah, 16) Immer, 17) Hezir, 18) Happizzez, 19) Pethahiah, 20) Jehezekel, 21) Jachin, 22) Gamul, 23) Delaiah, 24) Maaziah.

These are numbered according to their order of service decided by lot rather than according to order of birth or parentage. Lot number 8 is the division of Abijah. An example of a priest who was serving during his allotted time is Zacharias, father of John the Baptist. Luke 1:5 tells us that he was of the division of Abijah. Luke 1:8 - 9 says:

> So it was, that while he was serving as priest before God in the order of his division, according to the custom of the priesthood, his lot fell to burn incense when he went into the temple of the Lord.

The temple musicians as well as the priests were divided into 24 divisions (see 1 Chron. 25:1-5). These were all Levites. There were four sons of Asaph, six of Jeduthun, and 14 of Heman, a total of 24 whose descendants were the divisions that were charged with prophesying with harps, stringed instruments, and cymbals.

There are 24 elders in Rev. 4 because there were 24 divisions of the priesthood. This has symbolic significance for us today since all believers in Christ are members of the priesthood. The 24 divisions included all the priests. The 24 elders are symbolic of all the saints of God who serve as priests before the throne of God. In Revelation the functions of the musicians and the singers are combined with the function of the 24 divisions of the priests. In 5:8 the 24 elders not only have bowls of incense to offer as priests, they also have harps, indicating the sacrifice of praise (see Heb. 13:15).

Heb. 6:19-20 is a significant passage in understanding our standing before God:

> This *hope* we have as an anchor of the soul, both sure and steadfast, and which enters the *Presence* behind the veil, where the forerunner has entered for us, *even* Jesus, having become High Priest forever according to the order of Melchizedek.

Because Jesus entered the Holy of Holies behind the veil, now the way is open for us to enter the throne room of God. When Jesus died on the cross, the veil in the temple was torn in two, from top to bottom (Matt. 27:50-51). This event was declaring the fact that with Christ's death the true Holy of Holies was no longer barred to His servants (priests of God). Death is the true veil, but Jesus opened the grave not only for Himself but for us as well. Jesus our Great High Priest entered through the veil and tore it open so that we could enter before the throne of God. Heb. 10:19-22 says:

> Therefore, brethren, having boldness to enter the Holiest by the blood of Jesus, by a new and living way which He consecrated for us, through the veil, that is, His flesh, and *having* a High Priest over the house of God, let us draw near with a true heart in full assurance of faith, having our hearts sprinkled from an evil conscience and our bodies washed with pure water.

Do you see how the writer draws from the symbolism of the temple in the Old Testament? The way was barred by the veil (curtain), but Jesus consecrated the way through the veil for us. We, as priests of God, must first consecrate and sanctify ourselves by washing in the laver. We must have the assurance of faith, the cleansing of our consciences (repentance), and the washing with pure water (baptism) in order for us to draw near to God. Heb. 4:16 admonishes us, "Let us therefore come boldly to the throne of grace, that we may obtain mercy and find grace to help in time of need." *The throne of grace* is another way of saying *the mercy seat*. Christ not only entered for us, He prepared the way so that now we can enter.

In the body of Christ every Christian is a priest of God (1 Pet. 2:5,9). We each are to offer up sacrifices and intercessions (1 Pet. 2:5; Heb.13:15-16; Rom.12:1-2). The 24 elders are figurative of our service as priests before the throne of God. We don't have to be in heaven literally in order to minister before His throne.

4. Multiples of Twelve. I believe there is another reason in addition to the 24 divisions of the priesthood for the number 24. It has significance because it is the sum of 12 and 12. There were 12 sons of Jacob from which came the Israelites, the chosen people of God. There were 12 tribes of Israelites, and 12 loaves of the bread of the presence, one representing each of the tribes. There were 12 gems on the ephod of the High Priest, again one for each of the tribes of Israel. Coming to the New Testament we see a multitude of references to the 12 apostles of Christ. In Rev. 21:14 the names of the 12 apostles are inscribed on the 12 foundations of the New Jerusalem. The names of the 12 tribes are inscribed on the 12 gates of the city. According to Heb. 12:22-23, the Jerusalem above (the heavenly Jerusalem) is the church, the body of Christ, the saints of God.

In God's plan the apostles were the beginning or foundation work of the church (Eph. 2:19-22). The gateway to the church was Israel. I do not mean that one has to be circumcised and become a Jew in order to be in the church, but that God worked through Israel to make salvation available to all mankind. Even the New Testament scriptures came to us through Israel. Through Israel Christ was born. The early church was composed of Israelites until certain Jewish Christians, namely Peter and Paul, were sent to the Gentiles. With the 12 apostles as the foundations and the 12 tribes of Israel as the gates, is it any wonder that the number 12 came to be a symbol for God's people? Perhaps the addition of the 12 apostles to the 12 patriarchs to give us the number 24 is a way of saying that Jews and Gentiles have been united in the one body of Christ, His church.

Here is something that will help in understanding some of the symbolism in the book of Revelation. Wherever the number 12, or 12 plus 12 (24), or 12 times 12 (144) appears it is **always a reference to the people of God**.

Twelve. In Rev. 12:1 the woman has a crown of 12 stars, identifying her as the people of God, combining both Old and New Testament saints in one figure. In 21:12,14 the New Jerusalem has 12 gates and 12 foundations. In

21:15, the length and breath of the city are each 12 thousand furlongs, or 144 million square furlongs. In 21:17 the wall is measured 144 cubits (presumably in thickness).

Twenty-four. In chapters 4 and 5 there are the 24 elders, a symbol of God's people as priests before God's throne. Why do I say they are priests? In Rev. 5:8 they have the golden bowls full of incense which are the prayers of the saints. The business of offering the incense was limited to priests. In Rev. 5:8, the 24 elders each had a harp as well as a bowl of incense. In the heavenly scene the function both of the priest and the musician are combined. Heb. 13:15 points out that the sacrifice of praise is one of the spiritual sacrifices Christians are to offer.

One-hundred-forty-four. In Rev. 7:3-4 there are 144 thousand people who are called "the servants of God." In 14:1,3-4 there are 144 thousand who have God's name and the Lamb's name. These are the redeemed from the earth and they are the followers of Christ the Lamb. Thus they are identified as the people of God. In the Old Testament temple, musicians as well as priests were divided into 24 divisions (see 1 Chron. 25:1-5). From each division of musicians 12 men were chosen by lot (1 Chron. 25:8-31) so that the total of the musicians is 288, or twice 144 (1 Chron. 25:7).

This Is Not Numerology. The symbolic meaning of these numbers is not *numerology*, which has its roots in mysticism and magic. It is simply the fact that numbers sometimes derive symbolic meanings because of association. For example, the number seven is the number of perfection or completeness. Seven days complete a week. God rested on the seventh day to wind up the very first week, the week of creation. We have also demonstrated the associations of 12, 24 and 144. I believe some go far afield when they begin to assign symbolic meanings to too many numbers. These meanings are too often drawn from numerology rather than from significant associations from scripture.

It seems that the focus in chapter 4 is primarily 1) God on His throne and 2) the 24 elders around the throne. The overriding theme of Revelation is God's relationship with His people. He is on the throne. He is over all and is the one in control. Everything that happens in Revelation is important only as it pertains to God's care for and protection of His people, and His direction of the events that affect them.

C. THE SEVEN LAMPS OF FIRE

Verse 5b goes on to say, "Seven lamps of fire were burning before the throne, which are the seven Spirits of God." Three things are said about these lamps: 1. they were burning 2. they were before the throne, and 3: they are the seven Spirits of God.

What is the significance of these lamps? We have already noted earlier in this chapter that there was in the tabernacle/temple a seven branched lampstand on which seven lamps of fire were kept burning. These were located on the left side of the Holy of Holies in the tabernacle as you enter. They were there, obviously, to provide light. But they were also symbolic of a higher reality. We have just been told that the seven lamps of fire are the seven Spirits of God. This has been explained fully in chapter one where the seven Spirits of God are first mentioned. Seven is the number of wholeness. The seven Spirits of God are in reality the one Holy Spirit of God in the fullness of all His functions—in this case as the giver of light.

Psalm 104:30 addresses God in this way; "You send forth Your Spirit, they are created." The Holy Spirit was active in creation, and He is active in the new creation. He was in the beginning, moving over the face of the waters. God said, "Let there be light," and there was light. The Holy Spirit is the giver of light—not only the light of the sun, moon and stars, but spiritual light as well. 2 Cor. 4:6 says, "For it is the God who commanded light to shine out of darkness, who has shone in our hearts to *give* the light of the knowledge of the glory of God in the face of Jesus Christ." The One Who imparts that knowledge is the Holy Spirit. He has given us the whole of the inspired writings which contains the mind of God. More than that God has given us the Holy Spirit in our hearts, and in these ways has shined in our hearts.

It is only through the work of the Spirit that we can begin to have an inkling of the knowledge of God's glory. The light given forth by these lamps of fire is enlightenment by the Holy Spirit. It is interesting that in the seven-fold description of the Spirit in Isa. 11:2, four of the seven characteristics have to do with giving light. These are the Spirits of wisdom, understanding, counsel and knowledge. The giving of enlightenment or

105

inspiration is only one of the Holy Spirit's functions. We shall see others later.

These lamps are before the throne of God. The curtain has been taken away, torn asunder at the death of Christ (Matt. 27:50-51). Now the lamps shine directly into the Holy of Holies. In fact, there is no more division between the Holy Place and the Holy of Holies. The Holy Place, where the priests serve, and the Holy of Holies where God's throne is, are now one. It is true that the throne room is in heaven and the church operates on earth, but the saints who come to God in prayer and offer up their sacrifices of praise and service do so in the presence of God. We come into His presence spiritually, while we long for the time when we can see him face to face. That part of the church which has gone on and has been redeemed from the earth is now literally in His presence. After 2000 years of Christians going to meet God, they are by far the largest part of the church.

In the temple the lamps rest on the lampstand with seven branches. The seven branches are seen in Rev. 1 - 3 as the seven lampstands. The church is the lampstand. It is commissioned to hold up the light. Jesus said of us in Matt. 5:14 that we are the light of the world. We are not the source of that light, but the bearers of it. In John 8:12 Jesus claimed to be the light of the world. Then in John 9:5 He said that He is the light of the world as long as He is in the world. He left, but He has come to dwell in us through the Holy Spirit (John 14:23). So His light must shine through us. The work of the Holy Spirit in us is to enable us to show forth the glory of God in the face of Jesus. We are the light bearers—the lampstand. So the lamps before the throne are also at work on earth giving their light. If we as the light bearers hide our light, how can it accomplish its purpose.

It amazes me that God has chosen to put this treasure in earthen vessels. 2 Cor. 4:7 says, "But we have this treasure in earthen vessels, that the excellence of the power may be of God and not of us." Paul is talking about the light of the knowledge of the glory of God which He has shone in our hearts. As earthen vessels we must hold up that light and let it shine to the world. God has put it there through His Holy Spirit. Now we must let it shine. The church's function as a lampstand is to hold up the light—to shine the light of the knowledge of the glory of God in Christ Jesus into a dark world.

The seven-branched lampstand is not mentioned in chapters 4 and 5, but it is reasonable to infer its presence in the vision. After all, lamps are normally on stands of some sort, not floating in the air or sitting on the ground. Of course, it is possible that the vision showed them in one of those ways, but it is not likely. The probable reason that the stands were not mentioned is because they were introduced in chapters 1 - 3, and their presence holding up the lamps would be understood. In Rev. 1 - 3 the focus is upon the lamp-bearers, the churches, and their function. In chapters 4 and 5 the focus is upon the lamps, the Holy Spirit in His function as light-giver. The lamps are not mentioned in chapters one through three, although we would naturally understand that the lampstands which are mentioned would be holding up lamps. In like manner, the lampstands are not mentioned in chapters four and five, although we would expect to see the lamps on lampstands.

IV. MORE THINGS JOHN SAW IN THE TEMPLE (Read 4:6-8)

A. THE CRYSTAL SEA

Before the throne John saw a sea of glass like crystal. This has its counterpart in the sea of bronze which stood before the temple in Jerusalem (1 Kings 7:23-39). This was a large basin made of bronze that was 10 cubits (approximately 15 feet) across, mounted on 12 bronze bulls, three on each side. From this basin water was drawn into 10 wash basins mounted on wheels. These were kept on the sides of the temple, five on each side. The priests had to wash their bodies in this water to prepare to go into the temple to perform their priestly functions.

The basin in the temple in heaven is seen as clear glass instead of bronze. I like to think that the cleansing agent in this basin is the blood of Jesus. After all, the blood is what cleanses the people of God. It washes them pure and clean from all spiritual uncleanness. This enables them to come before God's throne to minister as a nation of priest before Him (see also Eph. 5:25-27 regarding the washing of water). However, in the baptismal waters in which the Christians are washed, you cannot see the blood with the naked eye. It is nevertheless there, symbolically, since Paul says that we are baptized into His death (Rom. 6:3). So, perhaps the same is true for this symbol of our cleansing in the blood. In that case the water in the laver, like the laver itself, would be clear.

B. *THE FOUR LIVING CREATURES (THE CHERUBIM)*

John also saw beings called *living creatures.* These were in the midst of the throne and around it. These creatures are very closely associated with God's throne. They have four different faces. One is like a lion, one like an ox or calf, one like a man, and one like a flying eagle. They are also full of eyes all around and within. They each have six wings. (Isn't it curious that John was able to see the eyes inside these creatures as well as the ones on the outside? But anything is possible in a vision.)

1. The Seraphim in Isaiah. How are we to make sense of these creatures? Remember that the best interpretation of symbolism is that which comes from the scriptures themselves. This is the principle we have tried to follow so far. There are similar creatures found in the prophets. In Isa. 6 Isaiah was given a vision of the Lord in His temple. This is when God commissioned him as a prophet. He saw the Lord on His throne, high and lifted up. In verse 2 there were seraphim, an order of angels, above the throne. Each had six wings—two covering his face, two to cover his feet, and two with which to fly. These seraphim cried out, "Holy, holy, holy is the LORD of hosts; The whole earth is full of His glory!" This is a very similar scene to the one in Revelation 4:8 where they do not cease to cry, "Holy, holy, holy, Lord God Almighty, Who was and is and is to come!" These creatures who are continually around the throne of God never cease to be overwhelmed with the majesty, might, glory, and holiness of the God who created all things by the word of His power. They cannot help but cry, "Holy, holy, holy!"

2. The Living Creatures (Cherubim) in Ezekiel. Ezekiel is also helpful in interpreting the living creatures. In the first chapter he sees the chariot of the Lord coming. His throne is on the chariot which is like an expanse of crystal above the heads of the creatures. Each of the four wheels of the chariot was accompanied by a living creature similar to the ones in Revelation. The description of these creatures is a great deal more detailed than in Revelation. They each had four faces—the same four faces as the creatures in Revelation. The only difference is that each one had all four faces, while in Revelation each had one of the four faces. Differences like this commonly occur when symbolism is brought over from the Old Testament into the New. Such differences have no bearing on the meaning of the symbols. Another difference is that they have only four wings, whereas the creatures in Revelation have six. A final difference is that the eyes are in the wheels beside the living creatures. This is explained by saying that the spirits of the creatures were in the wheels.

The most helpful thing in Ezekiel is that the living creatures are identified as *cherubim*. In speaking of these same creatures in chapter ten, the word *cherubim* is used in place of *living creatures*. The singular is *cherub*; the plural is *cherubim*. Now we begin to see the significance of the living creatures in Revelation. In the temple in Jerusalem, the mercy seat which represented the throne of God had two figures of cherubim, one on each side, with their wings overshadowing the mercy seat. In Revelation there are four living creatures, or cherubim, around the throne instead of two.

Cherubim are a very high order of angels. In Gen. 3:24, when God drove Adam and Eve from the Garden of Eden, he placed cherubim at the entrance to guard it so that man could not return. The primary function of cherubim, however, seems to be associated with God's throne. In Ezekiel they conducted the chariot of God which carried His throne. In Revelation they are continually in contact with the throne. They, like the Seraphim, are constantly praising God. In Rev. 4:8 they continually cry out, "Holy, holy, holy, Lord God Almighty, Who was and is and is to come!"

The word *seraph* or *seraphim* is probably a descriptive term rather than the name of a different order of angels. It means, literally, *fiery* or *burning*. The word has been used to refer to fiery (poisonous) serpents. It is probable that the seraphim of Isa. 6 are another depiction of the cherubim. At any rate, I think that from the Old Testament references to the living creatures, we can safely conclude that in Revelation they are meant to portray the cherubim who wait upon God's throne. Let's not make the mistake of trying to interpret the images literally. I doubt if cherubim look like these living creatures are described. Would heavenly beings have faces like earthly animals? I doubt it.

3. The Four Faces of the Living Creatures. What, then, do the faces signify? My guess would be that they are intended to point to specific characteristics of the cherubim. Again, we rely on other scriptures to enlighten us.

A Lion. Jesus is portrayed as both a lion and a lamb in chapter five. The kings of Judah were called lions. The lion has certain characteristics which are often used in figures in the Old Testament. He is a fearsome creature. The lion is said to have great strength. In Jud. 14:18 this is the characteristic used by Samson in his riddle. The lion is also noted for its courage (2 Sam. 17:10; Prov. 28:1), its fierceness (Job 10:16; 28:8), its kingliness, majesty, stateliness (Prov. 30:29-30), its fearsomeness (Amos 3:8). A very large number of scriptures refer to characteristics of the lion. In several passages a person or nation is said to be like a lion, referring to one or more of these characteristics.

We have not given all the characteristics of a lion here, but just those which would pertain to a cherub. Some characteristics are negative. Satan is likened to a lion who goes about seeking whom he may devour. The characteristics that would pertain to cherubim are the ones named above—strength, boldness or courage, fierceness, regality, stateliness, and fearsomeness. Angels are often pictured as strong, courageous, fierce, and majestic.

An Ox. The second cherub had a face like an ox. The ox is known mostly as a domestic beast of burden. It is a symbol of service. It is noted for its strength (Num. 23:22), service, and profit to its owner (Prov. 14:4: 1 Cor. 9:9). When the pioneers came across plains and mountains to the western states, the ox was the preferred animal to pull the Conestoga wagons. They were slower than horses, but steadier, stronger and surer footed. Oxen were ceremonially clean animals, acceptable for food and for sacrifice upon the altar to God. I believe the face of an ox is a symbol of strength and willingness to serve.

A Man. The third cherub had the face of a man. What are the characteristics of man that fit an angel? Man is a spirit being clothed in a human body. Man was created with intelligence, will and emotions. Above all, he was created in the image of God. Angels are spirit beings, and they serve God willingly. Those who were unwilling lost their place in heaven and are the fallen angels who are under the control of Satan, the chief of the fallen angels. The cherub has great intelligence and knowledge, as indicated by the multitude of eyes.

An Eagle. The fourth cherub had the face of a flying eagle. Eagles are noted for swiftness (Deut. 28:49). They are also known for their sharpness of vision, as when an eagle, from a great height, is able to see a small mouse on the meadow below. Finally, it is noted for its lofty environment—soaring higher than other birds, and making its nest in the high cliffs (Jer. 48:40).

4. The Significance of the Faces. What is the significance of the faces of the cherubim? In the Old Testament, when someone was said to be like a lion, or ox, or eagle, it is intended that we see that person as having certain characteristics like these creatures. So it is here. The cherubim are like a lion in their fearsome strength, courage and regal bearing. They are like an ox in their strength, endurance and service. They are like a man in their spirit nature, their free will, their god-likeness and their intelligence. They are like an eagle in their swiftness, keen sight and loftiness. Whatever characteristic is good about these four earthly creatures may be ascribed to the cherubim.

The cherubim have eyes within and all around. Eyes are used for seeing. The significance is that the cherubim have great knowledge and wisdom. They are able to see many things. Our eyesight is more limited because we have only two eyes. We do not have the knowledge or wisdom that the cherubim have. From their great height, like a soaring eagle, and with a multitude of eagle eyes, they are able to see what no earthbound creature can see.

V. JOHN HEARS EXUBERANT PRAISE (Read 4:9-11)

In the description of the cherubim it says in Rev. 4:8: "...they do not rest day or night, saying: 'Holy, holy, holy, Lord God Almighty, Who was and is and is to come!'" Their praise is incessant. Living constantly in the awe of God's presence, they are compelled to express their emotions in exuberant praise to God. The praise in this chapter is all directed to God upon His throne. He is the self-existent one. He was, is, and will be. He comes from eternity past, and continues through eternity future. Although He is the beginning and the end, He has no beginning nor end.

The 24 elders join with the cherubim to praise Him. They fall down before the throne of God and cast their crowns down at His feet, as if to say,

"Our victory belongs to God." They were acknowledging that victory is theirs only by the grace of God, not by their own accomplishments.

They join with the cherubim in offering this sacrifice of praise: "You are worthy, O Lord, To receive glory and honor and power; For You created all things, And by Your will they exist and were created." Worthiness! Glory! Honor! Power! These are the things they ascribe to God. Why? Because He is the creator of all things. All things, all worlds, all angels, all men, all nature exists only because God willed it so. PRAISE HIS HOLY NAME!

Chapter 5

PRODUCER, DIRECTOR, AND SCRIPT
Rev. Chapter 5

In Rev. 4 John was called up to heaven to observe the things which were "to happen after this." We were introduced to the temple scene in heaven which was the theater in which he would view the unfolding drama of the age. In chapter five things begin to happen in preparation for the drama.

If we follow the drama motif we should look for certain things. Who is the producer of the drama? Who is the director? What about the script? What are the themes dealt with? What is the plot? Who are the actors? What are the scenes where the action takes place? These are all revealed as the preparation for the drama unfolds.

I. THE PRODUCER AND THE SCRIPT OF THE DRAMA(5:1-4)

The first thing seen in this chapter is God on His throne. In His right hand is a book, a scroll, full of writing on both sides, and sealed with seven seals. In the fourth chapter the one on the throne is described in terms of the brilliance of precious jewels. Here He seems to have a form, for John speaks of seeing His right hand holding the scroll. This indicates that God is in control. He is both the author of the script and the producer of the drama. The scroll, once opened, will reveal the things which are to take place in the future from John's day.

The seven seals must be removed in order to open the scroll and reveal its contents. To seal a letter or scroll, heated wax would be dripped on the edge of the folded letter or the exposed edge of the scroll, and an impression would be made in the wax by a seal made for that purpose.

A seal represents the authority of the one who possesses it. A seal was often a signet ring worn on a finger, or a cylinder with the seal on one end. In this way the seal would be readily available for use when needed. Gen. 41:39-42 tells how Pharaoh made Joseph ruler over all Egypt by putting his own signet ring on Joseph's hand. This gave him authority to give decrees as if he were Pharaoh himself. To violate a seal impressed by such a signet ring was a very serious offense. Only one with the proper authority could legally break such a seal.

Some have the idea that this scroll had one seal on the outer edge with the other six positioned at intervals on the inside of the scroll so that the opening of each seal revealed a portion of the book. This is not likely, since it is not the manner in which scrolls were sealed, and would be difficult to do. John was not given the scroll to eat and digest until it was completely open. It was his job to reveal the contents of the scroll. That was not done until after the seals were completely removed. The visions which John saw in the opening of each seal were only preparatory, giving hints as to the content of the book.

Matt. 27:59-65 gives the record of the burial of Jesus, including the securing of the tomb. Pilate authorized the sealing of the stone. Before the stone could be moved away from the door of the tomb the seal would have to be broken. Anyone who broke the seal illegally would have been subject to severe penalty. In this case the penalty would probably have been death. Of course, the seal was broken by a higher authority than Pilate. God sent His angels to roll back the stone to reveal the empty tomb.

The seals on the scroll in God's hand were there by the authority of God. Only one who had His authority could remove them. A search was made in heaven and earth for one worthy (with the proper authority) to break its seals and open the scroll. No one was found. This distressed John so much that he wept bitterly until one of the 24 elders comforted him. He let John know that there was one who was worthy, who had the authority of God to break the seals and open the scroll to reveal its contents.

II. THE DIRECTOR – THE LAMB OF GOD (Rev. 5:5-7)

Who was found worthy to break the seals and reveal the contents of the scroll? He was called, ***"The Lion of the tribe of Judah, the root of David."*** When John looks for this Lion, he sees a Lamb. He is in the midst of the throne with God and the four cherubim. In Rev. 22:3-4 the Lamb shares the throne with God. It is called, *"The throne of God and the Lamb."* It is interesting to note that the passage refers to these two by the singular pronouns ***His*** and ***Him,*** i.e., *"His servants shall serve Him."* This seems to indicate that God the Father and the Lamb who is Jesus the Son are in essence one.

A. THE LAMB OF GOD AS OUR PASSOVER

The Lamb appears as one who had been slain, but He is alive! Here is another of the items found in the Old Testament tabernacle/temple—that is, the lamb that was killed as a sacrifice for the sins of the people. It had to be a lamb[1] without spot or blemish of any kind. Jesus is, "The Lamb of God that takes away the sins of the world" (John 1:29,36).

The 14th day of Abib (Nisan), the first month of the Jewish religious calendar, was the day on which the Passover lambs were sacrificed. The lambs, brought by the people to be sacrificed and then eaten as the Passover meal, would be set aside on the 10th day of the month.[2] Then when the time came, each person would point out his own lamb, and, as the custom was, the priest would point to the lamb and say, "Behold, the lamb of God." John the Baptist, being the son of the priest Zacharias, was himself a priest by inheritance. He pointed to Jesus and said, **"Behold, the Lamb of God which takes away the sins of the world."** Jesus was, in this way, designated as our Passover offering. In 1 Cor. 5:7b Paul says, "For indeed Christ, our Passover, was sacrificed for us."

---

[1]*Lamb* refers to either a goat or sheep. Exod. 12:5: "Your lamb shall be without blemish, a male of the first year. You may take it **from the sheep or from the goats.**" For the Day of Atonement (Yom Kippur), the once a year sacrifice in the Most Holy Place, the blood of a goat was specified, but for the Passover lamb either a sheep or a goat was acceptable.

[2]In Exod. 12:1-11 in giving the initial instructions for the Passover Moses specified the tenth day of the first month as the time to set aside the Passover lamb, and the 14th day just before sundown as the time to kill the lamb. They were to roast it and eat it that night.

B. THE ATONING BLOOD TAKEN INTO THE HOLY OF HOLIES

Jesus was not only our Passover, but He was also the atonement whose blood was taken into the Holy of Holies by the High Priest. In the Old Testament this was done once every year on the day of atonement (Yom Kippur), but it was done once for all by our High Priest, Jesus Christ. It was by His own blood, the blood of the Lamb of God, that He atoned for our sins once for all. Heb. 9:12 says, "Not with the blood of goats and calves, but with His own blood He entered the Most Holy Place once for all, having obtained eternal redemption."

C. THE BODY OF CHRIST AS THE BREAD OF LIFE

The Lion of Judah/the Lamb of God (Jesus Christ) is both our Great High Priest and the sacrifice for our sins. In addition he is the bread of life. He Himself is the bread of the presence for in Him dwells the fullness of the presence of God. In John 6:32-33 we read:

> Then Jesus said to them, "Most assuredly, I say to you, Moses did not give you the bread from heaven, but My Father gives you the true bread from heaven. For the bread of God is He who comes down from heaven and gives life to the world."

Again, in John 6:35, "And Jesus said to them, 'I am the bread of life. He who comes to Me shall never hunger, and he who believes in Me shall never thirst.'" Then in verse 51 Jesus said:

> I am the living bread which came down from heaven. If anyone eats of this bread, he will live forever; and the bread that I shall give is My flesh, which I shall give for the life of the world.

His flesh is this living bread. This is a direct reference to the fact that He was to be the sacrificial Lamb of God. Partaking of the benefits of His sacrifice upon the cross is to eat of this bread. But only the priests were allowed to eat the bread of the presence. This means that only those who belong to Christ and are a holy priesthood can partake of the life that He gives.

In this chapter so far we have seen three of the items on the list of temple/tabernacle items (see chapter four for the list), all of them being represented by Jesus the Son of God—i.e., the Great High Priest, the sacrificial Lamb of God, and the Bread of the Presence of God. There are two more to come. We will identify them when we get to them.

D. THE SEVEN HORNS OF THE LAMB

The Lamb is said to have seven horns and seven eyes which are the seven Spirits of God. We have previously seen that the seven lamps of fire are also the seven Spirits of God. The explanation of the seven Spirits of God has been given in chapter one and in chapter four. I suggest you go back and read these if you need to review. In Rev. 1:4-5 the seven Spirits of God are named in the greeting, together with the Father and the Son, Jesus Christ. This would indicate that *the seven Spirits* is a way of characterizing the Holy Spirit. The significance of the number seven has already been explained several times. At the risk of being over-repetitive, the number seven is a symbol of wholeness or completeness. It stands for all of a thing. In chapter four the seven Spirits of God are seen as lamps of fire. Lamps give light. The Holy Spirit is the source of all inspiration, all enlightenment, and all revelation.

The horn is a symbol of power. A king or kingdom may be represented as a horn, but the horn is a generic symbol of power, whether king or kingdom, or just power in general. A ram's horn, when hollowed out, is used in the Old Testament for a trumpet, and as a container, especially for oil. However, when used figuratively it refers to power, might and authority. Deut. 33:7 is Moses' blessing on the descendants of Joseph, the tribes of Ephraim and Manasseh:

His glory is like a firstborn bull, And his horns like the horns
of the wild ox; Together with them He shall push the peoples
To the ends of the earth; They are the ten thousands of
Ephraim, And they are the thousands of Manasseh.

With his horns Joseph was to extend the peoples (of Ephraim and Manasseh) to the ends of the earth. In the last part of 1 Sam. 2:10 Samuel writes of God, "He will give strength to His king, And exalt the horn of His anointed." This verse, in poetic form, is using what is called synthetic or equivalent parallelism. The first clause is repeated using other words in the second clause. *Exalting the horn of His anointed* is the same thing as *giving*

117

strength to His king. Psalm 18:2 is an example of many passages in the Psalms and elsewhere which uses *horn* to mean strength or power: "The LORD is my rock and my fortress and my deliverer; My God, my strength, in whom I will trust; My shield and the horn of my salvation, my stronghold."

Now put the symbols together—the Lamb is Jesus Christ, seven equals all, horn equals power and authority. This is a figurative way of saying that Jesus has all power and authority. In Rev. 3:1, Jesus said to the church in Sardis, "These things says He who has the seven Spirits of God...." Jesus is the one who has the seven Spirits of God. He is the one who was anointed with the Holy Spirit and power (Acts 10:38). When it was time for Jesus to enter His three and one-half years of ministry before fulfilling His ultimate goal of dying for mankind, the Holy Spirit came upon Him after his baptism to empower Him. He was given all power and all knowledge. These are characteristics of God. In becoming a man Jesus emptied[3] himself of His equality with His Father according to Phil. 2:7.

Having emptied Himself of various divine characteristics, Luke 2:52 tells us that He had to grow in wisdom and in favor with God as well as in physical stature. One of the attributes He left behind was His omniscience (having all knowledge), or else He would not have had to grow in wisdom. As a human He was limited as to his location, traveling from place to place to get where He wanted to be. When He became a human He emptied Himself of His omnipresence (being everywhere present at once). He also left behind His omnipotence (having all power) because He depended on the anointing of the Holy Spirit for His power. We can see, then, why it was necessary for Him to have the seven Spirits of God. Because He had the seven Spirits (the totality of the Holy Spirit), He not only had the light of all knowledge, but all power as well. This is the meaning of the seven lamps and the seven horns.

E. THE SEVEN EYES OF THE LAMB

The Lamb also has seven eyes. These also are said to be the seven Spirits of God. The obvious use of eyes is to see. We saw in chapter 4 that the cherubim (living creatures) are full of eyes all around and within. This

---

[3] κενόω (*kenoo*, pr. *ke-noh'-oh*)—literally, *to make empty.* King James Version and New King James Version translate Phil. 2:7 to say *"...made Himself of no reputation."* Most later versions say, *"...emptied Himself."* NIV translates, *"...made Himself nothing."*

indicated tremendous seeing ability. As a result they are able to observe and know many things. But the Lamb has seven eyes. In this case, the seven eyes are more than all the eyes of the cherubim combined, because seven is the figure for completeness. The Lamb sees all and knows all. Lamps give inspiration and enlightenment so that eyes can see. If a person's spiritual eyes are blind, the light does him no good.

Jesus has the Spirit and He gives the Spirit (Rom. 5:5). Jesus has all inspiration and He gives inspiration (2 Tim. 3:16-17). But we must have our spiritual eyes open to see in order to receive and understand the knowledge He gives. Jesus has all power, and He gives power through the Holy Spirit (Eph. 3:16,20). Eph, 1:17-19 says:

> ...that the God of our Lord Jesus Christ, the Father of glory, may give to you the spirit of wisdom and revelation in the knowledge of Him, the eyes of your understanding being enlightened; that you may know what is the hope of His calling, what are the riches of the glory of His inheritance in the saints, and what is the exceeding greatness of His power toward us who believe, according to the working of His mighty power....

Because Jesus has the seven Spirits of God which are the seven lamps, He can give us enlightenment. Because the seven Spirits are the seven horns, he can give us power. Because they are also the seven eyes, He can open our eyes to understand. All that Jesus left behind when He became a man, He now has taken up again. He has all power, all knowledge and wisdom, and He is omnipresent, being everywhere He wants to be, especially in the hearts of every Christian in the person of the Holy Spirit. Only God has all power and knowledge. Only God is everywhere at once. Jesus is God. The Holy Spirit is God.

F. THE SEVEN SPIRITS OF GOD SENT OUT TO ALL THE EARTH

As the church we are the lampstand that holds up the seven lamps of fire. It is our task to share the enlightenment of God's Holy Spirit to all the world. "Go into all the world and preach the gospel . . ." (Mark 16:15). We who have been given power through the Spirit must show the power of God in our lives. We must be living demonstrations to those around us of the power of

God at work. We, who have had our spiritual eyes opened by him who sees all and knows all, must be engaged in helping others to see. Through His church, the seven Spirits of God are sent out to all the earth. This is not to say that He does not or cannot exercise His powers apart from the church, but we who are His body are the earthen vessels through whom God intends to give the light of the knowledge of the glory of God in the face of Jesus to the world (2 Cor. 4:6-7).

G. THE SCROLL IS GIVEN TO THE LAMB OF GOD

"Then He came and took the scroll out of the right hand of Him who sat on the throne" (Rev. 5:7). The lamb is now in possession of the script. When God chose to create the heavens and the earth with all things in them, it was the Word, the preexistent Christ, who carried out that creation. When it was time to make a new creation, it was the resurrected Christ who brought that into being. When it is time to make all things new, it will be the coming Christ who does that also. Jesus said in John 14:2 "...I go to prepare a place for you." When He has finished that preparation of the New Heaven and New Earth, He will come and take us there to live with Him forever. When God has a plan to carry out, Christ is the one who carries out the task. This task of opening the seals is no exception.

He gives the scroll to the Lamb who takes it from God's right hand. He is the one who has the authority to open the seals. He is the one who will open the book and reveal it's contents. But His task is not just to show us what it says. His job is to make what is prophesied come to pass through the work of the Holy Spirit in this world. Remember that He is the director of the drama. This does not mean that He is going to make all the choices for everybody and every nation, but it does mean that there is a general script to follow in what is to take place from John's day on, a script that culminates in the return of Christ, the judgment of all men, the rewarding of the saints and the destruction of the destroyers. Jesus the Lamb is the director as well as the star of the show.

We have just been introduced to God as the Producer; Christ the Lamb as the director; and the script—i.e., the scroll taken from the hand of God by the Lamb. The contents of this script will be revealed to us later, after it has been opened. At the bidding of the director the actors in this drama will come upon the stage and play their parts. The lamb has all the authority, knowledge, wisdom and power to be the director of this Divine Drama of the Ages.

III. PRAISE TO THE LAMB (Read Rev. 5:8-10)

In Rev. 4 the cherubim and elders extolled the glory and worth of God on the throne. Now they voice exuberant praise to the Lamb who was slain. The song that they sing is a new song. It is new, because never before could this song be sung. It has only been since the sacrificial death of Christ the Lamb that we could proclaim redemption by His blood. This is an ongoing theme. The Great High Priest, the Lion of Judah, has offered the sacrifice—Himself, the Lamb of God. He has come to the throne of God with His blood as a payment for our sins. We can sing this new song throughout the ages to praise the Lamb for what He has done.

The elders and cherubim extol His worthiness to open the seals of the scroll. The reason given for this is that He was slain, and by His blood he redeemed people to God. The 24 elders each has a harp and a golden bowl full of incense. Here are two more items in the pattern for the tabernacle/temple—the golden incense bowls and the incense. In the Old Testament only the priests were allowed to offer the incense. Here the incense is the prayers of the saints.

These elders are offering up to God the incense of prayer. They are the priests of God. They represent all those who are redeemed by the blood. These are the people of God who have sacrifices to offer (1 Pet. 2:5). One of these is the sacrifice of prayer. Another is the sacrifice of praise (Heb. 13:15). In the Old Testament a separate group of Levites were appointed to offer up musical praise to God. Like the priests, they were organized into 24 divisions, 12 men in each division. Their job was to stand in the temple, singing and playing their instruments to God. In the heavenly temple/tabernacle both jobs are combined and included in the work of the twenty-four elders, who have the harps of God as well as the bowls of incense. They offer both the sacrifices of praise and prayer. But that is not all. They have the sacrifice of service to offer (Hebrews 13:16). Whatever else they might do in service to God, their bodies are to be offered as a living sacrifice. This is their spiritual worship to God (Rom. 12:1).

Preparing for the Drama

With Jesus as the High Priest, the Lamb of God as the sacrifice, and the body of Christ as the bread of the presence of God, the golden bowls and the prayers as incense, we have five of the items in the tabernacle/temple pattern. There were ten in chapter four. This makes fifteen in all. There are four left. All but one will show up later. This temple of God in heaven is foreshadowed by the tabernacle in the wilderness and the temple in Jerusalem.

In verse 9 in the *NKJV* the song of the elders and cherubim is translated, "And have redeemed us to God by Your blood." There is some variation in the Greek manuscripts on the pronoun *us*. The redemption by the blood of Jesus was not for angels (see Heb. 2:16) but is limited to humans. It is doubtful that the cherubim would be saying *us*.[4] While the elders could say that, the cherubim could not. Add to this that those who were redeemed were from the people on earth, "...out of every tribe and tongue and people and nation...." There are several discrepancies in the translation of verse 10. The preponderance of the evidence is for the following translation: "And have made them a kingdom[5] and priests to our God; And they shall reign on the earth." Certainly the angels are not the ones to reign on the earth, nor are they the kingdom of priests which was prophesied in the Old Testament and fulfilled in the New (1 Pet. 2:5,9).

While the expression *kingdom* in this verse, as opposed to *kings*, does not have as much support here as in chapter one, yet it conforms to the parallel statement in 1:6 as well as elsewhere in scripture.

---

[4] While the majority of the manuscript evidence is for the pronoun *us* in this verse, this is not the case with the same pronoun in verse 9. It is translated, *"...made us kings...."* In many versions. However, both the Nestle/UBS and Majority texts use the Greek word αὐτούς (*autous*—pr. *ow-toos'*)—*them*. Thus it reads, *"...made them a kingdom...."* In like manner, the preponderance of evidence is on the side of *they* instead of *we* in verse ten—thus *"...and they shall reign on the earth."*

[5] See chapter one page 35, footnote 6. The Majority text, while supporting *kingdom* in chapter one, reads *"kings"* in this verse, while Nestle/UBS reads *"a kingdom."* It is my opinion that the better reading, and most textual evidence, is on the side of *kingdom*. The concept of a kingdom of priests is found in several places in the Bible (See 1 Peter 2:5, 9).

IV. THE FULL CHORUS OF PRAISE (Read 5:11-14)

Now something else is seen in the temple scene in heaven—a chorus of angels said to be 10,000 times 10,000, and thousands of thousands on top of that. The first factor comes to 100 million. How many millions or billions of angels do you suppose there are? These surround the throne, the cherubim and the 24 elders. The song they sing is, "Worthy is the Lamb who was slain To receive power and riches and wisdom, And strength and honor and glory and blessing!" The praise here continues to be for the Lamb. Worthy is the Lamb! What is He worthy of? Power. Riches. Wisdom. Strength. Honor. Glory. Blessing. The host of angels is praising the Son of God. I am reminded of the statement God made to the angels in Heb. 1:6: "But when He again brings the firstborn into the world, He says: 'Let all the angels of God worship Him.'" The angel in Rev. 22:8-9 tells John that he is not to worship angels—only God. But the angels themselves worship the Lamb. Why? Because He is God, along with the Father and the Holy Spirit. The Father says to the Son in Heb. 1:8, "Your throne, O God, is forever and ever."

Then, added to these voices in verse 13 are every living creature in heaven and earth, under the earth, and in the sea. They give blessing, glory and honor both to God upon the throne and to the Lamb. Then the four cherubim say "Amen!" This is an expression which means, "Let it be so." Can you imagine the swell of praise rising up to the throne from the earth and sea? Wow! Once again the 24 elders fall down to worship Him who lives for ever and ever.

The Lamb that was slain has reached out and taken the scroll from the right hand of the One who sits on the throne—God the Father. The producer (God) has given the script (the scroll) to the drama's director (Christ) who is now ready to remove the seals. Remember that the contents will not be revealed until the seals have been broken and the book is open. There are seven seals to be removed before we get to that point. Chapters six through eight tell of the removing of the seals. With the breaking of each seal a vision is given to John dealing with the theme or themes with which the book is dealing. Let's take a look at these and see what we can learn. Meanwhile, from time to time we will return to the temple scene and see more of the temple's furniture, along with visions that relate to this furniture, including the altar of burnt offering, the altar of incense and the ark of the covenant. Are you ready?

Chapter 6

THE SEALS—THE THEME OF THE DRAMA
Rev. Chapter 6

I. VISIONS OF THE SEALS—WHAT THEY TELL US

A. THE THEME OF THE DRAMA

In Rev. 6-8 the Lamb removes the seals from the scroll one at a time. As each is removed John is given a vision which reveals part of the theme of the script. This theme will be played out in the drama when the book is finally opened. We should not think of these visions as a succession of events. They are all symbols presenting different aspects of the overall theme. Each vision adds to the others to present a complete picture of the theme. They all pertain to the fortunes of the servants of God, either in terms of what they must suffer, or in terms of judgment upon their persecutors and victory over the world.

B. THE FOUR HORSEMEN

The first four of the seven visions are of a kind. They are four horses with their riders. The fourth rider is Death, followed by Hades. Death and Hades are not persons, but they are states presented as persons. This gives us a clue as to the nature of these riders. They are not literal persons, but personifications. Each rider represents a state or condition.

The horse is commonly used to signify warfare or conflict. Moses, in Exod. 15:1, and Miriam, in Exod. 15:21 both refer to the triumph of God over the armies of Pharaoh when they were drowned in the Red Sea: "I will sing to the LORD, For He has triumphed gloriously! The horse and its rider He has thrown into the sea!" Solomon wrote in Prov. 21:31, "The horse *is* prepared for the day of battle, But deliverance *is* of the LORD." In Jer. 51:21 Israel (Jacob) is the weapon God will use against His enemies: "With you I will break in pieces the horse and its rider...." Revelation uses the horse and rider to depict the various aspects of the spiritual warfare which is the first emphasis of the Drama of the Age. As the book is being opened we begin to understand that it is dealing with the conflict of Christ and His followers with the forces of evil.

What is the meaning of the colors of the horses? There is a reference to red, black, white and dappled horses in the book of Zechariah (Zech. 1:8; 6:2). They are spiritual troops who have the assigned task of going to and fro on the earth to bring quietness and peace. There is no explanation of the meaning of their color, and their mission does not seem to have any connection with the mission of the horses and their riders in Revelation. Perhaps the meaning of the colors can be determined from things with which the colors are associated—i.e., victory, bloodshed, starvation, and death.

C. OBSERVATIONS ON INTERPRETING THE VISIONS OF THE SEALS

In interpreting these things we should not read more into the visions, or any other part of Revelation, than what appears in the text. It is legitimate to use deductions, scriptural references, and historical data to help in the interpretation, but it is not legitimate to create an interpretation out of thin air by speculation. Now let us watch as the Lamb (Jesus Christ) opens the first six seals.

II. THE RIDER ON THE WHITE HORSE (Read 6:1-2)

When John removes the first seal one of the living creatures (a cherub) shows him a vision of a rider on a white horse.

A. NOT THE PERSON OF CHRIST

When we see the rider on the white horse and hear him described, our first impulse is to interpret this as a picture of Jesus Christ. That is what I did at first. I gave evidence of this interpretation by pointing to Jesus on the white horse in Rev. 19:11. Then I noticed in 19:14 that the whole army of heaven on white horses, not just Jesus. There are some notable differences between the rider in Revelation 19 and the one here. In chapter 19 the rider is identified as a person—the Word of God and the King of Kings, and He has a two edged sword coming out of His mouth. In chapter 6 the rider is not named, and has a bow rather than a sword. In chapter 19 Jesus has on his head many crowns (*diadems—crowns of rulership*), indicating that He has conquered the kingdoms of the world. He is King of kings and Lord of lords. In chapter 6 the rider has a single crown of victory (*stephanos—laurel wreath*).

The only similarity is the white horse, which, in both cases, is a symbol of victory and conquest. The rider in chapter 6 is not a person but a personification. He represents the victory that shall be ours—i.e., the victorious cause of Christ. This is played out in the scene in 19:11 ff. There we do not see a personification, but the persons of Jesus Himself and His army of angels riding on white horses as they bring destruction to the beast and false prophet, and to the kings and armies who follow the beast.

B. NOT THE "ANTICHRIST"

Instead of seeing the rider of the white horse in chapter six as a symbol of the victory of the saints, some have interpreted him as representing "the Antichrist" or the seemingly victorious forces of evil. I see nothing in the context to warrant this interpretation. In fact, the visions of the seals, in one way or another, all pertain to the saints of God.

C. IDENTIFYING FEATURES OF THIS RIDER

What makes up this picture of the rider on the white horse? There is, of course, the white horse; then the rider is wearing a victory crown and carrying a bow; and there is the statement by John about the rider's mission, "...he went out conquering and to conquer." The interpretation must also be consistent with the other three horsemen in this chapter. Since the fourth horseman represents Death, an obvious personification, I see all of these horsemen as personifications. The three horsemen are the same in nature. If one is a personification, they are all personifications. Since that is the case, the rider on the white horse is obviously the personification of victory. All the parts of the picture point to it.

127

1. He Goes Forth Conquering. He has no other purpose than to conquer, and he goes forth *to conquer*—i.e., he is destined to be victorious.

2. He Wears the Crown of the Victor. In Rev. 2:10 Jesus told the church in Smyrna:

> Do not fear any of those things which you are about to suffer.
> Indeed, the devil is about to throw some of you into prison,
> that you may be tested, and you will have tribulation ten days.
> Be faithful until death, and I will give you the crown of life.

The crown the Christians in Smyrna were to receive is the same kind of crown of victory worn by the rider on the white horse—the *stephanos*.[1] He lets us know that we are to go through a battle with evil forces. This will result in suffering, persecution, and even death, but we should not fear what men or devils can do to us. God has assured us of a victory which will result in everlasting life. In Matt. 10:28 Jesus said, "And do not fear those who kill the body but cannot kill the soul. But rather fear Him who is able to destroy both soul and body in hell."

3. He Rides the White Horse that Symbolizes Victory. In the days of John the white horse was a recognized symbol of victory. Whenever a Roman Caesar or his appointed general returned to Rome victorious from a war, he would announce his victory by leading his army into Rome riding on a white horse or driving a chariot drawn by white horses.

The bow is an instrument of warfare (see Zech. 9:10). This rider is a picture of a conquering warrior. The crown is the laurel wreath used to crown the head of the one who is victorious in the games or in war. Notice that this crown is given to him; he doesn't earn it. Our victory is a gift of grace. The end is pre-determined.

Why is victory the first thing pictured? The rider on the white horse stands in stark contrast to the other three riders. Revelation shows time and again that God's people will face severe suffering and even death at the hands of Satan's forces, as signified by the other three riders. But why does He put

---

[1]The word here is στέφανος (*stephanos—victory crown*). It is the laurel wreath that was used to crown the victors in the games or in the wars. It is the symbol of victory. The royal crown of kingship is διάδεμος (*diademos—diadem*)

this symbol first rather than last? Before showing the shocking reality of persecution and death, He wants to reassure us that the victory is ours. Christ has already won the victory and given it to us. "But thanks *be* to God, who gives us the victory through our Lord Jesus Christ" (1 Cor. 15:57). "Now thanks *be* to God who always leads us in triumph in Christ...." (2 Cor. 2:14).

In the first act of the drama (Rev. 12) the first thing presented is the victory of the forces of good (Michael and his angels) over the forces of evil (the Dragon and his angels). That defeat took place at the beginning of the Christian era, for it was the blood of Christ's sacrifice and the proclamation of the gospel by the brethren which defeated Satan and cast him down so that he could not stand before God to accuse the saints any longer. The victory is already assured before the drama goes on to depict the persecution of the servants of God. Apparently God wanted them to know that the victory was already won before they were ever called upon to face tribulations. I believe that it is for this reason that the theme of victory is the first thing presented. With this assurance we can face the riders on the red horse, the black horse and the pale horse with confidence.

III. THE RIDER ON THE RED HORSE (Read 6:3-4)

A. THE IDENTIFYING FEATURES OF THIS RIDER

As the Lamb removes the second seal another cherub directs John's attention to the vision of a fiery red horse and rider. This rider is allowed to take peace from the earth so that people would kill one another. He is given a great sword. This great sword is not the long sword of most soldiers, but the short sword[2], like those worn by the Roman foot soldiers. This is also the word for the knife used for slaughtering sacrifices, and the word from which we get the name for the *machete*.

B. WHAT THIS RIDER SIGNIFIES

The rider signifies slaughter and bloodshed. The things which indicate the nature of this rider are:

1. The Blood-red Color of the Horse

---

[2]The Greek word is μάχαιρα (*machaira*). This is the word from which *machete* is derived.

2. The Short Sword—the Instrument of Slaughter

3. It Was Given to Him to Take Peace from the Earth

4. He Was to Cause People to Kill One Another

He is given this task, and the sword with which to accomplish it. He is the purveyor of violence. Bloodshed fits the picture whether we are talking about the brutal killing of defenseless people, or killing in warfare during a pitched battle.

C. A TIME OF VIOLENCE AND BLOODSHED

This vision, like the first, pertains to the people of God. Bloodshed is one of the kinds of suffering and persecution Christians will undergo. When Christ returns there will have been many martyrs for the cause of Christ. The people of God are going to have to live in times and among people where violence and killing are commonplace. We are now living in just such a time, and it seems that matters are getting worse and worse.

How many Christians lost their lives on September 11, 2001? From the reports many of them were believers. These were killed by those who are professed enemies of Christianity. How many in our time have been killed because of their faith in Jesus Christ? I was stunned to learn that there have been more Christians martyred for their faith since the beginning of the 20th century than in all the centuries since His crucifixion. It is still going on in the first years of the 21st century.

God decided to destroy mankind and start over with Noah and his family because of the violence that existed in the days of Noah. A time is coming when God will once more bring a halt to the violence of men. Meanwhile, this is one of the things Christians must suffer—i.e., a world where there is no peace, and where men kill one another. The rider on the red horse has been riding for centuries, and he still rides today.

IV. THE RIDER ON THE BLACK HORSE (Read 6:5-6)

A. THE RIDER DESCRIBED

When the Lamb breaks the third seal a third cherub shows John a black horse and his rider. The rider is holding a pair of balance scales in his hand.

This is the kind of scales used in the old fashioned apothecary to measure out chemicals and drugs, and in produce markets of years gone by to measure out food stuffs. They are still used today for certain measurements for accuracy. That is what is going on here. A quart of wheat is measured out for a day's wages, or three quarts of barley for a day's wages. And don't touch the oil or the wine, because the average person couldn't afford it. A quart of wheat is barely enough to sustain one man for one day. What of the man who has a family? His only recourse is to get the coarser barley. For a day's wages he can get three quarts of barley. This is a picture of great want.

B. THE SOURCE OF THIS SYMBOL

The symbol of extreme economic hardship and hunger probably comes from the history of the destruction of Jerusalem. The things that took place in the city were reported by Josephus.[3] This Jewish historian lived through the siege of Jerusalem that resulted in the fall of that city in 70 A.D. The siege lasted for three and a half years and caused severe shortages of food supplies.

People resorted to stealing food from others, while thousands died of starvation. There was no commerce into or out of the city. Food supplies ran so low that Josephus reported a case of a woman eating her newborn child.[4] Moses prophesied that such things would come upon Jerusalem if they failed to keep the commands God had given them at Sinai. You can read this prophecy in Deut. 28:15-68 (notice especially verses 52-57).

Was John prophesying the fall of Jerusalem? No, for John was writing some 25 years after Jerusalem was destroyed by Titus (Titian), the Roman general who later became the emperor of Rome. Revelation is using imagery from those things familiar to Christians of that day to symbolize the hardship that was to come upon Christians. Just as the Romans surrounded the city of Jerusalem, so in Rev. 20:7-9 the forces of Satan surround the beloved city, New Jerusalem, also called the Heavenly Jerusalem and the Jerusalem which is above (see Gal. 4:26; Heb. 12:22). In Rev. 21:2 the bride of Christ, the church, is called *the New Jerusalem.*

---

[3]Flavius Josephus, *The Wars of the Jews,* Bk 5, Ch 12, ¶ 3; also Bk 6, Ch 3, ¶ 3.

[4]Op. Cit., Bk 6, Ch 3, ¶ 4.

C. HUNGER AS A MEANS OF PERSECUTING GOD'S SERVANTS

One of the persecutions that Satan brings upon Christians is economic deprivation and hunger. In some instances they would not be allowed to buy and sell. The starvation would not necessarily be because of natural famines which made food scarce, but they would be deprived of available food supplies as a means of persecution. In Rev. 13:16-17 the beast and the false prophet (the two horned beast) use this as a means of causing men to worship the beast and his image. In my own lifetime I have known of people in another country, seeking to escape the clutches of a false religious system, who were blacklisted and not allowed to buy or sell. The businesses as well as the government in that country were so dominated by this false system that they would not sell even necessary provisions to these individuals, even though they might want to do so. If it had not been for help which came from missionaries from other countries, they would have perished from hunger.

Black is worn as an indication of mourning. It is also the color of starvation. Artists have traditionally used black to depict starving peoples. The rider on the black horse is the symbol of persecution by starvation and economic oppression.

V. THE RIDER ON THE PALE HORSE (Read 6:7-8)

The four visions are presented by the four cherubim. Each of these living creatures has some part in presenting the four visions to John. It is as if there were four separate movie or television screens with a cherub standing by each one. Each in his turn calls to John to come and see the picture portrayed on the screen.

There has been unwarranted speculation about the visions of the four horsemen. According to one view the four horsemen are seen as representing the events of four time periods. Another view is that the living creatures each represent the four directions and thus four regions or continents of the earth. Therefore, the visions of the horsemen they are seen as symbols of four periods of history characterizing each of these four regions.

This is going beyond what can be found in the visions themselves. Notice that each vision is set forth simply, and all the things described in each vision focus on one theme, whether that is victory, bloodshed, economic deprivation and hunger, or death. This is all we can ascertain from the text. We can all recognize the themes associated with the horsemen. If they mean more than this we cannot know it except by speculation.

A. *This Rider is Death Personified*

The fourth horseman is named *Death*. We are not left to guess or surmise or speculate about this. This symbol is explained for us. It is my belief that the meaning of the fourth rider is limited to what appears in the text.

There is another figure in this vision—that of a person called *Hades*. Again we are dealing with a personification of an impersonal state. Hades is said to follow Death. In Greek mythology Hades was the name of the god of the underworld. He ruled over the nether world of darkness, the abode of the dead.

B. *The Meaning of Hades*

The word *hades* was adopted by the New Testament writers to refer to the abode or state of the souls of the dead, roughly corresponding to the word *sheol* in the Old Testament. As the rider Death claims the bodies, Hades comes behind and gathers up the souls. The word *hades* makes sense in the context of this vision only as the receiver of the souls of the dead.[5] Hades, like death, is a temporary state which will no longer exist after judgment. Rev. 20:14 says that both Death and Hades will be cast into the lake of fire. If Hades itself were the lake of fire, how then could Hades be cast into itself? For a more thorough study of the meaning of *hades* go to *Appendix A Hades and Hell.*

Death rides his horse with the gloomy pallor of death, while behind him comes Hades and gathers up the souls of the dead. In this vision Death kills one-fourth of mankind through warfare, famine, pestilence (plague) and wild beasts.

---

[5]*An Extract out of Josephus's Discourse to the Greeks Concerning Hades* is an interesting presentation of Josephus' understanding of hades, found in *Josephus—The Complete Works,* William Whiston, A.M. Tr., 6. *Thomas Nelson Pub.*, Nashville, 1998, p. 974.

C. THE CAUSES OF DEATH BY THE RIDER OF THE PALE HORSE

1. The Sword. This is the long sword of warfare[6] in contrast to the short sword of the rider on the red horse. Death is meted out by warfare in this vision.

2. Hunger. Famine is often a result of the devastation of warfare. This causes even more deaths. The word here translated *hunger* indicates hunger that is connected with famine.[7] This cause of death coincides with the starvation of the black horse and rider.

3. Pestilence. Most scholars believe that the word *death,* given as a third cause of death, is referring to pestilence such as the bubonic or black plague. Many translations use the word *pestilence* instead of *death*; otherwise it would seem redundant to speak of killing by death. Obviously various causes of death are being listed. To say that death is caused by death doesn't make much sense unless it refers to a specific cause of death.

When resistance has been lowered by starvation, disease and pestilence usually follow. When great disasters occur, whether by slaughter in warfare or starvation by famine, or by floods or other natural calamities, the multitude of dead bodies putrefy and cause disease and death unless they are quickly disposed of. In such disasters this is not usually possible, thus subjecting the survivors to pestilence and death. Just recently South-East Asia suffered a catastrophic tsunami, caused by a massive earthquake. The death toll reached into the hundreds of thousands. A primary concern was disposing of the dead bodies before they could decay and cause pestilence, and as a result, more deaths. In this sense we could certainly say that death causes death. This only confirms the idea that the third cause, given as *death,* is actually death through disease.

4. Wild Beasts. The last cause of death listed is wild beasts. When warfare has taken the lives of many, often starvation follows to take the lives of many of those left from the war. Then pestilence comes against those who survive the starvation, resulting in more deaths. Finally, when people are left

---

[6] ῥομφαία (*hromphaia*)—*Young's Greek Dictionary* gives the meaning as: "...a *sabre*, that is, a long and broad *cutlass* (any *weapon* of the kind, literally or figuratively):—sword."

[7] λιμος (*limos*)—dearth, famine, hunger.

helpless because they have been decimated by wars, famines, and disease, the wild beasts grow bold and move in to be a further threat to their life. By this process one-fourth of mankind lose their lives.

Pale is the color of death because of the pallor of the dead bodies. The rider on the pale horse is Death who claims the bodies of men, and following is Hades who claims the souls.

D. HOW DOES THIS AFFECT CHRISTIANS TODAY?

The saints have to live in the world and suffer the same trials that afflict the world as a whole. While they are subject to the persecutions of violence and starvation, they are not immune to the wars, the famines, the plagues, and the wild beasts which threaten all men. These form part of the tribulation which the saints must undergo.

These four horsemen represent the things that the saints will be subjected to. First of all they are promised the victory in this spiritual warfare. Meanwhile, the methods which Satan uses against them are bloodshed, economic oppression (starvation), and death.

Heb. 2:14 tells us that Jesus shared in our humanity, "...that through death He might destroy him who had the power of death, that is, the devil." Satan has been given the power of death, but through the death of Christ he will be destroyed. In 1 Cor. 15:25-28 Paul says of Christ, "For He must reign till He has put all enemies under His feet. The last enemy *that* will be destroyed is death." Christ defeated death for Himself by rising from the dead. His death and resurrection assures us that we will rise from the dead. This is the ultimate defeat of death. If we are Christ's we shall never die again. We will be immune to the second death. Rev. 20:13-15 shows us the final judgment scene:

> The sea gave up the dead who were in it, and Death and Hades delivered up the dead who were in them. And they were judged, each one according to his works. Then Death and Hades were cast into the lake of fire. This is the second death. And anyone not found written in the Book of Life was cast into the lake of fire.

When that day comes it will be the end of Death. He will ride his pallid horse no longer. Praise God for His unspeakable gift. We will rise again! For those of us whose names are written in the Book of Life it will be a glorious, never-ending day. Hallelujah!

VI. THE SOULS OF WITNESSES UNDER THE ALTAR (6:9-11)

A. THE ALTAR OF SACRIFICE

When the Lamb removed the fifth seal from the scroll John was shown the altar of burnt offering which would have been near the crystal sea in the temple scene. The altar of burnt offering is the sixteenth item in the list from the Old Testament tabernacle/temple (see Rev. 4). This is the altar upon which the sin offerings and thank offerings were offered. This is the altar upon which the Passover lambs were sacrificed.

First, this was the altar upon which the once a year atonement sacrifices of a bullock and a goat were offered by the high priest. The altar of burnt offering prefigures the offering of Christ. It is a figure of the sacrifice of Christ Who was nailed to the cross, shed His blood, and died. Jesus was killed in the outer court, i.e., in the world. From there His blood was figuratively taken into the Holy of Holies by the Great High Priest (Jesus Himself) when He rose from the dead and ascended to the throne of God. There His blood was offered at the mercy seat (throne of God) as the atonement for the sins of the whole world, not once every year, but once for all (Heb. 9:11-14).

Secondly, this was also the altar upon which the various sacrifices were offered by the priesthood. We as priests of God have our sacrifices to offer—that is, the sacrifices of praise and service and various other spiritual sacrifices, including offering ourselves as a living sacrifice (1 Pet. 2:5; Heb. 13:15-16; Rom. 12:1).

B. THE SOURCE OF THIS SYMBOL

In this vision the souls under the altar are figuratively the blood of the martyrs given in sacrifice. In the Old Testament, when animals were sacrificed on the altar the priests were instructed to pour out the blood under the altar—i.e., at its base. These instructions are repeated many times in

Leviticus. We will use only one verse for our purpose here since they are quite repetitive. Lev. 4:34 says, "The priest shall take *some* of the blood of the sin offering with his finger, put *it* on the horns of the altar of burnt offering, and pour all *the remaining* blood at the base of the altar." This Old Testament altar with blood poured out at its base is the source of the imagery here.

C. THE SOULS AS THE LIFE'S BLOOD OF THE SLAIN WITNESSES

When John looked closely at the alter he saw the souls of those who had been killed for the word of God and for their testimony, as if their life had been poured out like blood at the base of the altar. Jesus our High Priest gave himself as a sacrifice. He poured out His blood for us. Isa. 53:12 says that He poured out His soul unto death. The saints who are slain are seen as having offered themselves up as sacrifices on the altar. Their souls, like blood, are poured out at the base of the altar for their testimony, just as Jesus' soul was made an offering for sin (Isa. 53:10, 12).

These souls under the altar are the witnesses who give testimony to the word of God and are killed because of it. The word *martyr* comes for the Greek word for *witness*.[8] The word came to be used for those who were killed because of their testimony. These souls represent the saints of God who undergo tribulation because of their faith and testimony.

D. *THE MEANING OF THE SYMBOL*

It would be difficult to explain how this picture could be interpreted literally. The altar is so obviously a symbol of the sacrifices of the lives of the saints. John could not have seen literal souls since souls are invisible. On the other hand the symbolism is a beautiful picture and its meaning easy to ascertain. What better way to give a figurative picture of the persecuted church? The saints are to suffer persecution in this world. In 2 Tim. 3:12 Paul wrote. "Yes, and all who desire to live godly in Christ Jesus will suffer persecution."

The souls under the altar are the objects of the persecution represented by the second, third, and fourth riders. They will also be the recipients of the

---

[8] μάρτυς (*martus*)—a witness. μαρτύριον (*marturion*)—a testimony.

victory represented by the first rider. They will undergo bloodshed, economic hardship, and death by various means. But they do not need to despair because they will be victorious in the end. In fact, Christ has already given them the victory.

E. MARTYRS AWAITING ULTIMATE VINDICATION AND VICTORY

The souls under the altar know that the victory will ultimately be theirs, but they don't know when. They cry out to God, "How long, O Lord, holy and true, until You judge and avenge our blood on those who dwell on the earth" They are told that they must wait for vindication until the rest who are to suffer martyrdom have been killed. Meanwhile, they are given white robes—the garments of imputed righteousness—and told to rest until the number of martyrs is complete. In the 20th chapter of Revelation we will see a complete reversal of the condition of these souls (see 20:4). Here they are as blood under the altar; there they are as kings, reigning with Christ. Meanwhile they are told to rest. They have come to the rest promised in Revelation 14:13:

> Then I heard a voice from heaven saying to me, "Write: 'Blessed *are* the dead who die in the Lord from now on.' Yes," says the Spirit, "that they may rest from their labors, and their works follow them."

F. CRY FOR JUDGMENT AGAINST "THOSE WHO DWELL ON THE EARTH"

We should note that the cry of the martyrs is for judgment and vengeance on *those who dwell on the earth*. This is a phrase that is used throughout Revelation to refer to those who do not belong to Christ, who have aligned themselves, whether willingly or by default, with the world system controlled by Satan. There is another category we shall discuss more fully when we get to it—i.e., *those who dwell in heaven.* These are the strangers and pilgrims here on earth. The Martyrs could well sing the old gospel song; "This world is not my home; I'm just a-passing through."

VII. JUDGMENT ON THOSE WHO DWELL ON EARTH (6:12-17)

When the sixth seal is broken the vision is one of judgment upon the world. This vision also pertains to the servants of God in that it pictures their vindication and victory over the world.

A. A FIGURATIVE PICTURE OF JUDGMENT

With the opening of this seal John sees a vision of the earth and its environs. There is a great earthquake. The sun turns pitch black. The moon becomes blood. The stars all fall to the earth. The sky is rolled up like a scroll. What we are seeing is a figurative picture of God's judgment. Some of the things mentioned in the above passage could possibly happen literally, but not all. Every star is hundreds or thousands of times larger than the earth. If just one of the stars literally fell to the earth it would instantly annihilate the earth and everything and everyone in it.

The universe is pictured as coming unglued. Every star and planet and galaxy is held in place by the power of Christ. He upholds all things by the word of His power (Heb. 1:3). When He releases His grip and lets go, chaos and destruction follow (Job 34:14-15). Our text likens it to a fig tree full of fruit, only to have the fruit shaken loose by a violent wind.

B. WHAT THE LITERAL DESTRUCTION OF HEAVEN AND EARTH WILL BE LIKE

Peter tells us about the literal destruction of the heavens and earth in 2 Pet.3:7,12. They are to be dissolved with intense heat and burnt up. If this should be referring to the fires of nuclear chain reaction, then the end result is that all matter in this universe would cease to exist as matter and be wholly transformed into energy. Matter is entirely made up of energy and is known in science to be a form of energy. Men have discovered how to transform very small portions of radioactive matter into energy. This resulted in the uranium, plutonium and hydrogen bombs which have unbelievable destructive force. What if God disassembled every atom completely into its basic energy? What would happen to our world? Our universe? It would literally be dissolved with fervent heat and vanish.

C. THE MEANING OF THIS VISION

The sun and moon are part of the firmament and the sun is itself a star. Our text says, "...the sun became black as sackcloth of hair, and the moon became like blood." There are times when the sun has literally become darkened and the moon appeared as blood. An example of this is the day Christ died. What is signified by this in the vision? I doubt that it is speaking literally since the vision is basically figurative.

When God created the sun and moon we are told that He created them to rule over the day and night (Gen. 1:16). Darken the sun and the world becomes dark. The atmosphere, if taken away, would no longer diffuse the light. The world's knowledge and wisdom are eclipsed. The wise men and strong men of the world no longer have the "light" of their philosophical and pagan religious systems to guide them. Their environment collapses around them.

The blood moon is a portent of evil upon the world. The moon's turning to blood is a sign of evil and violence. In this case, the atmosphere in which the wicked flourish (false religions and philosophies of men) is darkened and evil and violence are brought upon the world. That atmosphere is removed like a scroll being rolled up and stars (dignitaries) in the firmament fall to the earth. Kingdoms fall and nations are overturned. The people run to hide and beg to be hidden from the wrath of God and the Lamb. Who are these people? They are *those who dwell on earth.*

Stars are used in various places in scripture as a symbol for dignitaries, such as kings, governors and angels, both good and evil. Jesus is Himself called *the bright and morning star* in Rev. 22:16. The name *Lucifer* means *Day star.* Seven stars in chapter one are symbolic of the angels (messengers) of the seven churches. To speak of the stars falling to earth is a fitting way of referring to the fall of the great and important men of the earth, and perhaps even the angels of Satan. Even in today's society we refer to dignitaries such as famous actors and athletes as stars.

The use of this figure is so common that it is natural that it should be used to refer to the fall of people of power and influence. This would be "the kings of the earth, the great men, the rich men, the commanders, the mighty men" of verse 15. No king or emperor is powerful enough to escape the judgment of God. Those in opposition to God are destined to fall.

The sky is pictured as a vast sheet stretched above the earth. One end curls over and begins to be rolled up into a scroll. In this way the heavens pass away in the vision. "...the sky receded as a scroll when it is rolled up." Think of the sky as being man's environment. He lives in the atmosphere. He breathes it. It sustains his life. Take away the sky and you take away his ability to exist. But after the sky is removed in this picture men are still running from God and trying to hide from Him. This indicates that the picture is symbolic and not literal. Just as people thought of the sky as supporting the stars, so also the men of power and influence are supported by an environment that sustains their ambitions. Think about the political, moral and economic environment that sustains the corrupt world system we live in. Take away that atmosphere and the stars fall.

Mountains are used as symbols of kingdoms or governments in various places in scripture, while islands may be understood as nations. "...every mountain and island was moved out of its place...." In the midst of the announcement of Babylon's fall in 16:18-21, verse 20 uses an expression similar to the one in this scene of judgment. It says, "Then every island fled away, and the mountains were not found."

Isa. 2:2-3 speaks of the establishment of the mountain of the Lord's house. It was destined to be the highest of the mountains. This means that the Kingdom of God is greater than all kingdoms. All nations shall flow into it. Mountains and islands being moved out of their place is a picture of the fall of kingdoms and nations of men. As for the kingdoms of this world, remove the stars that govern the kingdoms and nations, and each will fall— or as verse 14 says, be moved out of its place.

In verse 15 we are told that all men (dwellers on earth—those who are subjects of God's wrath) hide themselves in the caves and rocks in the mountains. This is a picture of the awesome prospect of facing the judgment of God. But nothing, absolutely nothing, can hide men from the eyes of Him who sees all things and knows the hearts of all men. The attempt is completely futile. And by the way, if the picture is literal instead of figurative, after the first star falls to earth there would be no rocks or caves or mountains in which to hide. Even the smallest star is many times the size of the earth. There would be no more earth. All those who dwell on earth would be dead. Paul wrote in Gal. 6:7, "Do not be deceived, God is not mocked; for whatever a man sows, that he will also reap."

The cry of mankind to the rocks and mountains is, "Fall on us and hide us from the face of Him who sits on the throne and from the wrath of the Lamb! For the great day of His wrath has come, and who is able to stand?" This is a picture of judgment in general, and the final judgment in particular. There are several lessons we can learn. Judgment is sure, judgment is final, and judgment cannot be escaped by any means devised by man. The only escape is to accept the gracious gift of God—eternal life through Jesus Christ and the righteousness which is by faith in Him, accepting Him as Savior and obeying Him as Lord.

D. JUDGMENT AS AN ANSWER TO PRAYER

The prayers of the persecuted church, of the saints under the altar, called for judgment and vengeance upon those who dwell on earth (verse 10). Those who dwell on the earth stand in opposition to those who dwell in heaven—i.e., God's people, the followers of the Lamb. A good question for each of us to ask is, "Am I one of the dwellers on earth, or is my citizenship in heaven?" The answer to that question will determine whether I am one of those upon whom this judgment will fall.

E. THE GREAT DAY OF GOD'S WRATH

There are several great days in scripture. There was the great day of the outpouring of God's love in sending His Son to be born in a stable in Bethlehem. There was the great day of the outpouring of God's wrath on our substitute who died upon a cross to save us from wrath. He took the judgment for us. There was the great day when victory over death was proclaimed by the resurrection of Jesus the Christ. There was the great day of the Lord when He poured out His Spirit upon all flesh on the day of Pentecost following the resurrection. Then there will be the great day of His wrath, when He will pour out His wrath on all who have rejected Christ and those who have brought persecution against the servants of God. The pouring out of God's wrath is part of the victory given to the saints. This wrath is played out in the drama in chapters 14 through 20. As the seals are broken, the theme of judgment is presented as part of the overall theme of the drama of the ages.

VIII. THE THEME OF THE DRAMA OF THE AGE

From these six visions of the seals we see the theme of the scroll. It includes persecution and suffering, and even death for those who faithfully bear witness to the Word of God. It includes victory over sin, death and the world, including vindication by God's judgment upon the world. How shall we word this theme? How about, "THROUGH PERSECUTION AND SUFFERING TO VICTORY!"

There is yet one seal to be opened in chapter 8. The result is a half hour of silence depicting the silence of eternity—the eternal peace that is for those who love and serve the Lord. Following this the theme of judgment is pursued further in another series of seven symbols—the trumpets of judgments. Meanwhile in chapter 7 there is an interlude---a preparatory vision, actually two visions, showing the preparation of the saints for judgment, and the final outcome.

Chapter 7

GOD PROVIDES FOR HIS SERVANTS
Rev. Chapter 7

In this chapter there are two parts. First is the preparation of the servants of God for the judgments to be revealed against "those who dwell upon the earth." The judgments are held back by four angels during which time the servants of God are given a mark or seal on their foreheads (7:1-8). Second is the scene of the victorious saints before God's throne in the temple of God. In this scene the conflict is over and the multitude of the redeemed are around the throne of God. The theme of the first part is the preservation of God's people from judgment (2 Pet. 2:9), and the theme of the second part is their ultimate victory over, and redemption from, the world.

The seventh and last seal is about to be removed from the scroll. This, in addition to completing the opening of the book, will introduce another set of seven symbols which expand upon the theme of judgment. These are the trumpets announcing God's warning judgments upon the earth. In these God directs His wrath against those on earth who have rejected Him and have persecuted His saints.

Between the removal of the sixth and seventh seals a time out is taken; call it an intermission, interlude, or whatever you like. In this interlude we are first allowed to see how God prepares his servants for these judgments. The process of sealing the servants of God is pictured, a process that has been going on since the day of Pentecost following Christ's death.

144

I. SEALING THE 144,000 ON EARTH (7:1-8)

A. THE ANGELS HOLD BACK WINDS OF DESTRUCTION (Read 7:1-3)

John sees a scene in which the winds of destruction are about to blow upon the earth, but they are held back until the saints are sealed against the destruction. An angel comes from the east with the seal of the living God. He calls out to the four angels holding the winds of destruction not to let the winds blow until he has finished his job of marking the servants of God with the seal.

B. THE SEALING OF THE SERVANTS OF GOD (Read 7:4-8)

1. The Source of the Symbolism of the Sealing. The vision of Ezek. 9:1-7 is the source of the figure of the sealing of the servants of God. In Ezekiel's vision God has come to Jerusalem with the intent of bringing judgment on those who had forsaken him and turned to idols. Ezekiel sees a man clothed in linen (presumably an angel) with an ink horn. This man is told to go through the city and put a mark on the forehead of all those who weep for the condition of Jerusalem and the temple. After he does this there are six men with swords (presumably angels) who are sent to execute God's judgment. They kill everyone except the ones who have received the mark. The swordsmen are not to touch the ones with the mark because they are under the protection of God. Both the marker and the slayers are told to begin at the sanctuary. This is significant. 1 Pet. 4:17 says: "For the time has come for judgment to begin at the house of God; and if it begins with us first, what will be the end of those who do not obey the gospel of God?"

The priests of the temple were not immune to this judgment. The basis for judgment is what is in the hearts. This should cause those who call themselves Christians to think seriously about their position. If God's judgment begins at the house of God, then not everyone in that house has been sealed with the seal of God on his forehead. Some are evidently imposters.

As soon as the angel finishes his job of sealing the servants of God, the four angels will release the winds of destruction to blow upon the earth and bring the judgments of God against those who dwell upon earth. Everyone will be in one of two categories—those who have been sealed and are protected from the judgments, or those who have not been sealed. Those in the second category are called *those who dwell upon earth.* They are the ones who will undergo the judgments.

2. 144,000 Are Sealed. The number of those who are sealed in the vision is 144,000. Who are they? We don't have to wait for the answer to this question. Those who are sealed are the servants of God. Verse 3 has already told us this. It does not say they are "some of the servants of God," or "a special group of the servants of God," as taught by one sect, nor does it say that they are "the servants of God from the Jewish race," as taught by many Christian teachers. It just says, "the servants of God." By this we can understand that the angel is talking about all those who are the true followers of God. What follows in 7:4-8 is not meant to modify or contradict this by limiting the number to exactly 144,000. It is intended to be a symbolic picture of the sealing of all of God's servants.

3. The Twelve Tribes of Israel. Twelve thousand out of every tribe of Israel are said to be sealed. Twelve times twelve is one-hundred-forty-four—thus, 144,000. Now if the vision were to be interpreted literally, out of the millions of Israelites born from Jacob onward, only 144,000 are chosen to be sealed. Only 144,000 are the servants of God. Not only would this rule out most of the Israelites, but all of the Gentile Christians as well. There are those who do a lot of speculating when dealing with the symbols of Revelation. Some assume that this is talking about a special group of Jews who are to be used for a special purpose. Where does it say it? This idea is pulled out of thin air. Nothing is said in Revelation about such a group.

Twelve tribes are named. If the writer were speaking literally then he made some mistakes. He did not name all the right tribes. In Num 1:1-50, Moses and Aaron, along with certain men from each tribe, were charged with numbering the tribes of Israel. The twelve tribes that were named are: Reuben (v.21), Simeon (v.23), Gad (v.25), Judah (v.27), Issacher (v.29), Zebulun (v.31), Ephraim (v.33), Manasseh (v.35), Benjamin (v.37), Dan (v.39), Asher (v.41) and Naphtali (v.43). Verses 49ff specifically says that the tribe of Levi shall not be numbered, because the Levites were to be set aside to serve the people in sacred matters. Joseph is not named because he is the one given the double portion by his father Jacob. As a result he has a tribe named for each of his two sons, Ephraim and Manasseh.

There are changes in the list in Rev. 7:5-8. It makes no mention of Dan or of Ephraim. Levi is substituted for Dan, contrary to God's instructions to Moses excluding Levi (Num. 1:47-50), and Joseph is put in place of his son Ephraim. Why is this? It does not say. In my opinion it is because Ephraim and Dan were centers of rebellion and idol worship. When Jereboam led the rebellion that resulted in the secession of the ten northern tribes (Israel) from the two southern tribes (Judah), he made Samaria in Ephraim his capitol. He placed an Egyptian idol—a golden calf—in Bethel in the south of his kingdom, and another in Dan in the tribe of Dan in the north of Israel. He urged the people to go to these centers of worship rather than going to Jerusalem in Judah to worship at the temple. In this way he established idolatry as the worship of the break-off kingdom of Israel—a condition that stayed with the northern kingdom until it was destroyed by the Assyrian army. Ephraim was the leading tribe of the northern kingdom.

Dan's association with idolatry dates from the time of the judges. When the land of Canaan was apportioned to the twelve tribes of Israel Dan was assigned its portion in the coast land west of Ephraim. The tribe of Dan was unfaithful in pursuing God's instructions to take the land and drive out its inhabitants. As a result, they were unable to hold their allotted territory. Because of this, they migrated to the far north of Canaan where they settled as the northernmost tribe of Israel.

The idolatrous practices of Dan can be seen from the story of their migration to the north. This story is found in the 18th chapter of Judges. Chapter 17 tells of a man named Micah in Ephraim who made household idols and hired a priest from Bethlehem to serve as his personal priest. Chapter 18 tells of how the scouts from the tribe of Dan found out about the idols and the priest in their stay with Micah on their way to find a suitable place for relocation of their tribe. It also tells how they found a suitable place and reported back to the tribe. Then it tells how the tribe, in its migration, stole the idols of Micah, and his priest, and took them to their new home in the north where they worshiped these idols under the ministry of the priest.

These two tribes, Ephraim and Dan, have much to answer for. I don't wonder that they were excluded from this list of tribes that were the symbols

147

of God servants. Since the list of tribes is not a literal list of the twelve tribes of Israel, it must be figurative. If the writer is speaking literally, is it a coincidence that exactly 12,000 people in each of the twelve tribes are designated as servants of God? Remember that there is no indication that they are chosen from among the rest of Israel for a specific purpose or task as some say, but simply that they are the servants of God. If it is speaking literally then surely this is an extreme case of the sovereign election and predestination of God, to arbitrarily choose exactly twelve thousand out of each of the twelve tribes of Israel and none from among the Gentiles. Are there no servants of God among the Gentiles?

4. The Meaning of 144,000. If we remember that Revelation was written in symbolic language then we should be able to discern the meaning of this figure. In the symbolism of numbers, 12 is the number of God's people. That number added to itself is 24, as in the 24 elders in chapters 4 and 5. 12 multiplied by itself is 144, as in the redeemed city of New Jerusalem in the new heaven and earth in chapter 21. The city is four square, 12,000 furlongs to a side. This equals 144 million square furlongs. The measurement of the wall (presumably its thickness since its height was said to be 12,000 furlongs) was 144 cubits. The names of the 12 tribes of Israel are inscribed on its 12 gates and the names of the 12 apostles are written on the 12 foundations. That city is the symbol of the people of God, the church of Jesus Christ (see Heb. 12:22-23). In chapter 21 it is called *the bride of Christ.* We see, then, how the number 144 is associated with the servants of God.

There are also numbers which we call round numbers. 1000 is used to represent many, and ten to represent a few. Psalm 50:10 uses 1000 in this way: "For every beast of the forest is Mine, *And* the cattle on a thousand hills." If the psalmist were speaking literally then the cattle on all the rest of the hills after hill number 1000 would not belong to the Lord. 1000 hills is only a tiny fraction of the hills in this world that have cattle on them, but they all belong to the Lord. We understand that the psalmist means the cattle on all the hills. 1000 is used to represent a great number, a multitude, or the totality of some large number of things.

In Psalm 90:4 we read, "For a thousand years in Your sight *Are* like yesterday when it is past, And *like* a watch in the night." This is the psalmist's poetic way of portraying the timelessness of God's existence.

Peter uses a similar statement in 2 Pet. 3:8: "But, beloved, do not forget this one thing, that with the Lord one day *is* as a thousand years, and a thousand years as one day." There are even some who want to interpret the last half of this verse literally—that exactly one thousand years equals one day on God's calendar. Of course, according to the first half of the same verse, this would have to mean that one day of our time is literally one thousand years on God's calendar. This is a contradiction. It can't work both ways; there is no way to make this literal. What Peter is saying is that time means nothing to God. A thousand (or a million) years and one day are the same to Him. He lives outside of time, for time is a part of the universe which He created.

How, then, are we to interpret the 144,000 without doing a lot of speculating about things not revealed in the text? If we interpret according to the symbolism of numbers, as they are used elsewhere in Revelation, we see that 144 is the number 12 squared. This is the number of God's people, or as the angel puts it in verse 3, "the servants of God." 1000 is the number of a multitude or of the totality. As Cinderella's fairy godmother sings, "Put 'em together and what have you got?" The answer here is *the multitude of the servants of God*, or *all of God's people*. 144,000 is simply a figurative way of saying *the multitude of God's people*. In Rev. 14:1-5 there is more said about the identity of the 144,000. There they are seen on Mount Zion with the Lamb. The 144,000 are there called, "...the ones who follow the Lamb...." They are the saints who have been redeemed from the earth. On earth they were called the servants of God. Who can they be but the multitude of the people of God? When Revelation itself gives us the meaning, as it does in this case (i.e., the servants of God, the followers of the Lamb), we should not seek further meaning in our own speculations. (For a fuller explanation of God's Israel, go to *Appendix D*.)

5. The Seal on Their Forehead. What does it mean that they are sealed on their foreheads? In Exod. 28:36-38 we read the words of God quoted by Moses:

> You shall also make a plate of pure gold and engrave on it, *like* the engraving of a signet: HOLINESS TO THE LORD. And you shall put it on a blue cord, that it may be on the turban; it shall be on the front of the turban. So it shall be on Aaron's forehead, that Aaron may bear the iniquity of the holy

149

things which the children of Israel hallow in all their holy gifts; and it shall always be on his forehead, that they may be accepted before the LORD.

This passage is in the context of God's instructions for the garments of the priesthood, and especially for the high priest. There was a plate put on his turban in such a position that it would be on his forehead. It read, "Holiness to the Lord." It was to be always on his forehead that they may be accepted before the Lord. This sign on his forehead was a sign of the acceptance of the people he represented—i.e., Israel. In Christ there is no mediator between God and man except Christ. We are each a priest of the most high God (1 Pet. 2:5,9). We must each have the seal of acceptance on our own foreheads. Paul writes in 2 Tim. 2:19a, "Nevertheless the solid foundation of God stands, having this seal: 'The Lord knows those who are His.'"

What is the significance of the forehead? Where do you point when you want to indicate your mind? The forehead is where most people point. It is the seat of the biblical heart—the emotions, will and intellect. An example may be found in Jer. 3:3b: "You have had a harlot's forehead; You refuse to be ashamed." In this context the Lord is talking about the heart of Israel. This is the significance of referring to the forehead.

While the forehead (heart) is the only acceptable place for the seal of God, in Rev. 13:16 the Beast and False Prophet are satisfied to have the beast's mark on the forehead **or** on the hand. Satan doesn't have to possess your heart as long as he has your service. Whether you serve him willingly or unwillingly he still has you. Such is not the case with the seal of God. He must have your heartfelt service.

6. The Meaning of the Seal. The seal of God is the Holy Spirit in the hearts of His people. Let us remember to let the scriptures interpret the symbols wherever possible. Are there scriptures which tell us what the seal of acceptance of God's servants is? Indeed there are. Paul writes in 2 Cor. 1:21-22, "Now He who establishes us with you in Christ and has anointed us *is* God, who also has sealed us and given us the Spirit **in our hearts** as a guarantee." Notice that we are sealed with the Spirit in our hearts. Paul writes in Eph. 1:13-14:

> In Him you also *trusted*, after you heard the word of truth, the gospel of your salvation; in whom also, having believed, you were **sealed with the Holy Spirit** of promise, who is the guarantee of our inheritance until the redemption of the purchased possession, to the praise of His glory.

Paul also says in Eph. 4:30, "And do not grieve the Holy Spirit of God, by whom you were sealed for the day of redemption." Is there any doubt as to what the seal of God is? The picture of the sealing of the servants of God on their forehead in Rev. 7 is a graphic picture representing the sealing of the servants of God with the Holy Spirit in their hearts. Ever since the day of Pentecost, whenever a person believes in Christ and yields obedience to Him as Savior and Lord, he is sealed with the Holy Spirit in his heart as the guarantee of his acceptance and protection. That mark is not visible in the sense that you can see a literal mark on the Christian's forehead. The seal is seen in subtler ways—i.e., by the fruit of the Spirit in the life of the believer. But whether or not the people of the world see the seal, God knows who are His. Paul tells Timothy in 2 Tim. 2:19a, "Nevertheless the solid foundation of God stands, having this seal: 'The Lord knows those who are His.'"

7. Why the Symbol of the Twelve Tribes of Israel? One thing more remains to be explored in this part of chapter seven. What is the significance of the twelve tribes of Israel? Is this to be understood literally, or is it also figurative? I am convinced that it, too, is symbolic, not only for the reasons given above, but because of God's ultimate purpose for Israel. The nation of Israel was one of many types found in the Old Testament which have a corresponding antitype in the New Testament.

From the sacrifices offered by Cain and Abel on down through the Old Testament just about everything pointed to a spiritual fulfillment in Christ. Israel is no exception to this. When God gave the covenant of promise to Abraham He promised that Abraham's seed would bless all nations, not just the Hebrew nation. According to Gal. 3:16 the seed (descendant) to which God was referring was Christ. In verse 14 that blessing culminates in the giving of the promised Holy Spirit to those who believe. Just as the other institutions and events of the Old Testament are foreshadows of a greater spiritual reality, so also the nation of Israel is a foreshadow of the holy nation of priests mentioned in 1 Pet. 2:5-10. Verses 9-10 say:

> But you *are* a chosen generation, a royal priesthood, a holy nation, His own special people, that you may proclaim the praises of Him who called you out of darkness into His marvelous light; who once *were* not a people but *are* now the people of God, who had not obtained mercy but now have obtained mercy.

Who Are the True Israelites? Several times the New Testament points to the fact that those who are in Christ are the true children of Abraham by faith. In other words, it is not the physical but the spiritual descendants that count. Gal. 3:29 says, "And if you *are* Christ's, then you are Abraham's seed, and heirs according to the promise." Rom. 9:6-8 states:

> For they *are* not all Israel who *are* of Israel, nor *are they* all children because they are the seed of Abraham; but, *"In Isaac your seed shall be called."* That is, those who *are* the children of the flesh, these *are* not the children of God; but the children of the promise are counted as the seed.

For a fuller discussion of this subject see *Appendix D—The Israel of God* at the end of this book.

II. THE VICTORIOUS SAINTS BEFORE GOD'S THRONE (7:9-17)

A. THE PRAISE OF THE REDEEMED (Read Rev. 7:9-12)

The second vision John sees in this chapter is of the redeemed around the throne of God. They have come through everything that Satan has thrown at them on earth and have come out victorious. In this vision John's eyes are turned again to the throne-room. The spiritual warfare has been won and the saints join the elders, the cherubim, and the host of angels around the throne of God. In this vision John is not looking at a different group of people. These are the servants of God who were sealed with the Holy Spirit as a guarantee of their inheritance. However, in this scene they have entered into their inheritance. They are before God's throne praising Him ecstatically. In the first vision they are seen on earth and still must go through trials. In this second vision the multitude of God's people are no longer on earth. They have been transported to the presence of God.

1. The Redeemed in the New Heaven and New Earth. This vision is a kind of preview of Revelation 21 where the Holy City, New Jerusalem (the saints of God), comes down out of heaven to the new heaven and new earth. There they dwell in the presence of God. On earth they are symbolized by the 144,000, and by the twelve tribes of Israel. In their eternal home they are literally the saved of God out of every nation and tribe and tongue and people. This expression is used several times in the book of Revelation to refer to the saints of God drawn to him from every nation and race and ethnic group. They are the ones who make up the Israel of God. "And they shall bring the glory and the honor of the nations into it" (Rev. 21:26).

These stand before the throne and before the Lamb. All striving and warfare have ceased. Their praise is for God and for the Lamb. In the New Jerusalem the throne is occupied by God and the Lamb, and they share the glory. Rev. 22:3-4 says, "And there shall be no more curse, but the throne of God and of the Lamb *shall be* in it, and His servants shall serve Him. They shall see His face, and His name shall be on their foreheads." Notice that they are His servants—i.e., "the servants of God." That is the same terminology used in 7:3 to refer to the 144,000 who are sealed on their foreheads.

2. White Robes of Righteousness. These are arrayed in white robes, i.e., the righteousness imputed to them by the grace of God. These robes have been washed and made white in the blood of the Lamb. There is no sin in them for it has all been washed away in the blood of Christ. These are the bride adorned for her Husband, arrayed in fine linen, pure and white (19:7-8).

3. The Meaning of the Palm Branches. The redeemed have palm branches in their hands. This is reminiscent of the triumphal entry of Jesus into Jerusalem when the Jews waved palm branches and spread them as a carpet for Jesus' donkey to tread on (John 12:12-13; Matt.. 21:8-9). In the law of Moses the use of palm branches was commanded as part of the rejoicing on the first day of the feast of tabernacles. Lev. 23:40 declares:

> And you shall take for yourselves on the first day the fruit of beautiful trees, branches of palm trees, the boughs of leafy trees, and willows of the brook; and you shall rejoice before the LORD your God for seven days.

153

Later the carrying of palm branches became a symbol of freedom and of victory over the enemies of God's people from the time of the revolt of the Maccabees against Greco-Syrian control of Israel. In 1 Maccabees 13:51, after expelling the enemy from the citadel of Jerusalem, we read:

> On the twenty-third day of the second month, in the one hundred seventy-first year, the Jews entered it with praise and palm branches, and with harps and cymbals and stringed instruments, and with hymns and songs, because a great enemy had been crushed and removed from Israel.

In 2 Maccabees 10:1-8 the Jews under Judas Maccabeus recovered the Temple, and after cleansing the sanctuary, throwing down the pagan altars that had been built, and reestablishing the temple worship, they held an eight day feast in which they carried beautiful branches including palm fronds in celebration of the victory.

The waving of palm branches was a declaration of resistance to Roman rule in the time of Christ. In this way the Jews announced their intention of casting off the yoke of the oppressors. This is why they conducted Jesus triumphantly into the city of Jerusalem using palm branches. They were mistaken in thinking that it was the intent of Jesus to overthrow the Roman legions. He had a different kind of victory in mind.

Psalm 118:25-27 in the NIV reads as follows:

> O LORD, save us; [Hosanna]
> O LORD, grant us success.
> Blessed is he who comes in the name of the LORD.
> From the house of the LORD we bless you.
> The LORD is God,
> And he has made his light shine upon us.
> With boughs in hand, join in the festal procession up to the horns of the altar.

This is sometimes referred to as *the Hosanna prayer.* At least a portion of it was used by the crowd that ushered Jesus into Jerusalem. Notice the reference to carrying branches with rejoicing up to the horns of the altar. This passage is probably the source of the symbolism of the multitude having palm branches in their hands in Rev. 7:9-10. In the picture painted there the redeemed saints have done as this Psalm says, "With boughs in hand, join in the festal procession up to the horns of the altar."

The palm branches possibly signify all these uses. 1) They are used as a part of the rejoicing and praise of the redeemed before the throne. 2) They are perhaps intended as a declaration that God has overcome the enemies of His people. 3) They are also a proclamation by the saints of the victory God has given them, as they enter into their final dwelling in the presence of God.

This multitude of the servants of God cry out with a loud voice in praise to God and the Lamb, "Salvation belongs to our God who sits on the throne, and to the Lamb!" Then the angels, the 24 elders and the four living creatures (cherubim) join with them in praise; "Amen! Blessing and glory and wisdom, Thanksgiving and honor and power and might, *Be* to our God forever and ever. Amen."

B. THE MULTITUDE AND THEIR FATE *(Read Rev 7:13-17)*

John is often puzzled as to the meaning of the visions given to him. One of the 24 elders then comes to explain things. This happened in chapter 5. It happens here in chapter 7. It happens again in chapter 11 where all 24 elders reveal the explanation as part of their praise of God.

Here an elder asks John if he knows who those in the white robes are? John expresses his opinion that the elder knows. So the elder tells him. These are the ones who have come out of the great tribulation. Remember that these are the redeemed of all ages. In whatever period of time they were living on earth they experienced persecution and suffering. Jesus told His disciples in Matt. 24:9, "Then they will deliver you up to tribulation and kill you, and you will be hated by all nations for My name's sake."

1. What Is the Great Tribulation? Three times in the New Testament the term *great tribulation* is used: Once in Matt. 24:21 with reference to the sufferings of Jerusalem under the siege of the Romans prior to, and including, the destruction of the city in A.D. 70; once in Rev. 2:22 with reference to the judgment of the woman in Thyatira, the false prophetess called Jezebel; and once here in Rev. 7:14 with reference to the persecution of Christians.

Three times the word *tribulation* is used in Matt. 24. Two we have already noted (verses 9 and 22). The other is in verse 29. Here, as in verse 9, it refers to the persecution of Christians.

The reference to *"the great tribulation"* in our text is probably not referring to a limited time of persecution near the end such as three and one-half years. It is more likely a reference to the persecution that God's people have had to suffer and will continue to suffer in this world.

Remember that the multitude before the throne, "a great multitude which no one could number," is composed of God's people throughout the ages. Only a few of them, relatively speaking, would be involved in a persecution near the end, but they have all come out of the great tribulation. Each was involved in it during whatever time period they lived and served on earth. These are the ones who have endured to the end. They are those who are victorious over sin, suffering and death.

2. The White Robes. The elder further tells John that these who wear white robes have washed them and made them white in the blood of the Lamb. It is because of the white robes, because of the cleansing in the blood of the Lamb, that they are before the throne of God. Will you be among these when they stand before the throne of God praising His name? Do you see yourself in this multitude? Will your robes be white? Will you have endured to the end?

3. Continued Service Before the Throne. Then the elder tells John something that will be a surprise to some of us. He says that they serve God day and night in His temple. This is a return to the temple scene described in chapters five and six. I say this will surprise some of us because some have the notion that there won't be anything to do except sing praises. These were the servants of God on earth, and they gladly serve Him in heaven. In our resurrected bodies we will need no rest, but can keep on serving as well as worshiping Him day and night. Does this sound like a drag? In no way! It will be the joy of our hearts to serve Him who redeemed us. We won't be able to think of anything else we would rather do.

4. God to Dwell among Them. The elder continues by saying that God who sits on the throne will dwell among them. This is the ultimate fulfillment of the promise of God's dwelling with us. Jesus told his disciples that He was going to send the Holy Spirit, and by this means both He and the Father would dwell with them (John 14:15-17, 23). Eph. 2:20-23 tells us that we are the temple of God in which God dwells through His Spirit. He dwells with us now in the person of the Holy Spirit, but this is just the guarantee or down payment on our inheritance. The time is coming when God will personally dwell with us and walk among us, and we will see His face. Rev. 21 tells us of the time when there will be a new heaven and new earth—the place that Jesus has gone to prepare for us (John 14:1-3). In Rev. 21:3-4 we read:

> And I heard a loud voice from heaven saying, "Behold, the tabernacle of God *is* with men, and He will dwell with them, and they shall be His people. God Himself will be with them *and be* their God. And God will wipe away every tear from their eyes; there shall be no more death, nor sorrow, nor crying. There shall be no more pain, for the former things have passed away."

5. Eternal Blessings to Be Theirs (Ours). Furthermore, the elder says that they will never go hungry or thirsty again, or get sunstroke, or get overheated. Instead, the Lamb who occupies the throne will be their shepherd (what an irony—the Lamb of God is Himself the Shepherd of the lambs) and He will lead them to fountains of the water of life. In Rev. 22, in the continuing description of the New Jerusalem on the new earth, there is a river of water of life flowing from the throne. Verses 1-4 tell us:

> And he showed me a pure river of water of life, clear as crystal, proceeding from the throne of God and of the Lamb. In the middle of its street, and on either side of the river, *was* the tree of life, which bore twelve fruits, each *tree* yielding its fruit every month. The leaves of the tree *were* for the healing of the nations. And there shall be no more curse, but the throne of God and of the Lamb shall be in it, and His servants shall serve Him. They shall see His face, and His name *shall be* on their foreheads.

What is the water of life? John 4:10, 13-14 gives us an insight:

> Jesus answered and said to her, "If you knew the gift of God, and who it is who says to you, 'Give Me a drink,' you would have asked Him, and He would have given you living water."

> Jesus answered and said to her, "Whoever drinks of this water will thirst again, but whoever drinks of the water that I shall give him will never thirst. But the water that I shall give him will become in him a fountain of water springing up into everlasting life."

With this water one will never thirst again. It is the water that gives eternal life. In John 7:37-39 John explains what this water is:

> On the last day, that great *day* of the feast, Jesus stood and cried out, saying, "If anyone thirsts, let him come to Me and drink. He who believes in Me, as the Scripture has said, out of his heart will flow rivers of living water." But this He spoke concerning the Spirit, whom those believing in Him would receive; for the Holy Spirit was not yet *given*, because Jesus was not yet glorified.

Now we see! The water that is thoroughly satisfying, that gives eternal life, is the Holy Spirit whom Jesus gives to all who truly believe in Him. We can have that water even now, because the Holy Spirit is given to us as a guarantee of our inheritance of eternal life. Then, however, as we look upon the face of God and are shepherded by the Lamb who provides us with the living water, we can drink to the fullest of the Holy Spirit of God throughout the eternal age.

6. No Tears For the Redeemed. The last thing that the elder tells John is that God will wipe away all tears from their eyes. Is there any doubt that the scene here is the same as the one described in chapters 21 and 22? The same descriptive terminology is used. We are looking here at the ultimate victory of the saints and their eternal reward in the presence of God and the Lamb on the throne. Now let's go with the Lamb as He removes the seventh and last seal.

Chapter 8

TRUMPETS OF JUDGMENT—THE FIRST FOUR
Rev. Chapter 8

The script is almost open. The first six seals have been removed. The scroll is filled with writing on the front and back of the sheets. I can just see John wanting to lift the freed corner, anxious to get a peek at its contents. It did not happen since the scroll was part of a vision in which the book isn't given to John until chapter 10 after the book is fully open.

I. REMOVING THE SEVENTH SEAL (Read 8:1)

Only one verse deals with the seventh seal. It says, "When He opened the seventh seal, there was silence in heaven for about half an hour." There is no vision that proceeds immediately from the opening of the seventh seal. The message is contained in the half hour of silence.[1] What is it saying? John sees nothing or hears nothing for 30 minutes; then the revelation continues with further visions. What does the half hour of silence indicate?

Perhaps we can get a clue to the significance of the seventh seal by looking at the seventh symbol of each of the groups of seven. The seventh trumpet is the last trumpet. Rev. 10 7 declares, "...but in the days of the sounding of the seventh angel, when he is about to sound, the mystery of God would be finished, as He declared to His servants the prophets." In other words, when the last trumpet blows it will be all over for this world.

---

[1] σιγή *(sige* – pr. *see-gay')* Young's Greek Dictionary says, "Apparently from σίζω *(sizo* (to *hiss,* that is, *hist* or *hush)*; *silence:*—silence" just as a mother hushes her child to assure him that everything is now all right.

The seventh bowl of wrath is also the end. Rev. 16:17 says, "Then the seventh angel poured out his bowl into the air, and a loud voice came out of the temple of heaven, from the throne, saying, 'It is done!'" That is all that it has to say. 17:18 then gives the portents that frequently introduce a new set of visions in Revelation.[2] "It is done! It is finished!" I believe that this is also the message of the silence in Rev. 8:1. In other words, the seventh of each set of symbols brings us to the end of this age. The seals speak of the theme(s) to be found in the script, including the silence of eternity. This is not the silence of nothingness or cessation of existence, but the quietness of peace, of the ceasing of conflict, of rest in the bosom of God.

The overall theme revealed in the opening of the seals is *through persecution and suffering to victory*. The end result is silence of warfare over. Rev. 14:13 puts it this way, "Write: 'Blessed *are* the dead who die in the Lord from now on. Yes,' says the Spirit, 'that they may rest from their labors, and their works follow them.'" Heb. 4:9-11 points out that the sabbath rest for which we strive is to come when we have ceased from our labors. The silence of the seventh seal is the silence of peace and rest just as the seventh day was the sabbath of rest for the Israelites.

The warfare is over. The dwellers on earth have been judged. The saints are before the throne of God with the seal of God on their foreheads, dressed in white robes of righteousness, made pure and white in the blood of Christ. They have come through their great tribulation and have now entered their sabbath rest. At the end of each of the three sets of seven visions we have the same message. It is over! The striving has ceased. The suffering and death have ceased. The destroyers have been destroyed. The mystery is finished. What remains for the saints is eternity in the presence of God serving and worshiping Him together with all the saints of all ages.

---

[2]Rev. 4:5 uses lightnings, thunders and voices to introduce the scenes around God's throne, and to announce the visions that were to take place in the removing of the seals. Rev. 8:5 uses noises, thunders, lightnings, and an earthquake to announce the blowing of the seven trumpets. In Rev. 16:18 there are noises, thunders, lightnings, and the worst earthquake ever known, to announce the events to follow—i.e., the destruction of Babylon the harlot, the beast and false prophet, and Satan himself, the great red dragon.

II. PRAYERS ON THE ALTAR OF INCENSE (Read Rev. 8:2-6)

As John's visions continue he sees seven angels who are given seven trumpets. Before they can blow their trumpets they must wait for the prayers of the saints. With these verses the temple scene is almost complete. These seven angels are standing before God who is on the throne and now, for the first time, John's attention is drawn to the altar of incense which also stands before the throne.

A. THE ALTAR OF INCENSE

In the Old Testament tabernacle/temple the golden altar of incense was situated at the place where the curtain (veil) would be drawn back for the high priest to enter once a year with the blood of atonement. On this altar the priests would burn a specially prepared incense whose aroma would waft to the mercy seat (throne of God). This incense was offered daily. We have already learned in chapter five that the incense was symbolic of the prayers of the saints which rise like sweet-smelling incense to the the throne of God. Thus the Old Testament altar of incense was a symbol of the offering of the prayers of the people of God.

B. INCENSE ADDED TO INCENSE

In this scene there is something else of importance. The golden censer which the angel held contained the prayers of the saints, but this was not enough! To these prayers was added more incense. This was divinely provided incense that was to ascend to the throne of God together with the prayers of the saints. I see in this a picture of God's grace. As Paul writes in Rom. 8:26-27:

> Likewise the Spirit also helps in our weaknesses. For we do not know what we should pray for as we ought, but the Spirit Himself makes intercession for us with groanings which cannot be uttered. Now He who searches the hearts knows what the mind of the Spirit is, because He makes intercession for the saints according to *the will of* God.

The added incense is the intercession of the Holy Spirit as He helps our prayers to be effective before God. It is only by the grace of God that our prayers can ascend to the throne of God and be effective in influencing His actions and moving His hand. The grace of God makes up the lack. Because of this help we can come before the throne of grace with boldness (Heb. 4:16). Even when we make stumbling, bungling attempts at prayer, those prayers go up to God with the intercession of the Holy Spirit. God hears a beautiful, well worded prayer that asks Him for the very thing that is needed to bring about His will on earth. What a beautiful realization; as a Christian I can pray an effective prayer if my heart is in the right place.

C. IMPORTANCE OF THE PRAYERS OF THE SAINTS

In Revelation the prayers of the saints play a key role in the warfare between good and evil, between Christ and Satan. When saints fail to pray, Satan prevails. But the angels of heaven are sent by God to press the battle and win when the saints engage in fervent prayer.

The censers in the hands of the twenty-four elders (Rev. 5:8) are filled with the prayers of the saints. At the opening of the fifth seal the souls under the altar (the persecuted church) cry out in fervent pleas to God (Rev. 6:9-10). The result of the prayers of the souls under the altar was the answering judgment of the vision of the sixth seal. This presented the theme of judgment in a general sense, with focus upon the great day of the wrath of God and the Lamb. It is probably intended to be a condensed version of all of God's judgments.

The prayers being presented here as incense on the altar probably represent the same thing—i.e., the cry of the persecuted saints for judgment. This conclusion is based on the fact that the results of these prayers are the seven trumpets which announce the judgments of God. After the bowl of incense is offered on the altar the angel takes the bowl and fills it with the burning coals from the altar. Then he throws these coals upon the earth. This is another way of showing that the prayers are being answered, for the bowl from which the prayers are offered is the same bowl used to cast the coals of fire on the earth.

When the angel throws the fire upon the earth there are noises, thunders, lightnings and an earthquake—a figure that is used several times through the book of Revelation before earth-shaking events occur. It is a way of announcing momentous things to come. So the seven angels prepared to blow their trumpets.

III. THE FIRST FOUR TRUMPETS SOUND (Read 8:7-12)

The first four trumpets deal with judgments against the habitat of mankind. This includes the earth, the sea, the fresh water sources, and the heavens. Each of these is an essential part of our existence on earth. Remove any one of them and mankind could not survive. The judgments of these trumpets are not final. They do not affect the whole of man's habitat, but only one-third of each area named above. As a result, most of mankind survive these judgments.

Although the trumpets are blown one at a time in the vision, we should not think of them as a succession of judgments coming chronologically. They reveal different aspects or different areas of God's judgments rather than different events. They are intended to give more detail to the theme of judgment which will be played out in the drama.

Trumpets are used to announce and to warn. Obviously they are announcing the judgments that follow their blowing, but since the destruction is not total or final it also becomes obvious that they are intended as warnings. They are warnings of the coming final judgment of all mankind, when the destruction will not be just one-third, but total.

How shall we apply this? Calamities are allowed to strike the earth from time to time. These include wars, pestilence, meteorological disasters, and so forth. People often overlook the fact that such calamities could well be a judgment of God, intended to warn people to repent and turn to God. Instead most see them only as natural disasters which have nothing to do with God. In the Old Testament God's judgments on Israel and upon the nations around served not only to avenge God's people, but to wake people up and turn them back to the will of God.

How successful such judgments are depends on the response of the people being judged. Too often the result is like that stated in Rev. 9:20a, "But the rest of mankind, who were not killed by these plagues, did not repent of the works of their hands...." In other words, the world as a whole continues in its rebellion against God. A plague comes upon mankind such as Bubonic Plague or AIDS. God is saying, "Repent!" Mankind does not usually hear, but ascribes the plague just to natural causes and thinks that God has nothing to do with it. They forget that even when natural causes produce calamities, God turns them to His own purposes. These calamities, such as wars, such as the first and second world wars, affect all of man's habitation, his health and his life.

A. *THE FIRST TRUMPET Is Blown* (Read Rev. 8:7)

Trumpet number one brings destruction to one-third of the earth and its vegetation. The symbolism of this judgment, like those of all the trumpets as well as the bowls of wrath, is taken from the record of the ten plagues brought upon Egypt to convince Pharaoh to let God's people go. The result of those plagues was that the Israelites were freed from their bondage as slaves in Egypt. The hail and fire of this first trumpet judgment is reminiscent of the seventh plague brought upon Egypt (Exod. 9:22-26). The result here is the destruction of the green grass and one-third of the trees. What is the message of this trumpet judgment? I do not think that it is referring to a specific event where judgment is brought upon the earth. Rather I see it as a representation in a general way of calamities that come upon the earth and destroy some fraction of its surface.

During the second world war metallic hailstones filled with explosives (we call them bombs) devastated a portion of the earth's surface, shedding much blood and setting fires that consumed many buildings and trees. Was this perhaps one of the calamities which this trumpet was intended to symbolize? Over the centuries large meteorites have crashed into earth digging huge craters and scorching large areas around them. Are these some of the hailstones? The text says that the hail and fire are mingled with blood. Such calamities as those just mentioned usually cause some bloodshed, although the judgment is primarily aimed at the earth itself. When Adam and Eve rebelled against God in Eden God cursed the ground so that it brought forth thorns and thistles. As a result Adam had to eke out a living by the sweat of his brow. God was sending a warning message to mankind—rebellion has its consequences. If we see the calamities of the first trumpet as warning judgments of God, then they will have served their purpose in our lives. Others will miss the point altogether.

B. *THE SECOND TRUMPET IS BLOWN (Read Rev. 8:8-9)*

The first plague in Egypt was the turning of the waters to blood (Exod. 7:19-21). Here, just such a plague is brought upon the sea at the blowing of the second trumpet, something that looked like a burning mountain is thrown into the sea producing this effect. One-third of the sea becomes blood. As a result one-third of the sea creatures die and one-third of the ships are destroyed.

The sea is very important to the existence of mankind. The surface of the waters moderates the temperature of the earth. Three-fourths of the earth's surface is water. If this were not so mankind could not live. The seas also drive the weather. The winds depend upon the seas for their energy. The waters evaporate and form clouds which deposit water in the form of rain, snow and ice on the land. The snow-pack which builds up in the mountains thaws into streams and rivers and lakes to provide fresh water sources, some going underground to provide springs of fresh water.

Many people depend upon the sea for food. The harvest of fish is a necessary and thriving industry. When one-third of the sea creatures die this is a heavy burden on the fishermen, as well as those who depend on the fish for their food.

The sea lanes also provide commerce in the form of ocean-going ships which carry goods from continent to continent, from country to country, and from city to city. The destruction of one-third of the ships would deal a devastating blow to our economy.

As a result of the immense importance of the sea to man's life, the significance of this judgment becomes clear. Calamities that affect the sea should serve as a warning to mankind. As this partial judgment has affected many lives, so the final judgment is coming. Mankind needs to repent, or be condemned at the final judgment. God sends warning after warning in the form of partial judgments. What is our response to them? Do we see them as messages from God?

C. *THE THIRD TRUMPET IS BLOWN (Read Rev. 8:10-11)*

In the first plague of Egypt when the fresh water was turned into blood men could not find water to drink. Likewise, in this third-trumpet judgment one-third of the earth's fresh water sources are affected. The waters become so bitter that men die from drinking it. A burning star falls from heaven onto a third of the rivers and springs. The star's name is *Wormwood*. This produces the problem of the bitter water. Usually a star falling from heaven is a symbol of a fallen angel. If that is the case here, and I believe that it is, the angel's name here is *Wormwood*, a synonym for *bitterness*.[3] Perhaps the Lord uses a fallen angel, one of Satan's angels (as He does on occasion), to cause the condition of bitterness mentioned here.

In Exod. 15:22-25, just after the Children of Israel were saved from the Egyptians by crossing the Red Sea, they came to Marah (*bitterness*) where there was a well or spring of water. The water could not be drunk because of their bitterness. They may have been strongly alkaline as some ponds are in the deserts. To drink such water would cause death. God showed Moses how to remedy the situation. He threw a certain tree or shrub into the water and it became sweet, providing the Israelites with water. The results of Moses' actions were exactly the opposite of the plague of the 3rd trumpet. There are several species of bitter shrubs with the name *wormwood*. Perhaps this is the reason the fallen star is called *Wormwood*.

In our present day thousands are dying because of the pollution which has made its way into our drinking water. Even though water systems destroy the microbes through chlorination, this does not remove the inorganic poisons which make their way into the water from pesticides, chemical fertilizers, industrial waste, and even the chlorination itself. Without realizing it many are slowing being poisoned, so that diseases of all kinds are rampant. Many diseases that were not widespread a century ago are now commonplace. Could these be part of what is symbolized by the falling of the star Wormwood on the rivers and springs of water?

If a third of the drinking water became bitter and poisonous what would be the result? Many men would die. The supply of fresh water is in such delicate balance that mankind can hardly afford to lose a third of the supply. Nevertheless, not everyone dies. Not all of this area of man's habitat is

---

[3]For examples of the use of the term *wormwood*, see Deut. 29:18; Prov. 5:4; Jer. 9:15; 23:15; Lam. 3:15,19; Amos 5:7; 6:12. The *International Standard Bible Encyclopedia* assigns five species of shrubs to the genus *artemisia* or *wormwood*. These have a bitter taste, giving rise to the term's significance of bitterness.

affected. It is not total but is another warning judgment. It is calling for men to repent. Any calamity which affects mankind's source of fresh water should be considered a judgment from God, letting us know that the final judgment is coming, and may be just around the corner.

D. THE FOURTH TRUMPET IS BLOWN (Read Rev. 8:12)

The ninth plague in Egypt was the plague of thick darkness. Here, the blowing of the fourth trumpet results in the darkening of a third of the sun, a third of the moon, and a third of the stars. Also a third of the day was without any sunlight, and a third of the night was without any light of moon or stars. Again, the judgment is partial. The reason is because it is a warning judgment. There is coming a day when the sun, moon and stars will not shine at all. They, along with the earth, will be totally destroyed. That day will be announced by the final trumpet.

The sun is the source of earth's light, warmth, and energy. From the sun's energy plants are caused to grow, giving mankind food. If the earth were a little farther from the sun men would freeze to death. If the earth were a little closer to the sun, men would burn up. In either case life could not exist. The influence of the moon upon the tides, the weather, and the growing seasons is well known. Any disturbance in the balance that exists in the heavens would bring disaster to mankind. Volcanoes have at times shut out the light of the sun, moon, and stars by the dark clouds of smoke and ash which they spew into the atmosphere when they erupt. Eclipses of the sun have, in times past, frightened people into thinking the end of the world was upon them. Remove such protective defenses as earth's ozone layer and the existence of life itself would be threatened by the deadly radiation that would reach us from the sun.

How delicate is the balance of nature. Bring disaster upon any of the four areas of man's habitat represented by the judgments of the first four trumpets, and you bring disaster on man himself. Such disturbances, while not total, should serve as a warning, a trumpet blast, if you will, calling us to run for shelter from the wrath of God. How do we do that? In the judgment of the opening of the sixth seal the people of earth ran to the rocks and mountains seeking to hide from the wrath of God; but the only effective way to run from the wrath of God is by running to God our Rock, turning from our rebellious ways to serve the living God. He is our only safe refuge.

IV. WARNING OF THE TRUMPETS YET TO BLOW (Read 8:13)

Rev. 8 ends on an ominous note. The trumpets yet to sound are three woes upon the inhabitants of the earth. John sees an angel flying through the air crying out these woes to the earth dwellers. Remember that the phrase, *the inhabitants of the earth* does not refer to the people of God, but those who belong to the world system. This earth is their home. As for the children of God, the gospel song, *This World Is Not My Home* expresses it well. "This world is not my home; I'm just a-passing through. My treasures are laid up somewhere beyond the blue."

This will become increasingly clear as we proceed further in our study of the book. God's people are in the world, but not of it. When someone asks an American who is in France, "Where do you live?" He answers, "I live in the United States. I don't live here in France." We should make that same distinction here. We are strangers and pilgrims in this world. We are not part of those who dwell upon the earth. Our dwelling is in heaven.

The reason that the last three trumpet blasts are so devastating to those who inhabit the earth is that all are directed against their persons. They have rebelled against God. They have rejected His will and word. They have lived contrary to every principle of right and wrong that His word sets forth. They are thieves, murderers, slanderers, revilers, adulterers and fornicators, liars, and idolaters, to name a few things. They have not repented but have continued in their evil ways right up to the end—either their death, or the Lord's coming in final judgment. It is such people that are the subjects of these last three judgments. In the next chapter we will see the blowing of the fifth and sixth trumpets, bringing the first and second woes. The third woe will come at the blowing of the seventh and last trump.

Chapter 9

TRUMPETS OF JUDGMENT--TRUMPETS 5 AND 6
Rev. Chapter 9

In the blowing of trumpets five and six the judgments are focused on mankind. When man's habitat is affected, as in the first four trumpet judgments, man suffers. But in trumpet five tribulation is sent upon men who have not the seal of God. In trumpet six the judgment is violent death to a third of mankind.

I. THE BLOWING OF THE FIFTH TRUMPET (9:1-12)

A. A LOCUST PLAGUE FROM THE ABYSS TO TORMENT MAN (Read 9:1-6)

The eighth plague brought upon Egypt was a plague of locusts which devoured grass, trees, and every green thing. As a result the crops of Egypt were destroyed. The plague of locusts described in the fifth trumpet judgment is different. The locusts were forbidden to harm the vegetation, but to attack man himself—i.e., those who have not the seal of God.

John begins by telling about a star falling from heaven. In the third trumpet judgment the dirty work of poisoning the waters was done by a star fallen from heaven whose name is *Wormwood*. The fallen star of the fifth trumpet is called *the angel of the bottomless pit* whose name is *Abaddon* or *Apollyon,* meaning *Destroyer*. I mention this to show that fallen angels are spoken of as fallen stars. This angel is given the key to the bottomless pit. Notice that the key is given to him. He has authority to open the pit only because he is allowed to. He has been given that authority, otherwise he would not be able to open it. God allows this in order to accomplish His own purpose of judging those who do not have the seal of God.

The bottomless pit, translated *the abyss* in some versions, is mentioned several times in Revelation. It is where evil spirits are consigned, where they are kept in chains of darkness awaiting judgment (2 Pet. 2:4). It is thought, by many authorities, to be the lowest region of Hades, the abode of the dead. Jesus is the one who has the keys of death and Hades. Apparently, then, He is the one who gives the key of the Abyss to the Destroyer to allow him to release his agents upon the world. From there they are apparently allowed to come forth to do their mischief on the earth. For more information concerning the abyss see *Appendix A: Hades and Hell.*

In our current text the Pandora's box of demons which the fallen star releases from the abyss is turned loose upon the world. God uses this as a judgment upon mankind and a warning to them of impending doom. The evil which comes up out of the abyss is pictured as huge clouds of black smoke like the smoke from a great furnace. This is a fitting symbol for evil since it is often compared to darkness. "...men loved darkness rather than light, because their deeds were evil" (John 3:19). Saul of Tarsus (Paul) was told what he was to do when Jesus confronted him on the road to Damascus. According to Acts 26:17-18 this task included going to the Gentiles, "...to open their eyes, *in order to* turn *them* from darkness to light, and *from* the power of Satan to God." Darkness is equated with the power of Satan, and God is seen as light.

The evil which ascends from the abyss is like a smoke so dense that it darkens the sun and the air. Satan wants to blot out the light of righteousness so that people will walk in the darkness of sin. Sin not only brings darkness, but it poisons even the spiritual air that we breath. While living in the mountains, I sometimes experienced the results of nearby forest or grass fires. The smoke hangs over the little mountain valley like a pall, and breathing becomes hard. When I breath the air that is thick with smoke from the fires, it affects my lungs. Sin is like this.

Our social atmosphere becomes darkened by the constant barrage of stories, advertisements, and programs on television, on the radio, and in the movies and magazines. They promote all kinds of sin and darkness. Social institutions, education, and even government are enlisted by Satan in this work of polluting the spiritual atmosphere. Like the proverbial frog in the pot of water, the temperature has been raised so gradually that we haven't even realized that we are boiling to death. Sin is subtle. It encroaches on our lives and thinking so gradually that we don't even realize it. It poisons our atmosphere until we are no longer bothered by the things that would have appalled us a few years earlier. Things become acceptable that grieve the heart of God. Sin is darkness, and when we get involved in it eventually we realize that in the darkness are "locusts" which inflict torment like the sting of scorpions.

In our text verse 3 says, "Then out of the smoke locusts came upon the earth. And to them was given power, as the scorpions of the earth have power." These odd creatures have bodies like horses, faces like men, hair like women, teeth like a lion's teeth, breastplates like iron, tails like scorpions with stingers, wings that sound like rushing chariots, and they wear victory crowns of gold. We will get to the meaning of these things shortly. These locusts sting like scorpions, and their task is to torment men for five months. Unlike the locust plague in Egypt, they are not to harm the grass or trees or any green thing. Their target, according to verse four, is "...those men who do not have the seal of God on their foreheads."

Verse five talks about the locusts' given task. Just like the fallen angel, they are allowed to do certain things, and forbidden to do others. All creatures ultimately receive their authority from God. These demons from the abyss are not allowed to kill anybody, but to torment them for five months. This is similar to what Satan was allowed to do to Job (Job 2:4-6). During this time men will want to die, but death will elude them according to verse six. This torture must be severe indeed. There is no torment so painful as the torment of sin in the heart and mind, and in the consciences of men. Sin holds out its allurements to draw men into its clutches. It soon enslaves them and holds them in its grip. Then the pangs of conscience and remorse take over. The mental and emotional pain that grips the heart of men is terrible to see.

Perhaps the most obvious examples of this truth are found in alcohol and drug addiction. Is there anyone who has not known someone who lived in torment because he/she was in the clutches of one of these addictions? Although other sins may not be so obvious, yet once they have the sinner in their clutches the torment can be just as severe. Greed, sexual addiction, hatred and envy, the pursuit of pleasure, etc.—all eventually have their sting. Death is the ultimate sting of sin (1 Cor. 15:55-56), but this fifth trumpet judgment is not final, for it, too, is a warning for mankind to repent. These scorpion-tailed locust are not allowed to kill them.

Many times God has used evil men to accomplish His purposes. This is also true of spirit beings, for He also uses Satan and His angels to bring about judgments on man, just as He used wicked Babylon to bring judgment on Israel. I think that the basic message of this fifth trumpet is not that God makes men sin, but that He brings the torment of sin on those who give themselves over to sin. He uses the messengers of Satan to do this.

B. DESCRIPTION OF THE LOCUSTS FROM THE ABYSS *(Read 9:7-11)*

In symbolism descriptions are not intended to be taken literally, but are intended to set forth the characteristics of the thing symbolized through analogy. For instance, if you call someone a pig, you don't mean he is literally a pig, but that he is filthy or gluttonous like a pig, or has the boorish manners of a pig. Let's see what we can make of this description. "The shape of the locusts was like horses prepared for battle." Literally the original language says "The likeness of the locusts...." They are said to be like horses prepared for battle. Horses often symbolize warfare. The battle in which we are engaged is a spiritual warfare between the forces of good on the one hand, and the forces of evil on the other.

Satan has been waging this warfare from the beginning. He promised Eve many things in Gen. 3, but his real purpose was to conquer her. He was not her friend. He was actually making war on her. This has been the case ever since. He promises people riches, power, pleasures, but his real purpose is to fight against them, capture them, and destroy them.

These locusts are the messengers (angels) of Satan, sent by him, and permitted by God to bring torment to mankind—i.e., those who do not have the seal of God. On their heads are crowns (victory wreaths) of gold. They are victorious over those who have not received the seal of God, the Holy Spirit, in their hearts.

Their faces appear like the faces of men, and their hair is like that of women. The faces of men represent intelligence. Just as one of the four faces possessed by the living creatures in chapter 4 was the face of a man, indicating that these cherubim were highly intelligent creatures, so also one of the characteristics of these demons is that they have intelligence like man.

The hair of a woman is said to be her glory (1 Cor. 11:15). Like a woman, they have a fatal appeal to those who belong to the world. How do we apply this? Sin is very alluring and enticing. Even Satan was said to be very beautiful. The woman's hair probably represents the appeal of sin. It looks very pretty, but take it into your bosom and you get stung. What the world has to offer appears to be very glorious, but in the end it is very disgusting and hurtful. These locusts have teeth like lions teeth. Lions tear and devour with their teeth. Remember that the devil goes about as a roaring lion seeking whom he may devour (1 Pet. 5:8). The devouring here, however, is not physical, but spiritual. A man engulfed in sin can come to the point of being devoured by it. When that happens he begins to experience the sting of sin. Often his life becomes a living hell.

These locusts are prepared for war. They have breastplates of iron. Locusts, like many insects, have breastplates made up of segments that are like scales. The main purpose of these hard breastplates is the protection of the insect. The same is the case with locusts. The breastplates of these locusts are like iron, like the armor of a warrior. Their wings make an awesome sound like the sound of chariots rushing into battle. What is being pictured here is the fact that these locusts form an army rushing in to do battle with those who dwell on earth.

Sinners think that Satan is on their side. There are some who even worship him. Imagine their consternation when they find that Satan is really their enemy, and his forces are sent to overcome them and harm them. These forces like nothing better than to use Satan's ultimate weapon, death. Satan is the one who wields the power of death (Heb. 2:14-15). But in this case they are not allowed to go that far. God's purpose is to warn, not to destroy.

Their tails are like a scorpion's tail with a stinger in the tail. This stinger does not kill, but is very, very painful. These demons have the power to inflict severe suffering, like a scorpion's sting. Their power is to hurt men five months. What is the significance of this? I don't think the five months is a literal period of torment for sinners. It comes from the fact that the adult locust (migratory grasshopper) has a life span of five months. Like the life of a locust, the torment is of limited duration. This does not mean that if you can last it out you will be all right. Remember that God is warning you to repent.

You may eventually sear your conscience as with a hot iron so that you don't feel its sting anymore. You may eventually settle down into sin without further torment of mind, but don't deceive yourself. Judgment is coming, and everyone will stand before God to receive the things done in the body. "He who sows to his flesh will of the flesh reap corruption" (Gal. 6:8). "...all that are in the graves will hear His voice and come forth; those who have done good to the resurrection of life, and those who have done evil to the resurrection of condemnation" (John 5:28-29). The characteristics of the locusts are symbols of the characteristics of the angels of Satan who are used by God to bring torment to sinners.

The leader of this horde of creatures that comes up from the abyss is none other than the angel of the bottomless pit. He is their king. His name is *Abaddon* in Hebrew and *Apollyon* in Greek. These words have the same meaning, i.e., *Destroyer*. This is a name for the devil himself. Our only defense against him is to receive Christ and the gift of the Holy Spirit as the seal and guarantee of our inheritance, the mark of the children of God. "One woe is past. Behold, still two more woes are coming after these things." (9:12)

II. THE BLOWING OF THE SIXTH TRUMPET (9:13-21)

A. ONE-THIRD OF MANKIND KILLED BY WARFARE (Read 9:13-16)

The first four trumpet judgments destroyed one-third of the earth, sea, fresh water, and firmament. The fifth trumpet judgment is directed against all men who do not have the seal of God, but they are not killed. They suffer greatly for a time, but they survive. Now in the sixth trumpet one-third of mankind is killed. Orders to the four angels to bring this judgment come from a voice originating at the golden altar—i.e., the altar of incense seen in the beginning of chapter eight.

The Old Testament altar of incense stood in front of the mercy seat, separated from it by a heavy curtain. So far there is no mention of this curtain in the temple in heaven. That is probably because Jesus tore it down at His death on the cross. All we know is that the altar stands in front of the throne of God. The altar of burnt offering and the altar of incense in the Old Testament were each made with horns at the four corners (Exod. 27:1-2; 30:1-2) . Each was probably something like an ox's horn. A horn is a symbol of power. This symbol represents the power of the prayers of the saints as they cry out for judgment and vindication.

The prayers of God's people have much power. So also do the orders that come from these horns. The fact that the orders come from the altar of incense is an indication that they come in answer to the prayers of the saints offered upon the altar in Rev. 8:3-4. In Rev. 6:9-10 the souls of the martyred saints cried out to God, ". . .And they cried with a loud voice, saying, 'How long, O Lord, holy and true, until You judge and avenge our blood on those who dwell on the earth?'"

The orders were given to the sixth angel who blew the sixth trumpet call. He was told to release the four angels that were bound at the great river Euphrates. Remember that there were four angels who held the four winds of destruction in chapter 7. They were not allowed to release this destruction until the servants of God had been sealed. Assuming that these are the same four angels, they are now given leave to release the winds of destruction, to kill one-third of mankind. They have been prepared for the hour, day, month and year of this destruction.

What is the significance of the river Euphrates? Many times in history armies were assembled at the Euphrates to strike southward through Syria, Palestine (Israel) and Egypt. The armies of Assyria amassed there and conquered Syria, and the northern kingdom of Israel, as well as most of the territory in the kingdom of Judah. This is also the direction from which the armies of Babylonia and Persia came, as well as the direction from which the Greeks under Alexander the great came as they conquered these same regions. The river Euphrates has been very important in great battles. Because of this the Euphrates is chosen to represent the mobilization of the forces of destruction that are to be released on mankind. We'll see more of the Euphrates when we get to the sixth bowl of wrath in chapter 16.

What is the significance of the hour, day, month and year? This is a way of pointing out that God does not do things haphazardly. He is very precise in His planning, and He is punctual. He is never too early or too late. What

God does, he does at exactly the right time. The statement does not point to a particular date in history, but to the precise timing of God.

Verse 16 tells us that there is an army of 200 million horsemen that is released to bring the destruction upon mankind. That is a huge army. There has never been an army that large in the history of the world. Very few nations even approach that number in total population. There are, of course a few that exceed that number several times over, but the vast majority of nations do not. But even China and India, the most populous nations, could not afford to field an army that size. I believe the number of these horsemen represents the devastation of warfare brought upon mankind not by one specific war or army either in the past or future, but the totality of the destruction of warfare over the age, just as God repeatedly brought the destruction of warfare and death upon the people of Israel when they forsook His ways. This destruction is intended to be a warning to those who dwell on earth.

We make a mistake if we think that one-third is a literal 33⅓ percent of earth, sea, fresh water, the heavens, and mankind that are destroyed. The idea is that the judgments are incomplete or partial. We also make a mistake to suppose that 200 million is a literal 200 million. In the original Greek text it is "twice ten thousand times ten thousand." This is a symbolic way of saying "an immensely great number". Its purpose is to emphasize, not to be literally precise. This army is God's means of bringing death to a significant portion of those who dwell on earth. Its soldiers are all those who are used by God to bring about these partial judgments on the dwellers on earth. It's purpose is to call men to repentance—to warn of the coming final judgment.

We saw the winds of destruction restrained until the servants of God were sealed. This may sound like God is waiting for a particular point in history. I think it is more likely that the sealing is taking place throughout this age, and as the citizens of heaven are sealed, warning judgments are released upon the dwellers on earth. God knows how to preserve his chosen ones until they are sealed to God. Then nothing can harm them, not even death. Even if they should die in some conflagration that is intended as a judgment upon the unrighteous, it is not they who are judged. They simply find themselves in the presence of God.

The sealing of God's people goes on throughout the age. God's warning judgments also go on throughout the age. There are not a literal seven judgments. This number symbolizes the totality of God's judgments, culminating in the final judgment. Perhaps we should see these first six trumpets of judgment as the calamities that come upon mankind throughout the age, whether they are natural disasters (as in the first four trumpets) or the sting of sin in the heart and soul of men, or the disasters of war that kill a significant portion of mankind. God uses them all to remind men that the final judgment is coming when all must give account to God for the deeds done in the body.

B. DESCRIPTION OF THE RIDERS AND THEIR HORSES (Read 9:17-19)

The 200 million riders on the horses are said to have breastplates of three colors—fiery red, hyacinth blue, and sulfur yellow. Many translations say, *fire, jacinth and sulfur. Jacinth* is another spelling for the word translated *Hyacinth.* The New King James adds the words *red, blue,* and *yellow* because these are the colors of the items named. The original Greek does not name the colors. The King James Version and others simply say, "breastplates of fire, jacinth, and sulfur."

What is the significance of this? It is associated with the three things which come out of the mouths of the horses. These are fire, smoke, and brimstone. What does the smoke have to do with jacinth? Simply that thick smoke is usually the color of jacinth—i.e., a deep dark blue. The colors are portrayed on the breastplates, while the elements themselves come out of the mouths of the horses. This is, of course, symbolism. What is its meaning? We will see very shortly.

The heads of these horses are like the heads of lions. In the vision of the 5th seal the locusts had teeth like lions. Here the horses have whole lions heads. That would include the tearing teeth, the dreadful roar, and the fearful visage. These horses also have tails that are like serpents with heads that can bite and kill. Not only is their power in their lion-like heads, but also in their serpent-like tails.

Out of the lion-mouths of the horses came three things. These things are fire, smoke, and brimstone. These are called three plagues which kill mankind. It is interesting that the deaths are not caused by swords, or arrows, or lances wielded by the riders. The horses themselves are the weapons used by the riders to kill. The appearance of these horses is calculated to strike fear into the hearts of men. The lion head and teeth, the serpent tail, the fact that the horses' mouths are breathing out fire, smoke and brimstone like a fire breathing dragon—this would even be enough to scare some to death. But it is what comes out of the horses' mouths that does the killing. Again, what is the meaning of all this?

Fire and brimstone have been associated in scripture many times with the judgments of God. Psalm 11:6, "Upon the wicked He will rain coals; **Fire and brimstone** and a burning wind *shall be* the portion of their cup." With reference to the judgment on Gog and Magog, Ezek. 38:22 states, "And I will bring him to judgment with pestilence and bloodshed; I will rain down on him, on his troops, and on the many peoples who *are* with him, flooding rain, great hailstones, **fire, and brimstone**." Speaking of the judgment on Sodom, Jesus says in Luke 17:29, "but on the day that Lot went out of Sodom it rained **fire and brimstone** from heaven and destroyed *them* all." When Abraham went out and looked toward Sodom after its destruction he saw the smoke ascending like the smoke of a furnace. In Rev. 14:10b-11 fire and brimstone are joined with smoke in the final judgment of those who worship the beast and his image and receive the mark of the Beast; "...He shall be tormented with **fire and brimstone** in the presence of the holy angels and in the presence of the Lamb. And **the smoke** of their torment ascends forever and ever...." The final punishment of sinful man is in the **lake of fire and brimstone**, which is the second death (Rev, 20:10; 21:8).

The army of riders on fearsome horses with lion heads and serpent tails is the symbol of God's warning judgments on mankind through warfare and violence. The destruction of those who belong to the world is not complete, but only partial. The fire, smoke, and brimstone tell us that these wars are not just incidental, but are deliberate judgments of God, as was the judgment on Sodom and Gomorrah. The tenth plague in Egypt was the death of the firstborn of every household in Egypt not protected by the blood of the lamb on the doorposts and lintel. Here the plague of death is brought by the three plagues of fire, smoke, and brimstone which represent the overthrow of the people of the world by violence as a means of God's judgments. Thus, death by violence overtakes one-third of those who are not under the protection of the blood of Christ.

One thing yet remains in this vision. By means of the horses' mouths and tails they harm mankind. Normal horses do not hurt with their tails. However the horses ridden by the cavalry regiments today are such things as hummers, trucks, tanks, and armored carriers. Many of these have cannons facing to the rear as well as to the front. Machine guns, Gatling guns, etc., enable them to do harm to the rear as well as to the front. There have been suggestions that these horses of the sixth trumpet judgment are prophetic symbols of such weaponry. The belching of fire and smoke from the cannons on tanks could well be pictured as fire, smoke and brimstone coming out of the mouths of the horses to kill ⅓ of mankind. I don't think we need to be too concerned about finding a specific fulfillment of these figures. I believe they are intended to set forth a general truth that through the slaughter of a portion of mankind in warfare God is warning mankind and announcing the coming final judgment, just as trumpets warn and announce.

III. DWELLERS ON EARTH DO NOT REPENT (9:20-21)

In my opinion the most logical and likely meaning of the visions of the first six trumpets is that they represent the theme of God's warning judgments, rather than pointing to a specific time period or specific event for each trumpet. Whenever and wherever catastrophic events occur, they would fit into the meaning of these trumpets.

The drama will not start until chapter 12. Chapters 4 - 11 are dealing with the preparations for the drama. First is the opening of the seals of the script, with accompanying visions revealing the themes of persecution, judgment and victory for the saints. Then comes the blowing of the trumpets, further exploring the theme of judgment in terms of partial judgments, warning mankind to repent. The curtain is not opened to signal the beginning of the drama until after the seventh trumpet is blown at the end of chapter 11.

The seventh trumpet, the last trump, announces the final judgment. Meantime the warnings of the first six trumpets go unheeded by mankind as a whole. Those who are not killed by the warning judgments refuse to repent of their demon worship, idolatry, murders, sorceries, sexual immorality or thefts. It is too easy for them to attribute the judgments to accidents, natural causes, or the natural course of events. They do not admit that there is any relation of the events to the deliberate judgments of God, or to their own wicked lifestyle. So they do not repent, and will continue in this state unless something even more drastic happens.

Before the last trumpet is blown we come to another interlude in which some other things are explained. We'll see these things in Rev. 10 - 11.

Chapter 10

THE OPEN BOOK GIVEN TO JOHN
Rev. Chapter 10

Between the opening of the sixth seal in chapter 6 and the seventh seal in chapter 8 there was an interlude (chapter 7). In like manner there is an interlude between the blowing of the sixth trumpet in chapter 9 and the seventh trumpet in chapter 11. The visions of this interlude encompass chapter 10 and most of chapter 11, after which the seventh trumpet is blown..

I. THE GIANT ANGEL WITH THE OPEN BOOK (Read 10:1-4)

A. THE ANGEL DESCRIBED

Another angel comes down from heaven. Let us see His description: 1) He comes from heaven; 2) He is clothed with a cloud; 3) There is a rainbow on his head; 4) His face is like the sun; 5) His feet are like pillars of fire; 6) He cries out with a loud voice.

B. WHAT DOES THIS ALL MEAN?

1. He Comes from Heaven. The giant Angel does not fall from heaven. Wormwood fell from heaven (Rev. 8:10-11). Abaddon the destroyer fell from heaven (Rev. 9:1-10). This Angel does not fall. He comes from heaven with a mission.

2. Clothed with a Cloud. The cloud is associated with divinity, and is usually the symbol of the presence of the one known in the New Testament as the Son of God. When the children of Israel came out of Egypt they were protected and led by a pillar (or column) of cloud by day and fire by night. Exod. 13:21 says, "And the LORD went before them by day in a pillar of cloud to lead the way, and by night in a pillar of fire to give them light, so as to go by day and night." The Lord was with them in the cloud. The apostle Paul speaks of that cloud in 1 Cor. 10:1-4 in which he identifies the one who accompanied the Israelites in the wilderness as Christ the Rock.

The fifth kingdom to appear in Daniel's vision (Dan. 7:13) comes on a cloud. Unlike the previous four who came from the earth and looked like beasts, this one comes from heaven and looks like a man. The cloud indicates the divine origin of this kingdom, whose King is none other than the Son of God.

When Jesus ascended to heaven He did so in a cloud, and the angels said He would come in like manner (Acts 1:9-11). Matt. 24:30 and 26:64, as well as parallel passages in Mark and Luke, speak of the Son of Man coming with the clouds. Rev. 1:7 tells us He is coming with the clouds. When Jesus came up out of the Jordan River after His baptism, and again on the mount of transfiguration, the voice of God spoke from a cloud that overshadowed them. The cloud is the symbol of divinity and is associated with the presence of God the Son.

3. The Rainbow of Covenant. The Angel is not only clothed with a cloud, but there is a rainbow on His head. The rainbow is the sign of God's covenant of promise. As stated in Chapter 4, the rainbow around God's throne is the symbol of God as a covenant keeping God. It came to have this meaning because God gave the rainbow in the clouds as the sign of the covenant of promise He made with mankind in Gen. 9:8-17. The rainbow also identifies the angel as the Angel of the Lord.

4. His Face Like the Sun. The face of this Angel is like the sun in its brightness. When Jesus was transfigured in Matt. 17:1-2 He was revealed in His glory, for His face shone with His glory. The description of Christ in Rev. 1: 16 also speaks of this.

5. The Feet Like Pillars of Fire. In both Old and New Testaments when a vision of God is described in human terms, His feet and legs are presented as brilliant fire or burnished bronze (see Ezek. 1:27-28, Rev. 1:15). This is part of the picture of God's glory.

6. The Loud Voice. The Angel cries out with a loud voice. In Rev. 1:10 the voice of Christ is said to be loud, like the sound of a trumpet (See also 4:1). In 1:15 it is described as being like the sound of many waters. The description of this Angel is so like the description of the figure of Christ in Rev. 1 that I am inclined to believe this Angel is intended to be a representation of the Christ.

C. THE ANGEL OF THE LORD

In the Old Testament, when God made His appearance in the form of a man, He was called *the Angel of the Lord.* He appeared several times throughout the Old Testament, as He did to Abraham in Gen. 18. This Angel, unlike other angels, did not forbid men to worship Him. Most conservative Bible scholars believe that the Angel of the Lord in the Old Testament was the appearance of the pre-incarnate Christ. I am inclined to agree with this.

There is one major difference between the Old Testament appearances and those in Revelation. In the Old Testament He, as the Angel of the Lord, literally appeared in the form of a man. In Revelation the appearances are part of the vision given to John, and are symbolically stylized. The different appearances of Christ thus far in Revelation are as a Son of Man in chapter 1, as a Lion and Lamb in chapter 5, and as an Angel in chapter 10. These are symbolic appearances rather than literal.

For a period of 33 years Christ lived among us in the form of a man. He did not merely look like a man; He was indeed a man and not an angel. He was conceived in the womb of Mary and born as a baby in Bethlehem., actually becoming a man and living among us. When He ascended to heaven He did not leave His humanity behind, but will continue to exist and reign as a man with His Father on the throne throughout eternity. He was always God, and will always be God, but He became a man on our behalf, so that He could die for our sins. It is by that man that God will judge the world (Acts 17:31).

This mighty Angel in Rev. 10 is described with the symbolic attributes of deity and He speaks with authority. Not only that, He holds the book in His hand. It was the Lamb, Jesus Christ, who received the book from the hand of God on the throne in chapter 5. He proceeded to remove the seven seals, and now that they are all removed the book is open. There are other angels who deal with John in Revelation, but it is Christ Himself who opens the book by removing its seals. He appeared in John's vision in chapter 1 as a figure described much like this Angel. He appeared in chapter 5 as a Lamb that had been slain. Since Christ removes the seals from the book, it is only logical that He is the one, appearing this time as the giant Angel, who places it in the hand of John.

This giant Angel of the Lord, like the Lamb, is part of the vision. Both are symbolic, not literal. Neither is intended to be a literal representation of what He looks like. When the Angel of the Lord literally appeared directly to men in the Old Testament, He did so in the form of a man, not as an exceedingly large angel who stood with one foot on the earth and one in the sea.

D. THE OPEN BOOK

There are those who argue that the book in the Angel's hand is not the same book as the one with the seven seals. The reason given for this is that the word here means a *little book (or little scroll)* whereas the book with the seven seals is simply called *the book* (or *scroll*).[1] One might as well argue that the Lamb of Revelation is not the same as the Lamb of the gospel of John since two different words are used, one meaning *a lamb* of undetermined size or age, while the other means *a little lamb*.[2] However, it is undisputed that both words refer to the Christ as the sacrificial Lamb of God. The book in the hand of a giant Angel who has one foot on earth and one in the sea would look very small indeed. No wonder it is called *a little book* by John.

The scroll, when first seen, was tightly sealed with seven seals. The seals are removed one at a time, and then a book is seen lying open in the hand of the Angel, with the seals removed. It logically follows that the book in chapter 10 is the same as the one which had the seven seals. The emphasis

---

[1] βιβλίον *(biblion)* – *bill, book, scroll, writing,* and βιβλιαρίδιον *(bibliaridion)*– *little book.* The first has no reference to size while the second refers to the book as little.

[2] ἀμνός *(amnos)* – *lamb,* the word use in the gospel of John as in John 1:29. The word used in Revelation, as in Rev. 5:6 is ἀρνίον *(arnion)* – *lamb. or lambkin.* The first has no reference to size whereas the second refers to it as a little or young lamb. There is no doubt that both refer to the Christ as the sacrificial Lamb, slain to take away the sins of the world.

there was the opening of the closed book. The emphasis here is on the fact that the book is now open..

E. THE VOICE OF THE SEVEN THUNDERS

When the Angel cries out, the seven thunders speak. John hurries to write the message of the seven thunders. This tells us that John was writing the visions as he saw them, not waiting until a later time when he could sit down and calmly write them from memory. Before he starts to write, however, he hears a voice from heaven forbidding him to write what the thunders uttered, but commanding him to seal them up.

Whose voice was it? It was either the voice of the same Holy Spirit who spoke to the apostles and prophets about what they should do or speak or write as in Acts 13:2, "As they ministered to the Lord and fasted, the Holy Spirit said, 'Now separate to Me Barnabas and Saul for the work to which I have called them,'" or it was the voice of the Father who spoke from heaven on several occasions, as in Matt. 3:17, "And suddenly a voice *came* from heaven, saying, 'This is My beloved Son, in whom I am well pleased,'" or it was the voice of the giant Angel who is a symbolic representation of Christ. Since the Father, the Son and the Holy Spirit are all God it doesn't make a lot of difference which it was.

What did the thunders speak? How can we know? John didn't tell us, by order of the voice from heaven. The things that are revealed belong to man, but the hidden things belong to God; man cannot know them until the time when God chooses to reveal them. There are some things given for us to know, and some things we will just have to wait on. This is one of those things we will have to wait on. John was the only one who heard and knew what the thunders said. One day, when we're all around the throne of God, perhaps we'll ask John what those thunders said, and maybe he will tell us.

II. THE LAST TRUMPET IS TO BRING THE END (10:5-7)

A. TIME WILL BE NO MORE

John sees this giant Angel raise His hand and take an oath. He swears by God who lives forever and ever and who created all things in heaven, earth and sea. What does He swear? The New King James Version says, "...that there should be delay no longer." The King James Version says, "...that there should be time no longer:" The original carries the meaning of the KJV—"time no more."[3] I believe that what the angel was saying was that when the last trumpet sounded, time, as we know it, would cease to exist. Our time is a part of the creation of this universe. When it all melts with fervent heat everything about this universe will come to an end, including time.[4] What will bring time to an end? The angel says that will happen when the seventh angel blows his trumpet.

B. The Finish of the Mystery—God's Eternal Plan

When that trumpet blows God's eternal plan will be finished. There were things about God's eternal plan that have been kept secret through the ages. On the other hand, the heart of that mystery has been revealed to His apostles and prophets who have then passed it on to us in their writings. Paul wrote in 1 Cor. 2:7-13:

> But we speak the wisdom of God in a mystery, the hidden *wisdom* which God ordained before the ages for our glory, which none of the rulers of this age knew; for had they known, they would not have crucified the Lord of glory. But as it is written: *"Eye has not seen, nor ear heard, Nor have entered into the heart of man The things which God has prepared for those who love Him."* But God has revealed them to us through His Spirit. For the Spirit searches all things, yes, the deep things of God.... These things we also speak, not in words which man's wisdom teaches but which

---

[3]Rev. 10:6 literally says, "...that there should be time no more (or *no longer*)." This is a literal translation of the Greek—χρόνος οὐ ἔτι.

[4]Much of the theory of relativity set forth by Albert Einstein has been verified by experimental evidence in nuclear proton accelerators. One of the things which has been confirmed is the fact that as a proton is accelerated to near the speed of light it ages much more slowly indicating slower passage of time, its mass increases tremendously, and its length in the direction of travel greatly decreases. This demonstrates the fact that the passage of time is not at a fixed rate, but is relative to the velocity of the object on which time is measured by an observer. If the velocity could be increased to the constant velocity of 286,000+ miles per second, time would stand still. If the universe, which is the matrix of time, were to be annihilated, so also time, as we know it, would cease.

the Holy Spirit teaches, comparing spiritual things with spiritual.

Obviously, according to 1 Cor. 2:7-8, the hidden things of God had to do with the crucifixion of Christ. The things provided for those who love God through that sacrifice are those things that were revealed to the apostles and prophets following the resurrection and ascension of Christ. Paul writes in Eph. 3:3-6:

> ...how that by revelation He made known to me the mystery (as I have briefly written already, by which, when you read, you may understand my knowledge in the mystery of Christ), which in other ages was not made known to the sons of men, as it has now been revealed by the Spirit to His holy apostles and prophets: that the Gentiles should be fellow heirs, of the same body, and partakers of His promise in Christ through the gospel.

The mystery revealed to Paul was that all men, Jews and Gentiles alike, should become fellow partakers of the promise in Christ. The gospel is the good news about this mystery, which Paul and others have preached to us. This is the mystery of salvation, now no longer a secret, but revealed to all who are spiritual enough to receive it. Paul writes further in in Eph. 3:9-11:

> ...and to make all see what is the fellowship of the mystery, which from the beginning of the ages has been hidden in God who created all things through Jesus Christ; to the intent that now the manifold wisdom of God might be made known by the church to the principalities and powers in the heavenly places, according to the eternal purpose which He accomplished in Christ Jesus our Lord.

The mystery was kept secret from the beginning of the ages until the time was right to reveal it to all men. This was first the task of the apostles, then of the church as a whole. This was all according to God's eternal plan which was accomplished by and in Jesus Christ. Paul refers to this mystery further in Col. 1:25-27:

> ...of which I became a minister according to the stewardship from God which was given to me for you, to fulfill the word

of God, the mystery which has been hidden from ages and from generations, but now has been revealed to His saints. To them God willed to make known what are the riches of the glory of this mystery among the Gentiles: which is Christ in you, the hope of glory.

Paul emphasizes that the mystery of the ages has been revealed to God's saints. This involves God's provision to take up residence in His saints. "Christ in you." Herein lies our hope of sharing in the glory of Christ. Now what have we learned about that mystery?

1. This was God's eternal plan, hidden from the foundation of the world.

2. It pertains to Christ's coming and dying on the cross as a sacrifice for our sins.

3. It is for all nations whom God would draw together in His fellowship, i.e., that they can become partakers of this fellowship through the gospel.

4. It means that the Father and the Son planned to take up residence in the saints through the Holy Spirit. This indwelling is the guarantee of our inheritance, the hope of sharing the glory of Christ in eternity.

5. It means that the mystery has now been revealed to the apostles and prophets who in turn gave it to us by their preaching and writings.

6. It means that not only the apostles, but the church as a whole has the responsibility to make known by word and deed this manifold wisdom of God, so that the principalities and powers in the heavenly places might see the plan of God.

Paul summarizes this great mystery in 1 Tim. 3:16:

And without controversy great is the mystery of godliness: God was manifested in the flesh, Justified in the Spirit, Seen by angels, Preached among the Gentiles, Believed on in the world, Received up in glory.

There remains one more aspect of this mystery which has not yet been accomplished, that is, the consummation of all things. The plan of God which was kept secret before the ages will all be finished when the last trumpet sounds. This has all been spoken of in the prophets, but we will understand it better when that time comes. Perhaps there are some aspects of this part of the mystery that are still kept secret. Could it be that these things are what the seven thunders uttered? If so, it is too early for them to be revealed, for they are kept secret until the appointed time.

III. JOHN TOLD TO PROPHECY TO THE NATIONS (Read 10:8-11)

A. John Told to Take the Scroll From the Giant Angel

The voice from heaven speaks to John again and gives instructions to him. In verse four the voice told him not to write what the seven thunders said. Here the voice tells him to go and take the little book from the Angel's hand and eat it up. Up to this point the Lamb (Christ) was in the process of opening the book by removing the seven seals. Now the open book is given to John so he can reveal its contents.

In Rev. 1:1 God gave the revelation to Christ who sent it by His angel to John who then must deliver it to the servants of God. Notice that Christ sends the revelation by His angel rather than bringing it in person. Now think about what we have seen. God on the throne gives the scroll to the Lamb (Christ) in chapter five. The Lamb (Christ) proceeds to open the book in chapters six through eight. Then the book is given to John by the hand of His Angel in chapter 10. John is then told to devour it and prophecy its message to the nations. What we have briefly in Rev. 1:1 is what we see played out in greater detail in 5:1-10:11.

B. THE ANGEL COMMANDS JOHN TO EAT IT UP

In verse 9, as instructed by the Voice, John goes to the Angel and receives the book. Then the Angel commands John to take it and eat it up. This apparently symbolize John's absorbing the contents of the book so as to be able to carry the prophecy to the nations. He first had to digest the message and make it a part of his very being, just as food is eaten and digested to become a part of one's body.

We are told that we are what we eat. This is true not only of what we eat physically, but it is especially true of what we eat spiritually. In His temptation in Matt. 4:4 Jesus said, "Man shall not live by bread alone, but by every word which proceeds from the mouth of God." Psalm 119:97-104 extols the word of God as food for the soul:

> Oh, how I love Your law!
> It is my meditation all the day....
> I have more understanding than all my teachers....
> How sweet are Your words to my taste,
> Sweeter than honey to my mouth!
> Through Your precepts I get understanding;
> Therefore I hate every false way.

When we devour the word of God, not only does it produces life-giving benefits in our own lives, but it also prepares us to share that word with others, just as John was expected to do with the contents of the scroll.

C. THE BITTER-SWEET BOOK

We don't always like the food we should eat. This was the case with the book which John ate. It was sweet to his taste, but it made his stomach bitter. The message of Revelation is exciting to read, but when understanding sets in there are some bitter things to digest—things not so pleasant, such as the sufferings and tribulation that we, the servants of God, must undergo. How sweet to the taste is the knowledge of salvation through Christ, and of things to come. How bitter is the realization that some things we must undergo are not at all pleasant.

The book is about a bitter warfare between good and evil. How sweet to be assured at the outset that the good will prevail—that the servants of God will be victorious (the white horse and rider); but how bitter to realize that before victory there will be persecution, suffering and even death (the red, black and pale horses with their riders). The taste is especially bitter when we see the souls of the saints of God as blood poured out in sacrifice under the altar, but the sweet taste returns in the realization that in the end the saints will be vindicated and rewarded, while the enemies of Christ will be judged and destroyed.

D. JOHN TOLD TO DELIVER ITS MESSAGE

Verse 11 tells us that John's assignment is to deliver the message—i.e., to prophesy. The contents of that prophecy was to be about many nations, people, languages, and kings. This drama takes place in the world, and its players, besides the saints of God, are the nations, people and kingdoms of the world. Since John is about to begin revealing the contents of the book, everything up to this point has been preliminary and preparatory, like previews of coming attractions, or like the abundance of work that goes into the preparation and production of a play. As the script was being opened we were given glimpses of the themes which would be carried out in the drama. The over-riding theme is *through persecution and suffering to vindication and victory.* The victory will include not only the reward of the saints, but also the vindication of the saints through judgment against their oppressors.

There is one trumpet yet to sound—the final trumpet which is to wind up the mystery of God, and bring all things to their conclusion at the end of time and the transition to eternity. But before that trumpet is blown and the curtain opens to begin the drama there is one more preparatory step. Call it presenting a synopsis of the contents of the book which John had just devoured, or call it the presentation of the plot of the drama, a summary of the play's action. This is given to us in chapter 11 before the last trumpet is blown.

Chapter 11

THE PLOT OF THE DRAMA
Rev. 11:1-18

The interlude between trumpets six and seven continues in chapter 11. John is given the opened book, he devours the book, and digests its contents. After this the first thing he does is to summarize the action of the drama for us, a condensed picture of the plot. It may help to see a brief summary of this plot before noticing its details.

I. A SUMMARY OF THE PLOT OF THE DRAMA IN REV. 11

A. PERSECUTION OF GOD'S PEOPLE, HIS CHURCH

This is symbolized in two ways—first, by the Holy City being trodden under foot for 42 months, and secondly, by two witnesses who prophesy in sackcloth for 1260 days. The two periods are the same. 42 months times 30 days to the month is 1260 days.

B. TEMPORARY DEFEAT OF THE CAUSE OF CHRIST

This is presented as the killing of the two witnesses by a beast which is coming up out of the abyss. This occurs at the end of the period of persecution, and is the final act of persecution prior to the reign of the saints on earth.

C. REVIVAL OF THE CAUSE OF CHRIST

This is presented as the resurrection of the two witnesses after a short period of three and a half days. These witnesses are exalted in the sight of all

192

men as they rise into the clouds of heaven to be seen by all. One-tenth of those in the city of the world are destroyed while the rest glorify God..

D. THE DOMINION OF THE WORLD IS TAKEN BY CHRIST

The Lord takes His great power and begins to reign. This is presented in chapter 20 as the 1000 year reign.

E. THE REBELLION OF THE NATIONS

The nations rage against Christ and His saints in a last ditch effort to overthrow His reign on earth.

F. THE LAST TRUMPET

The time comes for the dead to be judged, for rewarding the saints and prophets, and for destroying the destroyers of the earth.

We will see this plot unfold as the drama is played out in Rev. 12 - 22. Now let us do a more detailed study of the chapter to see what it has for us to learn.

II. JOHN TOLD TO MEASURE THE TEMPLE (Read 11:1-2)

In Rev. 4 - 5 we learned of the temple of God in heaven, the theater where John is shown these visions. We returned to the temple scene from time to time in earlier chapters. In Rev. 6 we saw the altar of sacrifice. In Rev. 7 we saw the saints of God in white robes around the throne. In Rev. 8 there was the golden altar of incense which stands before the throne of God. Now once again we return to the temple in Rev. 11:1-2 and again in verse 19. This is not talking about Solomon's temple, or the temple of Zerubbabel or of Herod. The temple in the earthly Jerusalem, in all its splendor, was but a poor representation and foreshadow of the real temple in heaven. That temple was totally destroyed in A.D. 70, 25 years before John wrote the book of Revelation.

Preparing for the Drama

A. MEASURE THREE THINGS

The giant Angel gives John a measuring rod and tells him to measure three things: the temple itself; the altar; and the worshipers. In Ezek. 40 - 43 the prophet Ezekiel records his vision of a man who measured the temple in Jerusalem including all the items of that temple. The measuring rod which the man used was six cubits in length. The cubit was the *royal* cubit which was a regular cubit (17 or 18 inches) plus the breadth of a man's hand (about four to five inches). This cubit was therefore about 21 to 23 inches long. That means that the measuring rod was approximately 126 inches (3 ½ yards or 10 ½ feet) long. The imagery in Rev. 11:1 is probably drawn from Ezekiel's vision of measuring the temple. John was given a similar rod to measure the temple in his vision. For a fuller explanation of the temple in heaven go to *Appendix B: The Temple of God.*

John is told that the outer court of the temple belongs to the nations (Gentiles). As a result he was not to measure that. On the other hand, there is no need to measure the Holy of Holies because it is God's throne-room with its furniture. That is all out of our hands. We have no part in building the throne room of God. On the other hand, although it is Christ who builds His church, we are honored to be given a part in the work of building it, as we have seen in 1 Cor. 3:10-15. This is the temple that requires measuring— i.e., the church of our Lord, the Holy Place as seen in the church on earth.

Again, the things to be measured are the temple itself, the altar, and the worshipers. The temple is composed of Christians—the Holy Place reaches into heaven itself where Christians on earth have the authority and boldness to enter in before the throne of God, the mercy seat, in order to obtain mercy in time of need. Heb. 4:16 says, "Let us therefore come boldly to the throne of grace, that we may obtain mercy and find grace to help in time of need."

A measuring rod (today we would probably use a tape measure) is used to make sure that the thing being measured conforms to the requirements of the blueprint. What is the rod by which the church is to be measured? What else but the word of God revealed through the apostles and prophets? God planned and gave the pattern for the tabernacle/temple in the Old Testament. That pattern serves as the foreshadow for the church. We all, as Christians, have a part in building this temple. Each of us is a living stone in this spiritual house (1 Pet. 2:5). Each of us is a priest in this house. Each of us serves at the altar to offer up spiritual sacrifices (see Eph. 2:20-22).

In the building of Solomon's temple the workers worked with great care. The building stones were cut with such precision that when they were brought from the quarry to the temple site they fitted together perfectly. As a result, the walls went up without the sound of a hammer or chisel or any such thing. Any faulty blocks were cast aside at the quarry before they reached the temple site, because they did not measure up.

As we are built into God's temple, so we are instrumental in building others into that temple (1 Cor. 3:9-17). We need to be careful how we build on the foundation laid by the apostles. The church is built of human stones. Are they gold, silver or precious stones? These will survive the refining fires and remain as part of the completed temple. Are they wood, hay, or stubble (see 1 Cor. 3:12-15)? The trial by fire will consume these.

The life, commitment, and works of the church are to be measured according to the standards set in God's word. What are the materials being built into this temple? What are the temple's dimensions? When we get right down to it, the builder is Christ. However, He honors us by giving us a part in His work. Now let us look at these three ways God wanted the temple measured.

1. Measure The Temple Itself. Among the things subject to measurement by God's word are: 1) the foundation of the church; 2) the doctrine of the church; and 3) the plan of salvation taught by the church. You may think of others, but let us take a look at these.

Measure The Foundation of the Church. In Matt. 16:18 Jesus said, "...on this rock I will build My church...." That rock was the foundation truth Peter had confessed—"You are the Christ, the Son of the living God." Jesus sent His apostles to lay that foundation by preaching the gospel. This foundation was laid by the apostles and prophets (Eph. 2:20). According to 1 Cor. 3:10-11 there is only one foundation. The apostle Paul says:

> According to the grace of God which was given to me, as a wise master builder I have laid the foundation, and another builds on it. But let each one take heed how he builds on it.

> For no other foundation can anyone lay than that which is laid, which is Jesus Christ.

As an apostle, Paul was a wise master builder who laid that foundation. John is asked to measure the temple. The foundation is part of the temple. What are we building our churches upon? What is the foundation? Is it the foundation truth of Jesus Christ? Many who lay claim to being Christians have changed the foundation upon which they build. In order to measure up to the blueprint, the foundation upon which we build must be the one laid by the apostles—i.e., Jesus Christ and Him crucified. The foundation truth is that He is the Christ, the Son of God.

Measure The Doctrine Taught by the Church. Some churches preach a different Christ than the one preached by the apostles. Does your Christ conform to the teachings of the Bible about Him? John wrote in 2 John 7-11:

> For many deceivers have gone out into the world who do not confess **Jesus Christ *as* coming in the flesh**. This is a deceiver and an antichrist. Look to yourselves, that we do not lose those things we worked for, but *that* we may receive a full reward. Whoever transgresses and does not abide in the doctrine of Christ does not have God. He who abides in **the doctrine of Christ** has both the Father and the Son. **If anyone comes to you and does not bring this doctrine**, do not receive him into your house nor greet him; for he who greets him shares in his evil deeds.

If a church does not measure up to this standard in its teachings about the person and work of Jesus who is its foundation, it will most certainly not be recognized by Christ. The doctrine of Christ—His divine/human nature is of primary importance. Without this there is no valid basis for salvation. To fail to abide in this doctrine is to lose the things for which we have worked. It is to become antichrist (1 John 2:22; 4:3; 2 John 1:7). So important is the doctrine of Christ that if someone comes proclaiming a different Christ, we are not to receive him into our house or greet him.

Measure the Plan of Salvation Taught By the Church. Some churches teach a different plan of salvation than that given by Christ. God's plan was ordained before the foundation of the world. That plan is called *the gospel of*

Christ—i.e., the good news about Christ. There are two parts to God's plan. It includes what God has done, and it includes how we must respond.

God's Grace. God's part is called *grace*. Grace is not just a way of feeling, but it is active in providing what is necessary for the salvation of mankind. It involved God's giving His Son to die for our sins.

Man's Response. Man's response to the plan is called *faith*. Faith is not just a mental acceptance of facts about Jesus Christ. It, like God's grace, must be active. It must reach out to receive the salvation that God is offering to him. It is an obeying faith which includes the belief of the truth about Jesus; repentance (turning away from sin); confession of that faith with the mouth; and obedience to God's command to be baptized. This means trusting God to the point that you will do whatever He asks. For a more thorough study of this plan consult *Appendix E*: *The Plan of Salvation*.

In measuring the temple we have noted three things: 1) The foundation of the temple, the church, is Jesus Christ; 2) The doctrine of the church is the truth about Jesus Christ, who He is and what He did. 3) The eternal plan of salvation as it is given to us in scripture includes active grace on God's part, and man's response—i.e., an obedient faith. The yardstick for measuring these things is the word of God.

2. Measure The Altar. The altar, which was the center of the worship of Israel, symbolizes the worship of the church—of Christians. We are to offer up spiritual sacrifices (1 Pet. 2:5). These include: the fruit of our lips—the sacrifice of praise (Heb. 13:15); service rendered to others in doing good and sharing—sacrifices well pleasing to God (Heb. 13:16); and offering up our own bodies as living sacrifices to God—our spiritual service of worship (Rom. 12:1). In John 4:23-24 Jesus points out to the woman at the well in Samaria the following truth:

But the hour is coming, and now is, when the true worshipers will worship the Father in spirit and truth; for the Father is seeking such to worship Him. God is Spirit, and those who worship Him must worship in spirit and truth.

There were times in the Old Testament when the Israelites permitted other things to be brought into the temple—things that were not allowed—things which had been condemned by God through His law and His prophets.

Among these things were idols that were set up in the sanctuary for the people to worship. Sometimes unclean animals would be offered as sacrifice on the altar. As a result of these defilements the temple had to be cleansed on several occasions.

Does your worship measure up to the standard of His word? Has your private worship been defiled by things in your life that don't belong—your own private idols? The injunction, "Thou shalt have no other gods before Me" still stands. What about the worship in your church? Has it been polluted by things which don't belong—by the doctrines and commandments of men, created by human traditions? Jesus said in Mark 7:6-8:

> Well did Isaiah prophesy of you hypocrites, as it is written: *"This people honors Me with their lips, But their heart is far from Me. And in vain they worship Me, Teaching as doctrines the commandments of men."* For laying aside the commandment of God, you hold the tradition of men—the washing of pitchers and cups, and many other such things you do.

In this context Jesus told the Jewish leaders that when their traditions conflict with the commandments of God they would rather keep their human traditions than the commandments of God. This is vain worship. There are three kinds of human traditions:

1) There are traditions which are wrong because they conflict with God's commands;

2) Some traditions may not conflict with any command of God, but they become wrong by being bound upon the consciences of men as if they were laws of God;

3) There are some traditions which do not conflict with God's commands and are recognized for what they are—human traditions. These may be practiced as long as they are not bound and made a necessity for all to follow.

Such traditions, established by man and not God, are: church ownership property; building church buildings; a general church treasury; the offering of an invitation at the conclusion of a sermon; Sunday school classes; and many, many more. These traditions, although of human origin, serve a valid purpose, and do not violate God's commands, provided they are not bound as essentials.

The first and second categories of traditions are unacceptable. Men sin by practicing traditions that conflict with God's commands. They also sin by binding human traditions of any kind upon the consciences of man. When the measuring stick of God's word is applied to your church, how does it measure up in regard to worship?

3. Measure The Worshipers. Christians are the priests who offer sacrifices on the altar. They are a holy nation, a royal priesthood. What is to be measured about individual Christians? Are we being an effective witness to the world? Are we practicing unity with all true believers in Christ? Are we practicing sacrificial love for others? This is the new commandment Jesus gave. All the law is fulfilled in this command. John 13:34-35 says:

> A new commandment I give to you, that you love one
> another; **as I have loved you**, that you also love one another.
> By this all will know that you are My disciples, if you have
> love for one another.

Old Testament priests had to conform to a rigid set of rules as to how they offered their sacrifices and how they prepared themselves to serve at the altar. We, too, must be measured to conform our life and worship to His standard. This standard is not a legalistic set of rules and regulations, but has to do with the commitment and devotion of our heart to God's will and word. As Christian priests, our task is that of ministering to the souls of the lost—to help them bridge the gap between their sins and God's forgiveness. We are intercessors for mankind, not mediators that go between God and man. There is only one such mediator, that is Christ the righteous one. 1 Tim. 2:1-5 says:

> Therefore I exhort first of all that supplications, prayers,
> intercessions, *and* giving of thanks be made for all men, for
> kings and all who are in authority, that we may lead a quiet
> and peaceable life in all godliness and reverence. For this is
> good and acceptable in the sight of God our Savior, who
> desires all men to be saved and to come to the knowledge of
> the truth. For *there is* one God and one Mediator between
> God and men, the Man Christ Jesus....

God has a standard of living for His saints. They are to be in the world, but not of it. The temple was holy in all its parts. It was sanctified, separate, cleansed. What does all that mean for the heavenly temple? 1 Pet. 2:9-10 puts it this way:

> But you *are* a chosen generation, a royal priesthood, a **holy** nation, His own special people, that you may proclaim the praises of Him who called you out of darkness into His marvelous light; who once *were* not a people but *are* now the people of God, who had not obtained mercy but now have obtained mercy.

How does your life measure up in your worship, in your ministry, and in your holiness?

III. THE HOLY CITY AND THE TWO WITNESSES (Read 11:2b-6)

A. THE HOLY CITY (11:2)

The temple of Solomon was situated in Jerusalem. The heavenly temple is also situated in the heavenly Jerusalem. The city mentioned here is not the earthly city where David reigned. It is the city of God, the Holy City, New Jerusalem.

1. Paul's Allegory—Two Jerusalems and Two Covenants. In Gal. 4:21-31 Paul compared the old covenant, given through Moses, to Hagar, and he compared the Israelites to her son Ishmael. Hagar was a slave woman and gave birth to Ishmael who was born in slavery. Paul's point was that the Israelites were in bondage under the old covenant just as Ishmael was in bondage. Not only does Hagar represent the old covenant, she also corresponds to the earthly city of Jerusalem. Verses 25-26 say:

> For this Hagar is Mount Sinai in Arabia, and corresponds to Jerusalem which now is, and is in bondage with her children—but the Jerusalem above is free, which is the mother of us all.

On the other hand, Sarah represents the other covenant—the new covenant. She also corresponds to the Jerusalem which is above, and her son Isaac represents the children of the new covenant—i.e., Christians. Whereas

Hagar represents the earthly Jerusalem which is in bondage under law, Sarah is the Jerusalem above which is free. This Jerusalem is the mother of us all. This is the same Jerusalem spoken of in Heb. 12:22-24:

> But you have come to Mount Zion and to the city of the living God, **the heavenly Jerusalem**, to an innumerable company of angels, to the general assembly and church of the firstborn *who are* registered in heaven, to God the Judge of all, to the spirits of just men made perfect, to Jesus the Mediator of the new covenant, and to the blood of sprinkling that speaks better things than *that of* Abel.

2. The New Jerusalem—the Church, the Bride of Christ. Eph. 5:25-27 admonishes men to love their wives as Christ loves the church, which He cleansed by the washing of water with the word in order to present her to Himself a glorious church without spot or wrinkle. The comparison of the church to the bride of Christ here is carried out in several places in Revelation. In Rev. 19:7, after the destruction of Babylon the Harlot, John writes, "Let us be glad and rejoice and give Him glory, for **the marriage of the Lamb** has come, and **His wife has made herself ready.**" Then in Rev. 21:2 John says, "Then I, John, saw the holy city, **New Jerusalem**, coming down out of heaven from God, prepared as **a bride adorned for her husband.**" Is there any doubt that the bride of Christ is the church? Can we doubt that the bride of Christ is also the heavenly Jerusalem, the Jerusalem from above, the new Jerusalem? It then follows that the new Jerusalem is the church.

This Jerusalem is the one depicted in Rev. 11:1-2. Just as the heavenly temple is the church, as seen in these verses, so also the Jerusalem shown here is the church, the bride of Christ. The heavenly Jerusalem depicted in chapter 11 has not yet descended to the new earth. That takes place after the final judgment. Here that portion of new Jerusalem which is the church on earth is under persecution. The outer court of the temple is trampled by the Gentiles. They also trample the holy city. What does this mean? It means the church will go through a period of severe persecution by the nations (non-Christians). This is represented as being for 42 months. It should be pointed out that the word translated *Gentiles* is the word for *nations*.[1] Here it obviously means the people of the world who are in opposition to Christ and Christianity.

3. What Is the Meaning of 42 Months? What is the period of 42 months? What does it represent? Is it literal? This number is found in one other place. It is the period of time during which the seven-headed beast makes war upon the saints in Rev. 13:4-5. However, there are several other references to time periods that are equivalent. A Jewish month was 30 days. 42 months was therefore 1260 days, as found in chapters 11 and 12. 42 months is also three and one-half years, or "a time, times and a half time." This is found in Dan. 7 and 12 as well as in Rev. 12. They all refer to the same period of time, the time of the persecution of the saints. At the end of the persecution they would be victorious.

We have seen symbols of the persecution of saints in the opening of the seven seals. The fifth seal vision is of the martyred saints under the altar of burnt offering (6:10), crying "How long ...until You (God) judge and avenge our blood on those who dwell on the earth?" In chapter 11 the persecution is seen in the symbol of the gentiles trampling the outer court of the temple, and the Holy City being trampled under their feet for 42 months. We will wait until the exposition of Rev. 12 and 13 to give an explanation as to the meaning of the 42 months or 1260 days. Meantime let us see another symbol of this persecution.

B. THE TWO WITNESSES (11:3-6)

1. 1260 Days of Prophesying in Sackcloth. The first thing we notice about this picture is that two characters called *witnesses* prophesy in sackcloth for 1260 days. This period is the same as 42 months, and is obviously referring to the same period of time as that in which the holy city is trodden under the feet of the gentiles. Wearing sackcloth was a common way of showing severe distress of mind, such as mourning, or as in the case of Job, severe suffering (Job 16:15-17). The figure of the two witnesses

---

[1] ἔθνος *(ethnos)* plural ἔθνοι *(ethnoi)*, according to *Young's Greek Definitions*—gentile, *heathen, nation, people.* Sometimes in the New Testament, especially in 1 Corinthians, the term is used to denote the people of the world as opposed to Christians, just as it was used by the Jews to denote the people of other nations.

prophesying in sackcloth for 1260 days is another way of symbolizing the period of time when the church is under severe persecution. In my opinion the 42 months or 1260 days are not to be taken literally but figuratively. There are several things alluded to by these figures. We will deal with them more fully in chapter 12. Meanwhile I will say that I believe 1260 days to correspond to a time approximating 1260 years—i.e., each day representing a year. For a more thorough explanation of the *day-for-a-year* theory go to *Appendix B*.

2. Two Olive Trees and Two Lampstands. Let us take a closer look at these two witnesses. They are characterized in two ways. First, they are two olive trees and two lampstands who stand before the God of the earth. Please notice that the God of the earth is not the same as the god of this world. Satan is called the god of this world, but there is a difference between the world and the earth. The world, as used in the New Testament, usually refers to the world system and not to the earth itself. The things that make up this world, according to 1 John 2:15-16 are the lust of the flesh, the lust of the eyes, and the pride of life. The earth, on the other hand, was created by God and still belongs to God. Psalm 24:1 says, "The earth is the LORD'S, and all its fullness."

The reference to the two olive trees and two lampstands is taken from Zech. 4, although the figure is slightly altered, as is often the case when symbols in the New Testament are drawn from symbols in the Old Testament. In Zechariah there is only one lampstand and two olive branches or trees. In Zech, 4:4-6 we read:

> So I answered and spoke to the angel who talked with me, saying, "What are these, my lord?" Then the angel who talked with me answered and said to me, "Do you not know what these are?" And I said, "No, my lord." So he answered and said to me: "This is the word of the LORD to Zerubbabel: "Not by might nor by power, but by My Spirit," Says the LORD of hosts."

Zerubbabel, governor of Jerusalem when the Israelites returned from Babylonia, was given the task of rebuilding the temple and reestablishing the worship of God in the temple. He had as his partner in this undertaking the high priest Joshua (or Jeshua). This prophecy is about them. In verses 11-14 the olive trees are identified. Verse 14 says, "So he said, 'These are the two anointed ones, who stand beside the Lord of the whole earth.'" The two anointed ones are, in all probability, referring to Joshua and Zerubbabel. How does this relate?

The olive trees are the source of the oil which fills the lamps on the lampstand. The lampstand is probably to be understood as the seven branched lampstand that would be returned to the temple when it was rebuilt. Actually the two anointed ones are not themselves the trees, but branches through which the oil flows (Zech. 4:12). They are not themselves the source of the oil. The oil is a symbol of the Holy Spirit. The Holy spirit is the source of light or enlightenment. The Holy Spirit, working in Joshua and Zerubbabel, was the source of the power by which they were to accomplish the rebuilding of the temple. Verse 6 says, "This is the word of the Lord to Zerubbabel: 'Not by might nor by power, but **by My Spirit**,' Says the LORD of hosts."

The two witnesses in Revelation are like lampstands receiving and burning the oil of the Holy Spirit. This was the source of their prophesying. This was the source of the power by which they could continue to build the church while under persecution. They are those anointed by God to this task. Who are they?

3. Witnesses Like Moses and Elijah. Let us take a look at the other figures applied to them. These are obviously referring to Moses and Elijah. "These have power to shut heaven, so that no rain falls in the days of their prophecy." Elijah is the one whose prayer stopped the rain from falling. This interesting story is found in 1 Kings 17 and 18. James 5:17 says, "Elijah was a man with a nature like ours, and he prayed earnestly that it would not rain; and it did not rain on the land for three years and six months." Three and one-half years is the same as 1260 days. "...they have power over waters to turn them to blood, and to strike the earth with all plagues, as often as they desire." It was Moses who brought the plagues on Egypt. The first of these was turning the water into blood. Exod. 7:20 states:

> So he lifted up the rod and struck the waters that *were* in the river, in the sight of Pharaoh and in the sight of his servants. And all the waters that *were* in the river were turned to blood.

What is the point? These witnesses, like Joshua and Zerubbabel, like Moses and Elijah, are the anointed of God. They draw their strength from the Spirit of God. Through this power, they can do whatever is necessary to finish their testimony—i.e., to finish their prophesying. If need be, fire can come out of their mouths to destroy those who would harm them during the 1260 days. Are these witnesses two literal men? No more than they are two literal olive trees or two literal lampstands. Who, then, are these two witnesses?

3. The Church As a Witness. In Rev. 6 the People of God are represented as the persecuted church by the symbol of souls under the altar. These are said to be the souls of the martyrs (witnesses) who were beheaded because of their testimony. As individuals they are witnesses. As a unit they are one witness—i.e., the church, the body of Christ. Paul represents the church as a primary witness for revealing the mystery of God's wisdom which had been hidden before. The church served as a demonstration of this mystery, not just to the world, but even to the spiritual powers that are in the heavenly places—those who rule over the world system.

> Although I am the very least of all the saints, this grace was given to me to bring to the Gentiles the news of the boundless riches of Christ, and to make everyone see what is the plan of the mystery hidden for ages in God who created all things; so that **through the church the wisdom of God in its rich variety might now be made known to the rulers and authorities in the heavenly places.** This was in accordance with the eternal purpose that he has carried out in Christ Jesus our Lord....[Eph. 3:8-11, NRSV]

Jesus is still in this world in the form of His Body, the Church. Just as His works—i.e., His miracles and teachings—testified of Him while He was here in person, so now the works of the body of Christ—i.e., the miracle of changed lives, resulting in the ministry of the church to human needs as well as the ministry of the word, continue to testify of Jesus.

4. The Written Word As a Witness. When the church was in its infancy it had no New Testament to give men so they could read and know the word they were to preach. Apostles went here and there to deliver the revealed word to them. Members of Christ's body had the Old Testament, but needed help in applying it to their Christian life and responsibility. The apostles imparted to some people in each congregation the gifts of prophecy and knowledge. With this the Lord would guide them into the things to which they needed to bear witness. If there were people of other tongues to whom they could testify, the gift of tongues would come into play. Meanwhile the apostles and prophets were engaged in setting down the words inspired by the Holy Spirit in writing. With the New Testament added to the Old Testament, the completed word of God was able to lead. Why was the Bible given? It was to bear testimony to God and to Jesus Christ.

Jesus identifies the scriptures as a primary witness of His identity and work in John 5:39-40. "You search the Scriptures, for in them you think you have eternal life; and these are they which testify of Me." If this was true of the scriptures, which at that time only included the books of the Old Testament, how much more is it true since the Holy Spirit has added the New Testament books. These bear even greater testimony to Jesus.

5. Why Two Witnesses? By the end of the first century A.D. the Holy Spirit left two institutions in this world to bear witness—i.e., **the church** and **the Bible**. Neither is sufficient in itself. The two stand or fall together. The church needs the guidance of the word, and the word will not be proclaimed by any but the church. The book of Revelation has many personifications in it. Death is personified as the rider of the pale horse. Hades is personified as the one who follows death to receive the souls of the dead. We will notice others as we proceed in the book. Here personification is used to represent the body of believers and the written word as two persons bearing witness in the world.

These two witnesses are a torment to the world system since they are opposed to everything the world stands for. The world wants to get rid of the scriptures and the church, to kill them like their Lord was killed. But like their Lord, they won't stay dead either. They will rise again.

The Law of Two Witnesses. But why present them as two witnesses instead of a single witness? The law makes it clear that only at the mouth of two or three witnesses could a word be established. Deut 19:15 says, "One witness shall not rise against a man concerning any iniquity or any sin that he commits; by the mouth of two or three witnesses the matter shall be established." Jesus was referred to this requirement when he said in John

5:31, "If I bear witness of Myself, My witness is not true." He was saying that according to the law His claim to be the Son of God was not to be counted true if there were no other witnesses; but He proceeded to give a list of witnesses besides himself that give evidence of who He was. These include John the Baptist, the works (miracles) that He did, the Father Himself Who spoke from heaven, the scriptures, and His own words.

An Apostle and the Holy Spirit Make Two Witnesses to Jesus' Resurrection. In John 15:26-27 Jesus told the apostles that as they bore their witness they would also have the witness of the Holy Spirit:

> But when the Helper comes, whom I shall send to you from the Father, the Spirit of truth who proceeds from the Father, He will testify of Me. And you also will bear witness, because you have been with Me from the beginning.

As each apostle carried his eye-witness testimony of the death, burial, and resurrection of the Christ, he did not go alone. The Holy Spirit was with him and bore witness with him. In Acts 5:32 Peter states this same truth; "And we are His witnesses to these things, and so also is the Holy Spirit whom God has given to those who obey Him."

The Holy Spirit and Our Spirit—Two Witnesses to Our Sonship. Paul inserts this truth into Rom. 8:16 while assuring Christians of the presence of the Holy Spirit in their lives. He said, "The Spirit Himself bears witness with our spirit that we are children of God." Notice that in this verse Paul says that the Spirit bears witness **with, not to,** our spirit. Paul is talking about a joint witness here as a Christian bears testimony to the world, backed up by the testimony of the Holy Spirit.

The Holy Spirit Is the Source of the Testimony in the Word. The primary witness of the Holy Spirit is found in the written word. He is the one who inspired the scriptures. Like the apostles, the church, through the power of the Spirit, bears its own testimony while the Holy Spirit through the word bears His testimony. When the two testimonies agree they are powerful. It is my conviction that the two witnesses in Revelation 11 are the church and the Bible. Both are left in this world to bear testimony. The Holy Spirit is the source of the power of both witnesses as well as the source their testimony.

6. The Seven Lampstands Joined as One Lampstand. In Rev. chapters 1, 2, and 3 the churches were represented as seven lampstands. Each congregation is a branch in the seven-branched lampstand. The churches (congregations) are in reality one church, just as the seven branches form one lampstand. The church as a whole is seen as the lampstand holding up the seven lamps of fire. The Bible is another lampstand that holds up the lamps of fire. The Holy Spirit is said to be the seven lamps in chapter four. The Holy Spirit is the source of the testimony in both the church and the Bible. They operate by His power. If anyone is disturbed about there being more than one seven-branched lampstand, please notice that while there was only one in the tabernacle, there were ten in the temple in Jerusalem—five on each side of the holy place.

The testimonies of the written word and the church agree when the Holy Spirit is the source of the testimony. He will not contradict Himself. When the Spirit is the source, the church flourishes, even under persecution—or perhaps we should say especially under persecution. But when the church bears a different testimony, one from another source, one that does not agree with the testimony of the Bible, then the church does not flourish. In order to present a united front to the world and to Satan's forces we must get our testimony from the Holy Spirit. The church relies on the scriptures for its direction, and the scriptures rely on the church to proclaim the word.

7. The Witnesses Under Attack. The witnesses are pictured as wearing sackcloth, a sign of great anguish. The church and the Bible undergo attack from the world—i.e., from Satan's forces. Satan knows that as long as the Bible stands the church will stand. He also knows that as long as the church stands and continues to proclaim the word that the Bible will stand. In order to defeat them Satan knows that they must fall together.

IV. THE BEAST KILLS THE TWO WITNESSES (Read 11:7-10)

A. THE PERSECUTOR—THE BEAST TO ASCEND FROM THE ABYSS (11:7)

Here is the first appearance of the Beast of persecution. This is a stage of the same Beast that appears in chapter 13 as the seven headed beast, and in chapter 17 where John explains what this Beast represents. His end is found in chapter 19 when he is cast into the lake of fire. For now, suffice it to say that the Beast in its sixth head stage, with the crowns on its ten horns, represents the kingdoms arising out of the Roman Empire which persecute the servants of God for a period of 1260 days (years). The beast succeeds in killing Christians during this period, but cannot kill the church which is protected by God. After the 1260 days the seventh stage of the beast succeeds in killing the church and the Bible, i.e., the two witnesses, just prior to his being cast into the bottomless pit. For a full explanation of the beast go to *Appendix F.*

He is here called "the beast that ascends out of the bottomless pit." This is the one who kills the witnesses. Notice that 11:7 does not say that the killing takes place after the Beast ascends out of the bottomless pit, but that the Beast that does the killing is the one who is coming up out of[2] the abyss. This is given to identify the Beast as the one spoken of in Revelation 17:8. John is told, "The beast that you saw was, and is not, and will ascend out of the bottomless pit and go to perdition." As we shall see in chapters 19 and 20, the Beast does not have time to kill the witnesses when he comes out of the abyss, because he is almost immediately cast into the lake of fire.

John wants us to understand that it is this beast that does the killing—i.e., the one that will ascend out of the abyss and go into perdition. 17:11 also says, "The beast that was, and is not, is himself also the eighth, and is of the seven, and is going to perdition." The beast that ascends from the bottomless pit is the same one who descends into it. He goes in as the seventh and comes out as the eighth. Since he will not have time to do his dirty work when he comes up, he must do it before he goes in. As a result, I conclude that the Beast that kills the witnesses does so in the seventh head stage. This is the same beast that later comes up out of the abyss. A fuller understanding of this must await the playing out of the drama.

B. THE KILLING OF THE TWO WITNESSES

What does it mean that the witnesses are killed? If the witnesses represent the church and the Bible, apparently there is to be a time when they are dead. This does not mean that all members of the church are killed, or that there will be no more believers. In that sense the church and the Bible

---

[2] τὸ ἀναβαῖνον ἐκ—*the one coming up out of*—the verb is 3rd person present participle.

will never cease to exist. There will still be some around to prevent the bodies from being buried.

I remember a time in my earlier years when a professor in a liberal seminary declared that God is dead. Of course, true believers know better than this. If God were dead this universe could no longer exist. But he was voicing an opinion that has been voiced by many members of the intelligencia, that belief in God has become irrelevant. The world declared the Bible to be invalid—just a book of myths and stories, and that the church was on its way out as a relic of past superstitions. When these things were being said there were still many who believed in God and the Bible. Many still professed faith in Christ and were members of His body the church.

How Near Are We to the Killing of the Two Witnesses? In the United States the popular attitude toward the church and the Bible has gone from respect to disinterest to open hostility. Over the last several decades there is a frantic attempt to exclude the church from having a voice in public policy, and the Bible is being banned from public life. We have come to the point where the Beast is making war with the church and the Bible, and plainly expects to kill them. That has already been done in many nations of the world already. Communism ruled two-thirds of the world's surface in which the church and the Bible had been banned. In places like France the popular view is that the church is a fringe element with no relevance, and that the Bible is no longer recognized among educated people as having any educational, moral or religious value—i.e., in effect, dead.

Whether or not we have actually reached the point of the killing of the witnesses as set forth in this verse, for some decades most of the world has looked upon the church and the Bible as dead. There are, however, signs of revival. Let us pray diligently that the church and the Bible will take their rightful place in this world, and that the kingdom of this world will finally become the kingdom of our Lord Jesus Christ.

C. THE BODIES OF THE WITNESSES LIE IN SODOM AND EGYPT (11:8)

The bodies of the witnesses are allowed to lie in the streets of the great city. What is this city? Some think it is talking about the literal city of Jerusalem because it says that this is where the Lord was crucified. This city is also called *Sodom*, but this could not be literal since Sodom no longer existed in John's day, nor does it today, and it will never exist again. It is also called *Egypt,* but Egypt is a country and not a city. What is the meaning of all this?

1. The Meaning of Sodom and Egypt. Egypt has long been used as a figure for the world of sin. The delivery of Israel from Egypt by Moses was a type of our delivery from sin by Christ. Sodom, while no longer existing, is still used as a figure for the sinful world. In Isa. 1:9-10 God calls the nation of Israel *Sodom and Gomorrah* because of its sinful condition, but I know of no passage that calls the literal city of Jerusalem *Sodom* or *Egypt,* or that even likens it to Sodom and Egypt. If there is one I shall be glad to know it.

It is more likely that these figures mean *the sinful world.* The statement about the Lord being crucified there does not have to mean the literal city where He was crucified. Jesus was sent into **the world** because God loved the **world**, and sent Him to be the payment for the sins of **the world**. To **the world** He came and in the city of **the world** He was crucified.

2. The City of the World as Opposed to the City of God. The counterpart to the city of God, the heavenly Jerusalem, is the city of the world, spiritual Sodom and Egypt. If the witnesses are the church and the Bible, they could hardly be killed in one literal city and lie there, because the church is world-wide. There is yet another figure used later to represent the city of the world—i.e., Babylon the Harlot.

D. THE PEOPLE OF GOD PRESERVE THE BODIES OF THE WITNESSES (11:9)

1. God's People Are From All People, Tribes, Tongues, and Nations. The expression *those out of every people, tribe, tongue, and nation* is used many times in Revelation to refer to those called out of the world into Christ. The word *from* in this verse is literally *out of.* The believers left on earth after the beast has killed the witnesses (we may call them *the remnant*) will not accept the world's evaluation of the situation. They will not let the church or the Bible be buried under the teachings and philosophies of this world. They are expecting these two to get up on their feet and take their rightful place on God's earth. They know that a reversal of the situation is coming, so they preserve the bodies of the witnesses.

2. The World Rejoices Over the Death of the Witnesses (11:10). The rejoicing of the world is unrestrained. They considered the church and the Bible their enemies. They are elated that the prophecies of these witness no longer accuse and torment them. Their evil consciences cannot stand the light of the gospel, for it calls them to repentance. They love the ways of the world. They love the darkness. It infuriates them when anyone calls attention to their wickedness. While this chapter was being written the forces of Satan prevailed upon our government to remove the ten commandments from a courthouse in Alabama. The world doesn't want their consciences pricked. They have dulled the accusations of their own consciences and will not tolerate the Bible or Christians pointing a finger of accusation. This is torment to them. They are understandably overjoyed to know that these tormenters will no longer bother them. But just wait.

V. The Witnesses Rise and Men Glorify God (11:11-13)

A. The Witnesses Come to Life and Ascend to the Sky (11:11-12)

The witnesses remain dead only three and a half days! This is a short period of time for someone to stay dead. This is comparable to the period of time that Jesus stayed dead. The breath of life from God enters them and they stand on their feet. In the beginning God breathed into the nostrils of the clay body that He had formed and man became a living soul (Gen. 2:7). In Acts 2 the Holy Spirit was poured out for all mankind. The Spirit entered into the newly formed body of the church and it became a living thing. The written word of God was inspired by the Holy Spirit. This might be likened to God's molding Adam's body from the dust and breathing into it the breath of life. His Spirit gave form and life both to the church and the word. It is said in Hebrews 4:12, "For the word of God is living and powerful."

It is through the ministration of the Holy Spirit, the Breath of Life, that the two witnesses now stand upon their feet and live. Before, they had been persecuted and hounded by the forces of evil in this world. They prophesied in sackcloth. Now they are not wearing sackcloth anymore but royal robes. Everyone who sees them are seized by terrible fear.

The witnesses heard a loud voice from heaven saying, "Come up here." I wonder whose voice this was. Was it the same one heard by the apostles when God acknowledged Jesus as His Son with whom He was well pleased? Perhaps. Perhaps it was Jesus Himself who was calling them. It doesn't say, so we don't know whose voice it was. These two witnesses rose into the air in a cloud and all their enemies saw them. They did not ascend out of the sight of men. They ascended to a position where they could be seen of all men. They were exalted in the eyes of the nations. Just think of what this would do to those who had been unbelievers. They could respond in one of three ways: 1) They could deny the evidence of their own eyes just as they have denied the plain evidence of the existence of God; 2) They could believe, but resist doing anything about it; 3) They might be caused to repent and seek after God. At any rate the stage is set for a new era, a period of time when righteousness reigns supreme upon the earth—when the dominion of the world would come into the hands of our Lord and His saints.

But what about the three and a half days? This is probably a figure. I found nothing in the Bible referring to three and a half days other than this passage. The symbolism of periods of time is sometimes found in the significance of the number itself, as in the number seven, or the number 1000. Sometimes it is with reference to some event which uses the same number, with perhaps a different unit of time. For instance, three and a half is the number of years during which it did not rain in Israel during Elijah's day. It was also the number of years of the siege of Jerusalem which ended in its destruction in A.D. 70. It may be that a day stands for a year, in which this period would be three and a half years. This is more plausible than a literal three and a half days. It may be that it is only to be understood as a short time, however many months or years are actually involved. Who would notice the death of the church and the Bible in just three and one-half days? Very few. But the whole world was aware of their demise in this account. They had time to throw parties and send congratulations to one another.

When God acts, he doesn't have to take forever. Remember how swiftly the iron curtain fell. Many of us believe that was a work of God. It will definitely be a work of God when His people, the church, together with His word, the Bible, are retrieved from the junk heap and given a position of honor in the world.

The events depicted here are reminiscent of the death and resurrection of Christ. He was killed by the forces of Satan who are led to think that they had won. But Jesus stayed dead for just three days, then God raised Him from the dead. Several days later He went up into heaven in a cloud. Only His apostles and two angels saw Him go on that occasion, but everyone will witness the revival and exaltation of the witnesses, just as everyone will see Jesus returning on a cloud when He comes to judge the living and the dead.

B. DESTRUCTION OF THE CITY OF THE WORLD (11:13)

In the same hour that the witnesses are raised and exalted the city is shaken by an earthquake which destroys a tenth of the city and kills 7,000 people. A small portion (1/10th) of the city is in ruins. 7,000 probably takes its meaning from the two symbolic numbers seven, meaning complete, and thousand, meaning a multitude. The destruction of this multitude who have resisted, thwarted, and rebelled against God is complete. But there are many more left. What happens to them? They are afraid, and they give glory to the God of heaven. The fear of God is lacking in most of the people of this world. When that fear is instilled, people will learn to give glory to God. This is the beginning of the dominion of Christ and His saints in the world.

Now the interlude ends and the vision returns to the seventh of the seven trumpets. In fact, there is one other thing that takes place before the trumpet is blown, but it is not revealed until after the vision of the seventh trumpet, when the elders around the throne explain to John what has happened. With the events related by these elders the plot is completed.

VI. THE LAST TRUMP FINISHES GOD'S PLAN (11:14-18)

A. THE SEVENTH TRUMPET SOUNDS (11:14-15)

The third woe is announced and the seventh angel blows his trumpet. This is the last trumpet. 1 Cor. 15:51-54 reveals what will happen when the last trumpet blows:

> We shall not all sleep, but we shall all be changed—in a moment, in the twinkling of an eye, at the last trumpet. For the trumpet will sound, and the dead will be raised incorruptible, and we shall be changed.

We don't really have to wonder about who will be raised or when. The Bible makes it clear. In John 5:28-29 Jesus Himself tells us:

Do not marvel at this; for the hour is coming in which all who are in the graves will hear His voice and come forth—those who have done good, to the resurrection of life, and those who have done evil, to the resurrection of condemnation.

In the hour of the resurrection all the dead will be raised to receive their eternal reward or judgment. It will be either life or condemnation. Jesus proclaims in John 14:2-3:

In My Father's house are many mansions; if *it were* not so, I would have told you. I go to prepare a place for you. And if I go and prepare a place for you, I will come again and receive you to Myself; that where I am, *there* you may be also.

The reason for His coming again is to take us to be where He is. He will take us to the place He has prepared for us. The location of this place is revealed in Rev. 21—the new heaven and new earth. The beauty of that place and the great joy that those who go there will have is described for us. I want to go there—Don't you?

Paul describes the events of that last trumpet in 1 Thess. 4:13-17. He is seeking to comfort those who are concerned about their loved ones who have "fallen asleep." Will the living saints have an advantage over them? Will they get to go to that place Jesus has prepared before the dead? Paul tells us not to worry. We that are alive at His coming will not go before the dead in Christ. First the dead will be raised, then we all will go together to meet the Lord, to be with Him forever.

In Matt. 25:31-34 we learn that when Jesus comes all the nations will be gathered before Him to be judged. He will divide the saved from the unsaved, to his right and left. He will then pronounce the reward of the saved to His right. "Come, you blessed of My Father, inherit the kingdom prepared for you from the foundation of the world." Then in verse 41 He pronounces the punishment of the wicked. "Then He will also say to those on the left hand, 'Depart from Me, you cursed, into the everlasting fire prepared for the devil and his angels.'" This everlasting fire is called *the lake of fire and brimstone* in Rev. 20.

When Jesus was about to leave He promised to return in order to receive those who belong to Him and take them to be with Him forever. In Acts

1:10-11, when Jesus went up to heaven, the apostles saw Him going in a cloud as He ascended out of their sight. On that occasion two men (angels, no doubt) said, "This same Jesus, who was taken up from you into heaven, will so come in like manner as you saw Him go into heaven." In Rev. 1:7 John is told, "Behold, He is coming with clouds, and every eye will see Him, even they who pierced Him. And all the tribes of the earth will mourn because of Him. Even so, Amen."

When Jesus returns He will be seen by all, not just the saved. When He comes the graves will be opened and all will come forth, not just the saved. At that time the saints and prophets as well as all who fear the Lord will be rewarded and the destroyers of the earth will be destroyed. These are the events ushered in by the last trumpet.

B. ELDERS WORSHIP GOD, AND DECLARE HIS MIGHTY WORKS (11:16-18)

When the trumpet blows the 24 elders fall down to worship. As they praise God they not only tell of the last trumpet judgment, but also of events that lead up to it. The three things for which the elders praise God are: 1) "The Lord has taken His great power and reigned [begun to reign];"[3] 2) "The nations were angry (raged);" and 3) "Your great wrath has come, and the time of the dead, that they should be judged." It is the third item, the great wrath of God, that is the result of the blowing of the last trumpet. However, the elders are praising God for the events leading up to the final judgment.

1. The Lord Has Taken His Great Power and Has Begun to Reign. When the seventh trumpet was blown there were loud voices from heaven proclaiming, "The kingdom of the world has become the kingdom of our Lord and of his Christ, and he will reign for ever and ever" (NIV). The voices are proclaiming what had already occurred, not what is about to occur now that the trumpet has blown. The dominion of Christ over the kingdom of

---

[3] *ἐβασίλευσας (ebasileusas)*, from *βασιλεύω (basileuo)* , to *reign* is in the aorist tense. This may be likened to the simple past tense. Its action is point action unless indicated otherwise by the context. In this case the reign of Christ did not just happen at some point in the past. His reign is eternal. The aorist tense here is undoubtedly the *inceptive aorist*. It speaks of the beginning point of the reign. "You have taken your great power and **have begun to reign**." (Dana and Mantay's *A Manual Grammar of the Greek New Testament,* The MacMillan Co., 1948 calls this use of the aorist tense *the ingressive aorist. See page 196 (2).*

the world is the first thing for which the elders praise God. According to the best authorities the word *kingdoms* in the KJV and NKJV should be rendered *kingdom*, (singular).[4] This is the reading in most translations. The word *kingdom* basically means *dominion*. The dominion of the world is destined to become the dominion of Christ.

With the resurrection of the two witnesses, the destruction of a tenth of the great city, and the killing of 7,000 people, the rest are caused to fear and give God the glory. Here is where God takes His great power and begins to reign. He takes back the dominion of the world so that it becomes the dominion of the Lord. This reign is referred to as the thousand year reign (millennium) in Revelation chapter 20. But the reign does not stop at the end of the millennium. His reign goes on into eternity in the new heaven and earth. He shall reign throughout eternity, forever and ever.

2. The Nations Raged. The second thing mentioned by the elders is the fact that the nations were angry. In Psalm 2:1-3 David writes:

> Why do the nations rage, And the people plot a vain thing? The kings of the earth set themselves, And the rulers take counsel together, Against the LORD and against His Anointed, saying, "Let us break Their bonds in pieces And cast away Their cords from us."

The anger of the nations against God can be traced throughout history. But there is one time in particular when the anger of the nations causes them to rage against God. Rev. 20:7-9 tells us of the rage of the nations at the end of the thousand years reign when Satan is loosed. Just prior to the final judgment in Rev. 20 the nations are deceived by Satan, who emerges from the abyss, and they are turned against God and His people. As a result the nations rage against the Lord and His anointed. This is the signal for their destruction and the final judgment.

3. God's Great Wrath Has Come. The blowing of the final trumpet heralds the coming of the wrath of God. It ushers in the final judgment in which the righteous are rewarded and the wicked are destroyed. The wicked

---

[4]*The Textus Receptus,* from which the KJV was translated, has βασιλείαι *(basileiai – kingdoms)* in the plural while the Majority Text and the Nestle/UBS text have βασιλεία *(basileia - kingdom)* in the singular.

will have to pay for all their sins by their own suffering in the lake of fire. The righteous, on the other hand, will stand before God spotless, because they have been continually cleansed from their sins (1 John 1:7-10; 2:1-2). God erases the sin from their past so that it does not appear in the book of the record of their life. Because of the blood of the Lamb, they are saved by the grace of God, and will enter into eternal joy in the presence of the Father, the Son, the Holy Spirit, and all the angels. This is a future worth going all out for! I want to be among the righteous, those saved by grace. How about you?

VII. THE CURTAIN OPENS TO BEGIN THE DRAMA (Read 11:19)

Prior to this, only one article of temple furniture was yet to be introduced. Now John sees the ark of the covenant, completing the symbolism of God's temple. The covenant represented by the ark of the covenant in heaven is not the old covenant of laws given by Moses, but the new covenant of grace and truth which came in the person of Jesus Christ (John 1:17). God says to the Messiah in Isa. 42:6-8: "I, the LORD, ...will keep You and give You as a covenant to the people...." In the vision this ark was probably situated under God's throne, since the ark of the covenant was under the mercy seat, the symbol of God's throne, in the Old Testament temple.

John was already in the temple in his vision. What did he mean when he said, "the temple of God was opened in heaven"? It was like saying that the curtain was opened in the theater. The play is about to begin. The lightning, noises, thunderings, earthquake and hail are announcing the beginning of the play.[5] Such phenomena are used in Revelation as portents of the momentous things which are about to happen. Think of these things as the drums and loud music of the overture, depicting the sounds of war, like Tchaikovsky's *1812 Overture* which depicts the explosions of gunfire and cannons and the loud noises of the war of 1812. God's overture is played by the forces of nature—lightning flashes, loud noises, great rolls of thunder, the heaving

---

[5]Although we are dealing with symbolic imagery the figures are drawn from a real event. When the covenant was given at Mount Sinai such signs occurred in reality. Exodus 20:18 states, "Now all the people witnessed the thunderings, the lightning flashes, the sound of the trumpet, and the mountain smoking; and when the people saw it, they trembled and stood afar off." See also Hebrew 12:18-24.

earth, the hailstones which threaten life and limb. This is a fitting overture for the war of the ages that follows in this drama. Now let the play begin!

THINGS THAT ARE TO HAPPEN
Part Two: DRAMA OF THE AGE IN SEVEN ACTS

Rev. 12:1 – 22:5

Chapter 12

ACT 1: THE CONFLICT IN HEAVEN
Rev. Chapter 12

THE DRAMA'S CAST OF CHARACTERS

The players in this drama include, in order of appearance:

1. The Woman wearing the crown of twelve stars, also called, and *the bride of Christ, the New Jerusalem, and a witness*;

2. The Man-child—also called, *the Lamb, the King of kings, the Word of God*, and *the Son of Man*;

3. The great red Dragon with seven heads and ten horns, with a diadem on each head, also called *the Devil and Satan*;

4. The fallen angels of the Dragon;

5. The angelic army of heaven led by the angel Michael;

6. The Servants of God, the children of the Woman who bear the testimony of Christ, also called *the 144,000, those who dwell in heaven,* and *witnesses*;

7. The Beast with seven heads and ten horns with a diadem on each horn;

8. The False Prophet, the beast with 2 horns, like a lamb;

9. The followers of the Beast and False Prophet, also called *those who dwell on earth*;

10. The Image of the Beast created by the False Prophet;

11. Babylon the Great, the mother of Harlots

12. Various kings and kingdoms, captains and merchants of the earth;

13. Various angels;

14. Birds of prey, meat eating scavengers;

15. God.

Some of the words, such as *Woman, Dragon, Beast, False Prophet,* and *Harlot* are not capitalized in the Bible quotations, but they are in this volume since they are presented here as the names of actors in the divine drama. Others, such as *Death* are capitalized because they are presented as persons (personified) in the drama.

Although some scenes in this act are be set on earth, yet the conflict in this chapter is on a spiritual or heavenly plain. For example, when the woman with the crown of twelve stars bears the Man-child, we are looking at a symbolic representation of the coming of Christ. The woman in the symbol is not Mary, but the Israel of God. While Mary on earth brings forth the Christ, the reality behind the scenes is that this was all done in heaven.

SCENE 1: THE WOMAN, THE MAN-CHILD, AND THE DRAGON

Setting—On Earth (Read 12:1-6)

A. THE STARS OF THE SHOW—THE MAN-CHILD AND THE WOMAN

We are introduced to the stars of the play in this scene. The Man-child has appeared in different forms in previous visions. In chapter 1 He is an awesome white-haired person with a sword coming out of His mouth, with eyes that were flames of fire and feet like highly polished bronze, and with an overwhelming voice that was like the sound of many waters. In chapter 5 He is the Lamb with seven horns and seven eyes Who had been slain, but now is alive. In chapter 10 He is the giant Angel with one foot on earth and one foot in the ocean. Now we see him as a Man-child, born of a Woman who is wearing a victory crown of 12 stars.

The Woman in this scene is the co-star in the drama. She has the sun for her robe, the moon for her footstool, and a crown (*stephanos*)[1] of twelve stars on her head. She is pregnant with a Man-child. Like the crown promised to those who overcome in Smyrna (2:10) and in Philadelphia (3:11), like the crowns worn by the 24 elders in chapter 4, the rider on the white horse in chapter 6, and like the crown that Christ Himself will wear when He comes to reap the harvest of His people in chapter 14, this crown is the victory wreath. There is a notable difference, however. This is a wreath containing twelve stars. It indicates that she is a symbol of God's people, Israel. God chose to bring the Christ into the world through Israel.

The woman who is the symbol of Israel bears the Man-child who is the Christ. The stars in her crown may well represent the twelve patriarchs, the sons of Israel (Jacob), or perhaps the twelve tribes of Israel. In either case the number 12 is a symbol of God's people. Through the drama she is presented in different forms, as is Christ also. At the end of the drama she is seen as the bride of Christ.

B. THE ANTAGONIST—THE DRAGON

There is someone else waiting for the birth of this Man-child—waiting to devour him. He is the great fiery red Dragon with seven heads and ten horns, with a crown (diadem)[2] on each head. His tail drew one-third of the stars of heaven and cast them down to earth. What does this symbol represent? Verse 9 tells us that this Dragon represents none other than Satan, that ancient serpent seen in the garden of Eden. The stars, therefore, would be the angels who joined Satan in his rebellion and subsequent fall.

C. THE DRAGON'S ATTEMPTS TO DEVOUR THE MAN-CHILD THWARTED

The first thing seen in this scene is the pregnant woman with the Dragon waiting to devour the Man-child as soon as He is born. When the Man-child is born He eludes the Dragon by being caught up to the throne of God. In this one statement the whole of Christ's life, death, resurrection, and ascension is encapsulated. He escapes all the attempts of Satan to destroy Him.

---

[1] στέφανος *(staphanos)*—laurel wreath worn by victors in the games and in war. Roman Caesars frequently wore them proclaiming their victory over the nations.

[2] διαδήματα *(diademata—diadems)*. These are the regal crowns of authority worn by kings.

While Jesus was on earth He seemed to be in danger of being devoured by the Devil. Through King Herod Satan had every male child under age two around Bethlehem murdered (Matt. 2:16). Herod failed to kill Jesus, the target of his slaughter, because He escaped to Egypt. We don't know how many times Satan tried to destroy Christ, since they are probably not all recorded. We know Satan tried to destroy Him through temptations, and he tried to kill Him by having Him thrown off a cliff. All his efforts were in vain.

Finally, when Satan influenced the Jewish leaders to crucify Jesus with the help of the Roman officials, he thought he had succeeded in thwarting God's plan. He thought he had devoured the Man-child through his most powerful weapon—death. He was wrong. Yes, Jesus entered the realm of death, but then He broke the bonds of death and the grave, and He arose victorious.

He defeated death for Himself and for us also. Because He arose, we have the hope of resurrection from the dead. In 1 Cor 15:20 Paul writes, "But now Christ is risen from the dead, *and* has become the firstfruits of those who have fallen asleep." In verse 22 he says, "For as in Adam all die, even so in Christ all shall be made alive." What a glorious hope. Finally, after a little more than a month following His resurrection, He ascended to the throne of God and sat down with Him on His throne, "For He [Christ] must reign until He has put all enemies under His feet. The last enemy *that* will be destroyed is death" (1 Cor. 15:25-26).

The Man-child is destined to rule the nations with a rod of iron. The word for *rule* is ποιμαίνῃ (*poimaine—to shepherd*). The shepherd's rod was used to govern and protect the sheep. The nations are to be the ones who benefit from this rule, whereas the human governments which oppose Christ are to be broken to pieces as if they were pottery (See Rev. 2:27; 19:15; Isa. 11:4; Psalm 2:9).

D. THE DRAGON'S ATTEMPT TO DESTROY THE WOMAN FAILS

Every good drama is based upon a conflict to be resolved. Here the conflict is caused by Satan's desire to destroy Christ—to prevent Him from carrying out His mission, the redemption of mankind. The protagonist is

Christ, represented here as the Man-child, and elsewhere as the Lamb, et. al. The antagonist is Satan, the Dragon.

Now that Christ is caught up to heaven and is personally beyond Satan's reach, Satan tries to destroy the Woman and her children—i.e., Christ's representatives on earth—His servants. The Woman is not caught up to heaven as the Man-child was, but she is, never-the-less, under divine protection (Matt.16:18). She flees to the wilderness where God nourishes her for 1260 days, just as God nourished Israel in the wilderness when she fled from Egypt (v. 6). Although all the adults but two who came out of Egypt died in the wilderness, Israel survived. We will return to the picture of the woman in the wilderness in Scene 3.

This picture is represented as taking place symbolically. The reality is played out on earth. As Israel gives birth to the Man-child in the symbolic picture, a young daughter of Israel, Mary, gives birth to the Christ-child in a stable in Bethlehem, and she wraps Him in swaddling clothes and lays Him in a manger. As the Dragon tries to devour the Man-child by eating Him up, Satan uses evil men to try to destroy Jesus Christ in Bethlehem, Nazareth, and Jerusalem. This should help us see that the counterpart of the warfare on earth is a spiritual warfare. There is a greater spiritual reality behind the physical.

SCENE 2: WAR BETWEEN MICHAEL AND THE DRAGON

Setting—In the Heavenly Realm (Read 12:7-12)

A. THE FORCES OF EVIL—THE DRAGON AND HIS ANGELS

Satan is himself a rebellious angel. He is a created being since only God has no beginning. All things were created by God. All that was created by God was good, otherwise God would be the source of evil. Satan, then, must have originally been part of God's good creation; but angels and men are moral creatures (i.e., with a free will, the power of choice). Some angels, like men, are good beings gone bad by choice. Satan and his angels chose to rebel against God, and so became adversaries, enemies of God.

The third of the stars which the Dragon drew with his tail are the angels who followed him in his rebellion. Satan himself is called *the day star* (*Lucifer*—Isa. 14:12-15). The angels who followed him in his rebellion are his forces, marshaled and commanded by him. Lest we doubt the identity of the Dragon, we are told that he is that ancient serpent (who tempted Eve in the garden) the Devil and Satan. The dragon (Satan) is depicted as having seven heads and ten horns. Heads are the symbols of governments or kingdoms. Horns are generic symbols of power. Seven is the symbol of completeness, and ten is a small indefinite number. These symbols are more fully explained in Rev. 17 in the explanation of the Beast.

The war in heaven has its counterpart on earth. As the Dragon with seven heads and ten horns wages war in the spiritual realm the Beast with seven heads and ten horns of chapter 13, his agents, governmental powers wage war against the saints on earth. Satan manifests himself through world governments by which he persecutes the saints. They are, you might say, "created in his image." He used Herod, for instance, to try to destroy Christ at his birth.

The seven heads represent all of the kingdoms of the world which he presses into His service to fight against the plan of God in all ages. Therefore the crowns are on the heads. Also included are the governmental powers which arise out of these kingdoms (the horns). Another plausible interpretation of the ten horns is that they represent limited power. Satan has considerable power, but all power (seven horns) belongs to the Lamb, who is the Christ, God incarnate. Just as Satan was manifest in Eden in the body of a serpent (the Dragon is the serpent—12:9), so he is embodied in the kingdoms and other institutions of this world which he uses to promote his own evil cause.

B. THE ARMY OF HEAVEN—MICHAEL AND HIS ANGELS

Michael is the archangel who served as the prince of God's Israel in the Old Testament (See Dan.10:13,20-21; 12:1; Jude 9). Some see Michael here as a symbol of Christ, the Prince of Peace, the prince of Spiritual Israel. Michael is the commander of the army of God's angels, the host of heaven. Satan and his forces had no chance against these forces.

C. THE SPIRITUAL PLANE OF OUR WARFARE

The war in heaven depicts the forces that are behind the war on earth. Our battle is really a spiritual one. We may think evil men are our enemies.

They are only the victims of Satan's deceit, used by him to accomplish his purposes. The ones we really have to fight are Satan and his spiritual forces of Evil. Eph. 6:12 declares:

> For we do not wrestle against flesh and blood, but against principalities, against powers, against the rulers of the darkness of this age, against spiritual *hosts* of wickedness in the heavenly *places*.

From this perspective we are better able to see that our earthly conflicts are only part of the larger spiritual battle.

D. SATAN DEFEATED AND CAST DOWN TO EARTH (12:8-12)

What are the results of this battle? "Now salvation, and strength, and the kingdom of our God, and the power of His Christ have come." What are the weapons that won this battle? "And they overcame him by the blood of the Lamb and by the word of their testimony." While the battle scene is in heaven, i.e., a spiritual battle pictured symbolically, it is events on earth which bring about Satan's defeat—i.e., the death of Christ and the preaching of the gospel. These two things are also what brought about salvation, strength, the kingdom of God, and the power of Christ.

1. By the Blood of the Lamb. Imagine the bewilderment and consternation of Satan when he learned that by crucifying Christ he helped in his own defeat. He fell prey to a colossal trap that was carefully laid and kept secret from the foundation of the world. Paul tells us in 1 Cor. 2:7-8:

> But we speak the wisdom of God in a mystery, the hidden *wisdom* which God ordained before the ages for our glory, which none of the rulers (princes) of this age knew; for had they known, they would not have crucified the Lord of glory.

The rulers of this age are not human rulers, but the spiritual principalities of Satan. He didn't know what he was doing when he had Jesus crucified. God had planned all along that Jesus should die for the sins of the world. This is the plan of salvation, devised and kept secret by God before the worlds were framed. If Satan and the spiritual rulers of this age had known this, they would have turned heaven and earth upside down to keep Jesus alive. When Jesus suffered and died, the sins of all men were paid for.

Anyone can now come to Christ and be forgiven. By this means all who accept Christ are snatched out of Satan's hand. What a blow to the forces of Satan!

2. By the Word of Their Testimony. The Dragon is filled with consternation and anger when the message of the gospel dawns upon him. He had helped in his own defeat, because he worked so hard to kill the Man-child. When Jesus was put into the grave, Satan probably threw a celebration party. He didn't know that Sunday was coming and all his plans would be overthrown.

The message of the gospel is "the word of their testimony" that played a necessary part in the defeat of Satan. If that message had never been proclaimed, there would never have been anyone saved by the blood of Christ. Belief of that message prompts us to yield our lives to Christ to receive salvation and sonship. In 1 Cor. 1:21 Paul puts it this way: "For since, in the wisdom of God, the world through wisdom did not know God, it pleased God through the foolishness of the message preached to save those who believe."

If Jesus had stayed in the grave there would have been no salvation, no redemption, no justification, no resurrection to eternal life. In like manner if the message of His death and resurrection had never been preached, there still would be no salvation, no justification, and no resurrection to life for mankind. Paul declared in 1 Cor. 15:1-2 that we are saved by the gospel, unless we have believed in vain. What is he talking about? In verse 14 he says, "And if Christ is not risen, then our preaching is empty and your faith is also empty." The word *vain* means *empty*. This is the same word used in verse two. In other words, we have believed in vain if Christ has not risen. Why? Verse 17 tells us, "And if Christ is not risen, your faith is futile [vain]; you are still in your sins!" If Christ has not risen, then we are not saved. Our sins are still upon us, and we are destined for eternal destruction.

But take heart. Three days after He died Jesus rose from the dead, giving validity and power to His death. Rom. 1:4 says that He was, "...declared *to be* the Son of God with power according to the Spirit of holiness, by the resurrection from the dead." As the Son of God, He was able not only to die for our sins, but to rise from the dead. It took the resurrection to validate His death. If He had stayed dead He would not have been God in the flesh, and His death could not have paid for our sins. 1 Cor. 15:20-23 declares:

> But now Christ is risen from the dead, *and* has become the firstfruits of those who have fallen asleep. For since by man *came* death, by Man also *came* the resurrection of the dead. For as in Adam all die, even so in Christ all shall be made alive. But each one in his own order: Christ the firstfruits, afterward those *who are* Christ's at His coming.

Death could not hold Jesus because of who He is. Acts 2:23-24 says of Jesus:

> Him, being delivered by the determined purpose and foreknowledge of God, you have taken by lawless hands, have crucified, and put to death; whom God raised up, having loosed the pains of death, because it was not possible that He should be held by it.

Neither will it be possible for death to hold those who belong to Christ, who have been redeemed by His blood. Jesus was the firstfruits to be raised from the dead, never to die again. Afterwards, at His coming, all His servants will be raised to eternal life. Heb.2:14-15 states:

> Inasmuch then as the children have partaken of flesh and blood, He Himself likewise shared in the same, that through death He might destroy him who had the power of death, that is, the devil, and release those who through fear of death were all their lifetime subject to bondage.

E. THE RAGE OF THE DRAGON

Satan, having been cast down to earth, is in a rage because he knows he is defeated. He also knows that he has only a short time left, and he knows that he is destined for the lake of fire prepared for the Devil and his angels (Matt. 25:41). How does he know this? Because the apostles whom Jesus appointed as special witnesses of His resurrection bore their testimony which revealed the mystery of the plan of God, the results of Christ's death, burial and resurrection. All the apostles suffered death because of their testimony with the exception of John who is writing this book of Revelation. "They did not love their lives to the death." This testimony is called *the gospel (good news) of Christ*. This is God's power to save all who put their trust in Christ (Rom. 1:16).

1. Dwellers in Heaven Told to Rejoice. Praise God! Now salvation has come and I am redeemed, justified, and destined to be raised to eternal life. Now I am a member of His kingdom, under His power and strength—a servant of Christ and a child of God who is the Lord of the universe. I am one whose dwelling is in heaven, not on earth.

2. Woe to Inhabitants of Earth and Sea! "The devil has come down to you, having great wrath, because he knows that he has a short time." The inhabitants of the earth are those whose dwelling is on earth and not in heaven. Where do you live? Where is your home? If it is in heaven you need have no fear of the angry devil who prowls about "like a roaring lion seeking whom he may devour." Don't get me wrong. You must always be sober and watchful so that Satan will not deceive you and take away your crown. But you don't have to be afraid of him. He may be able to kill your body, but he cannot kill your soul. You should rather fear him who is able to destroy both body and soul in hell (Matt. 10:28).

Satan has great wrath because he knows he is defeated. This battle was the decisive one and it took place at the time of the Jesus' death, resurrection, and ascension. When the good news was proclaimed to mankind men began to escape from Satan's bondage by being washed in the blood of the Lamb.

Although the decisive battle is already won it is not over. We still have battles to fight because Satan keeps on fighting in his anger. He persecutes, deceives, and entices God's people, doing all the damage he can while he still has time. He and his forces also work hard to keep the people of the world from accepting Christ. First he tries to keep them from believing in Christ. If he fails in this, he tries to convince them that true repentance is not necessary. Finally he tries to deceive them into believing that as long as they just believe the facts about Jesus they don't have to commit their lives to Him as Lord by obeying Him. Whenever he fails in this, Satan has lost another soul to Christ. The result is the everlasting salvation of the believer, and this makes Satan very angry.

F. THE ACCUSER REPLACED WITH AN ADVOCATE

Formerly in the court of heaven Satan was the prosecutor accusing the brethren. His names, the *Devil* and *Satan* mean *slanderer* and *adversary*. In Job 1:6-12 and 2:1-6 he came before God to accuse and slander Job. In Zech. 3 :1 he served the same function in accusing Joshua the high priest. Now Satan has lost that privilege (v. 10), "...for the accuser of our brethren, who accused them before our God day and night, has been cast down." Now Satan can no longer stand before God as my accuser. In his place is my advocate, Jesus the righteous (1 John 2:1-2), and no one can successfully prosecute an accusation against me. Paul writes in Rom. 8:33-34:

> Who shall bring a charge against God's elect? *It is* God who
> justifies. Who *is* he who condemns? *It is* Christ who died,
> and furthermore is also risen, who is even at the right hand of
> God, who also makes intercession for us.

SCENE 3: SATAN PURSUES THE WOMAN AND HER CHILDREN
Setting—On Earth (Read 12:13-17)

A. AN OVERVIEW OF THE SCENE

The dragon, having been cast down to earth, persecutes the woman. She flees into the wilderness but the Dragon pursues her and tries to destroy her as with a flood of water. He is pictured as spewing the water out of his mouth in order that she might be caught up in the deluge. This, however, fails. The earth is pictured as opening up to swallow the water Satan spews after the Woman. She reaches a place where she is protected and nourished for 3½ years or a time, times, and a half time from the face of the Dragon. During this time she cannot be destroyed for she is under divine protection.

The Woman with the crown of twelve stars has children who bear testimony to Jesus Christ. Who is this Woman? We have already pointed out that she is God's Israel. She is, however, both physical Israel before the cross and spiritual Israel after the cross. The prophets did not view Israel and the church as two separate institutions but as one—i.e., two stages of the same institution. Jesus was born of the Jews; but Christians also are children of this Woman. In Gal. 4:26 she is represented in these words, "...the Jerusalem above is free, which is the mother of us all." The *us* in this verse refers to Christians.

Perhaps the 12 stars in her crown now refer to the 12 apostles of Christ. At the resurrection of Christ and the beginning of His church the woman went through a metamorphosis. Before this the people of God were identified by their physical lineage, being descended from Abraham, Isaac and Jacob in the flesh. After the cross, the unbelievers are pruned from the tree of Israel (Rom. 11:17-26) and believers from among the Gentiles are grafted in with the remnant of Israel who are believers. Israel, including both Jews and Gentiles, is now known as the church, the community of believers in Christ. For a more complete study of this subject go to *Appendix D: The Israel of God.*

B. A PLACE OF REFUGE PREPARED FOR THE WOMAN IN THE WILDERNESS

Earlier, in verse 6, we were told that the Woman who bore the Man-child fled into the wilderness where she had a place prepared for her by God. She was to be fed there for a period of 1260 days. Now we see why she had to flee. The dragon was after her. Verse 6 was a kind of preview of what was to happen after a very angry Satan was cast down to earth.

C. THREE WAYS OF REPRESENTING THE PERIOD OF PERSECUTION

Although the number 42 is not used in chapter 12, it is used in chapter 11 as the period of time that the Holy City was to be trodden under the feet of the Gentiles (11:2). This city, like the Woman, is a symbol of the people of God. The 1260 days of 12:6 is the same period of time as the 1260 days that the witnesses prophecy in sackcloth (11:3). These are different ways of representing the same truth–i.e., the persecution of the people of God (also called *servants of God* and *witnesses*). Another way of representing this period is *a time and times and a half time.* This can be translated into three and one-half years. 1260 days at 30 days to the month is exactly 42 months. 42 months at 12 months to the year is exactly three and a half years. They are all the same period of time.

Our text says that when the dragon was thrown down to earth he persecuted the woman who bore the Man-child (12:13). As a result the woman was given two wings like an eagle so she could fly into the wilderness to her place where she would be nourished for a time and times and a half time from the presence of the serpent (12:14). In Dan. 7:25, a parallel prophecy speaks of the persecution of God's people for a time and times and a half time (see Daniel 12:7 where the same time-period is given).

D. The Source of the Wilderness Symbol and the Number 42

The wilderness refuge is a symbol taken from Israel's escape into the wilderness from Egyptian bondage. They were there for 42 years. It is the number 42 itself, not the unit of time (month or year) that is important here. After escaping from Egypt Israel stayed in the wilderness at Sinai until the second year (Num. 10:11-12), and some time later that year they were assigned 40 more years in the wilderness because of unbelief (Num. 14:34). Their sojourn in the wilderness was a period of trial and tribulation. The 1260 days of the woman's sojourn in the wilderness is appropriately symbolized as a wilderness experience like that of the Israelites.

E. Source of the Symbol of "A Time and Times and a Half Time"

The symbolism of three and a half years is taken from many sources in the history of the Israelites. Most prominent among these is the three and a half years of the siege of Jerusalem before its conquest and destruction by the Romans in A.D. 70. It also corresponds roughly to the abomination of the temple in Jerusalem when Antiochus Epiphanes of Syria (the Seleucid Empire) abolished the true worship during the 2nd century B.C. Three and a half years was also the period of time that rain did not fall in Israel due to the prayer of Elijah. We have already noticed that 42 is the number of years the Israelites spent in the wilderness.

F. What About the Number 1260?

The numbers three and a half and 42 are both associated with the sufferings of God's people, thus the symbolic significance of these number; but the number 1260 is not associated with any period of suffering or anything else in scripture. Perhaps it is intended to represent a specific period of time in which the church in this world would suffer persecution and tribulation. In other words, since 1260, as a number, has no other relationship to the suffering of God's people, perhaps we are to understand it as an indication of the length of the period of suffering. That period of time might be applied generally, as a principle of church history, representing an indefinite period of time, or it may be applied specifically to a historical occurrence of persecution during this time period. It is my opinion that it could be both. Perhaps there is a double meaning in some of these prophecies. Symbolism, however, is involved with this number.

I believe that the 1260 days are to be understood as a period approximating 1260 years. I base this upon the day for a year interpretation found several times in Old Testament symbolism. For a more thorough treatment of this theory go to *Appendix B: The "Day For a Year" Theory.* I also believe that this period stands generally for the whole of the persecution of God's people throughout the Christian age. It is interesting to note that 1260 is a multiple of twelve, the number of God's people.

G. THE DRAGON PURSUES THE WOMAN'S CHILDREN

Because Christians are the Woman's children, they are the brothers of the Man-child that she bore. Those who have the testimony of Christ are the children of God, and therefore the brothers of Christ. Jesus was born of Israel, and we are the children of Israel, the church, who is our mother. This also makes us the brothers of Christ (see Heb. 2:11-12).

The Dragon is very angry because the Man-child is out of his reach, and he cannot destroy the Woman, so he goes after the Christians, those who have the testimony of Christ and keep God's commands. We can assume that the time frame of this persecution will be the same period that the woman (church) is in the wilderness. This will be born out in the next chapter. In this drama we are dealing with a specific period of persecution called 1260 days (years?).

236

Chapter 13

ACT 2: THE SAINTS PERSECUTED ON EARTH
Rev. 13:1- 14:5

With the escape of the Man-child and the Woman who bore Him, the Dragon (Satan) turns his attention to the followers of Christ to make war on them. In the first act there was war in heaven between the spiritual forces of good and evil. In the second act the agents of Satan are waging war against the servants of God on earth. The time frame of this persecution is represented as three and a half years, or 42 months, or 1260 days. The church is being protected from destruction during this period of time. In chapter 11 she is the Holy City being trampled by the Gentiles and two witnesses prophesying in sackcloth. In chapter 12 she is the woman in the wilderness.

SCENE 1: THE BEAST MAKES WAR ON THE SAINTS
Setting—On Earth(Read 13:1-10)

A. *THE DRAGON CALLS FORTH THE SEVEN-HEADED BEAST*

In verse 1 the King James Version and New King James Version both have John saying, "Then **I** stood on the sand of the sea." The Nestle/United Bible Society text and most other translations say, "Then **he** stood on the sand of the sea."[1] The pronoun *he* refers to the Dragon. This makes sense,

---

[1] It would have been easy to change the second person accidentally to the first person since in the Greek *he stood* is ἐστάθη *(estathe)*, while *I stood* is ἐστάθην *(estathen)*. The only

237

since the Beast is in Satan's employ, the leader on earth of the war against the saints. The Dragon had been thrown down to earth and now goes to make war with the children of the Woman. He would be expected to call forth his agent through whom He would carry out this warfare.

Verse 1 continues, "And I saw a beast rising up out of the sea, having seven heads and ten horns, and on his horns ten crowns...." The sea is a symbol of peoples, multitudes, nations, and tongues (See 17:15; Dan. 7:2-3). The sea is always in motion, often in turmoil—a fitting symbol of the people and nations of the world from which the kingdoms and governments of men arise. This Beast represents persecution of God's people through the governmental powers of the world. These governments lend themselves to Satan's opposition of God, to His Anointed One, and to the people of God.

Out of the sea comes a monster that looks like he is straight out of science fiction, or out of some of the ancient tales of adventure with beasts having several heads. It reminds us of creatures from Sinbad's adventures in *the Arabian Nights*, or of the adventures of Ulysses in Homer's *The Odyssey*.

The Beast seems to have been created in the image of the Dragon. Each has seven heads and ten horns and each is red in color (see 12:3 and 17:3), but one is a Dragon while the other, the Beast, is a mixture of a leopard, bear, and lion; and the crowns[2] of the Beast are on the horns instead of the heads, indicating that the ten-horn kingdoms are in power during this period of 42 months or 1260 days.

Whereas the heads and horns of the Dragon represent the persecuting powers in a general sense throughout time, the Beast in chapter 13 represents a specific period of persecution. The events of this act are future to John's day since he is seeing visions of the things to take place afterward. Although John received the Revelation during the days of Rome, the sixth head, the kingdoms represented by the horns had not yet come into existence.

Whereas the seven heads of the Beast represent the world powers throughout the ages which are persecutors of God's people, the Beast in John's day was the Roman Empire, the 6th head. This head had ten horns.

---

difference is the addition of one letter v (*nu*).

[2] διαδήματα (*diademata—diadems*). These are the regal crowns of authority worn by kings.

The horns are persecuting kingdoms which arise out of Rome. This is explained further in the exposition of Rev. 17, and in *Appendix F*. The 13th chapter concerns the ten-horn phase of the Beast, the time when the kingdoms arising out of Rome are in power. This is indicated by the fact that the crowns are on the horns. These horns all come under the unifying leadership of another beast, called *the False Prophet*. This beast is introduced later in the chapter.

"...and on his heads a blasphemous name." It was characteristic of world powers to claim divinity. Often the emperor was worshiped as a god. This is blasphemy. When Jesus claimed to be the Son of God he was accused of blasphemy by His enemies. If He were not who He claimed to be, it would indeed have been blasphemy, but it is not blasphemy for God to claim to be God. On the other hand, the king of Babylonia made such a blasphemous claim, and was severely judged by God. Isa. 14:13-14 declares of the king of Babylon:

> For you have said in your heart: "I will ascend into heaven, I will exalt my throne above the stars of God; I will also sit on the mount of the congregation On the farthest sides of the north; I will ascend above the heights of the clouds, I will be like the Most High."

Even as John was writing the book of Revelation the emperor Domitian had images of himself in all the cities of the empire, and his agents were forcing the people to worship him through these images. The people were required to look upon Domitian as a god. This was truly blasphemy. The same thing applies to other kings in the Roman Empire. Even in Paul's day emperors Caligula and Nero demanded worship as gods. This blasphemy continues in the ten-horn stage of the Beast. The name of the Beast is called *a name of blasphemy* because of the claims of the Beast. Instead of exalting God, the rulers of this empire exalt themselves and blaspheme the name of God.

B. REFERENCE TO THE FOUR BEASTS OF DANIEL

Watch closely as this Beast emerges from the sea. He has ten horns, looks like a leopard, has the feet of a bear and the mouth of a lion. Apparently the Holy Spirit wants us to connect this Beast with the four beasts in Daniel. Dan. 7:3-7 tells us, "And four great beasts came up from the sea, each different from the other. The first *was* like a lion ...another beast, a second, like a bear ...another, like a leopard ...a fourth beast ...had ten horns." These four beasts of Daniel, like the seven-headed Beast of Revelation, came up out of the sea.

Daniel begins where he is, with the Babylonian Empire represented as a lion, and goes forward through the bear (Medo-Persia), the leopard (Greece), and the ten-horned beast (the Roman Empire). John, on the other hand, sees them in reverse order since he is prophesying during the fourth beast, the ten-horned beast of Rome. From there he looks backward to see the leopard, the bear and the lion as part of the description of the seven-headed Beast. The four beasts of Daniel represent four specific governments. The seven-headed Beast is the symbol of persecution, and is embodied in all persecuting governments. The four beasts of Daniel are probably to be understood as four of the seven heads of the Beast of Revelation.

As Daniel saw the Lion, the Bear, the Leopard, and the ten-horned beast, the Bear (Medo-Persia) had three ribs in his mouth, indicating he had devoured the three preceding empires—i.e., Babylonia, Assyria, and Egypt. These make up the first six heads that are described in Rev. 17:9-10, "Five have fallen, one is, and the other has not yet come." The five that had fallen in John's day are Egypt, Assyria, Babylonia, Medo-Persia, and Greece. The one that exists in John's day is Rome. All these were all involved in oppressing the people of God.

The number *seven* is a symbol for completeness or perfection. The seven-headed Beast is a symbol for all persecuting governments. Just as the seven churches of Asia in Rev. 2 and 3 are seven specific congregations, they serve to represent the whole church. Each head of the Beast is a specific persecuting power while the seven, taken together, serve to represent all the persecuting powers, however many they may be.

The angel in Daniel explains that the four beasts are four kings (verse 17). Then he says that the fourth beast is a fourth kingdom and would be different from the other kingdoms (Verse 23). The fourth beast, one of four kings, is a fourth kingdom. That sounds like a contradiction. Now which is it? King or kingdom? The resolution to this contradiction is found in the fact that a king and his kingdom are so closely related that often one is put for the other. This is a figure of speech called *metonymy*. *King* equals *kingdom*. Read Dan. 2:37-40; 7:17,23; 8:20-22 for examples of this use of *king* for *kingdom*. This is important because it will help us understand the explanation of the seven-headed, ten-horned beast in Rev. 17. For more information on Daniel's vision of the beasts go to *Appendix G* at the back of this book.

C. SOURCE OF THE BEAST'S POWER AND AUTHORITY

Verse 2 continues, "The dragon gave him his power, his throne, and great authority." The Beast is Satan's agent, working under his authority and doing his bidding. To serve the Beast, then, is to serve the Dragon (Satan).[3] Rom. 13:1-6 and 1 Pet. 2:13-14 teach us that human governments are ordained by God and receive their authority from Him. When they fulfill their proper function they do so by God's authority, but when they pervert their power to fulfill Satan's purposes, they do so not by God's authority but by the authority of Satan. When a government becomes a persecutor of God's people and sets itself up as a god, and allows itself to be used to propagate false teachings and anti-Christian philosophies, then it is functioning under Satan's authority, not God's. That government becomes part of the seven-headed Beast and an agent of Satan.

D. THE HEAD HEALED FROM THE DEATH WOUND (v. 3)

"And *I saw* one of his heads as if it had been mortally wounded, and his deadly wound was healed. And all the world marveled and followed the beast." After the Beast emerges from the sea a mortal wound is given to one of the heads, but then the Beast revives from this death blow. From the explanation of the Beast in Rev. 17:9-10 we learn that five heads had fallen in John's day. The Roman Empire of John's day is, therefore, the sixth head, and the ten horns arise out of that head. This corresponds to the ten-horned beast of Dan. 7. For a further explanation of this go to *Appendix F: Explanation of the Beast and False Prophet*.

Since the Beast of chapter 13 is the sixth head, then this head must be the one that was wounded and healed. This head with the ten horns is in power in this chapter. Let us see if we can make sense of this statement. The

---

[3]The principle of Rom. 6:16 applies here. "Do you not know that to whom you present yourselves slaves to obey, you are that one's slaves whom you obey...."

Roman Empire fell (received a death wound) after the barbarians invaded Rome and set in motion its downfall. From its ashes rose other kingdoms (horns). For a period of time, however, the whole empire was chaotic with no rule but anarchy. It was eventually solidified under the influence of the Roman church through the work of Charles Martel, his son Pepin, and his son Charles who was crowned Holy Roman Emperor in A.D. 800 by the Pope of Rome.

These kingdoms were brought together under one ruling religious power as the revived head. Seen from this perspective the Beast in chapter 13 is the revived sixth head, made up of the kingdoms which arose out of the Roman Empire.

Dan. 8:8,21-22 gives a precedent for interpreting the horns. There we see a male goat, representing Greece with a single great horn, representing its first king. Alexander the Great was the only king of this empire. You might say He **was** the empire. The horn was broken off, representing His fall. In its place grew four horns. The four kingdoms which arose out of Greece are still represented as the one beast (Greece) with four divisions (horns). These divisions of the empire are known as Greece, Thrace, Syria (the Seleucid Empire), and Egypt under the Ptolemys. According to this precedent the ten horns are probably to be understood as several divisions of the one head (Rome). In other words, the kingdoms which arise out of Rome are still recognized as part of Rome.

E. THE BEAST IS WORSHIPED AS A GOD (13:3b-4)

Can you imagine what the world thought looking on at this scene? "...the world marveled and followed the beast." This revived beast is a world dominating power (see verse 7-8). This was also true of each of the kingdoms of Daniel 7. Rev. 13:4 says, "So they worshiped the dragon who gave authority to the beast; and they worshiped the beast, saying, 'Who *is* like the beast? Who is able to make war with him?'" This world power relishes being worshiped. There was no earthly power that could withstand him.[4]

---

[4]See Dan. 2:37-38; 2:39; 7:23. None of these kingdoms had actually invaded and annexed the whole earth, but it is enough that no nation on earth was able to withstand them.

"And he was given a mouth speaking great things and blasphemies." We have already noticed that he has a name of blasphemy on his heads. Now John reemphasizes this. Listen to the things coming out of his mouth—the boasting, his claims to be a god. He desires to be worshiped; indeed he is worshiped. The idea that the emperors of Rome were gods was promoted in the Roman Empire. This same arrogance continued in the revived head as the power controlling the horns claimed to speak with the voice of God.

F. THE BEAST TO CONTINUE FOR 42 MONTHS (13:5)

"...and he was given authority to continue for forty-two months." Here is that number again. This is the period of the persecution of the saints. Act Two (Rev. 13) is mainly about the events of this 42 month (1260 day) period.[5] The Beast does some terrible things, but his time and power are limited.

G. THE BEAST OPPOSES AND MAKES WAR ON THE FOLLOWERS OF CHRIST

Verse 6 says, "Then he opened his mouth in blasphemy against God, to blaspheme His name, His tabernacle, and those who dwell in heaven." This beast opposes and blasphemes the name of God. Not only that, he blasphemes God's tabernacle. The tabernacle is God's dwelling place. In the tabernacle is the holy of holies in heaven where God's throne is. In it also is the holy place, where God's priests, His people serve. This is the church. The beast also blasphemes **those who dwell in heaven**. This is an expression used in Revelation as opposed to *those who dwell upon earth*. This is Revelation's way of referring to those in Christ's kingdom in contrast to those in Satan's kingdom (see Eph. 2:6; Rev. 12:12; 6:10). The beast was making war on God and His church by persecuting and killing His people, just as Saul was persecuting Jesus when he was imprisoning and killing Christians (Acts 9:4-5).

Verse 7 says, "It was granted to him to make war with the saints and to overcome them. Authority was given him over every tribe, tongue, and nation." The Beast persecutes God's people, His servants, the saints. It is very depressing to learn that he is destined to overcome them. But take heart;

---

[5]For a treatment of this 1260 day period and the day for a year symbolism see *Appendix B* at the end of the book.

this is not permanent, any more than the death of Christ was permanent (Dan. 7:21-22,25-27; Rev. 11:7-12). We have already learned from Rev. 11 that there is going to be a reversal of fortunes. The slain witnesses are raised and exalted to heaven. The kingdom of the world is destined to become the kingdom of our Lord and of His Christ. Before this we have a period of persecution to undergo. This drama is, after all, about us who are Christians. Meanwhile the Beast has the power to carry out his purposes, because authority is given to him over every tribe, tongue and nation. He is the dominant world power in the world during his 42 months.

H. DWELLERS ON EARTH VS. DWELLERS IN HEAVEN (13:8)

Verse 8 says, "All who dwell on the earth will worship him, whose names have not been written in the Book of Life of the Lamb slain from the foundation of the world." There are two kinds of people on this earth—*those who dwell on earth* and *those who dwell in heaven.* The former group are those who make this earth their goal. They have made it their home. Their names are not written in the Book of Life. The second group, while sojourning on the earth, are strangers and pilgrims here. They are those who claim heaven as their home. Their names can be found in the Book of Life.

The whole world—i.e., those who make this world their home—will worship the Beast. Those whose names are written in the Lamb's book of life will not yield to the pressure to worship the Beast. They will be faithful, even if it costs them their lives. For this faithfulness they will eventually conquer and receive as their prize eternal life in the new heaven and new earth where there will be no more sorrow or pain or suffering or dying. No tear will ever dim the eye, and no heartache will ever cast its shadow. They will enjoy the love of God and the fellowship of the saints throughout eternity. Dear reader, where have you made your home? Is your name in the Lamb's book of life?

I. ADMONITION TO PAY HEED, BE PATIENT AND TRUST (13:9-10)

As we come to the end of Scene 1 we are given an admonition and some consolation. Verses 9 and 10 declare: "If anyone has an ear, let him hear. He who leads into captivity shall go into captivity; he who kills with the sword must be killed with the sword. Here is the patience and the faith of the saints." The admonition which we read in each of the seven letters in chapters two and three is "If anyone has an ear, let him hear." Here is this phrase again. I guess that means me, because I have an ear. What is the Lord saying? He is letting us know that the things he has been talking about in this chapter apply to us. We are the church which has to undergo the persecution. We are the saints who will be hated, persecuted and killed.

What awaits the captors? What will happen to the persecutors? They are going into captivity themselves. What is going to happen to those who kill? They are going to be killed themselves. This assurance is "the patience and the faith of the saints." What does this mean? Realizing that the victory is ours helps us to be patient and remain faithful. Let us keep watching now as we view the second scene.

SCENE 2: THE TWO HORNED BEAST TAKES CONTROL
Setting—On Earth (Read Rev. 13:11-18)

A. THE EARTHLY ORIGIN OF THE 2-HORNED BEAST

Verse 11 says, "Then I saw another beast coming up out of the earth, and he had two horns...." This beast comes up out of the earth.[6] In Daniel 7:13-14 the one like a son of man comes riding on a cloud, indicating the divine origin of the kingdom of Christ. In contrast to this, the two-horned beast has its origin from earth. Its origin is not noticeably different from that of the seven-headed Beast. In Dan 7:2-3, 17 the four beasts are said to arise both out of the sea and out of the earth. Out of the earth means an earthly origin as opposed to a heavenly origin. Out of the sea is explained in Rev. 17 as originating among the peoples and nations. The two-horned beast, like the first, is also an agent of Satan. His purpose and method of operation are different, but the ultimate objective is the same—the overthrow of the cause of Christ on this earth.

---

[6]In Daniel's vision in chapter seven he describes the four beasts as coming up out of the sea (Daniel 7:3); but later in Daniel's vision the four beasts are said to arise out of the earth (Daniel 7:17). This is not a contradiction, but a means of emphasizing different aspects of the beasts. Coming up out of the sea means they arise from among the nations, people, tongues, and tribes of the world (See Revelation 17:15) while coming up out of the earth emphasizes their earthly or human origin.

Horns symbolize powers, whether political or otherwise. On the ten-horned Beast they are symbols of political powers since the ten horns are ten kings or kingdoms. The horns of the second beast are not directly explained, but the context tells of the kind of power wielded by this beast.

B. THE NATURE OF THE TWO-HORNED BEAST

1. He Looks Like a Lamb.[7] The horns on this beast probably looked like the horns of a ram. *Lamb* is the term used for Christ in Rev. 5:6; 14:1; and subsequent chapters. Christ is the true Lamb. This beast only looks like a lamb. He is a wolf in sheep's clothing (Acts 20:29-30; Matt. 7:15. See also 2 Cor. 11:13-15). In later chapters he is called *the False Prophet* (16:13; 19:20; 20:10). We will call him by that name most of the time and we will refer to the seven-headed Beast as *the Beast*. Jesus warned us about false prophets and false Christs who would come (Matt. 24:11,23-24; 2 Pet. 2:1-3).

Satan will go to any lengths to deceive—even to sending agents to imitate the Christ. Think how many times people have come claiming to be Jesus Christ. Some who have made this claim led large crowds of people to commit suicide by promising them eternal life. Others have been led to commit murder thinking that God was guiding them to do so. The False Prophet deceives some into believing they will have an eternity of sensual pleasures if they commit suicide in order to kill "unbelievers."

The False Prophet is the personification of deceit through false teaching. He is embodied in the false religions that he creates. Jesus came to show men the truth and to free them (John 8:32). This pretender came to deceive with false teachings, and to enslave mankind through falsehood.

2. He Speaks Like a Dragon. While pretending to be a spokesman for the Lamb, the False Prophet is actually speaking for Satan. His message is not that of the true Lamb but that of Satan. He is Satan's mouthpiece to speak false teachings and to deceive. Just as the Beast of persecution is embodied in the kingdoms of the world that make war on Christians, so also the beast of deceit (the False Prophet) is embodied in the false religions and philosophies of this world—i.e., in the institutions that promote false teachings and false religions. Later in this scene the false religion that is

---

[7]The word here is ἀρνίον *(arnion)*, the same word used for the Lamb that was slain in Rev. 5

predominant during the 1260 days (years) is established by the two-horned beast. It is called *the image of the beast.*

C. THE AUTHORITY OF THE BEAST IS GIVEN TO THE FALSE PROPHET

Rev. 13:12 says, "And he exercises all the authority of the first beast in his presence...." Now this is very interesting. Not only is the False Prophet a representative of Satan, as is the Beast, but he also exercises all the authority of the Beast in his very presence. Just as the Dragon is the source of the Beast's authority (13:2-3), so that authority is given over to the False Prophet (Verse 12). In other words, the False Prophet is in control. So the False Prophet is higher in authority than the Beast. He has his own authority as a deceiver, plus the power to exercise all the persecuting authority of the Beast. He is the one who calls the shots under the direction of Satan.

D. THE TWO HORNS—POLITICAL AND RELIGIOUS POWER

Now we begin to see the meaning of the two horns. Just as the Ram in Dan. 8 had two horns, so also does this beast which looks like a lamb. The two horns on the Ram represented two powers (Medes and Persians) with one higher than the other. Persia was the dominant power and was in control of the other. You might say that Persia exercised all the power of the Medes as well as its own power. So, also, the False Prophet, which is like a lamb, has two horns or two powers, its own and that of the Beast. What are these powers? We have already seen that the power of the Beast is political power. He is embodied in kingdoms or empires. His political power is used to make war upon the saints. The False Prophet exercises control of the persecuting political power through the Beast. The second horn represents religious or spiritual power.

E. THE WORK OF THE TWO-HORNED BEAST (Read 13:12b-14a)

What is the False Prophet doing? He is creating false religions and promoting false worship. He causes the Beast to be worshiped as a god, and convinces the world to worship this false god (see 13:4, 8). He has been given great power to deceive the nations, and he causes fire to fall from the sky to demonstrate his power. Paul declares in 2 Thess.2:9, "The coming of the *lawless one* is according to the working of Satan, with all power, signs, and lying wonders...." Some translations say "false wonders." It is my opinion that the signs performed by the second beast are not really miracles but false wonders, or illusions.

If you have watched many magic shows on stage or television you know that some artists are capable of performing some amazing illusions. The gullible are even caused to believe that they are really seeing magic. Of course most of these "magicians" admit that their work is illusion and not real. There are a few, however, who have haughtily claimed magical powers. Satan has a lot of power. If the False Prophet really has the power to perform genuine signs in order to deceive, we should be aware that all such things must be tested by the word of God. Those Christians who do not gain a thorough knowledge of the Bible are susceptible to being deceived by these agents of the Devil. Matt. 24:24 states, "For false christs and false prophets will rise and show great signs and wonders to deceive, if possible, even the elect."

Anyone who seems to work a miracle must be tested according to Deut. 13:1-3:

> If there arises among you a prophet or a dreamer of dreams, and he gives you a sign or a wonder, and the sign or the wonder comes to pass, of which he spoke to you, saying, "Let us go after other gods"—which you have not known—"and let us serve them," you shall not listen to the words of that prophet or that dreamer of dreams, for the LORD your God is testing you to know whether you love the LORD your God with all your heart and with all your soul.

If a miracle worker teaches a different Christ than the one found in the New Testament then he is not of God. Know the fundamentals of the faith—those teachings and beliefs that are essential to our salvation—and reject any teaching that is contrary to them, even if it is accompanied by great signs and wonders. Remember, Satan can use such signs to deceive even the very elect.

F. THE IMAGE OF THE BEAST

Verse 14b continues, "...telling those who dwell on the earth to make an image to the beast who was wounded by the sword and lived." As the action of this scene continues, the False Prophet uses deception to cause the people who belong to this world to build an image of the Beast (Rome) and to worship Rome by worshiping its image.

The worship of false gods dates all the way back to the beginning of Babylon at the tower of Babel. This was the work of Nimrod, a great grandson of Noah through his son Ham and Ham's son Cush. The story of the beginning of Babylon is found in Gen. 11. The Bible doesn't say much about Nimrod. It tells that he was a great hunter and that he founded many cities. It also tells of a rebellion against God's decree to populate the earth. This was probably led by Nimrod since Babel (Babylon) was his city according to Gen. 10:8-12. This city was founded by an attempt to build a huge tower (Gen. 11), a great accomplishment intended to keep men together contrary to God's will, and to provide a beacon, a landmark, so that those who go out over the desert will always be able to see the way to return.

Extra-biblical sources provide much information about Nimrod's influence. Cities were named for him. He became a god to many people and nations, and his counterpart is found in ancient pagan gods throughout Asia, Europe and Africa. All these worshipers made images of their gods and sinned by worshiping these idols. Throughout history since then, Satan has worked hard to convince all men to become idol worshipers. Even the Israelites in the wilderness, after having heard the command not to make or worship idols from the mouth of God Himself, built an idol to an Egyptian god—a golden calf—and worshiped it (Exod. 32:1-8).

After entering the promised land of Canaan they were influenced by the inhabitants to worship all sorts of false Gods, each represented by an idol. After the northern kingdom of Israel broke off from Judah, king Jeroboam, who led the rebellion, set up golden calves at Bethel and Dan and commanded the people to go to these places to worship instead of to the temple in Jerusalem (1 Kings 12:26-33). All the nations have been deceived by Satan to worship false gods, mostly represented by idols.

We are warned both in the Old Testament and in the New that to worship idols is to worship demons. In 1 Cor. 10:20 Paul warns against idolatry by saying, "...the things which the Gentiles sacrifice they sacrifice to demons and not to God, and I do not want you to have fellowship with demons." In Deut. 32:16-17a Moses declares, "They provoked Him to jealousy with foreign gods; With abominations they provoked Him to anger. They sacrificed to demons, not to God...." In the New Testament covetousness (greed) is called idolatry (Col. 3:5). Whatever we put ahead of God, whatever we worship that is not God, becomes our idol. This may be money, an automobile, pleasure, a loved one, or other possessions. All idols are made by the people who worship them. This is the case in Rev. 13. The dwellers on earth are deceived into making an idol of the Beast.

Verse 15 says, "He was granted power to give breath to the image of the beast, that the image of the beast should both speak and cause as many as would not worship the image of the beast to be killed." The two-horned beast had power to give the image breath (life) and the power of speech. This imagery is probably taken from events in the days of John. The pagan priests of the Roman empire rigged some of the idols so that they would appear to speak. It may be that Revelation drew its symbol of the image from this background. The Image of the Beast was also given the power to kill those who would not worship the beast.

G. THE FALSE PROPHET WORKS THROUGH FALSE RELIGIONS

How does the False Prophet exercise the power of the horns? The power represented by one horn is political power, used to persecute God's people. The power represented by the other horn is spiritual in nature. It is mainly the power to deceive. The Dragon has given the False Prophet the task of deceiving the world into believing falsehood. False philosophies, false religions, and false worship are its goals. He is a pretender, appearing to be a lamb. He is a diabolical substitute for the Lamb of God Who takes away the sins of the world. All the pagan religions of the world throughout history, both provincial and worldwide, including the so-called great religions of the world are the work of this deceiver.

How does he wield both religious and political power during the 1260 days? He exercises his religious power first by deceiving the nations into establishing false religions to draw away men from the true worship of the true God. God is the author of the true faith. Those who follow the true faith worship God who is its author. Those who follow false religions are in reality worshiping Satan or his demons (see 1 Cor. 10:20; Rev. 9:20; Deut. 32:17).

The beast of deception works through the religions that men have built. He speaks as a dragon because the false teachings and the false prophecies which he utters through these false religions are from the Dragon (Satan), not from God. By these teachings he deceives the nations. The false religions derive their power not from God but from Satan. They are doing the Dragon's work for him. The beast of deceit is his servant, his agent by which he deceives the world.

Religious power is represented by one of the horns. The other horn is the horn of political power. This power, by rights, belongs to the nations, to kings and governors who exist by God's ordination. In order for this power to be turned toward Satan's purposes the nations must first be deceived. This is the work of the horn of spiritual or religious power. When the False Prophet has accomplished his work, then he takes over in directing the political powers.

The False Prophet exercises all the authority of the Beast in his presence. How does he use this power? He causes all those who will not worship the beast or his image to be persecuted and killed. How does he do this? He directs the political power to use its authority to do this. In other words the kings and princes do the bidding of the false prophet embodied in the false religion (the image) by enforcing the false religion and false worship.

H. THE IMAGE OF THE BEAST DURING THE REVIVED SIXTH HEAD

Now let us focus on the image of the beast. The False Prophet deceives those of the world to "...make an image to the beast who was wounded by the sword and lived." This image is made in the likeness of the Beast. (After all, since he received a death wound, and yet lived, he must be a god.) It should be noted that the image looks like the Beast. What in history has been built in the image of Rome? There is a religion, based in Rome, which has all the organizational characteristics of Imperial Rome. Its high priest wears the same name that Caesar wore in his function as high priest of the religions of Rome—"Pontifex Maximus." It is organized with a hierarchical form of government patterned after that of the Roman Empire. Many of its officials wear the same titles as their counterparts in the Roman Empire. It copies the many levels of the Roman imperial hierarchy, right down to the local level, so that the religion is built in an almost exact image of the Roman government.

It even has its own political organization with its own political territory, and is recognized by the various nations as a nation of its own.

I. IDENTIFYING THE IMAGE OF THE BEAST

Just as the Roman Empire, during pagan Rome, exercised religious power as well as political, and just as its head wore a name of blasphemy (the emperor was called *god*), so also this false religion exercises political as well as religious power and wears the name of blasphemy, claiming for its head the title of *Lord God* on earth. Over the centuries this false religion has exercised its power over civil authorities, using them to persecute, torture and kill those who would not bow to the authority of its head. This religion claims not to be guilty of torturing or killing "heretics." This is because it had the civil governments do these things, but they were done at the bidding of the religious authority.

This religious system devised a doctrine called *the doctrine of the two swords*. According to this doctrine, one sword is the spiritual sword and the other is the civil sword. These are the religious power and the political power. The spiritual sword is wielded by the religious organization, and the civil sword is wielded by the political governments. The doctrine also states that the spiritual sword is higher than the civil sword. In other words, the higher authority is in control of the lower. The spiritual rules the civil. The governments are in subjection to the religion. Do you recognize the two horns of the beast in this doctrine? This false religion also has devised two other doctrines that it uses as weapons to force submission. One is called *excommunication* and the other is called *interdict*. This religion uses excommunication to control its members; it uses the interdict to control the nations.

The members are indoctrinated with the idea that unless they can receive the sacraments of the church, they are doomed to eternity in hell. Excommunication bars them from these sacraments. The hierarchy by exercising this power over them has been able to keep them in line. In many parts of the world people believe that if they do not bow to the authority of the priesthood, they are doomed to hell.

The interdict is the excommunication of a whole city, region or nation. The rulers of these political entities might want to claim their independence from the church. If they try it they are subject to the interdict. None of the people of that region or nation are allowed the sacraments, so the rulers are pressured by the people to bow to the authority of the hierarchy. These two weapons, excommunication and interdict, were powerfully, effectively, and widely used during a long period of time approximating 1260 years, while the nations which arose out of Rome were under the thumb of the Roman church. It is no coincidence that this period of time includes a long period referred to as "the dark ages."

In modern days this power has diminished, so that most western nations, while paying homage to the Pope of Rome, do not let their policies be dictated by the Roman church. The Protestant Reformation had a great deal to do with this, because with the spread of Protestantism the power of the Pope over nations was greatly diminished. Gone are the days when a king can be made to wait outside barefoot in the snow for three days before he is granted an audience with the Pope to beg for release from such excommunication or interdict.

It was the use of these means that led nations into such things as the Spanish Inquisition where heretics (those who would not submit to the authority of the Roman church) and their families would have their property confiscated while they would be tortured, maimed, and killed unless they would bow to the authority of the church. This included Christians, Jews, and all others who would not yield to the hierarchy. The Roman church claimed that the church did not do these awful things; but that they were done by the civil authorities. However these governments were under the authority of the religious leaders and were doing their bidding.

J. THE MARK OF THE BEAST (Read Rev. 13:16-17)

Bloodshed, starvation and death are the means Satan uses to force God's people to worship the Beast. In Scene 1 of this act we have seen the seven-headed Beast meting out bloodshed and death.[8] In Scene 2 the False Prophet directs the bloodshed and death, and he also causes the saints to starve.[9] He causes all to receive a mark in order to buy or sell. The necessities of life

---

[8] See the second and fourth riders and their horse—Rev. 6:3-4, 7-8.

[9] See the third rider and horse—Rev. 6: 5-6.

would be denied to those who would not submit to the mark. Economic oppression is directed against those who do not bear the mark (v. 17). Economic pressure is applied by the world to force conformity to the world. We are admonished, "Love not the world ..." (1 John 2:15-16), and "...friendship with the world is enmity with God" (James 4:4).

The mark is either the name of the Beast or the number of his name. It is the counterpart of the seal of God. We saw the 144 thousand as servants of God being sealed in Rev. 7. We will see them again in Scene 3 of this act, at the beginning of Rev. 14. The seal of God indicates those who belong to Him. There is only one place for the seal of God—i.e., on the forehead, indicating the heart. If a person has given his heart to God, the service of his hand will automatically follow. That seal is the Holy Spirit of God.[10]

A seal is a mark of ownership. Cattle are marked with a brand. Slaves are marked as a seal of ownership. Just as those belonging to Christ bear His mark, those enslaved to sin and Satan bear his mark. The mark of the Beast is Satan's seal on those who belong to him. It is no more a literal mark than is the seal of God. It is, after all, Satan's mark since the Beast and False Prophet are both his agents, and function under his authority.

There are two places the mark of the Beast can be worn—i.e., on the forehead or on the hand. The forehead indicates the heart, while the hand indicates service. Although there are many who have given their hearts to the works of Satan, there are others who serve him without their heart being in it. Satan doesn't care. As long as he has the service of a person's hand, he doesn't have to have the devotion of his heart. Satan's seal can be in the hand or in the heart. He has you either way.

This mark is called *the mark of the beast* because during the 1260 days of the Beast's reign he is the representative of Satan on earth. To worship and serve the Beast is to worship and serve Satan. But the term has a broader application.

The sixth-head stage of the Beast is not the end of the Beast's influence. There is also a seventh head. Throughout this age it can be said that those who give their heart and/or service to Satan have the mark of the Beast. Here

---

[10]To review the discussion of this subject see chapter 7

in chapter 13, however, the mark identifies those who are servants of the Beast during the 1260 day (year) period.

Verse 18 concludes, "Here is wisdom. Let him who has understanding calculate the number of the beast, for it is the number of a man: His number is 666." A name is said to have a number in the sense that the number represents the name. The number of the Beast's name is written out in the Nestle/UBS text as six-hundred and sixty and six.[11] In the Majority Text and the Textus Receptus it is written in the Greek as the numerals *xi, chi, stigma*—i.e., $\chi\xi\varsigma$.[12] Some say that the number 666 is symbolic of man because six is the number of man. This is based upon the fact that man was created on the sixth day, and that it falls short of the number seven, the number of perfection. It is pointed out that 666 is three sixes in a row, giving greater emphasis to the 6. This works well in Arabic numerals used today by the world, but it doesn't work in ancient numerals such as Roman or Greek numerals. This is because 600, 60, and 6 are not three sixes. 600 is the letter *chi*, 60 is *xi*, and 6 is *stigma*. Since the New Testament was not written using Arabic numerals the reasoning falls down.[13]

Unless *man* is itself the name represented by six-hundred sixty and six, then we must look for another name. It doesn't seem likely that John would tell us the necessity for wisdom in counting or computing the number of the name, and then turn around and tell us the name (*man*), thus eliminating the necessity of either computing or being wise to understand it. So the word

---

[11] In the Nestle/UBS text it is ἑξακόσιοι ἑξήκοντα ἑξ *(hexakosioi hexekonta hex,* pronounced *hex-ah-ko-see-oy hex-ay-con-tah hex)*, meaning *six-hundred sixty six.*

[12] In the Majority Text the number *666* appears as the numerals $\chi\xi\varsigma$. The letters are *chi, xi (pr. ksee) and stigma.* The last letter, *stigma*, which is the numeral *6,* is an obsolete letter that comes between the fifth letter *(epsilon)* and the sixth letter *(zeta).* The *stigma* looks somewhat like an enlarged *final sigma(ς).*

[13] Arabic numerals introduced to the world a revolutionary concept—i.e., the concept of zero as a place holder. The value of 0 depends on its placement. It turns one into ten (10), or a hundred (100), or a thousand (1000), depending on how many zeros are used. This revolutionized the science of mathematics by greatly increasing the ease of calculations. This made it possible to do with pencil and paper what the Chinese did with the abacus.

man is not itself the name, but is intended as a clue as to the nature or origin of the name.

Six-hundred sixty and six is said to be the number of (a) man. The word is not the word for a male person, ἀνήρ (*aner*), but the generic term ἄνθρωπος (*anthropos*), which indicates a human being, either male or female. The indefinite article *a* is not in the manuscript since Greek has no indefinite article. To translate into English one must determine from the context whether the indefinite article is implied. That is difficult to do in this case. The statement can mean 1) the number of mankind, 2) the number of a particular person, or 3) of human origin. The term *man* is sometimes used with reference to an organization or group, a body of people or division of mankind, as in Eph. 2:15 where two men (Jews and gentiles) are made into one new man (the church or spiritual Israel). This is the view I favor; *a man* equals *a division of mankind*. In this case the man is the revived Roman Empire. The name, then, must be one which identifies this man.

Notice that the number is the number of the Beast's name (verse 17). According to verse 1 the Beast's name is a name of blasphemy. Notice, also, that the mark can be either the number or the name (verse 17). The number is to be reckoned[14] (literally, counted or computed—verse 18). It requires counting or calculating. This probably means taking the numeric value of each letter in the name and adding them together. Men often counted the value of the letters in their name to establish their number. Those who practiced this had both a name and a number. In my opinion this is the calculating that is intended to determine the name of the Beast.

Many names have been set forth which add up to 666, however in most instances where the name would fit contextually this requires the altering of the name somewhat (as in the case of Nero Caesar put in the Hebrew language) or ignoring some of the letters, or manipulating the name in some way. Most names are put in some other language than Greek. I have seen attempts in Hebrew and in Latin. Since koiné Greek is the language of

---

[14] ψηφισάτω (*psephisato*) a form of ψηφίζω (*psephizo*)—to *use pebbles* in enumeration, that is, (genitive case) to *compute:*—count. The word comes from the word for pebble. A common practice was to use pebbles in adding numbers. Such a practice would result in taking the number of pebbles for the numeric value of each letter, then counting the total number of pebbles. The total would be the number of the name.

Revelation we should probably expect the name intended to be in the same language. Furthermore, the name should correspond to what we have already learned about the beast—more specifically the sixth head—Rome. It should be applicable to the ten-horn phase of the beast—i.e., to the revived Roman Empire under the aegis of the false prophet, and to the image he builds—i.e., the false religion of Rome.

I cannot claim to know for certain what this name is, but Irenaeus, a student of Polycarp, who was a student of the apostle John, the writer of Revelation, set forth λατείνος *(lateinos)* (the Greek for *Latin*) as the name which is intended. Irenaeus himself did not take a stand upon this name, but merely passed it on as a solution he had heard from those before him. If indeed he received it from Polycarp, then there is a good possibility that this is the correct answer since he could have received it from John himself. At any rate, it fits well.

Latin is a name which would apply equally well to the old Roman Empire, the revived Roman Empire, and/or the Roman Church. Further, it is a name which requires no manipulation, addition or subtraction. The simple name, spelled as it would be in the koiné Greek, equals 666.[15] It seems to this writer that this solution best fits all the facts. Yet I would not want to be dogmatic about it, or close my mind to other solutions. Whatever the specific meaning of the mark in this verse, it is virtually certain that the mark is intended to identify the persecuting power which is the sixth head, the one in power during the 42 months of persecution in chapter 13. The purpose of the mark, whatever its specific meaning, is to identify that persecuting power by use of the cryptic number six hundred sixty and six.

The world is divided into two classes—i.e. those who have the mark of the Beast, and those who have the seal of God (see 9:4; 14:9-12; 15:2; 16:2; 20:4; 22:3-5). The Beast, in general, is symbolic of world powers in opposition to Christ, persecuting the people of God; but a head is a specific world power. The sixth head, revived, with its ten horns, is the phase with which Rev. 13 deals. We, then, could expect this mark to have a specific

---

[15]The numeric equivalents of the Greek letters in λατείνος, taken from *A New Short Grammar of the Greek New Testament* by A.T. Robertson and W. Hersey Davis, ¶285, are: lambda - 30; alpha - 1; tau - 300; epsilon - 5; iota - 10; nu - 50; omicron - 70; and sigma - 200. This adds up to 666.

application in this context. Generically, those who have the mark of the Beast are all those who serve Satan's agencies in this world; more specifically, in Rev. 13, they are the ones deceived into serving the Beast and his Image during the ten-horn phase of the Beast. Those who do are marked as belonging to the Beast, and thus to Satan.

Those who have the seal of God were seen in chapter 7 as the 144,000, identified as the servants of God. These are the ones who are marked as belonging to God. In the final scene of this act these are seen with the Lamb.

SCENE 3: THE LAMB WITH THE REDEEMED ON MT. ZION

Setting—The Heavenly Zion (Read 14:1-5)

A. THE 144,000 WITH THE SEAL OF GOD (14:1)

The False Prophet sealed the servants of Satan with the mark of the Beast in the previous scene. In this scene John sees those who have the seal of God on their foreheads—i.e., they have the Holy Spirit dwelling in their hearts. They are standing with the Lamb on Mount Zion, in the temple of God, before His throne. These are the servants of God who were sealed in chap. 7.

The worshipers of the Beast had the name of the Beast, or the number of his name, on their foreheads or hands. The servants of God have the name of God and the Lamb on their foreheads.[16] They are the 144,000. 144 is 12 times 12, a symbolic number for God's people. 1000 signifies a great multitude or long period of time. Put them together and it is a symbolic way of saying *the multitude of the servants of God.*

B. THE PRAISE OF THE REDEEMED (14:2-3)

John heard a voice that roared like huge waves breaking on the rocks near the shore, and like the clap of loud thunder. This is the voice of the Lamb. The same imagery is used for the voice of Christ in Rev. 1:10,15. John not only heard the loud voice, but the sweet music of harps as well. The harpists are playing their harps. In chapter 5 the 24 elders are the ones who had the

---

[16]The *Nestle/United Bible Society Text* as well as the *Majority Text* read, "...having His name and the Father's name on their foreheads." This is the preferred reading.

harps. They are the symbols of God's people as the priests of God before His throne. The 144,000 are singing a new song before God's throne. They are the only ones who can learn that song, probably because they are the only ones who have experienced the grace and salvation of God.

Why are they standing before the throne? Because they have been redeemed from the earth. The resurrection has taken place and they await the completion of God's judgment to be taken to the place Christ has prepared for their eternal home—the new heaven and new earth. These are the New Jerusalem which is about to come down out of heaven to the new heaven and earth. The reference to Mt. Zion is another way of speaking of Jerusalem. The mountain in this scene is obviously in heaven, so the reference is to the Jerusalem that is above.

Their warfare is over, and they stand victorious as they sing their song of redemption and victory. What a chorus. At times I have worshiped where several thousand saints raised their voices to God in a harmony of praise. Wow! What an experience! I could envy those who have that experience week after week, but one day I hope to be in that heavenly choir as one of those who have been redeemed from the earth. Then I will have learned that new song, and will be able to raise my voice in exuberant praise to God. All the experiences we have now with earthly choirs and congregational singing cannot begin to compare with that experience.

C. THE IDENTITY OF THE 144,000 (14:4-5)

Chapter 7 tells us that the 144,000 are the servants of God. They are symbolized as the 12 tribes of Israel. All the saints belong to God's Israel. Now in chapter 14 we learn more about their identity. Not only have they been sealed with the Spirit of God, these also wear the name of God and of Christ—i.e., they are Christians. They are all those who have been, or ever will be, redeemed from the earth. This multitude will be many times greater than a literal 144,000. By this we know that the number is figurative and not literal.

1. They Are Virgins. This is not to be taken literally, but as a figure of their spiritual purity as the bride of Christ, as they wait for their marriage to the Lamb. The Bible does not represent marriage as moral impurity. Heb. 13:4 says, "Marriage *is* honorable among all, and the bed undefiled; but fornicators and adulterers God will judge." In our relationship with the world God wants us to be pure. Later the woman called Babylon the Harlot is introduced. She is a figure representing the allurements of the world. She stands in stark contrast to the virgin bride of Christ.

James 4:4 warns, "Adulterers and adulteresses! Do you not know that friendship with the world is enmity with God?" This is the significance of the symbol. Those who do not make friends with the world are the virgins who have not been defiled with women. This is a strong figure in the Old Testament. In the prophets God rebuked Judah and Israel for going after other lovers (idolatry and immorality) instead of being true to God their husband. Christ wants His bride to be a virgin.

2. They Follow the Lamb Wherever He Goes. They are the followers of Jesus Christ. 1 Pet. 2:21 tells us, "Christ also suffered for us, leaving us an example, that you should follow His steps." The servants of God are those who seek to be like Christ, to do what He would do in every circumstance, and to walk in His steps. There is a song of dedication that we sing which is entitled, "I'll Go Where You Want Me to Go." The chorus says:

> I'll go where you want me to go, dear Lord,
> Over mountain or plain or sea;
> I'll say what you want me to say, dear Lord.
> I'll be what you want me to be.

If you live the words of this song you will be among the multitude of the followers of the Lamb, singing the new song before the throne of God.

3. They Are Redeemed from among Men. In Matt 3:12 John the Baptist tells his audience that the Christ "...will thoroughly clean out His threshing floor, and gather His wheat into the barn; but He will burn up the chaff with unquenchable fire." He was speaking of what Christ would do at the final judgment. Later in chapter 14 we will see more about this harvest.

The redemption of the saved from the earth is spoken of as *the harvest of the firstfruits*. James 1:18 tells us, "Of His own will He brought us forth by the word of truth, that we might be a kind of firstfruits of His creatures." Jesus Himself is called the firstfruits of the resurrection (1 Cor. 15:20, 23). In the New Testament (KJV) the term *firstfruits* is used four times besides its use in Revelation. Christians are said to have the firstfruits of the Spirit

(Rom. 8:23). The first ones converted in a region are called the firstfruits of that region (Rom. 16:5; 1 Cor. 16:15). Only James 1:18 fits the context in Revelation where the redeemed are all referred to as the firstfruits from among men.

In the Old Testament there are many references to the feast of the firstfruits. Exod. 23:14-16 gives the following instructions to Israel concerning the three yearly feasts commanded by God:

> Three times you shall keep a feast to Me in the year: You shall keep the Feast of Unleavened Bread (you shall eat unleavened bread seven days, as I commanded you, at the time appointed in the month of Abib, for in it you came out of Egypt; none shall appear before Me empty); and the Feast of Harvest, **the firstfruits of your labors** which you have sown in the field; and the Feast of Ingathering at the end of the year, when you have gathered in *the fruit of* your labors from the field.

The Feast of Harvest, also called *the Feast of the Firstfruits*, is known today as *Pentecost*. It is also referred to as *the Feast of Weeks* from the counting of seven weeks following the offering of the first sheaf of grain. On the day after the seven weeks, a total of 50 days, the Israelites were to celebrate the harvest of the firstfruits. This referred to the harvest of the grain—mainly barley and wheat. *The Feast of Ingathering* in the late fall, also known as *the Feast of Tabernacles* celebrated the completion of the latter harvest—mainly the harvest of the wine grapes. This knowledge will be important later in Rev. 14 when dealing with the two harvests pictured there.

4. They Are People of Integrity. The last thing in this scene is the description of the redeemed as being people of integrity. They do not lie. The word *deceit* is translated *falsehood* in some translations. No deceit or falsehood is found in them. In fact, they are without fault of any kind. Does this mean that the redeemed from the earth will only be those who have lived without sin? Certainly not. If that were the case, there would be no one among them, because "all have sinned" (Rom. 3:23). They are faultless because the blood of Christ has made them faultless. Rev. 7:14 says they "...washed their robes and made them white in the blood of the Lamb."

When God looks at these, He sees them as sinless because Jesus has taken all their sins away. He sees the righteousness of Christ Himself which has been imputed to them. Phil. 3:8b-9 states:

> ...that I may gain Christ and be found in Him, not having my own righteousness, which *is* from the law, but that which *is* through faith in Christ, the righteousness which is from God by faith....

We have returned once again to the Temple in Heaven. In effect this is the same scene that we saw in Revelation 7:9-17. They who have washed their robes and made them white in the blood of the Lamb. They have gone through tribulation, and now they stand before the throne of God, having been redeemed from the earth. Do you see yourself in this picture? I pray you will be among them. I plan to be there.

Chapter 14

ACT 3: THE WRATH OF GOD

SCENES 1 AND 2

(Rev. 14:5-20)

In the first five verses of Rev. 14 we saw the victorious saints, redeemed from the earth, before the throne of God, singing the new song and praising the One on the throne. But what is the fate of the rest of the world? What about the nations, cities and people who served Satan? Most of the rest of the book of Revelation is taken up with the judgment and punishment of the wicked, and the victory and reward of the saints and prophets.

Whoever tries to interpret these chapters chronologically will have a hard time understanding the message since they give different pictures of the judgment of the forces of evil. In chapter 14 three angels give brief pronouncements of judgment, then two condensed pictures of the final harvest are seen. The first picture is of the reaping of the firstfruits; the second is of the latter harvest of the wine of God's wrath.

Chapters 15 and 16 presents God's judgment upon the world as the pouring out of seven bowls of wrath. These bring the wrath of God to its conclusion. In Rev. 17:1 - 19:10 God's judgment of Babylon the Harlot is given in detail. In the rest of chapter 19 God's judgment upon the Beast and False Prophet is shown as the final battle between the forces of Christ and those of Satan. In chapter 20 we have the judgment of Satan who is cast into the lake of fire along with the Beast and False Prophet. The last picture of judgment is of the resurrection of all people to stand before God's judgment throne. Those not found in the Book of Life are cast into the lake of fire.

Notice that each detailed picture of God's judgment ends up at the same point. We find the lake of fire waiting for the condemned and the marriage of the Lamb awaiting the righteous.

SCENE 1: ANNOUNCEMENTS OF GOD'S WRATH (14:6-13)

Setting—The Heavens

A. AN ANGEL PROCLAIMS THE HOUR OF GOD'S JUDGMENT (14:6-7)

John saw various angels from time to time in the previous visions. Now it says he saw another angel flying in the midst of the sky. This angel has "the everlasting gospel" which he preaches to those who dwell on earth. *Gospel* means *good news* or *glad tidings*. In other words, we are to understand that God's judgments against the wicked are part of the good news. It is not, however, good news to those who belong to the world system, for it is the news of their condemnation. Judgment is good news to the child of God because he has confidence for the day of judgment (1 John 4:17).

The persecuted saints cry out for God's judgment, as in 6:10 and 8:3-5. In the vision of the opening of the fifth seal the cry of the souls under the altar for judgment and vengeance is answered in the opening of the sixth seal by the wrath of God and the Lamb in judgment on those who dwell on earth. In the vision of the seven trumpets God answers the prayers of the saints with warning judgments, culminating in the last trumpet of the final judgment of God against the wicked.

Along with the destruction of the wicked, victory is given to the saints. Immediately after the wicked are sentenced the righteous receive their reward. The everlasting good news includes both the punishment of the wicked as well as the reward of the saints. Failure to punish the wicked for their wickedness would not be good news. There must be a time when all wrongs are righted and the righteous are vindicated, otherwise there would be no justice. On the other hand, when the wicked have repented and turned to Christ to receive forgiveness in the blood of Christ, that is indeed good news! They are no longer counted as wicked; instead, the righteousness of Christ is set down to their account by the grace of God. It is the only way that any of us can be saved.

The angel with the everlasting good news makes an announcement. He proclaims the arrival of the hour of the final judgment of God. This he proclaims to every nation, tribe, tongue and people.. His proclamation, is this, "Fear God and give glory to Him, for the hour of His judgment has come; and worship Him who made heaven and earth, the sea and springs of water." The coming of the hour of God's judgment is something to look forward to if we fear and serve Him. It is a cause for glorifying and worshiping Him. God made heaven and earth, and all things. He is also the one who will bring an end to this world.

B. A SECOND ANGEL ANNOUNCES BABYLON'S FALL (Read v. 8)

A second angel pronounces God's judgment upon Babylon. This is not another judgment being announced. It is the same judgment as it applies to Babylon. The cry, "Babylon is fallen, is fallen," is a direct quotation from Isaiah 21:6 where the prophet is foretelling the destruction of the city and kingdom of Babylon. This is the first direct reference to Babylon in the book of Revelation. Unlike the Babylon in the prophecies of Isaiah and Jeremiah, *Babylon* here is a symbol. The symbolism is not explained here; only the fall of it is announced. An explanation of the meaning of the symbol is given in chapter 17, where she is called Babylon the Harlot. The literal city of Babylon had long since been destroyed. It is that very destruction of literal Babylon from which the symbolism of the destruction of *Babylon the Harlot* is drawn. This will become apparent in chapter 18.

Like the beast and the false prophet of Rev. 13, she is also an agent of the Dragon (Satan). In 17:5 she is called Babylon, the mother of harlots. As the Beast is Satan's agent of persecution, and the False Prophet is His agent of deceit, so the Harlot is Satan's agent of enticement. It is her job, through the allurements of the world, to take captive the souls of men. She is allied with the beast and the false prophet. The three agents work together.

Satan has only three tools or methods to subvert the souls of men. These are all called *temptations* or *trials*. One is **enticement** to sin through the allurements that the world system presents. This is aptly represented by an alluring harlot, holding out her golden cup of abominations to men. A second tool is **deceit** through false teachings and philosophies of men which turn men aside from faith in the true God of the universe. This is represented by the two-horned beast called *the False Prophet*. A third tool Satan uses is **persecution** to pressure men into accepting what they do not believe. This is done mainly through the political powers of nations which have been deceived by the false prophet. This is represented by the seven-headed beast whose job it is to make war upon the saints.

It is said that Babylon makes all nations drink the wine of the wrath of her fornication. She causes them to become drunk with her excesses, as though involving them in drunken orgies. This wine is called *the wine of the wrath of her fornication* because it results in the wrath of God's indignation being poured out upon them. This idea is developed further as we move through the action of this scene. We will await our study of chapter 17 for a fuller explanation of Babylon the Harlot.

C. JUDGMENT ON THE WORSHIPERS OF THE BEAST *(Read verses 9-11)*

John sees yet a third angel who pronounces judgment upon the worshipers of the beast and his image—those who received the mark of the beast on their forehead or their hand. Those who refused to receive the mark of the beast and to worship him or his image were persecuted and killed in chapter 13. Now the angel proclaims judgment on those who yield to the pressure, accept the mark, and worship the beast and his image. This judgment is spoken of as drinking "the wine of the wrath of God." This wrath is poured out in full strength into the cup of God's indignation. In the application to Babylon the Harlot as well as in its application to the worshipers of the beast, God's judgment is spoken of as drinking the cup of the wine of God's wrath. This sets *God's Wrath* as the theme of all the visions of the final judgment.

What is the result of drinking this cup? It is torment with fire and brimstone in the presence of the Lamb and His holy angels. This torment is such that they have no rest, no respite from this torment, day or night. The results are eternal. It is said that the smoke of their torment keeps going up forever and ever. When one chooses to forsake the service of his maker for the service of Satan and the world he makes a choice that results in eternal consequences. The fire and brimstone spoken of here is called *the lake of fire and brimstone* later in Revelation. In Rev. 20:14 and 21:8 it is called *the second death.* In view of this, throughout the scriptures we are warned to "take heed."

In Matt. 24:4-5 Jesus said, "Take heed that no one deceives you. For many will come in My name, saying, 'I am the Christ,' and will deceive many." In this way He warns us against false teachings. Luke 21:34 records these words of Jesus, "But take heed to yourselves, lest your hearts be weighed down with carousing, drunkenness, and cares of this life, and that Day come on you unexpectedly." In this way He warns us against enticements of the world. In Col. 2:8 Paul says, "Beware lest anyone cheat you through philosophy and empty deceit." He writes in Eph. 5:6, "Let no one deceive you with empty words, for because of these things the wrath of God comes upon the sons of disobedience."

D. *SAINTS AND DEAD IN CHRIST ARE CONSOLED (Read verses 12-13)*

The cry of the persecuted saints under the altar in 6:9-11 brings a promise of eventual judgment upon their persecutors. Here is the basis for the patience of the saints as they wait for God's judgment. This same assurance is given in Rev. 13:10. Those who are obedient and faithful have a reason to be patient as they wait for vindication. The time is coming when the wrongs will be righted and the persecutors judged.

Those who die in the Lord are blessed—whether they are killed because of their faith or meet their death in some other way. They have rest from labor, and reward for their works. Paul speaks of such rewards in 1 Cor. 3:12-15. In verse 14 he says, "If anyone's work which he has built on it endures, he will receive a reward." In 1 Thess. 2:19-20 he refers to the ones he has brought to Christ as the reward he was hoping for. "For what is our hope, or joy, or crown of rejoicing? *Is it* not even you in the presence of our Lord Jesus Christ at His coming? For you are our glory and joy." Our works will follow us.

In Heb. 4:9-10 the writer speaks of this rest as the sabbath rest which we strive to enter. He says, "There remains therefore a rest for the people of God. For he who has entered His rest has himself also ceased from his works as God *did* from His." He goes on to say in verse 11, "Let us therefore be diligent to enter that rest, lest anyone fall according to the same example of disobedience."

After this brief interruption to console and reassure the saints the vision continues with the pictures of God's judgment.

SCENE 2: TWO HARVEST (14:14-20)

Judgment is pictured as reaping two harvests. In Matt. 9:37-38 the process of bringing people to Christ is likened to a harvest. Jesus said we ought to pray for laborers to be sent into this harvest. However, this is not the harvest at the end of the world, but the process of converting people to Christ throughout this age. On the other hand, when Jesus explains the parable of the tares, the harvest there is at the end of the world: In Matt. 13:37-43 we read:

> He answered and said to them: "He who sows the good seed is the Son of Man. The field is the world, the good seeds are the sons of the kingdom, but the tares are the sons of the wicked *one*. The enemy who sowed them is the devil, the harvest is the end of the age, and the reapers are the angels. Therefore as the tares are gathered and burned in the fire, so it will be at the end of this age. The Son of Man will send out His angels, and they will gather out of His kingdom all things that offend, and those who practice lawlessness, and will cast them into the furnace of fire. There will be wailing and gnashing of teeth. Then the righteous will shine forth as the sun in the kingdom of their Father. He who has ears to hear, let him hear!"

Jesus sends His angels to weed out all the wicked who are then gathered and burned in the fire. The rest, the righteous, will be gathered to the kingdom of God the Father. In this parable the righteous are the wheat and the wicked are the (tares) weeds.

In another illustration Jesus likens the harvest to the threshing of the grain. In Matt. 3:12 He puts it like this, "His winnowing fan *is* in His hand, and He will thoroughly clean out His threshing floor, and gather His wheat into the barn; but He will burn up the chaff with unquenchable fire." In this illustration the righteous are the grains of wheat after the threshing, and the wicked are the chaff which is to be burned up.

Chapter 14: Act 3, Scenes 1 and 2: Intro to the Wrath of God

In the harvest scenes of Rev. 14 the final harvest is seen as two separate kinds of harvest. The first is not specifically identified as grain, but Jesus gathers the righteous to himself. The second is the harvest of the grapes of wrath, the latter harvest. It follows, therefore that what John sees in the first picture is the former harvest, that of the firstfruits or the grain.

A. THE FIRST HARVEST (Read verses 14-16)

John sees One like a Son of Man, i.e., one with the appearance of a human being, referring, no doubt, to Christ himself. His favorite designation for himself was *The Son of Man*, emphasizing his own humanity. He rides on a white cloud, indicating His divinity. This strengthens the interpretation of the one like a son of man as being the Christ. This scene is also reminiscent of Dan. 7:13 where one like a son of man comes on a cloud to the Ancient of Days to receive the kingdom (dominion) of the world. When Jesus ascended to heaven He did so with the clouds (Acts 1:9-11). Those who saw Him were told that He would return in the same way. Rev. 1:7 also speaks of His coming with the clouds. It is His coming in judgment that is depicted in 14:14-16.

This One like a Son of Man has a golden crown[1] on His head. This is the crown *(stephanos)* of victory. Later, in chapter 19, He has many crowns of kingship *(diadems)*, as King of kings and Lord of lords; but here the emphasis is on His victory over the Beast and False Prophet and those who worship the Beast, as well as over Babylon the Harlot.

The One like a Son of Man has a sharp sickle in his hand. The sickle is used for cutting the stalks of grain. An angel out of the temple calls to Him and tells Him that it is time to reap the harvest. So the One on the cloud wields the sickle and reaps the harvest.

The coming of Christ is to be for judgment. 2 Thess. 1:7-10 says:

> ...you who are troubled rest with us when the Lord Jesus is revealed from heaven with His mighty angels, in flaming fire taking vengeance on those who do not know God, and on those who do not obey the gospel of our Lord Jesus Christ.

---

[1] στέφανος *(stéphanos)*, the laurel wreath of victory.

> These shall be punished with everlasting destruction from the
> presence of the Lord and from the glory of His power.

The emphasis of the first harvest, however, is not the judgment of the wicked, but the ingathering of the righteous. John 14:1-3 tells us that his second coming will be to receive his own unto himself: Verse 3 says, "And if I go and prepare a place for you, I will come again and receive you to Myself; that where I am, *there* you may be also." This first picture of the harvest is a picture of just that. Christ is gathering his own.

In Israel the harvest of the firstfruits was the harvest of grain. This occurred in the spring of the year. The day of Pentecost was a divinely ordained feast. called *the Feast of Weeks* or *the Feast of the First fruits*, which celebrated this harvest. It was the second of three feasts in which the men were required to journey to the House of God each year to offer their sacrifices (Exod. 23:14-17). The first sheaf of the firstfruits (Exod. 23:19) was to be offered to God on the first day of the week at the beginning of the harvest (Lev. 23:9-14). Beginning on that day they were to count 50 days (thus the name *Pentecost*) or, stated another way, seven weeks and one day (thus the name *Feast of Weeks*). This would bring them to another first day of the week. On that day they were to have a feast in celebration of the harvest of grain, or the harvest of the first fruits. 50 days gave time for the completion of that harvest before the feast (Lev. 23:15-22; Deut. 16:9-12).

There is a sense in which the harvest of God's people takes place throughout this age. The servants of God have a part in this work. Jesus spoke to His disciples in Luke 10:2, "Then He said to them, 'The harvest truly *is* great, but the laborers *are* few; therefore pray the Lord of the harvest to send out laborers into His harvest.'" It is significant that this harvest began on the day of Pentecost following the crucifixion of Christ (see Acts 2).

In another sense the harvest is seen as the gathering of the saints at the second coming of Christ. In Matt. 13:24-30, 37-43 Jesus explains the parable of the wheat and tares. In this he points to the end as the time of the harvest. It is in this sense that we see the harvests taking place here in Rev. 14.

The harvest of grain and *the firstfruits* are symbols of the righteous servants of God and followers of Jesus Christ. Those with Christ on Mount Zion in Rev. 14:1-5 are called *the firstfruits to God and to the Lamb* (v. 4). The picture of this first harvest is the Lord's coming to gather his righteous, the firstfruits unto God. Jesus is coming to do this himself (John 14:1-2). Judgment is not a fearful thing for the righteous. To them it is a blessed day (Matt. 25:34). This is when Jesus comes to gather His own and ultimately take them to the place He has prepared for them so they can be with Him forever (John 14:1-3).

B. THE SECOND HARVEST (Read verses 17-20)

While we were left to surmise that the first harvest is the harvest of wheat—i.e., the gathering of the righteous, here we are told that this second harvest is the harvest of the grapes which are to be cast into the winepress of the wrath of God. This is the latter harvest. The third of the yearly feasts was called *The Feast of Tabernacles*, and *The Feast of Ingathering* (Exod. 23:16; Lev. 23:33-43; Deut. 16:13-16). This feast celebrated, among other things, the competed ingathering of the years harvest. The latter harvest took place in the fall of the year, and its principal crop was the harvest of the wine. This harvest is used to symbolize the outpouring of God's wrath in judgment upon sinners. In the pronouncement of judgment on Babylon and on those who worship the beast and his image the figure of drinking the wine of God's wrath is used. Now we see God's wrath portrayed as the reaping of the grapes of wrath.

In the second harvest the reaper is not the Son of Man, but an angel who comes from God's temple in heaven, i.e., from God's presence. In the parable of the tares, it is angels who are sent to gather the tares for the burning (Matt. 13:36-43). Jesus comes with his angels to render vengeance (1 Thess. 1:7-9).

The angel with the sickle comes out of the temple in heaven, sent by God to complete the task of harvesting the grapes. Another angel comes from the altar. He is said to be the one with the power of the fire. He calls to the one with the sickle that it is time to swing the sickle and harvest the grapes, for they are ripe and ready.

Since this angel who came from the altar has the power of fire, he is probably the one who has the responsibility for the fire on the altar in this symbolic picture. The fire on both the altar of burnt offering and the altar of incense was to be kept burning day and night. The judgments in chapters 7 and 8 are a response to the prayers of the saints. In chapter 8 these prayers are represented as incense offered on the golden altar of incense. Perhaps this is the significance of the angel coming from the altar. He is announcing the time for the reaping of the grapes, those who are objects of God's wrath. Perhaps he is doing this in response to the prayers of the saints. Which altar is the one referred to here? Take your pick. It doesn't say. The altar of sacrifice is where we see the souls of the martyrs crying for judgment in 6:9-10. On the other hand, the golden altar of incense is where the prayers of the saints are offered calling for judgment. Either would fit the symbolism.

The reaping angel, like the Son of Man, has a sickle. The sickle that we know today is not used to gather grapes. However, the word translated sickle ($\delta\rho\epsilon\pi\alpha\nu\sigma\nu$ – *drepanon*) is defined as *a gathering hook, especially for harvesting*. This definition would apply equally well to the sickle used for grain harvesting and the grape knife used for gathering grapes. At times, In my youth, I worked with others in the vineyards gathering grapes. We used a hooked knife to sever the bunches of grapes from the vine with a quick pull of the blade. This knife would fit the definition of the word translated sickle.

In the action we see the reaping angel gathers the grapes and throws them into the great winepress of God's wrath. There they are trodden to crush them and release the wine. Although it does not say here, in 19:15b we are told that it is the Son of God who treads upon the grapes.

In Jesus' day criminals were executed outside the city of Jerusalem. Jesus took our sins to the cross outside the city of Jerusalem. He was led out, nailed to the cross, and lifted up as the cross was mounted upright. Jesus suffered and died there for our sins. The wrath of God was poured out on Him for us. All ungodliness and unrighteousness of men are subject to God's wrath (Rom. 1:18), but Jesus took our sins upon Himself and bore that wrath for us. Rom. 5:9 says, "Much more then, having now been justified by His blood, we shall be saved from wrath through Him." Those who fail to accept Christ's sacrifice as their own must themselves suffer the wrath of God. Just as Jesus bore the wrath for us outside the city, so the process of treading out the winepress of God's wrath will take place outside the eternal city.

John saw the wine which flowed from the winepress as human blood—an abundance of human blood—a flood of blood so deep that it was head high to the horses, and the stream was so long that it was 1,600 furlongs (approximately 200 miles) to the end of it. That is a lot of blood. This is the imagery used to picture the wrath of God being poured out on the wicked. I do not see any special significance to the number 1,600 except as a part of the picture of God's wrath.

RECAP OF SCENES ONE AND TWO

Let us review the action we have seen so far in Act Three. Scenes 1 and 2 have seven heavenly beings who present a symbolic picture of the final judgment. One is the Son of Man Himself while the other six are angels. In Scene One the first three angels fly through the heavens and herald the coming of the final judgment. The first angel proclaims the arrival of the hour of God's judgment upon the world. The second pronounces God's judgment on the great city called Babylon. The third proclaims God's judgment on those who worship the beast and his image, and who received the mark of the beast on their forehead or their hand.

A word of encouragement is then given to the people of God. They are told that they have a reason for patience as they await their reward. The blessing of rest and reward is pronounced upon those who have died in the Lord.

In Scene 2 the last four of the heavenly beings portray the final judgment as two harvests. The Son of Man (Christ), comes sitting on a cloud, with a victory crown on His head and a sharp sickle in His hand. An angel, comes out of the temple of God and calls to the One on the cloud that it is time to reap the harvest, so the Son of Man reaps the harvest of the earth.

Another angel comes out of the temple with a sharp sickle in his hand. An angel, the seventh heavenly being, comes out of the temple, from the altar, and calls to the angel with the sickle to gather the clusters of grapes. This he does, then he throws the grapes into a huge wine-press where the grapes are crushed by treading on them. A vast amount of blood flows out of the press, as high as a horse's bridle, and as far as 1600 furlongs. Since the number seven is the symbol of fullness, completeness, or perfection, we understand that these seven beings symbolize God's final and complete judgment on the world.

The picture given in these scenes is a general picture of God's final judgment. The picture of the two harvests should not be understood as occurring at different times. They are two parts of the same judgment. Two harvests are pictured to carry out the symbolism of the two feasts of the former and latter harvests presented in the Old Testament. The theme of the wrath of God is continued in scenes 3 and 4 with the vision of the seven bowls of the wrath of God—the last Plagues.

Chapter 15

ACT 3: THE WRATH OF GOD
SCENE 3: THE SEVEN ANGELS
Rev. Chapter 15

I. SEVEN ANGELS WITH THE SEVEN LAST PLAGUES (15:1)

In Scene 3 the first thing seen is a group of seven angels who have the seven last plagues. It doesn't say where these angels are when John first sees them, but later he sees them coming out of the temple in heaven. The reasonable conclusion is that he sees them in the temple before the throne of God. At this point nothing is said about their holding seven bowls. The angels have the seven last plagues—last because in them the wrath of God is completed or finished. These plagues of God's wrath are to be poured out from seven bowls. When the angels finish pouring out these plagues, the end will have come. The mystery of God's plan for this world will be completed, or as the voice from the temple in heaven says when the seventh bowl is poured out, "It is done!"

II. THE PRAISE OF THE VICTORIOUS SAINTS (Read 15:2-4)

Before the seven angels spring into action, the victorious saints are seen standing on (or by) a sea of glass. They are the ones who have been given the victory over the Beast, his Image (over his mark)[1] and over the number of his

---

[1]Neither the *Nestle/UBS* nor *Majority Texts* have the statement "and over his mark."

name. The sea of glass mingled with fire probably is not the same sea mentioned in Rev. 4:6 since it seems that John is seeing it for the first time: "I saw *something* like a sea of glass mingled with fire...." If he were merely referring to the same sea he had already seen he would have said something like, "I saw those who have the victory over the beast standing by the sea of glass." Yet here he refers to the sea in this scene as if it were something new.

The expression *on the sea* is translated in some versions as *by the sea* or *beside the sea.*[2] If the sea here is the crystal sea seen by John in 4:6, then it should be translated "*by, beside,* or *before* the sea," since that sea is the large basin which stood before the Holy Place, like the brazen sea in the temple in Jerusalem describe in 1 Kings 7:23-26.

I think it is more likely that the sea here is the expanse seen in Ezek, 1:22, 26-28. Ezekiel calls it a firmament (expanse). It is the platform on which the throne of God sits. In Ezekiel the four living creatures transport the throne of God on a crystal expanse. Ezekiel also refers to the appearance of fire in describing the appearance of the one on the throne in Ezek. 1:27. (See also Exodus 24:10.) John probably sees the victorious saints standing before the crystal expanse upon which the throne of God sits.

The victorious saints have harps of God, and they sing "the song of Moses ...and the Lamb." This is probably the same as the new song spoken of in chapter 14:3. It is a song of praise to God for his great and marvelous works which have been brought to completion in the redemption of the saints and their victory over Satan's forces.

Moses represents the Law of God while the Lamb portrays His Grace and Truth in the person of Jesus Christ (John 1:17). The work of Moses was very important, since it laid the groundwork for the coming of Christ (Gal. 3:24); but the foremost work was that of Christ, the Lamb, for Satan is defeated by the blood of the Lamb and by the testimony of the saints about Him (Rev. 12:11). The song of the saints extols God's mighty works. His deeds are marvelous and His ways are holy.

---

[2] KJV and NKJV have "**on** the sea," while ASV has "**by** the sea," and NIV and NRSV have "**beside** the sea." The Greek ἐπί *(epi)* with the accusative case may be translated *on, at, by, beside,* or *before* as in Acts 5:23, "standing at (or before or by) the door." certainly not upon the door. In Matt. 21:19 the tree stood "by the road," not on the road.

This song foretells the results of God's judgments—i.e., "...all nations shall come and worship before you." In verse three God is called *King of the nations*[3] The reason that all nations are to come worship is given: "For your judgments have been manifested." Christ refused to take over the nations as a vassal when Satan offered them to Him (Matt. 4:8-11). Yet it was Christ's purpose to take his great power and reign over the kingdom of the world (Rev. 11:15, 17; Dan. 7:13-14,26-27). Then, when the time for His final judgment comes, every knee shall bow before Him, from every nation, tribe and tongue (Rom. 14:10-11).

The saints in this scene are the righteous who have been faithful unto death. They await the resurrection in the disembodied state. They are in heaven before the throne where they await the resurrection, and the completion of God's final judgment. This is another picture of the scene of the redeemed in Rev. 14:1-5. There is a difference, however. The servants of God in chapter 14 have been redeemed from the earth—i.e., they have been raised from the dead and taken to heaven. There they await the completion of the judgment when they will be conducted to the new heaven and earth, their eternal abode. Those in the vision of chapter 15 have not reached that point. In 15:2-4 they are the righteous dead who await the resurrection. The judgment of the wicked had not yet taken place, for the saints are singing of things that were going to take place—i.e., all nations are going to come and worship before God, etc. At the last trump both the righteous and wicked are raised. The words of Jesus in John 5:28-29 state:

> Do not marvel at this; for the hour is coming in which all who are in the graves will hear His voice and come forth—those who have done good, to the resurrection of life, and those who have done evil, to the resurrection of condemnation.

The word *condemnation* is the same word as *judgment.* While the righteous are raised to receive eternal life, the wicked are raised for judgment, to receive the wrath of God. Before that time the wicked must face the last plagues here on earth. It is during these plagues that all the wicked are killed. They are killed by the first six of the plagues. The plagues are completed

---

[3]Whereas in verse 3, KJV and NKJV refer to God as being "King of **the saints**," the *Nestle/UBS* and *Majority Texts* have τῶν ἐθνῶν – **the nations**, as translated in the RSV and NRSV. ASV and NIV have **the ages**, as found in some ancient MSS.

when the last trumpet blows and the wicked are raised to stand before the judgment throne of God. From there they are cast into the lake that burns with fire and brimstone. The final judgment was at hand, but the angels who had the bowls of wrath had not yet poured them out. That will take place during the action of Scene Four.

III. PREPARING TO POUR OUT THE BOWLS OF WRATH (15:5-8)

The seven angels with the seven last plagues come out of the temple in heaven. This indicates that the source of these judgments is God since they proceed from His throne. These angels are dressed as priests, according to the Old Testament description of the priestly garments, with linen robes and golden breastplates (see Christ's garment in Rev. 1:13).

They are given bowls which are probably the incense bowls (censors) like the one used by the priest/angel of 8:3-5. There the incense of prayer in the bowl was offered as a sacrifice, then the censor was filled with coals of fire and poured out as judgment upon the earth. The symbolism here is the same, except here there are seven priest/angels pouring out seven censors full of judgments upon the earth. These bowls are given to them by one of the cherubim in v. 7.

Now the preparation is complete for the angels to pour out these bowls with the seven last plagues. As God judged Egypt with the ten plagues, so God will judge the world with the seven last plagues. No one can enter the temple until the judgment is completed (v. 8). It is only after the final judgment that the saints are rewarded and take up their residence in the new heaven and earth. The symbolism of the smoke filling the temple to represent the presence and power of God is taken from the Old Testament tabernacle and temple (see Num. 9:15; 16:42; 1 Kings 8:10-13; Exod. 19:18).

Chapter 16

ACT 3: THE WRATH OF GOD
SCENE 4: POURING OUT THE BOWLS OF WRATH
Rev. 16:1-17

I. THE COMMAND TO POUR OUT THE SEVEN PLAGUES (16:1)

Just as the command to reap in chapter 14 came from the temple, delivered by two heavenly messengers crying out to the reapers, so here also the command comes from the temple of God, indicating that it is God Himself who sets the time of judgment and the end, and sends forth the command when that time comes. No man knows that time. Not even the Son knew the time during His earthly life, but only the Father in heaven. In Matt 24:36, while discussing His second coming and the end of the age Jesus says, "But of that day and hour no one knows, not even the angels of heaven, but My Father only." These are things that God has set within His own authority, and no man can know them until they are revealed.

A. COMPARISON OF THE SEVEN BOWLS WITH THE SEVEN TRUMPETS

There is a great deal of similarity between the imagery of the seven last plagues in this chapter and the seven trumpets in chapters 8 and 9.

1. Plagues on Man's Habitat. The first four trumpets affect a third of the earth, the sea, the fresh water sources, and the firmament. These make up the habitat of man. The first four bowls of wrath are also poured out upon these same four areas of man's habitat, with, however, some notable differences in the effects.

279

Total, Not Just a Third. Unlike the trumpets, the last plagues are no longer affecting just a third of earth, sea, fresh water and firmament, but the whole of each.

Different Effects. When the first bowl is poured out on the earth, rather than destroying the vegetation as in the first trumpet, the earth is caused to produce foul and loathsome sores on all who dwell on earth. In the pouring out of the second and third bowls all the water in the seas and all the fresh water are turned to blood, not just a third, as in the second trumpet. All living things in the oceans die as a result, and "those who dwell on earth" have no drinkable water. When the fourth bowl is poured out, instead of the sun's being darkened, the angel uses it to burn men with fire and great heat. All those who dwell on earth suffer this burning.

2. Pain and Darkness. In the blowing of the fifth trumpet the sun and air are darkened by thick smoke from the abyss, and stinging locusts come out of the smoke and inflict great pain on the ones who do not have the seal of God. This is only for a limited time (Rev. 9:5). The fifth bowl of wrath brings darkness on the kingdom of the beast, and great pain upon men. However, there is no mention of this pain being temporary, as it was in the fifth trumpet.

3. The Death of All Men (Earth Dwellers), Not Just One-Third

When the sixth trumpet was blown men were faced with a great army which kills a third of mankind. The sixth bowl is similar in that it involves the preparation for a great final battle in which all the kings and worshipers of the beast are killed according to accounts elsewhere in the book. Rev. 16:12-16; 19:11-21; and 20:7-10 are all different symbolic pictures of the same final battle, and Rev. 17:12-14 allude to it. Unlike the sixth trumpet judgment, the destruction of mankind is total.

4. Seventh Bowl Brings the End. Just as the seventh trumpet finishes the mystery of God, and brings time to an end (Rev. 10:5-7; 11:15-18), the pouring out of the seventh bowl of wrath finishes the final judgment and brings the world to its end.

B. *CHRONOLOGICAL OR CONCURRENT?*

These final plagues, meting out God's wrath on the wicked, are probably not separate events happening chronologically. They are showing different aspects of the wrath of God. In whatever order they occur, chronologically or concurrently, they certainly must take place rapidly. The symbolism of having nothing but blood to drink indicates that men could only continue to live a very short time during these plagues.

Unlike the first six trumpet judgments which are taking place throughout the age, the first six bowls of wrath occur immediately before the final judgment, ending in the death of all the wicked. It pays to remember that these are symbolic pictures. There are seven bowls of wrath. The symbolism of the number seven indicates the completion of God's wrath, the finality of His judgment upon the wicked.

The symbolism of the seven last plagues, like that of the trumpets, is drawn from the ten plagues brought upon Egypt when Pharaoh refused to let the Israelites go free. These seven plagues, unlike the ten in Egypt, should not be viewed as a chronological succession of events. Of course, the seventh bowl, like the seventh trumpet, brings the judgment to an end, and is therefore the last event chronologically. The first six bowls are picturing different aspects of the wrath of God upon those who dwell on earth— plagues which occur just prior to the pouring out of last bowl. These plagues picture the life of the wicked on earth being brought to an end just prior to the resurrection and the judgment before the throne of God.

II. THE FIRST BOWL OF WRATH (Read 16:2)

The picture is of a festering sore. Can there be any more excruciating pain than the pain of flesh being eaten away by cancer, or the pain of a severe boil filled with the pressure of compacted puss? This is depicted as part of the punishment of those who wear the mark of the beast and worship his image.

This figure is taken from the sixth plague of boils brought upon the Egyptians in Exod. 9:8-12. The boils in Egypt were caused by ashes turned to dust that lighted on the people of Egypt. The first bowl of wrath was upon the earth producing grievous sores, perhaps this was caused by the dust of the earth lighting upon men, like the ashes in Egypt. In the third plague in Egypt dust filled the air and became lice upon all the people of Egypt. In this first bowl of God's wrath it is as if the earth upon which men live turns against them and causes them great pain.

III. THE SECOND BOWL OF WRATH (Read 16:3)

In the plague of the second trumpet in 8:8-9 a third of the sea is turned to blood. Here the whole sea becomes blood. The symbolism is drawn from the very first plague upon Egypt—the water turned to blood—found in Exod. 7:19-25. Whereas the turning of the Nile to blood in Egypt was a literal plague, here in Revelation the turning of the water to blood in both the second and third bowls of wrath is intended as a figure, depicting the severity of God's judgment upon those who would not repent of their opposition to God and His people. Much of the livelihood of people depends upon the sea. The fish of the sea provide a large part of mankind's food. Commerce depends much on the ships of the sea. All this comes to a halt when the whole ocean becomes blood. Every living thing in the sea and on the sea dies.

We should probably see this plague as relating to the harvest of the grapes of God's wrath in 14:18-20. There the blood results from trampling the grapes in the winepress of God's wrath. The grapes are the unrighteous, gathered by the angels in the final judgment. The blood of the second bowl of wrath is said to be like the blood of a dead person—i.e., it has congealed. The many waters from which the beast arises, and upon which the harlot sits represent peoples, multitudes and nations (Rev. 17:15). Perhaps, then, turning the sea into blood represents the slaughter of the people of the world, as if the sea were the blood of "those who dwell on earth."

IV. THE THIRD BOWL OF WRATH (Read 16:4-7)

The third bowl of God's wrath is poured out upon the fresh water sources (rivers and springs). They all became blood so there is no fresh water left to drink (v. 4). This, also, is reminiscent of the first plague in Egypt. In verse 5 an angel who is called *the angel of the waters* gives praise to God and expresses His righteousness in judging these things. Note what the angel says in verse 6: "For they have shed the blood of saints and prophets, and you have given them blood to drink. For it is their just due." This judgment is upon those who persecute the people of God. They shed the blood of the servants of God and now God gives them blood to drink.

Exod. 21:23-25 gives the following law; "But if *any* harm follows, then you shall give life for life, eye for eye, tooth for tooth, hand for hand, foot for foot, burn for burn, wound for wound, stripe for stripe." (See also Lev. 24:19-20 and Deut. 19:21.) The third bowl of wrath illustrates this principle. This law was given as a guideline for authorities who were to judge and punish wrongdoers. It was never intended for individuals to use as an excuse for revenge. Jesus teaches us to treat our enemies differently in Matt. 5:38-45. Rather than taking vengeance we are told to do good to them.

Vengeance must be left to God. In Rom. 12:19 Paul writes, "Beloved, do not avenge yourselves, but *rather* give place to wrath; for it is written, *'Vengeance is Mine, I will repay,' says the Lord."* Judgment and punishment are the Lord's business. God will avenge us in due time. He will give life for life, eye for eye, tooth for tooth, burning for burning, and in this case blood for blood.

Evil men have two choices. One is to repent and turn to Christ so that their sins may be taken away by the blood of Christ. When judgment day comes the one who has repented will stand with the righteous and not be condemned. The second choice is to resist and continue in evil as long as they live. In this case all their sins will be upon their own shoulders and their condemnation will be just. Their punishment will fit the evil, just as it indicates in this third plague. The wine of God's wrath which the wicked are made to drink is seen in these symbols as blood. The wine which came out of the winepress in chapter 14 was blood. The symbolism here is of being given blood to drink. This is the wine of God's wrath.

In verse 5 the expression "who is to come" is not found either here or in 11:17 except in a few late manuscripts. The reading should be, "The One who is and who was." Except for the King James and the New King James most versions read "the holy one" in place of "who is to come."[1] The reason

---

[1]Neither the *Nestle/UBS Text* nor the *Majority Text* have the expression "who is to come." Instead, both of these Greek texts have "the Holy One." *Nestle/UBS* is taken from the oldest available Greek manuscripts of the New Testament, while the *Majority Text* represents the reading found in the majority of the Greek manuscripts. Later copyists may have added the phrase "who is to come" to bring it into harmony with Rev. 1:8.

the phrase was not included should be obvious. This verse, as well as the one in 11:17, speaks of the judgment when Jesus comes to judge the world. At this point He is no longer the coming one. Having already come He is referred to as the eternal one—the one who always was, and who eternally is—YHWH, the eternal self-existing one.

Verse 7 says that John heard another from the altar[2] praise God for His judgment, and pronounce His judgment righteous. Most manuscripts omit *another* in this verse. They say instead that John heard the altar praise God. How is the altar praising God? Remember that in 6:9-10 the martyred souls under the altar were crying out for judgment and vengeance upon those who dwell on earth because they had shed the blood of the saints. Perhaps it is the blood of the martyrs from the base of the altar which John hears proclaiming the justice of God's judgment. This fits in well with the declaration that they have shed the blood of the saints and they have been given blood to drink.

V. THE FOURTH BOWL OF WRATH (Read 16:8-9)

The fourth plague is upon the sun. In the fourth trumpet judgment a third of the sun is darkened along with a third of the moon and stars. However, the results here are different. Power is given to the angel to burn men with great heat from the sun. This plague does not seem to have a counterpart in the plagues of Egypt. Burning, however, is often presented as a judgment upon the wicked. In the story of the rich man and Lazarus the rich man was burning in torment in the hadean world while Lazarus was comforted in Abraham's bosom (Luke 16:19-31).

The unfruitful tree is cast into the fire and the chaff is burnt up with fire (Matt. 3:10-12). The ultimate fate of the wicked is to be cast into the lake of fire and brimstone which is the second death (see Rev. 20:14-15 and 21:8).

The result of these first four plagues is not repentance and reformation, for the reaction of those who dwell on earth (the worshipers of the beast) is resistance. They do not repent nor glorify God (see Rev. 9:20-21). Instead they blaspheme God's name because of the plagues. There is a statement in

---

[2]Here, as in verse 15, the KJV and NKJV include the statement "another from (or out of) the altar." This is based on the *Textus Receptus* which is in turn based on a few late Greek manuscripts. The *Nestle/UBS* and *Majority Texts* do not have this phrase.

Rev. 22:11 which indicates the stubborn determination of the wicked to stick to their wickedness. "He who is unjust, let him be unjust still; he who is filthy, let him be filthy still; he who is righteous, let him be righteous still; he who is holy, let him be holy still." The time will come when the opportunity for repentance and reformation are past. In whatever state a person is found in the judgment, righteous or wicked, that is how he will remain throughout eternity.

VI. THE FIFTH BOWL OF WRATH (Read 16:10-11)

The fifth bowl of wrath brings darkness and pain to the throne of the beast. Darkness was the ninth of the ten Plagues brought upon the land of Egypt (Exod. 10.21-29). The Beast in John's day, the sixth head, was seen to be the Roman Empire. The throne of the beast would then be Rome. In the 13th chapter the beast is the revived Roman empire in the ten-horn stage. The ruling power governing these horns (nations) was still centered in Rome. What the throne of the beast will be during the eighth stage when the final judgment takes place remains yet to be seen.

There is yet another interpretation possible. Since the beast is the manifestation of Satan in the persecuting kingdoms of men, the throne of the beast may be wherever Satan holds sway. In Rev. 2:13 Jesus says to the church in Pergamum, "I know where you dwell, even where Satan's throne is...." The throne of the beast could be any city or region where the cause of Christ and His servants are persecuted.

Wherever the throne of the beast is, the result of the pouring out of the fifth bowl of wrath is that his whole kingdom is darkened. The people of his kingdom, all who wear the mark of the beast and worship his image, suffer great pain. God brings the suffering as a just punishment for their wickedness and opposition to the cause of Christ. The response of men to this plague is further resistance and blasphemy of God because of the suffering. There is no tendency on their part to repent and reform their lives.

There is a unity in the messages of these bowls of wrath. They are all interrelated. The suffering of the fifth plague is related to the first because the first brings the painful sores and the fifth shows the kingdom of the beast blaspheming God because of their pains and the sores. The second also is associated with the kingdom of the beast, because he came up out of the sea. That sea, according to Rev. 17:15, represents peoples, multitudes and nations. The treading of the grapes in the winepress of God's wrath produces a sea of blood—the blood of the peoples, multitudes and nations that support the beast and his evil work. The third and fifth both relate to the kingdom of the beast, because it is the beast that spills the blood of the saints and prophets, and so his kingdom is given blood to drink—i.e., the wine of the wrath of God. The fourth is related to the fifth in that the results of both are the same—blasphemy, resistance and unrepentance.

It is my conviction that these six bowls of wrath are a unit, portraying the wrath of God being poured out in various ways to bring an end to the life of all those who dwell on earth just prior to the resurrection and final judgment. As soon as these are completed then all men stand before the judge of all the earth to receive the things done in the body. This judgment is pictured in the 20th chapter.

VII. The Sixth Bowl of Wrath (Read 16:12-16)

The sixth bowl is the preparation for the downfall of the Beast, the False Prophet and the Dragon himself. It draws from the second Egyptian plague of frogs (Exod. 8:1-15). Out of the mouth of the dragon, the beast, and the false prophet, come evil spirits like frogs, and they go to enlist the kings of the earth in "the battle of that great day of God Almighty." The armies of the nations gather in the place called Armageddon. *The day of God*, or *the day of the Lord* is an expression used throughout scripture to refer to a day of judgment, or a time of the coming of God's judgment upon a nation or a people. This great day of God is the time when His judgment comes on all the nations and people in the final overthrow of evil.

The angel pours out the sixth bowl on the great river Euphrates. This river is significant because armies frequently assembled at the river as they prepared to strike across it to the lands of the south. Assyria, Babylonia, and Persia all lay north of this river. When Assyria invaded Syria (Aramea) and Israel, its armies crossed the Euphrates to accomplish this job. When the Babylonians came into Judea to conquer and destroy Jerusalem and the temple, they first crossed the Euphrates. Many times in ancient history armies were amassed at the river Euphrates. This is a fitting symbol of the preparation of the armies of the nations for the great final battle of Armageddon.

In this vision the waters of the Euphrates River are dried up, making it easy for the armies to cross. There was a historical event from which this symbol is probably drawn. When Darius the Mede brought the Medo-Persian army against Babylon, its last king, Belshazzar, was having a drunken feast and the city's guard was let down. Although the outer gates of the city were securely locked and guarded, the Euphrates River flowed through the midst of the city. The Babylonians felt no threat from that direction so the river walls were left open and unguarded. The army of the Medes and Persians diverted the waters of the river around the city, drying up the river bed under the city. The armies simply marched into Babylon along the river bed, made their way through the gates of the river walls, and conquered the city with little or no resistance. This historical conquest of Babylon provides a suitable symbol for the destruction of Babylon the Harlot.

In chapter 17 we learn that the Beast hated the Harlot and sought to destroy her using the kingdoms represented as ten horns (Rev. 17:16-7). It also tells us that the Beast, through the ten-horn nations, will make war with the Lamb and the Lamb will overcome them (Rev. 17:12-14). This is a reference to the battle for which preparations were being made in the symbolism of the sixth bowl of wrath. The reference to the armies at the Euphrates indicates that these nations are to be used to destroy Babylon the Harlot just prior to their own destruction.

The three frogs which come out of the mouths of the Dragon, the Beast and the False Prophet are demonic spirits whose job is to gather the nations of the earth. It is these nations that give their authority over to the beast, the world power that is opposed to Christ. The beast uses them to destroy the Harlot, and he uses them to make war on the saints. Although the nations are gathered together by Satan's forces to fight "the battle of that great day of God the Almighty," nothing is said here about the battle's taking place, or its outcome. There are other places in Revelation where this battle is described for us. It is enough to say here that the stage is set for that battle.

In response to this preparation Jesus tells us that He is coming like a thief would come. No one knows the day or the hour. It will be unexpected. You get the impression that the battle is not going to last very long. The armies are prepared to fight against the cause of Christ, but their intention is cut short by the coming of Christ. In 19:11-21 the final battle is depicted for us. Jesus comes just as the nations are gathered together for war. Jesus was hinting at this when He spoke of coming as a thief. Indeed the battle is a short one. The forces of the Beast don't even get to strike a blow. If you want to take a sneak peek at other scenes dealing with this battle, go to 17:12-14, 19:11-21 and 20:7-9.

The staging area for this battle is a place called Armageddon. This is why the battle is called *the battle of Armageddon*. Where does this name come from? There is a valley in the midst of the mountains of Israel called *Esdraelon*. It is also called the valley of *Jezreel*. This word means *judgment* or *decision* because many decisive battles were fought there between nations. The outpost guarding the entrance to that valley on the east was a garrison called *Megiddo*. *Armageddon (har-megiddo)* means *the hill of Megiddo*. This place is a symbol of the gathering place of the armies of the kingdoms who seek to fight against the Lamb and His saints. The name *Jezreel* is a fitting symbol for this final battle, because in this battle God's judgment will come upon the Dragon, the Beast and False Prophet and those who follow them. The battle will be even more decisive than the one fought in heaven between the Dragon and Michael. That battle ended with Satan's being cast to earth. This one will end with Satan, along with the Beast and the False Prophet, being cast into the Lake of Fire from which he will never emerge.

VIII. THE SEVENTH BOWL OF WRATH (Read 16:17)

When the seventh bowl is poured out a loud voice from the throne of God says, "It is done!" That is a simple statement. When the last plague is poured out it is all over. We would think that the curtain would come down on the drama. But the play is not over, because there are more scenes to come. This is just one more time that we come to the end. We will come to the end three more times in the following chapters. We have already seen the end twice in preceding chapters with the seventh seal and the seventh trumpet.

The first four plagues are directed against the worshipers of the beast—i.e., those who dwell on earth. They speak of the destruction of the habitat of mankind in terms of earth, sea, fresh water, and the heavens. The next two plagues are directed against the agencies of Satan—i.e., the Beast, the False

288

Prophet, and Babylon the Harlot. The fifth brings pain and suffering upon the throne of the beast, the sixth prepares for the final battle between good and evil, and the seventh brings the final and total overthrow of the forces of evil.
The judgments of these forces of evil are presented separately in this order: Babylon the Harlot (16:18 - 19:8), the Beast and False Prophet (19:11-21), the Dragon (20:7-10), and all whose names are not written in the book of life (20:11-15).

Chapter 17

ACT 4: THE FALL OF BABYLON
SCENES 1 AND 2
Rev. 16:18 – 17:18

SCENE 1: BABYLON'S JUDGMENT PROCLAIMED (16:18-21)

A. *NATURE'S ANNOUNCEMENT*

In Revelation, whenever there are momentous events about to occur they are frequently announced symbolically by catastrophic events of nature. This has happened several times in previous chapters. In Rev. 16:18 there are thunder, lightning, and the most violent earthquake the earth has ever seen. What is the message of this portent? Not only that momentous events are about to follow, but that those events will be such that the created world will be shaken to its foundation.

What God had created in the beginning He will destroy in the final judgment. Gen. 1:1 tells us, "In the beginning God created the heavens and the earth." "...the worlds were framed By the word of God," according to Heb. 11:3, and by the word of God they will be dissolved. 2 Pet. 3:12 says, "...looking for and hastening the coming of the day of God, because of which the heavens will be dissolved, being on fire, and the elements will melt with fervent heat." In Matt. 24:35 Jesus declares, "Heaven and earth will pass away, but My words will by no means pass away." The shaking of earth in this judgment will be followed shortly by the passing away of heaven and earth (20:11).

B. BABYLON TO BE MADE TO DRINK THE WINE OF GOD'S WRATH

Verse 19 speaks of the great city being divided into three parts. What is the great city, and what are the three parts? The first mention of this city is found in Rev. 11:8 where the two witnesses were killed and where their dead bodies lay for three and a half days; "And their dead bodies *will lie* in the street of the great city which spiritually is called Sodom and Egypt, where also our Lord was crucified." This great city was not literally the land of Egypt since Egypt was a country or nation, not a city. The great city is called Egypt because of its representation of the world of sin. The Israelites were called out of the bondage of Egypt. That was a foreshadow of the people of God being called out of the bondage of sin. The great city is the world system spoken of in 1 John 2:15-17:

> Do not love the world or the things in the world. If anyone loves the world, the love of the Father is not in him. For all that *is* in the world—the lust of the flesh, the lust of the eyes, and the pride of life—is not of the Father but is of the world. And the world is passing away, and the lust of it; but he who does the will of God abides forever.

It is from this world of sin that we have been called out. Rev. 11:8 also says that the city is called Sodom. This great city is not the literal city of Sodom. The city of Sodom had long before been destroyed and never rebuilt. Its exact location is even in doubt. Sodom was noted for its sinfulness. The great city is what Sodom symbolizes—i.e., the world of sin.

Some have said that *Sodom* is a figure of the literal city of Jerusalem, since 11:8 says that this city is where our Lord was crucified. Old Testament prophets referred to the rebellious nations of Israel and Judah as Sodom and Gomorrah, but the city of Jerusalem is nowhere referred to as Sodom. John 1:10 says, "He was in the world, and the world was made through Him, and the world did not know Him." Our Lord was crucified in the world of sin. The world system had Him put to death. The great city symbolizes the world system. This same city is called Babylon in 16:19. Again, it is not the literal city of Babylon but that for which Babylon stands.

What, then, are the three divisions into which the city (world system) was divided for the purpose of God's judgment? They are named in this passage—i.e., the cities of the nations, the islands (nations), and the

291

mountains (governments or kingdoms). Verse 19 says, "...the cities of the nations fell." Not only the city (*singular*), but the cities (*plural*) of the nations fall—i.e. all the cities which stand for the things represented by Babylon the Harlot. She must pay for her sins and her pervading evil influence upon the nations of the earth. She has made all nations drink the wine of God's wrath because of her fornication (Rev. 14:8). God remembers. Babylon herself must drink of the wine of God's fierce wrath (Rev. 14:19-20).

Verse 20 says, "Then every island fled away, and the mountains were not found." This is a picture not only of the destruction of Babylon the Harlot, but of all the cities, nations and governments of the earth over which she holds sway. When Jesus gave His great commission in Matt. 28:18-20 He decreed that we should make disciples of all nations. There is to be a time when the nations will come and bow to the authority of Christ, a time when it can be said that the nations have yielded to Christ (11:15,17; 20:4; Dan. 7:27). The bulk of the citizens in each nation will have become disciples of Christ and the leadership of those nations will acknowledge Jesus as Lord. It is the time when it will be said, "The kingdom of the world has become the kingdom of our Lord and of His Christ." However, at the end of that period many of the nations will rebel and rage against Christ and His saints. That will be the time when they will flee away and their governments will cease to exist.

One more word about the great city called *Babylon.* There are two contrasting cities in the book of Revelation. One is the city of God, called *the New Jerusalem,* and the other is called *Egypt, Sodom, and Babylon the Great.* These are two opposing systems. The New Jerusalem is composed of the people of God. They are her children according to Gal. 4:26. Rev. 12:17 tells us that they are the offspring of the woman clothed with the sun, with the crown of twelve stars. The two cities represent two systems—the system of righteousness, occupied by the people of God, and the system of the world with its selfishness and materialism, occupied by people of the world. They are **those who dwell in heaven** and **those who dwell on earth**. These cities are portrayed by two women—The glorious woman with the crown of 12 stars in chapter 12 and the scarlet robed harlot of chapter 17. One is the bride of Christ, the city of righteousness—the city of God. The other is the Harlot, the city of sin—the city of the world. The primary characteristic of the city of the world, Babylon, is the materialism and self seeking of the world. The Harlot appeals to the lust of the flesh, the lust of the eye, and the vain glory of life.

Following along with the theme of the plagues is the great hail which falls in 16:21. The symbolism of this plague is drawn from the seventh plague on Egypt in Exod. 9:13-35—i.e., the plague of hail. Although this plague is described after the pronouncement of the finish of God's wrath, it fits right in, and is, in fact, part of the seven. The judgments that are described in chapters 17 – 18 are to be understood as a further explanation of the plagues. These plagues symbolize the destruction of the people who dwell on earth. In the hail of Egypt, every person out in the field was killed by that hail. So here, those who are still in the world of sin, and not sheltered by the blood of Christ, die by the judgment of God, as if by giant hailstones. Yet, even in the process of this judgment, they continue to curse God because of the plague of the hail. For some reason they never consider that their plight is due to their own lives of unbelief, sin, and lack of repentance. Such is the blindness that envelops those who are slaves of sin.

SCENE 2: THE HARLOT AND BEAST EXPLAINED (Rev. 17)

A. AN ANGEL INVITES JOHN TO SEE THE GREAT HARLOT (Read 17:1-2)

The fact that one of the seven angels with the last plagues comes to show John the judgment of the great harlot indicates that this is part of the final judgment which was symbolized by the pouring out of the bowls of wrath. John is about to see God's wrath poured out on the various agencies of Satan in detail. The first agency whose judgment is pictured is called *the great Harlot*. Let us notice her description as given to John by the angel:

1. She Sits on Many Waters. The waters where the Harlot sits represent the people of the world—"peoples, multitudes, nations, and tongues" (v. 15). These are the same waters from which the Beast in Rev. 13 emerges. The kingdoms arise from the peoples, multitudes, nations and tongues. This woman has a controlling influence over the multitudes, and they, like the beast, support her. She sits on the heads of the Beast (v. 9), as well as on many waters, indicating that the world system is a controlling influence over both the kingdoms and the people of the earth.

2. The Kings of the Earth Commit Fornication with Her. The rulers of the earth are her consorts. She entices the nations with the things she has to offer. Whatever the wine of her fornication represents, the rulers and people of the earth are allured by her to partake in it. She holds out to them these abominations in a golden cup (v. 4).

3. Earth Dwellers Made Drunk with the Wine of Her Fornication. "Those who dwell on the earth" as well as the kings of earth are enticed by her. John sees her as a temptress, a seductress, and as such she is an agent of Satan. There only three ways Satan can subvert men. One is by the allurements and enticements of the world, another is by leading them astray through false teachings, and third is by the pressures of persecution by which he hopes to force men into renouncing Christ. The first of these is personified by the Harlot, the second by the False Prophet of deceit, and the third by the Beast of persecution.

B. WHAT JOHN SAW WHEN HE SAW THE HARLOT (Read 17:2-6)

In his vision the angel carries John in the Spirit into the wilderness. Is this the wilderness where the woman with the crown of 12 stars was carried, where she is protected from the Beast for 1260 days? It doesn't say, but the imagery of this wilderness probably stands for the barrenness of the world system—the wilderness of sin. Now let us notice the description of what John saw.

1. The Harlot Sitting on a Scarlet Beast. This Beast was full of names of blasphemy. This Beast is no doubt the same Beast we saw in chapter 13. It came up out of the sea. In chapter 13 the ten-horn stage of the sixth head was in power. Which head is in power in chapter 17? The description given here is not pointing to one of the seven heads. The woman sits on all seven of the heads. Whichever head of the Beast comes to power, there the Harlot is, supported by him, and influencing him with her allurements. The powers of the world that persecute the saints, and the enticements which the world has to offer, go together. It is precisely because the saints oppose the immoralities which the woman has to offer that she and the beast who supports her are so opposed to them.

2. Clothed in Purple and Scarlet, Gold and Gems and Pearls. The Harlot no doubt appears very beautiful to the nations and people of the earth.

Not only are they attracted to her, but to her luxuries as well. She is dressed in royal purple because she is found in the courts of royalty. She is dressed in scarlet because of her harlotry. Like an expensive harlot, the kings of the world ply her with gold and precious jewels.

3. A Golden Cup Full of Abominations. The Harlot holds her cup of abominations out to the kings and people of the earth. This is a picture of enticement. She is a fornicator and she entices the world to partake in her impurities. It is significant that she is never called an adulteress. This would be the word for her If she were a symbol of the apostate church, since the church is betrothed to Christ. God accused Israel and Judah, whom He had espoused to Himself, of being adulteresses because they went after other gods (Jer. 3:9-11).

4. Mystery, Babylon the Great, the Mother of Harlots. This woman is the great city called Babylon the Great, the one whose judgment was announced both in chapters 14 and 16. She is called *the mother of harlots.* She is the purveyor of all that appeals to the flesh, the eye, and human pride. The kings and people of the world commit fornication with her by making these—lust, greed, wealth, power, pleasure, fame, etc.—the center of their lives.

5. Drunk with the Blood of Saints and Martyrs. The things the Harlot represents (see 1 John 2:15-17) stand in opposition to the church and the Bible. Those who live righteously and teach righteousness are a torment to those who dwell on earth (11:10). As a result, when these agents of Christ (the church and the Bible) are seemingly killed the world rejoices (11:10). The Harlot becomes drunk with the blood of the saints who are martyred in her.

When John saw this amazing woman he was filled with wonder and amazement. What could all this mean? The Beast upon which the woman sat is apparently none other than the Beast we saw in Rev. 13. The great red Dragon gave him his power. Not only does he have seven heads and ten horns like the Dragon, but he also has the red color of the Dragon. He is a fitting representative of the Dragon on this earth. The Beast supports the woman who is closely associated with him.

C. THE ANGEL PROCEEDS TO EXPLAINS THE BEAST

Having described the figures of the Harlot and the Beast the angel proceeds to explain the Beast and then the Harlot for us.

1. The Sixth and Seventh Head in Revelation (verses 7-8). In order to understand the Harlot, we must understand the Beast with which she is associated, over which she wields controlling influence, and which supports her in her function as an agent of Satan. We must understand that John is seeing the Beast from the perspective of the day of judgment. Since John lived and prophesied during the Roman Empire, the Revelation deals only with the sixth and seventh heads, including the eighth phase of the beast which is one of the seven heads.

In chapter 13 the beast is the resurrected Roman Empire (the sixth head revived) with the crowns on the ten horns. The horns which made up the revived sixth head are the persecuting kingdoms which arose out of the demise of the ancient Roman Empire. This is the Beast that makes war on the saints for 1260 days (years). The sixth head and the ten horns do not outlive that period of time, for that is the time assigned to them by the sovereign providence of God. Here in chapter 17 the drama has progressed far beyond that point. We have already seen some pictures of the final judgment of the world, including the Beast. At this point in the drama the Beast is about to come up out of the abyss and go into perdition. Let's notice this description:

The Seven Heads Are Seven Mountains and Seven Kings. *Mountains* are symbolism for *governments*—i.e., kingdoms or empires. The heads are also called seven mountains in order to identify the woman who sits upon the heads in John's day. Verse 18 says that she is the great city which rules over the kings of the earth—none other than the city of Rome, the city which sits on seven mountains. The heads are also said to be seven kings. The term *king* is used figuratively for *kingdom*. This is a figure of speech called *metonymy*. It puts one thing for another, such as a part of a thing for the whole of it. A frequent use of this figure is that a king represents his kingdom. This was the case in Dan. 7. Both the four beasts and ten horns were variously called *kings* in some verses, and *kingdoms* in others. For a more thorough study of this subject see *Appendix G* on Daniel's Visions as well as chapter 13 of this book where the beast is introduced.

He Was and Is Not. The Beast has ceased to exist on earth at this point in the play. At this point in the drama the Beast has been defeated and confined to the abyss. At this stage in the play the Beast "is not". It is said that he "is not and yet is." What can this seeming contradiction mean? It means that although he has ceased to exist on earth for the time being, he is still in existence in the abyss. The Beast is Satan's agent of persecution. He exists to make war with the saints. When the Beast ceases to exist on earth, persecution ceases.

The Beast to Ascend from the Abyss and Go into Perdition. *Perdition* is *hell—the lake of fire,* or literally, *destruction.* We will learn more about this in chapters 19 and 20. The world marvels at the resurrection of the Beast. The world is composed of the ones whose names are not written in the Lambs book of life. These are the ones who will follow the beast in his brief rebellion when he ascends from the abyss. As a result, they will share in his condemnation (see 19:19-21; 20:7-10,15).

2. John Is Told How to Identify the Heads of the Beast (17:9-11). To a person watching a play there are two time elements—his own time and the time in the progress of the play. For example, if you go to see Wells' *The Time Machine* in a theater on June 15th, 2005, then your own time will be June 15th, 2005. However, the time in the movie begins in the 19th Century and progresses through hundreds of years. Then the time regresses to the 19th century again, then back to the future. The date at any given point in the movie depends on the progress of the movie. When you leave the theater your time is still June 15th, 2005.

The angel was speaking of the Beast's situation at this point in the drama—i.e., "he was, and is not." He is in the abyss but about to come out and go into perdition. In chapter 20 we will see that the Beast is in the abyss during the 1000 year reign of the saints. The angel is explaining the Beast that John saw in the wilderness from that point of view. Since the Beast of persecution is not, then persecution has ceased. The seventh head has already come and has fallen.

On the other hand, in verses 9 and 10 the angel describes the heads of the Beast in terms of John's time rather than from the play's time. He speaks of the Beast as existing, so it could not be the same time frame in which the Beast does not exist. Five of the heads are fallen (in John's day), one is (in

John's day), and one is yet to come (in John's day). The mind that has wisdom could identify these heads. John, no doubt had the wisdom to understand. It takes a knowledge of Old Testament history, which John had.

When we saw the Beast with seven heads emerge from the sea in Rev. 13:1, we noticed that the Beast was first described in terms of the four beasts of Dan. 7, beginning with the last and going in reverse order. Those were: 1) The ten-horned beast; 2) The leopard; 3) The bear; and 4) The lion. These beasts, in the order given in Daniel, were: 1) The lion—Babylonian Empire; 2) The bear—Medo/Persian Empire; 3) The leopard—Grecian Empire; and 4) The 10-horned beast—the Roman Empire. The first three of these had fallen. John lived in the days of the Roman Empire, the fourth beast.

There were two world powers prior to Babylonia which persecuted Israel, the people of God of that time. These were the Egyptian and the Assyrian Empires. These, along with Babylonia, are represented as three ribs in the mouth of the bear (Medo-Persia). When we add them to the list there are five persecuting empires, corresponding to the five heads of the Beast of Revelation that had fallen in John's day. These are Egypt, Assyria, Babylonia, Medo/Persia and Greece. The sixth head that existed in John's day was the Roman Empire. This corresponds to the fourth beast of Dan. 7.

In Daniel the ten horns were all on the fourth beast, which corresponds to the sixth head of the Revelation Beast. From this we can surmise that the ten horns of the seven-headed Beast are all on the sixth head, the symbol of the Roman Empire. This is the head that received the death-wound, and is revived in the ten-horn stage in chapter 13. This revived head is the one who makes war with the saints for 42 months or 1260 days (years).

In John's day the seventh head was yet to come, yet in Rev. 17 the drama had progressed to the point that the seventh head had already come, had carried out his dirty work, and then had been confined to the abyss. The seventh head is a short lived empire. This is the beast that kills the two witnesses in chapter 11, and then, following the resurrection of the witnesses, goes into the abyss (bottomless pit) for 1000 years (as we will learn more particularly in Rev. 20). Chapter 11 identifies the Beast that kills the two witnesses as the one that comes up out of the abyss and goes into perdition. Literally it is , "the one who is coming up out of the abyss."

Rev. 11:7 tells us that the Beast that ascends up out of the abyss overcomes the witnesses and kills them. It does not say that he kills them after he comes up out of the abyss; only that the Beast that kills them is the Beast who is coming up out of the abyss. The seventh head, whatever power he represents, is the Beast who kills the witnesses. This is the same head that comes up out of the abyss as an eighth. The witnesses, however, remain dead only a little while. Then they are exalted in the eyes of the world, symbolized by ascending into the heaven with all the world witnessing it.

The sixth head, the Beast with the crowns upon the ten horns, is in power only for the 1260 days (42 months). It is after that time in chapter 11 that the beast kills the two witnesses. It follows, therefore, that this is the beast in its seventh head stage. Those same witnesses are raised before the beginning of the millennial reign when the kingdom of the world becomes the kingdom of our Lord and of His Christ. Also, the beast of persecution goes into the abyss before that event, since persecution ceases during the millennium. Following the millennium persecution rears its head again. The beast (seventh head) who goes into the abyss comes up as an eighth. Before he can make progress in resuming his persecution he goes into perdition—i.e., he is cast into the lake of fire. We will pursue this further in the 20th chapter when we consider Satan's confinement and emergence from the abyss. It is interesting that nowhere does the text say the Beast goes into the abyss, but it logically follows that if he comes up out of the abyss, he has to go into it at some point. We'll see that point when we get to Rev. 20.

3. Explanation of the Ten Horns Under the Eighth Head (17:12-14). In chapter 13 the ten horns were part of the sixth head. They had arisen out of the Roman Empire and together made up the revived sixth head, unified by the religious power created by the False Prophet—namely, the Image of the Beast. The number ten is used symbolically of an indefinite number of nations. More than ten kingdoms arose out of the Roman Empire. More than ten were engaged in persecuting the people of God. Regardless of how many there were, they are identified as the ten horns of the sixth head. They were in authority, as indicated by the crowns (diadems) upon their heads. They made up the revived sixth head.

The 10 horns of chapter 17 are not precisely synonymous with the 10 horns of chapter 13. There they arose out of the sixth head. Here, while the

Beast "is not," these kingdoms have no dominion as yet. They are the nations that will receive their dominion from the Beast when he comes up out of the abyss. They give their authority to the Beast and receive their power and authority from the Beast. These horns had been on previous heads, but, except in the KJV and NKJV, are not said to be on the beast which is the eighth.[1] The angel told John that the Beast he saw in the wilderness was the one which did not exist (on earth) at that time, but that he was about to come up out of the abyss and go into perdition. He is identified as an eighth head, which is to be a repeat of one of the seven. In other words, the Beast who went into the abyss was the seventh head, and when this Beast comes out of the abyss he is called an eighth. We will attempt to identify heads seven and eight when we get to chapter 20.

These ten horns are all the kingdoms which will receive their power and authority from the Beast who is identified as an eighth. Here in chapter 17 the ten horns are said to receive authority as kings (kingdoms) from the Beast (the eighth) and give their power and authority to the Beast. What are the ten horns in this context? Obviously they are not horns growing out of the eighth head. They represent whatever kingdoms will give their power and authority to the Beast, and receive authority from the Beast. These are kingdoms which arise out of the previous fallen empires. It is possible that some, or all, of the kingdoms which make up the horns of the sixth head will be present at that time, as the horns which give their power to the Beast.

When the sixth bowl of wrath was poured out, the Dragon, the Beast and the False Prophet sent demonic spirits, like frogs, to the four corners of the earth to gather the nations together for the final war against Christ and the saints (Rev. 16:12-16). These are probably the nations referred to as the 10 horns in chapter 17. They are subservient to the Beast. They come and give their authority to the Beast and receive authority with the Beast. They are lackeys who do the bidding of the Beast. Their authority is short-lived. They receive authority for only one hour with the Beast. *One hour* indicates a very brief period of time.

---

[1] Whereas the *Textus Receptus* says *"on the beast,"* the *Nestle/UBS* and the *Majority Text* say *"and the beast."* The best authority is for *"the ten horns which you saw, and the beast."* The NRSV has it, *"And the ten horns that you saw, they and the beast will hate the whore."* With this translation most translations aside from KJV and NKJV agree.

The destruction and desolation of Babylon the Great was to come in "one hour" (see Rev. 18:10,17,19). The same is to happen to the Beast which comes out of the abyss. So short is the reign of the Beast that he "will ascend out of the bottomless pit and go to perdition." He is around just long enough to gather the nations together as allies with him to serve as God's tool to destroy the Harlot, and to fight the very short final battle against Christ. They will then be taken and cast into the lake of fire. As a result, the power of the ten horns will last only as long as the Beast that comes up out of the abyss—figuratively, one hour.

4. The Ten Horns United to Serve the Beast (Verse 13). Nations are not known very well for agreeing with one another. However, when they have a common cause they can be of one mind for the accomplishment of that cause. Here their common cause is their rebellion against the Lamb's reign of righteousness. The followers of Christ have cramped their style long enough. These nations arise which are bent on throwing off that reign and destroying the cause of Christ. After all, didn't the ten horns on the revived sixth head of the Beast succeed in persecuting the saints for a period of 1260 days (years)? Didn't the seventh head of the Beast effectively kill the two witnesses which God gave this world—i.e. the church and His word? So what if they came back to life. Couldn't the horns overcome them and kill them again? So what if the earth has been in the hands of the righteous for a thousand years. They have no guarantee. These rebels are determined to do it all again.

Ah! But the saints do have a guarantee! There is the promise that Christ shall reign forever and ever (Rev. 11:15). The locale of that reign will be moved to a new heaven and earth, but will continue throughout eternity. And they have the promise that the renewed efforts will be unsuccessful, and that the beast will go into perdition.

5. The Beast Destined to Lose the War (Read 17:14). This final war (Armageddon) is very short. It begins to look as if the beast and his cronies don't even get to strike a blow before they are consumed. We will return to this war in the latter part of chapter 19 and in chapter 20. Unlike the previous time (chapter 13), there is not a long period of persecution of the saints. The Lamb overcomes them because He is Lord of lords and King of kings. In chapter 19 this is symbolized by His riding on a white horse, wearing many crowns (diadems). Those who are with him (riders on white horses) are His angel warriors. 2 Thess. 1:6-9 is one of several passages which speak of Jesus coming with His angels to bring judgment:

> ...it is a righteous thing with God to repay with tribulation those who trouble you, and to give you who are troubled rest with us when the Lord Jesus is revealed from heaven with His mighty angels, in flaming fire taking vengeance on those who do not know God, and on those who do not obey the gospel of our Lord Jesus Christ. These shall be punished with everlasting destruction from the presence of the Lord and from the glory of His power.

D. THE HARLOT IS IDENTIFIED AND HER FATE TOLD (17:15.

As previously noted, the Harlot sits on many waters. The waters represent peoples, multitudes, nations and languages. This explains the sea from which the Beast arose in 13:1. Nations and kingdoms arise out of the troubled waters of humanity. But the Harlot is said to sit on the waters, just as she is said to sit on the seven heads of the Beast. Obviously these are symbols, because she could not literally sit in two places at once, and it would be difficult for her to sit on seven heads at once. What is intended by these figures? To sit on something is to be over it and/or to be supported by it. The Harlot wields her influence and power over the peoples, multitudes, nations, and tongues. Her power and influence are her ability to seduce the peoples and nations. She holds out her golden cup of abomination to them. In this way she exercises a type of control over them, getting them to do her bidding. This is not only true of the nations and peoples, but also of the Beast himself. If it were not for the influence of the Harlot, the Beast would probably not exist. The Beast is the means of upholding the values of the world system. This is what makes him the Beast. He is influenced by the Harlot.

E. THE BEAST USED BY GOD TO DESTROY THE HARLOT (Read 17:16-18)

God often uses sinful nations to bring about His judgments. Here is another example of that. The very system that seduces the nations comes to be hated by those nations. They turn on her and destroy her. This is no accident. God has put it into their hearts to do so. God has entered the picture and caused the nations to be of one mind, to give their kingdoms into the Beast's control, until God's purposes are fulfilled. This is really a reversal of earlier situations. The great city of Babylon, or Rome, or whatever city is at any particular time the seat of the empire, now becomes the target of the Beast and its vassals as they make her desolate and burn her with fire. This destruction is described for us in chapter 18.

The Beast of Rev. 13 has been identified by some as Nero. The fact that he burnt Rome (the harlot) is used as a verification of this. His burning Rome, however, did not destroy her. I think that Nero, who was famous for persecuting the Christians in Rome, and his burning of Rome, more likely serves as a source of the symbolism of Revelation, rather than its meaning. Another indication of this is the fact that the same Beast who destroys the Harlot is, immediately thereafter, taken and cast into the lake of fire as the conclusion of the final battle. The Beast which comes up out of the abyss lasts just long enough to be the instrument by which God judges the Harlot— i.e., one hour. Then, when he turns his attention to making war on the Lamb he is immediately taken. We'll see this in chapters 19 and 20.

In John's day the Harlot would be identified as Rome, the imperial city. That was not only the center of empire, but also the cultural center of the world. From her emanated the cultural influence that pervaded the Roman world. The world system was embodied in Rome. She was the seducer, the beautiful Harlot. She was known as the city which sat on the seven mountains. The heads of the beast upon which she sat are said to be seven mountains. This not only identifies the heads as governments or kingdoms which make up the Beast, but it also serves to identify the Harlot in the days of the sixth head of John's day as well as in the days of the revived sixth head when the ten horns were controlled by Rome.

In the days of Daniel, she would be identified as Babylon. This is why she is called *Babylon the Great.* It will pay to remember that these cities are but embodiments of the Harlot. She actually represents the principle of the seductions of the world to the things that the world system has to offer. She is the world system of adulteries, fornications, idolatry, and sins of every variety. The lust of the eye, the lust of the flesh, and the vain-glory of life are her stock in trade. She is the peddler of the darkness of the world, for she is

303

that darkness. This is why she hates the Lamb and Christians. They are a torment to her and expose her deeds. In John 3:19-20 Jesus said:

> And this is the condemnation, that the light has come into the world, and men loved darkness rather than light, because their deeds were evil. For everyone practicing evil hates the light and does not come to the light, lest his deeds should be exposed.

The city of Babylon had its beginning because of the rebellion of Nimrod against God's command to spread abroad over the face of the earth and to fill the earth. Scheming to keep the populace together he sought to build a tower reaching high into the heavens as a beacon to the travelers so they would find their way back to this spot. That tower on the banks of the Euphrates River was called *the tower of Babel*. It is from this that the city got its name *Babel* or *Babylon*. Although God stopped the building of that tower and scattered its people by confounding their language,[2] historians point to some very pervasive influences that spread from the work of Nimrod. Chief among them was the introduction of idolatry into the world following the great flood. Nimrod himself was deified along with his father Cush. Their counterparts can be found in most of the pagan idolatrous religions of the world.[3]

We have seen the Harlot robed in purple and scarlet riding on the heads of the Beast. One of the angels with the bowls of wrath has explained to John both the Beast in John's day, and the Beast which he saw in the wilderness—identified as the eighth stage which will arise from the abyss, with the ten horns which give their power to the beast. The angel has also explained the woman, who is called Babylon the Harlot, as being that great city which reigns over the kings of the earth, and we were told that her destiny is to be destroyed by the very nations which she had seduced.

Now it is time for us to proceed to the destruction of the Harlot in chapter 18.

---

[2]This story can be read in Gen. 11:1-9.

[3]See *The Two Babylons* by Rev. Alexander Hislop, published in America by Loizeaux Brothers, Inc., 1959, for some interesting historical facts about Nimrod and Babylon, and some examples of pagan gods who are identified with Nimrod.

Chapter 18

ACT 4: THE FALL OF BABYLON
SCENES 3 AND 4
Rev. 18:1 – 19:10

SCENE 3: DESTRUCTION OF BABYLON THE HARLOT (Rev. 18)

A. THE THIRD PROCLAMATION OF BABYLON'S FALL (Read 18:1-3)

Another angel of high authority proclaims, for the third time, the fall of Babylon. So radiant is this angel that the whole earth is lit up with his glory. He calls out with a voice that is very loud, loud enough for all to hear, and declares that Babylon is fallen. To emphasize the certainty of this he repeats, "is fallen." The language he uses is taken from the prophets Isaiah and Jeremiah as they describe the desolation of the literal city of Babylon (see Isa. 13:1 - 14:23 and Jer. 50 - 51). After the fall of the world system which is called Babylon the Harlot, she will be where she belongs—in the nether world of gloom and darkness with demons and evil spirits, as if these were vultures and scavengers and other birds of prey who are eaters of carrion.

The announcement was made the first time in Rev. 14:8, "And another angel followed, saying, 'Babylon is fallen, is fallen, that great city, because she has made all nations drink of the wine of the wrath of her fornication.'" The message is the same as the announcement here in chapter 18. The second time was in 16:19:

305

> Now the great city was divided into three parts, and the cities
> of the nations fell. And great Babylon was remembered
> before God, to give her the cup of the wine of the fierceness
> of His wrath.

Again the message is the same, although worded differently. The recurring theme of *the wine of her fornication* and *the wine of God's wrath* indicates the certainty of her utter doom. The world system which features lust and greed has characterized this world ever since the fall of man in Eden. It has wreaked its havoc on the world on a grand scale. Greed and avarice produce wars, murders, slavery, theft, debauchery, and every kind of evil. The lust of the eye, the lust of the flesh, and the pride of life have characterized the efforts of man throughout the history of the world. She has made the nations and kings to partake in her abominations and to drink of the wine of the wrath of her fornication. The merchants of the world have sold their souls to her as the price for sharing in her great wealth and luxuries. Like Esau of old, they have sold their birthright for a mess of pottage (Gen. 25:29-34).

Yet we have the promise of the Holy Spirit that all these things will pass away, according to 1 John 2:16-17:

> For all that *is* in the world—the lust of the flesh, the lust of
> the eyes, and the pride of life—is not of the Father but is of
> the world. And the world is passing away, and the lust of it;
> but he who does the will of God abides forever.

Here in Rev. 18 we see this promise being fulfilled. We also have the promise of a new heaven and new earth in which only righteousness dwells. 2 Pet. 3:13 says, "Nevertheless we, according to His promise, look for new heavens and a new earth in which righteousness dwells." Rev. 21:27 says of that place, "But there shall by no means enter it anything that defiles, or causes an abomination or a lie, but only those who are written in the Lamb's Book of Life." This is quite a different scene from this world where the Harlot continually holds out her golden cup of abominations. That cup contains the wine of her fornication which will result, for those who drink of it, in their also drinking of the wine of God's wrath.

B. *GOD'S PEOPLE CALLED TO COME OUT OF BABYLON (18:4-5)*

Sadly, it is true that some of God's people are in Babylon. They have been seduced by what the world has to offer. Although God has provided for their sanctification by the power of the Holy Spirit, in every generation there are Christians who are either unaware of the divine help that is available, or else they simply do not take advantage of that power. God will not force His will upon anyone, but there is a stern warning. If they do not come out of her they will share in her plagues—in her destruction. They will drink with her the wine of God's wrath. The call for God's people to come out of Babylon is drawn from statements made by the prophets Isaiah and Jeremiah as they prophesied concerning the destruction of ancient Babylon. In Jer. 51:6 God warns His people, "Flee from the midst of Babylon, And every one save his life! Do not be cut off in her iniquity, For this *is* the time of the LORD'S vengeance; He shall recompense her."

Don't think that God doesn't see, or doesn't know. The sins of the Harlot have been so great that they have become a pile that is heaped up to heaven.[1] God knows, and He remembers. He intends to punish her accordingly.

C. *THE STANDARD OF THE HARLOT'S JUDGMENT (Read 18:6-8)*

In Rev. 14:18-20 the angel who was sent to reap the harvest of the grapes threw them into the winepress of God's wrath. The blood that issued from that winepress is called *the wine of the wrath of God* (14:10; 16:19). Those charged with carrying out the Harlot's destruction are instructed to "render to her just as she has rendered". The Old Testament standard given to the judges of Israel was "life for life, eye for eye, tooth for tooth, hand for hand, foot for foot, burning for burning, wound for wound, stripe for stripe." In some things the offenders were made to pay double or more (See Exod. 22:7,9; Lev. 24:19-20). This is the standard God will apply to the judgment of the Harlot.

The wine offered by the Harlot is called "the wine of her fornication" (Rev. 17:2). It is also called, "the wine of the wrath of her fornication" (Rev. 18:3; 14:8), because the wine she offers incites God's wrath. He causes her

---

[1]*Nestle/UBS* and *Majority Text* both say the harlot's sins "have been heaped up to heaven" rather than they "have reached heaven."

cup to be filled with the wine of His wrath (Rev. 18:6; Rev. 14:10). As she made men drink of her fornications, she is to be made to drink a double mixture of His wrath.

As Jeremiah is prophesying concerning the fall of the city of Babylon, in Jer. 51:7 he says, "Babylon was a golden cup in the LORD's hand, That made all the earth drunk. The nations drank her wine; Therefore the nations are deranged."

According to the letter to the church in Thyatira (Rev. 2:18-29) there was a woman in that church called Jezebel. She was literally what Babylon the Harlot is figuratively. She taught the people of God to eat meat sacrificed to idols, and to commit fornication. She seduced them to commit fornication with her. Jesus said that he would cast her into a bed of sickness. Jesus uses her bed, the tool of her fornication and adultery, as a symbol of her judgment. In the same way God uses the cup of the Harlot's fornication as the symbol of her drinking of His wrath.

To the extent that she exalted herself in the eyes of the world, she shall be made to suffer torment and sorrow. She had boasted in her heart that she was a queen. In the Old Testament not only did the kingdom of Babylon exalt herself, but the king of Babylon exalted himself. Nebuchadnezzar is a prime example of this. In Dan. 4 King Nebuchadnezzar himself gives testimony to his own pride and boasting until God brought him low. God takes up a taunt against the king of Babylon in Isa. 14:11-20. I suggest you read this passage to see the boasting of the king of Babylon. He was called Day Star, son of the morning. But he became proud and very ambitious. Verses 13 and 14 read thus:

> For you have said in your heart: "I will ascend into heaven, I will exalt my throne above the stars of God; I will also sit on the mount of the congregation On the farthest sides of the north; I will ascend above the heights of the clouds, I will be like the Most High."

As it was with the king and kingdom of Babylon, so it is with Babylon the Harlot. She boasts and exalts herself. In Revelation Babylon is figurative since literal Babylon had been totally destroyed. The Harlot represents the things of the world that were characteristic of the city of Babylon. Rome's worldliness is also characteristic of the Harlot. She is represented as these two cities who enticed the kings and people of the world.

The Harlot is the agent of Satan for enticement, and is embodied in all such cities and systems. The Harlot is found in every succeeding generation. She is still alluring the rulers and people of the world. She offers people the pleasures, luxury, power and fame that the world has to offer. She entices people to the lust of the flesh, the lust of the eye, and the pride of life. She is the world system with all that it has to offer. She is the city of the world in contrast to the city of God. She can be found in all the sin cities of the world—cities which foster worldliness and world values.

She thought she would not see sorrow, but she was wrong. "...she says in her heart, 'I sit *as* queen, and am no widow, and will not see sorrow'" (v. 7). When she went against God's will to lead men away from righteousness by offering them the world, she sealed her own doom.

> Do not be deceived, God is not mocked; for whatever a man sows, that he will also reap. For he who sows to his flesh will of the flesh reap corruption, but he who sows to the Spirit will of the Spirit reap everlasting life. [Gal. 6:7-8]

"Therefore her plagues will come in one day—death and mourning and famine. And she will be utterly burned with fire, for strong *is* the Lord God who judges her" (v. 8). This judgment is still following the *plague* theme of the seven bowls of wrath—"the seven last plagues." The plagues we see in Act Four—the plague of huge hailstones in 16:21 and the plagues mentioned here must be considered part of the seven, or else the seven would not have been the last. Since seven is the number for completeness, these bowls refer to all the plagues that come upon the world at the end as a result of its sin. We are seeing the destruction of Babylon the Harlot as one aspect of the bowls of wrath. We will see another later—i.e., the destruction of the Beast and False Prophet.

Our text says these plagues will come upon her in one day (v. 8). The literal conquest of the literal city of Babylon took place in one day—in fact in one night, while a drunken feast was being held in King Belshazzar's palace. You can read this very interesting story in Daniel chapter 5. History tells of the diversion of the Euphrates River that night so that the armies of the

Medes and Persians could enter the city by the dry river bed and go through the open river gates to conquer the city.

The destruction of Babylon the Harlot is not a long drawn-out process. It comes upon her swiftly. Elsewhere in this same chapter the time of her destruction is shortened to one hour (Verses 10, 17, and 19). What does all this mean? Whether one day or one hour, these are just ways of emphasizing the swiftness and finality of the judgment of the Harlot. As it was with Sodom (Jude 7), her destiny, as with all the forces of evil, is the fire. "And she will be utterly burned with fire, for strong is the Lord God who judges her."

D. MOURNING OVER HER DESTRUCTION (Read 18:9-19)

The kings of the earth who depend upon what the world has to offer will be deprived of their luxuries when she is no longer around to provide them. They who gave themselves to her for the wealth, luxury, and pleasures she had to offer will not only be deprived of her favors, but will ultimately share in her judgment and destruction. Here it is said that her judgment comes in one hour. The retribution of God comes swiftly indeed.

The merchants of the earth who depend on her for their profit will weep and mourn. They will be deprived of their ability to sell their merchandise to those who demand luxuries. There will no longer be any demand for their goods. Those luxuries include precious metals, precious jewels, precious woods and other materials such as ivory and marble, fine foods of every kind, fragrant oils and incense, and merchandise of human slaves. These, like the kings, stand at a distance to watch her destruction. They see that everything she held dear has been taken from her forever. They wanted her favors, but they don't want to share in her judgment. Her great riches are consumed in one hour. They stand at a distance for fear of sharing in her destruction. This is in vain, for destruction will come upon them also.

The ship masters and traders who were paid to transport her goods and were made rich by her also cry out because of her destruction. They throw dust on their head—an act of utter grief. This act is still the way that the people in many lands react to great loss and grief, all the while weeping and wailing. In one hour her judgment has come (v. 10), in one hour her riches have come to nothing (v. 19), and in one hour she is made desolate (v. 19).

These are not three different hours, but the same hour. To this we might add that these mean the same thing as "her plagues will come in one day" (v. 8). All these are figures of the swift judgment of the Harlot.

E. A CALL FOR CELEBRATION OF HER FALL *(Read 18:20)*

Here a call is made for celebration over the downfall of Babylon. The celebration is told about in Rev. 19. All heaven is to join with the saints and prophets[2] in rejoicing. Babylon's destruction is the vengeance that the souls under the altar cried out for in 6:10. God has answered their prayers. The Harlot is among "the destroyers of the earth" who are to be destroyed (Rev. 11:18). The world system has been instrumental in persecuting the people of God, and God will bring vengeance on her for that. Just as the blood of saints and martyrs were found in ancient Rome as well as in the Rome that was ruled by the apostate church, so the blood of the saints is found wherever the world system holds sway. Her destruction is, therefore, great cause for rejoicing.

F. FINAL PICTURE OF THE FALL OF BABYLON THE HARLOT *(18:21-24)*

Millstones are stone wheels used for grinding grain into meal or flour and for pulverizing olives before pressing the oil out of them. Many of these stones are huge and very heavy. If one were to be thrown into the sea it would make a great splash and immediately sink out of sight. Jesus used a millstone as an illustration in Matt. 18:6:

> But whoever causes one of these little ones who believe in Me
> to sin, it would be better for him if a millstone were hung
> around his neck, and he were drowned in the depth of the sea.

Throwing a millstone into the sea is an apt illustration of the violence and speed with which Babylon the Harlot will be overthrown. Jer. 51:63-64 is a passage which relates to the destruction of Babylon from which the symbolism here is drawn. When Jeremiah completes his volume detailing God's wrath against Babylon, he is told:

---

[2]*Nestle/UBS* and *Majority Text* both agree in saying "saints and prophets" rather than "holy apostles and prophets."

> Now it shall be, when you have finished reading this book, *that* you shall tie a stone to it and throw it out into the Euphrates. Then you shall say, "thus Babylon shall sink and not rise from the catastrophe that I will bring upon her."

All festivities, including musical sounds of every kind will cease and be heard no more. The sound of workers such as builders and millers will cease to be heard. The lights of this great city will all go out. There won't be any more marriages with happy brides and grooms. All such happy occasions will no longer take place in Babylon. This description of her desolation is drawn from the prophecy of Tyre's destruction in Ezek. 26.

"...by your sorcery all the nations were deceived." The powerful influence which the Harlot wields over the nations of the earth—the alluring enticements of the world—are called *sorcery*, as though she were casting a spell over men. The appeal of the world is so strong that it requires divine help to overcome. Most of those without Christ are easy prey for her, and even those who are in Christ are not immune to her siren song. She wields a spell over the minds of people that is very compelling. They are led to believe the lie that in partaking of her sins they are doing nothing wrong. It is, after all, just the ways of the world. In this regard the Harlot is closely related to the False Prophet. By the false religions and false philosophies of the two-horned beast the world is led to accept the things of the world as good and right.

Here are just a few of those things: 1)There is no such thing as sin; 2) Morals are all relative; 3) Each person must determine for himself what is right; 4) Right and wrong are matters of viewpoint; 5) If a thing is done out of love it can't be wrong; 6) It can't be wrong when it feels right; 7) Some races of people are intended by God to be slaves of the rest; 8) A thing is wrong only if you believe it is wrong; 9) Might makes right; 10) Whoever has the gold makes the rules; 11) The ten commandments are really only ten suggestions; 12) All religions lead to God and are therefore right; 13) A woman has a right to choose what happens to her own body; 14) A fetus is not a living being, but just a mass of tissue; and 15) Business and religion don't mix.

This list of false teachings can be lengthened to book size, but the ones above have one thing in common—i.e., they are intended to justify the ways of the world. Lust of the eye, lust of the flesh, and the pride of life are sanctified through the false teachings of the False Prophet, and are motivated by the allurements of the Harlot. It is the False Prophet's job to deceive, and the Harlot's job to seduce. It is so much easier for one to be deceived if what he lusts after is represented as right and good.

"And in her was found the blood of prophets and saints, and of all who were slain on the earth." The truth is intolerable to the world system. John 3:19 declares, "And this is the condemnation, that the light has come into the world, and men loved darkness rather than light, because their deeds were evil." Further, John 3:20 says, "For everyone practicing evil hates the light and does not come to the light, lest his deeds should be exposed." That is why the world cannot tolerate the truth. The truth is the light which exposes their deeds as evil. That is why the world wants to get rid of Christians. In Rev. 11:10 after the two witnesses were killed we are told, "And those who dwell on the earth will rejoice over them, make merry, and send gifts to one another, because these two prophets tormented those who dwell on the earth." The truth does that to evil doers. The world system is condemned by the truth. The testimony of the two witnesses is truth, therefore the world hates them and kills them. The souls under the altar in Rev. 6:9 had been slain by those who dwell on earth as a result of their testimony.

Those who dwell on earth relate closely to the Harlot. She has enticed them. They are both deceived and justified in their deeds by the False Prophet. As a result they support the seven-headed Beast of persecution and the worship his image. These three are the weapons—the only weapons—which the Dragon (Satan) has by which he can subvert people. He can deceive them, he can allure them, and he can pressure them with persecution. That is why all three of them are destined to be judged and destroyed. Their fate will be the same as the Devil himself, for they will burn in the lake of fire which is prepared for the Devil and his angels. It will become populated for the first and last time at the final judgment when the last trumpet is blown, when the last bowl of wrath is poured out, when the Beast (the persecutor), False Prophet (the deceiver), and the Harlot (the seducer) are cast, along with Satan, into the lake that burns with fire and brimstone. All those who do not have their names written in the Lamb's book of life will also have their part in that lake of fire.

SCENE 4: THE SAINTS REJOICE (19:1-10)

A. PRAISES OF THE REDEEMED FOR THE HARLOT'S JUDGMENT (19:1-5)

The prayers of the souls of the martyrs under the altar[3] have been answered. Not only has God brought warning judgments at intervals throughout history upon the persecutors of God's people,[4] He has at last destroyed them so they will no longer persecute God's people. The redeemed in heaven rejoice with great exuberance, and they praise God for His judgments. They ascribe salvation and glory and honor and power to the Lord God. They proclaim that His judgments are righteous and true. There is no miscarriage of justice here. There is no ACLU to protest and declare that unfair treatment was given to the Harlot. God has avenged the blood of the martyrs which was shed in her. They call upon all the servants and those who fear God to praise Him.

The smoke of her burning is eternal, rising up forever and ever. This was also said of the destruction of Sodom and Gomorrah and the other cities of the plain in Jude 7:

> ...as Sodom and Gomorrah, and the cities around them in a similar manner to these, having given themselves over to sexual immorality and gone after strange flesh, are set forth as an example, suffering the vengeance of eternal fire.

When Abraham went out of his home in Hebron and looked toward Sodom and Gomorrah after their destruction, Gen. 19:28 says that he saw, "...the smoke of the land which went up like the smoke of a furnace." This destruction was said to be a destruction of eternal fire (Jude v. 7). The results of their destruction by fire was everlasting in its consequences. Those cities are obviously not still burning today. To say that the smoke of Babylon the Harlot ascends forever is probably a figure for the everlasting results of her destruction. It was said of ancient Babylon that she would be destroyed and never rise again. This destruction of spiritual Babylon, the Harlot will also be permanent. She will never rise again to seduce, deceive, and murder.

---

[3]The vision of the opening of the fifth seal—Rev. 6:9-11.

[4]The trumpets of warning judgments (see chapters 8-9).

B. *EXUBERANT PRAISE FOR THE MARRIAGE OF THE LAMB* (Read 19:6-9)

The judgment of the Harlot ends with the celebration of all the redeemed in heaven, and the coming of the marriage of the Lamb (see 21:1-2). We have come to the time when heaven and earth pass away, and the abode of the righteous is moved to the new heaven and earth. The voice of the multitude of the redeemed grows even louder when they realize that the time has come for the marriage of the Lamb. The sound becomes like the sound of many waters—like the roaring of the surf of the ocean against the rocks and cliffs along the shore, or like the roaring of a great waterfall such as Niagara. It also becomes like the sound of loud thunderings, so great is their exuberant praise. They shout, "Alleluia! For the Lord God Omnipotent reigns!"

The marriage of the Lamb has come and it is time to rejoice and be glad and give God glory. His beautiful wife has made herself ready and is clothed in the purest and brightest of wedding gowns. The fine linen of this robe is the righteous deeds of the saints. The bride of Christ is His church. Eph. 5:23 tells us, "For the husband is head of the wife, as also Christ is head of the church; and He is the Savior of the body." Christ's relation to the church is like that of a husband to his wife. Paul further writes in verse 25-27:

> Husbands, love your wives, just as Christ also loved the church and gave Himself for her, that He might sanctify and cleanse her with the washing of water by the word, that He might present her to Himself a glorious church, not having spot or wrinkle or any such thing, but that she should be holy and without blemish.

Notice that Christ prepared the bride for Himself: first He sanctified and cleansed her with the washing of water by the word. Because of this He can present her to Himself a glorious church without spot or blemish of any kind. In our text it says that His wife has made herself ready. In other words, the preparation of the bride is not without the cooperation of the bride. The church must submit itself to Christ, who then washes her in His blood, and prepares her by giving her a garment of fine linen, clean and bright. This garment is "the righteous deeds of the saints." This righteousness is not self-earned, but imputed. Paul wrote in Titus 3:5, "...not by works of righteousness which we have done, but according to His mercy He saved us,

through the washing of regeneration and renewing of the Holy Spirit...."
Paul also wrote in Rom. 4:6-8:

> ...just as David also describes the blessedness of the man to
> whom God imputes righteousness apart from works:
> *"Blessed are those whose lawless deeds are forgiven, And
> whose sins are covered; Blessed is the man to whom the* LORD
> *shall not impute sin."*

So, although the bride has a part in the preparation ("His wife has made
herself ready") still, we must admit that in the final analysis, our
righteousness is imputed to us through the grace of God. The bride has made
herself ready by putting on the garment of righteousness which Christ has
given to her.

This marriage is referred to again in Rev. 21:2. After the passing away of
the first heaven and earth John sees a new heaven and earth, "Then I, John,
saw the holy city, New Jerusalem, coming down out of heaven from God,
prepared as a bride adorned for her husband." The angel tells John to write in
19:9, "Blessed *are* those who are called to the marriage supper of the Lamb!"
They are blessed indeed, for these are the ones who have become the
followers of Christ, who have been redeemed by the blood of the Lamb and
have been washed pure and clean from all sin-stains in that blood. These are
the ones who are the beneficiaries of the covenant that provides eternal life
through Jesus Christ. These are the ones who have been redeemed from the
earth and now stand before God in exuberant praise. These are the church,
the holy city, New Jerusalem, the bride of Christ. The time has come for
them to unite eternally with their groom, and live with Him in the new
heaven and new earth throughout eternity. Indeed they are blessed. I want to
be called to the marriage supper. I hope you do too.

"These are the true sayings of God." God can be trusted. He cannot lie.
You can count on these things to be true.

C. JOHN'S ATTEMPT TO WORSHIP THE ANGEL IS REBUFFED *(Read 19:10)*

Man is permitted to worship only one Angel. In the Old Testament He is
called *the Angel of the* LORD *(Yahweh).* He was a *theophany*—i.e., an
appearance of God Himself as an angel. Also there is only one man who is
worthy of worship. He is the incarnation of God—God in the flesh—God

with us (Emanuel)—the only begotten of the Father—the one who is called *the Son of God.* The reason men are allowed to worship the Angel of Jehovah and Jesus Christ is that they are in truth God. Jesus Himself answered Satan's demand that Jesus worship him by saying in Matthew 4:10, "You shall worship the LORD your God, and Him only you shall serve." Because Jesus is the Lord God, He is to be worshiped.[5] In contrast, the angel who spoke to John was only a messenger bringing the testimony of Jesus which he calls the spirit of prophecy. He was one of the angels with the seven bowls of wrath. Angels are fellow servants with John and his brothers in Christ who have the testimony of Christ.

Let's go now to Act Five and see the final judgment of the Beast and False Prophet.

---

[5]In Heb. 1:6 the Father commands all the angels to worship Jesus the Son. In verse 8 the Father calls the Son *God.*

Chapter 19

ACT 5

BEAST AND FALSE PROPHET DESTROYED
Rev. 19:11-21

SCENE 1: CHRIST APPEARS IN HIS SECOND COMING
(Read 19:11-16)

A. A VISION OF THE RETURN OF CHRIST

In this vision John sees the awesome sight of the return of Christ from heaven. Heaven is opened and a rider on a white horse emerges. He is called *Faithful and True.* Rev. 1:7 tells us that He is coming with the clouds, and every eye shall see Him. Here we see Him leading a great army riding on white horses. These riders are all clothed in fine linen, white and clean. This is the same description as that of the robe of the bride of Christ earlier in this chapter. Angels also are said to wear such robes. For instance, in each of the four gospels the angels at the tomb of Christ were clothed in radiant white robes. Also the men (presumed to be angels) who appeared with the apostles on the Mount of Olives when Jesus ascended were arrayed in white garments. I see two possible interpretations to explain these armies clothed in fine linen.

1. Departed Christians Who Return With Christ?..The saints are portrayed as being soldiers of Christ (Phil. 2:25; 2 Tim. 2:3-4; Philem. 1:2). They are called upon to fight the good fight against sin and Satan (1 Tim. 6:12; 2 Tim. 4:7). God has even provided special armor for us in this battle against the spiritual host of wickedness in the spiritual realm (Eph. 6:10-17).

Christians are definitely an army. We even sing a song about this; "Onward Christian soldiers, marching as to war." The field of battle for Christians, however, is in this world while we are still living in it. Our sword is the word of God. It is the only weapon we have to use, although this warfare has sometimes been perverted by misguided believers to include slaughter and mayhem with physical swords and spears. This was not God's intent nor purpose, however well meaning the believers were. The word of God is living and powerful, and sharper than any two-edged sword according to Heb. 4:12. This is the only weapon with which we are commissioned to conquer the world for Christ. If we do not use this weapon—the word of God—in this life, we will not have opportunity to use it later. I do not see these riders as representative of Christians. They are a different kind of army with a different purpose.

2. Angels Sent Out in Judgment. The second possibility is that these armies arrayed in white are the angels of God who follow Christ to execute judgment. This is a more likely interpretation, being in harmony with several passages about the judgment. In 2 Thess. 1:7-10 we have a passage which throws light upon this:

> ...you who are troubled rest with us when the Lord Jesus is revealed from heaven **with His mighty angels**, in flaming fire taking vengeance on those who do not know God, and on those who do not obey the gospel of our Lord Jesus Christ. These shall be punished with everlasting destruction from the presence of the Lord and from the glory of His power, when He comes, in that Day....

According to this passage, when Jesus is revealed from heaven it will be with his mighty angels. They are the ones who will take part in the final judgment in which vengeance will be taken on those who do not know God and upon those who do not obey the gospel of Christ. In Rev. 14 it was **an angel who reaped the grapes of wrath** and threw them into the winepress of the wrath of God. In this symbol he represents all the angels of God who are to be involved in meting out God's wrath. In Matt. 13:39-43 Jesus explains the parable of the tares in this way:

> The enemy who sowed them is the devil, the harvest is the end of the age, and **the reapers are the angels**. Therefore as

319

the tares are gathered and burned in the fire, so it will be at the end of this age. **The Son of Man will send out His angels, and they will gather out of His kingdom all things that offen**d, and those who practice lawlessness, and will cast them into the furnace of fire. There will be wailing and gnashing of teeth. Then the righteous will shine forth as the sun in the kingdom of their Father. He who has ears to hear, let him hear!

The scriptures teach that when Jesus returns to judge the world His angels will accompany Him to accomplish the task of destroying those who are sinful. We have this message from the words of Jesus Himself as well as from the apostle Paul. We conclude, then, that the riders on the white horses that follow Jesus are His angels who follow Him to destroy the wicked on the last day.

3. The Rider on the White Horse is Described. Now let us focus our attention on the description of the rider on the white horse: 1) His name is called Faithful and True; 2) He is said to judge in righteousness, and to make war; 3) His eyes are like flames of fire; 4) He wears many crowns (diadems—the crowns of kings) on His head; 5) He has a name written (perhaps on His forehead) which He alone knows; 6) His name is The Word of God; 7) A sharp sword comes out of His mouth which He will use to smite the nations; 8) King of Kings and Lord of Lords is written on His robe, on His thigh.

Some of these descriptions are like that of the vision of Christ in chapter 1, such as the flaming eyes, the sword which comes out of His mouth, and His name, *the Word of God*. The eyes of fire are eyes that pierce and see, indicating His omniscience. The sword is the word of God. He is the Word of God not only because He is the highest expression of the person and will of God, but because He is the original cause (*logos*) of all things, and He will be the termination of all things in this earthly realm. He spoke the worlds into existence, and He will speak them out of existence when the time comes. The many crowns he wears indicates that the bulk of the nations have acknowledged Him as Lord and have yielded their allegiance to Him during the Millennial reign. Therefore He is called *King of Kings and Lord of Lords.*

In 17:14 we were told that the Beast and the ten horns would make war with the Lamb and the Lamb would overcome them because He is Lord of lords and King of kings. We are about to see that battle take place. It is a very short one, for it all takes place in one day—i.e., on the last day.

In that battle the only weapon Christ uses is the sword which comes out of His mouth—i.e., His word. By the power of His word he created all things, and by His word all things will come to an end. His word was all He needed to create heaven and earth; light and dark; land and seas; vegetation; sun, moon and stars; fish and fowls; and beasts and man. Why should He need anything more to destroy the forces of evil?

What is the name which He has written? Since no one knows, I cannot know. It must be a very special name by which we will know Him in our eternal abode.

B. CHRIST HIMSELF TO RULE THE NATIONS AND DASH THEM IN PIECES

"And He Himself will rule them with a rod of iron." He will not leave His reign to others. The emphasis is on Himself alone as the ruler of the nations. On the other hand, In Rev. 2:26-27 Jesus promises that the one who overcomes and keeps His works until the end will be given power to rule nations with a rod of iron. He is probably referring there to the millennial reign of the saints in this world. In Dan. 7:22 Daniel tells us that a time is coming when the saints will possess the kingdom. He speaks of the world dominion which passes from one kingdom to another. In its last stage that kingdom is received by the "one like a son of man" who represents a fifth kingdom in that vision—i.e., the kingdom of Christ. His explanation of this is found in Dan. 7:27a, "Then the kingdom and dominion, And the greatness of the kingdoms under the whole heaven, Shall be given to the people, the saints of the Most High."

At this point in the drama, we have come to the end of the reign of the saints. In Rev. 2:27, when Jesus says that those who overcome would have power to rule the nations with a rod of iron, He then says that the nations would be dashed in pieces. He does not say that the saints would do the dashing. He reserves that job for Himself. We have come to the point where the beast comes up out of the abyss and gathers the nations together to make war with the Lamb. At this point the Lamb, the rider on the white horse, takes over the business of ruling with the rod of iron. "He Himself will rule them with a rod of iron." We are about to see the nations dashed in pieces like a potter's vessel.

C. CHRIST WILL TREAD OUT THE WINE OF THE WRATH OF GOD

"He Himself treads the winepress of the fierceness and wrath of Almighty God." Once again the emphasis is upon what Christ Himself shall do. In Rev. 14:19-20 the reaping angel threw the grapes into the winepress of the wrath of God. Verse 20 tells us that the winepress was trampled, but it does not say who does the trampling. Here we are told that it is Christ Himself who treads the winepress. In other words, the army of God's angels gathers all the enemies of Christ and brings them to Him. He is the one who administers the final justice.

D. THE WHITE HORSE—A SYMBOL OF ASSURED VICTORY IN THIS FINAL WAR

One more question here—what about the white horse? Is the rider the same as the one in the opening of the first seal in 6:1? No, the rider there is not a person, but a personification of the victory of the saints. Here the rider is a person—Christ. The white horse, however, has the same significance. It is the symbol of victory. Since Christ comes riding on a white horse, and all His armies come riding on white horses, that is an indication that the victory over the forces of evil is certain. The angels scatter abroad over the face of the earth and gather together the forces of evil. Resistance is futile. They are immediately brought to the judge of the living and the dead, the King of kings and Lord of lords. He Himself is the one who slays them with the sword of His mouth. The symbolism of the white horse is the certainty of victory of Christ and His armies over the forces of evil.

SCENE 2: BIRDS OF PREY CALLED TO FEAST ON HUMAN FLESH
(Read 19:17-18)

John looks toward the sun and sees an angel standing there. He hears this angel call out loudly to the world. The angel is speaking to the birds. He is inviting them to a feast which he calls, *the supper of the great God.* The fare that will be served is human flesh—flesh of kings, captains, and mighty men, and the flesh of riders and their horses. The banquet will also include the flesh of all the free and the slaves, the small and the great. In other words, it will include the flesh of all whose names are not written in the book of life. In this way John is given a vision of the utter and complete defeat of "those who dwell on earth." Let's look in on the battle and see what we can learn.

SCENE 3: DESTRUCTION OF THE BEAST AND HIS NATIONS
(Read 19:19-21)

A. THE BEAST AND FALSE PROPHET CAST INTO THE LAKE OF FIRE

This scene looks very familiar, doesn't it? This is the battle that was prepared for when the sixth bowl of wrath was poured out in 16:12-16. Three demons, like frogs, came out of the mouth of the Dragon and the Beast and the False Prophet. These went out to gather the kings of the whole earth together for the battle of the great day of God the Almighty. The place of the gathering was called *Armageddon*. Nothing is said about that battle being fought. The next thing is the pouring out of the seventh bowl, and the statement, "It is done!"

Another reason this scene looks familiar is that we are told in Rev. 17:14 that the beast and the ten horns (kings or kingdoms) will make war with the Lamb, and the Lamb will overcome them. Again, there is no description of the battle except that the Lamb would overcome them. The Beast is identified as the Beast which comes up out of the abyss, the seventh head who returns as an eighth.

This Beast and those kingdoms which give their authority to him were to be used by God to destroy Babylon the Harlot. That would take place in one hour, since that is all the time they are given. The horns are given authority with the beast for one hour. The Harlot is brought to nothing in one hour. Now Christ comes to finish the task. While Rev. 17 only told of the coming of this time in the process of describing the Harlot and the Beast upon which she sat, now we have come to that time in the play. The beast was about to come up out of the abyss in chapter 17. Now he has come up and is here. Babylon the Harlot has been destroyed, and now it is the Beast's turn.

Here we are given a little more description of the battle, but we are still left with the impression that the battle had not even begun when it was over. "And I saw the beast, the kings of the earth, and their armies, gathered together to make war against Him who sat on the horse and against His army." John saw the results of the gathering that was portrayed in 16:12-14. There is the Beast (which has ascended from the abyss) with the armies of the kings (10 horns) of the earth. They are gathered together (in the place called Armageddon) to make war against the one on the horse (the Lamb) and His army.

The first thing seen in this battle is that the Beast is taken captive and the False Prophet along with him. This is the two-horned beast who worked wonders in the presence of the Beast, by which signs he deceived the kings and those who dwell on earth, the ones who received the mark of the Beast and worshiped his image. We saw what the mark and the worship of the Beast might mean in the time of the ten-horn phase of the Beast (during the 1260 days/years). What might they mean for the rest of the time—i.e., in the days of the seventh head, and in the days of the Beast which comes up out of the abyss? What do they mean in our own day?

For many of these things there is both a specific application, and a more general application. The seven heads of the Beast represent seven specific world powers involved in persecuting God's people, but they also represent all the kingdoms and institutions that persecute God's people. The bottom line is that the Beast is persecution personified, embodied in the governments that persecute the people of God, whenever and wherever they arise.

The image of the beast, in the days of the revived Roman Empire, represents a particular false religion set up by the False Prophet, who is the personification of deceit through all false doctrines and philosophies. Every false teacher, false philosopher, and false scientist is an embodiment of the False Prophet. Every false religious, scientific or philosophical system is an image set up by the False Prophet. For instance, we might see the false religious philosophy of Godless Communism (the economic philosophy of communism is socialism) as the image of the Beast in the latter half of the 20th century. At its base is the religion of humanism. The false religion of Islam can also be considered the image of the Beast. The Beast in this case is made up of the Islamic nations which persecute Christians. You can go on and look at the religious and philosophical teachings that have surfaced in the last century, and you can see the work of the False Prophet in setting up these institutions.

The mark of the Beast was something specific for one stage of the beast, such as the sixth head. We discussed this in the 13th chapter. On the other hand, all who do not have the seal of God end up with the mark of the beast, because it is the mark that identifies a person as belonging to Satan. All who serve him have his mark on their right hand. All who worship him have his mark on their forehead.

There is no middle ground for the followers of Christ. You are either for Christ, or you are against Him. If you are for Christ and have yielded to His claim on your life, you have the seal of God in your forehead, i.e., the Holy Spirit in your heart. If you do not serve God you serve Satan, and have his mark, i.e., the mark of the Beast in your forehead or in your right hand.

"These two were cast alive into the lake of fire burning with brimstone." The Beast and the False Prophet end up in the lake of fire. The Beast and False Prophet are not persons, but personifications. The Beast personifies persecuting systems and the False Prophet personifies systems of false teaching. Their being cast into the lake of fire is symbolic of the utter destruction of these systems. They will not rise again.

We saw Death personified as the rider on the pale horse, and Hades was personified as the one who followed him in chapter 16. In chapter 20 Death and Hades are cast into the lake of fire. The symbolism is the same. Since they are personifications they cannot be literally cast into the lake of fire. It is a figure for the total and irrevocable destruction of death and hades.

The Beast has come up out of the abyss (a term for the lowest part of the hadean world), and now in one day he goes into perdition, being cast into the lake of fire. This symbolism is like writing your bad character traits on pieces of paper, then throwing them into the fire and burning them, symbolic of a person's commitment to change. The fire is real enough, but you can't really burn up character traits. The lake of fire is real enough as we shall see in chapters 20 - 21.

B. THE NATIONS AND ALL WHO DWELL ON EARTH ARE DESTROYED

"And the rest were killed with the sword which proceeded from the mouth of Him who sat on the horse. And all the birds were filled with their flesh." The rest are the kings, captains, mighty men, soldiers, and all the dwellers on earth, every man who has not the seal of God on his forehead, and whose name is not written in the Lamb's book of life. Notice that the sword which comes out of Christ's mouth is the means by which they are killed. He has only to speak the word, and the job is done (See Isa. 11:4b). Now the birds of prey have their feast. "And all the birds were filled with their flesh."

Notice how quickly the battle is over. The forces of the Beast do not even get to strike a blow. John sees the coming of Christ on the white horse, then he sees the forces of the Beast gathered, then he sees the Beast and the False Prophet immediately taken and cast into hell, and by the word of Christ the rest are slain. How long does it take? A very brief time indeed. Just as the angel with the bowl of wrath told John in chapter 17, the Beast comes up out of the abyss and goes into perdition. We'll have more to add to this scene in Rev. 20.

Chapter 20

ACT 6

THE MILLENNIUM AND FINAL JUDGMENT
Rev. 20

Acts Three, Four and Five (Chapters 14 - 19) were about the final events just prior to the end of the world. The theme of the outpouring of the wrath of God is seen through all these. In the beginning judgment scene of Act 3 the grapes are trodden in the winepress of the wrath of God, and Babylon and the worshipers of the Beast are made to drink the wine of His wrath. The seven bowls of the last plagues are poured out, the final expression of God's wrath upon the sinful world. The results of this are seen in chapters 17 – 19 in which that wrath is meted out on the various forces of evil.

In Act 4 (Rev. 17:1 – 19:10) the wrath of God is directed against Babylon the Harlot. In Act 5 (Rev. 19:11-21) the King of kings treads out the grapes in the winepress of God's wrath as He brings destruction to the Beast and False Prophet. They are cast into the lake of fire. Act 6 (Rev. 20) gives the picture of the destruction of Satan, along with the Beast and False Prophet in the lake of fire. Then comes the resurrection of all the dead to stand before God's throne of judgment and be judged according to their deeds.

Act 6 is unique, however, in that it gives a flashback to 1000 years before the final judgment. The reign of the righteous is revealed prior to the final judgment. This reign corresponds to the reign spoken of in Dan. 7:18, 27. Satan, the great red Dragon, is bound and cast into the bottomless pit for 1000 years. The souls of the martyred saints under the altar are exalted to thrones. They reign with Christ for 1000 years.

After the 1000 years are up Satan is released from his prison for a brief time to resume his deception of the nations and persecution of the saints, and we return to the theme of final judgment.

SCENE 1: THE DRAGON IMPRISONED FOR 1000 YEARS
(Read 20:1-3)

An angel descends from heaven with a large chain in his hand and the key to the abyss. He seizes the great red Dragon, binds him with the chain, and throws the Dragon into the abyss. He locks the door over the Dragon and seals him in. For 1000 years the Dragon can no longer deceive the nations. After the 1000 years he will be released for a brief period of time.

There are three-stages to the defeat of Satan. The stages are:

1) He is **cast to earth by the blood of Christ and the testimony of the saints** (Act One—Rev. 12), so he can no longer accuse the saints before God's throne. This occurred at the crucifixion and resurrection of Christ, and the proclamation of the gospel.

2) He is **cast into the abyss for 1000 years** (Act Six, Scene 1—Rev. 20:1-3), so he can no longer deceive the nations and persecute the saints on earth. This occurs here at the beginning of the millennial reign.

3) He is **cast into the lake of fire for eternity** (Act Six Scene 3—Rev. 20:7-10), so he will never again be a threat to the people of God. This will occur at the last trump when Jesus returns to judge the world.

A. WHAT IS SIGNIFIED BY THE BINDING OF SATAN?

The Dragon is identified as "that serpent of old, who is the Devil and Satan." He has been confined to earth for a long time, because he was cast down to earth by the blood of the Lamb and the testimony of the followers of Jesus. Now the works of Satan on earth are brought to a halt for 1000 years. In John's vision an angel comes down from heaven holding a great chain. He binds the Dragon with the chain, and imprisons him in the abyss for 1000 years.

1. Chains of Darkness. In 2 Pet. 2:4 Peter writes:

> For if God did not spare the angels who sinned, but cast *them* down to hell [Gr. *tartarus—torment*] and delivered *them* into chains of darkness, to be reserved for judgment....

Notice that the angels who sinned are reserved in chains of darkness. However, there are times when some are allowed to roam the earth as evil spirits, to do the work of Satan. The Devil himself is a fallen angel, and the abyss of Hades is his rightful place prior to the final judgment. For God's purposes he has been allowed the freedom to roam the earth as the tempter of mankind. At the beginning of the 1000 year reign his freedom on earth is brought to an end and he is bound in one of those chains of darkness, and confined to the deepest region of hades.

2. Not the Binding of the Strong Man in Matthew. Matt. 12:29 says, "Or how can one enter a strong man's house and plunder his goods, unless he first binds the strong man?" Is the defeat of Satan at the cross what Jesus meant by binding the strong man? Some assume so, but in the context of this verse Jesus was talking about casting out demons, which was taking place even before His death on the cross. The strong man in this verse is the demon that is to be cast out. This verse is not talking about the binding of Satan.

3. Not What Jesus Did at the Cross. In a very real sense Satan was bound by the death of Jesus Christ, since by His death Jesus loosed the captives of Satan, and limited his power over those who have faith in Christ. Satan has no power to deceive or subvert those who are the servants of God, unless they give that power to him. "...because He who is in you is greater than he who is in the world" (1 John 4:4). The Holy Spirit who dwells in the child of God is able to give him authority over the Devil and over his wiles. But you must take hold of the advantage God has given you (Eph. 6:10-13).

Christ overcame Satan at the cross, but Rev. 20 could not be referring to that fact. First, it is an angel, not Christ, who does the binding. Second, the time of the binding is long after the death of Christ on the cross. At this time in Revelation he has been active deceiving and persecuting for many centuries since the cross. Satan will no longer be able to do so when he is bound and locked in the abyss. Third, Satan is to be released to roam the earth once more after the thousand years are up. On the other hand, what

Jesus accomplished at the cross will never be undone. The limitations imposed upon Satan by the cross will never be removed.

4. Bringing Deceit and Persecution to a Halt. The binding of Satan and his imprisonment in the abyss for 1000 years signifies curtailing his activities on earth for an extended period of time. During this time he can no longer deceive the nations and enlist them to persecute the servants of God. In Rev. 13 Satan was doing just that through the Beast and False Prophet. The binding of Satan, then, has to take place sometime during the Christian era, not at the beginning of it. The binding of Satan is at some point following the 1260 days (years) of the persecution of the saints of God.

B. SATAN CAST INTO THE ABYSS FOR 1000 YEARS (Verse 3)

The angel, having bound the Dragon, throws him into the abyss. To emphasize the certainty that Satan's work had ceased, he also puts a seal on him. When Pilate had a seal placed on the tomb of Jesus he wanted to insure that Jesus could not come out or be taken from the tomb. The authority of Pilate's seal was not strong enough to prevent His resurrection, for the authority of God was infinitely greater. The seal which the angel put upon Satan is by God's authority. It cannot be broken until the time God has set for Satan to emerge at the end of the 1000 years.

In 2 Pet. 2:4 the word *hell* is the Greek ταρταρώσας (*tar-tar-o'-sas*). This is the only place a form of this word is used in the Bible. It is translated in *Young's Literal Translation* as "cast them down to tartarus," and in *Darby's New Translation* as "cast them down to the deepest pit of gloom." This is the region where the angels who sinned as well as men who have died in sin are reserved for judgment. It is a place of torment—the same region where the rich man was confined in Luke 16:25. For a fuller study of the meaning of this word go to *Appendix A: Hades and Hell*.

1. Satan Can Deceive the Nations No More. The work of deceiving the nations comes to a halt for 1000 years. Since Satan's work of deceiving the nations is symbolized as a two-horned beast called *the False Prophet*, this means that the False Prophet will no longer be able to deceive the nations. When Satan goes into the abyss, with him goes the False Prophet who is the personification of deceit. This does not mean that there will be no falsehood at all, but that falsehood would no longer control the thinking of the nations as it does now.

Persecution is personified as the seven-headed Beast. Since the nations could no longer be deceived into persecuting the saints, the Beast of persecution could no longer function. This means that the Beast of persecution goes into the abyss with the Dragon and the False Prophet. This is why it was said in Rev. 17:8 that the Beast "was and is not and yet is." The same verse says that the beast is about to ascend from the abyss and go into perdition. The angel is telling John that the time frame for the Beast in chapter 17 is near the end of the 1000 year abyss confinement. We conclude that the Dragon, the Beast and the False Prophet are (figuratively) locked up together in the abyss for 1000 years.

2. How Long Is 1000 Years? Is this a literal period of 1000 years—i.e., not 999 nor 1001 but exactly 1000 years? I doubt it. 1000 is a round number that is often used to represent an indefinite number, i.e., a multitude, or a long period of time. In Psalm 50:10 God says, "For every beast of the forest *is* Mine, *And* the cattle on a thousand hills." How many cattle belong to the Lord? Does this mean that the cattle on all the hills from hill 1001 on do not belong to the Lord? There are many times more than 1000 hills that have cattle on them, and they all belong to the Lord.

In Deut. 1:11 Moses gives this blessing, "May the LORD God of your fathers make you a thousand times more numerous than you are, and bless you as He has promised you!" When Moses wrote this the Israelites were in the wilderness. They numbered over 600,000 able bodied men above the age of 20. When we add to this the number of the women, children and elderly, there were a few million. If God were to make them literally a thousand times more numerous, they would come to be numbered in the billions. The whole world had not reached a billion in population until some time during the 19th century A.D. Obviously the number 1000 was not used by Moses literally. In this case we may paraphrase by saying, "May the Lord God of your fathers make you many times more numerous than you are." This accurately portrays the meaning of 1000 here. So, in some instance 1000 means much more than 1000, as in the 1000 hills of cattle. In some instances it means much less than 1000, as in the multiplying of the populace of Israel. Other examples include Deut. 7:9, Psalm 90:4, Isa. 30:17, and 2 Pet. 3:8.

From all these passages it becomes apparent that 1000 years can be a very indefinite period of time. It can mean much more than 1000 years, considerably less than 1000 years, or approximately 1000 years. In the eyes of the Lord it is as one day. All we can know is that it stands for an extended period of time of indefinite length. Only the Lord knows exactly what that length will be. Whatever the actual length of time in years, Satan's activity will be curtailed for that period of time. During that same period of time the cause of Christ will flourish on earth and the saints will reign.

SCENE 2: THE 1000 YEAR REIGN OF THE SAINTS ON EARTH
(Read 20:4-6)

In the action of this scene John sees the souls of the martyrs raised to sit on thrones. They had been beheaded for the witness they bore to Jesus, and for the word of God. This is the first resurrection. They live and reign with Christ for 1000 years. During this time the Dragon is confined in the abyss. These martyrs are those who had not worshipped the Beast or his image, and had not received the mark of the Beast on their forehead or hand. They are blessed because the second death has no power over them. For 1000 years they minister as priests of God and Christ. The rest of the dead do not live again until the end of the 1000 years.

A. MARTYRS VINDICATED AND ENTHRONED (Verse 4)

1. Who Were on the Thrones? There are some errors in translation that need to be cleared up in order to understand what these verses are saying. In verse 4 *Young's Literal Translation* says:

> And I saw thrones, and **they** sat upon them, and judgment was given to **them, and** the souls of those who have been beheaded because of the testimony of Jesus, and because of the word of God....

Many translations fail to give us the true sense of this passage. The quotation from *Young's Literal Translation* presents exactly what the original Greek text says, except that the word ***and*** in the next to last phrase would make more sense if it were translated ***even***—i.e., "***even*** the souls of those who have been beheaded...."

Literally the verse says concerning the thrones, "and **they** sat upon them."[1] The pronoun *they* has no antecedent. How do we determine who sat on the thrones? Its reference must be determined by the context that follows. The ones for whom judgment was given are the ones who sat on the thrones. Who are they? The next statement in this verse, from *Young's Literal Translation* is "...**and** the souls of those who have been beheaded because of the testimony of Jesus...." Most versions insert *I saw* after **and** in this verse, making it say, "and *I saw* the souls...." Many versions use the convention of putting inserted words in italics, so that the reader can know that they were not in the original text. Without some such method the reader would have no way of knowing that the words are not in the original text without reference to the Greek text. In this case it is important to know this.

The NKJV does even greater violence to the original text by translating the *kai* (*and, also,* or *even*) as **Then,** *then adds "I saw,"* i.e., "then *I saw* the souls...." It implies that John saw the souls of the dead after he saw those who sat upon the thrones. This is unwarranted, because not only is it unnecessary, it also distorts the meaning. It makes the reader think that this is a different group than the ones on thrones.

Kai, translated *and* in the literal versions, can also be translated *also* or *even.*[2] Only **Even** makes sense linguistically without the insertion of *I saw.* John uses *kai* to mean *even* in other passages, as do other New Testament writers. In John 11:22, for instance, he writes, "But **even** now I know that whatever You ask of God, God will give You." *Even* in this verse is the same word as **and** in Rev. 20:4. It is so translated in many passages in the New Testament. *Young's Literal Translation* given above uses **and,** but it doesn't make sense. "...**and** the souls of those who have been beheaded"? What does that mean? But if we translate "...**even** the souls of those who have been beheaded...," that makes sense. It answers all the questions about who sat on the thrones, and to whom the judgment was given. The resultant translation would be:

---

[1] καὶ κάθισαν ἐπ' αὐτούς—literally "and (they) sat upon them." The pronoun *they,* although not expressed separately is required by the third person plural form of the verb.

[2] *The Analytic Greek Lexicon of the New Testament* says of the word καί that it not only means *and,* but used emphatically it means *even* or *also. Thayer's Lexicon* as well as *Arndt and Gingrich* also agree that καί often means *even.*

> And I saw thrones, and **they** sat upon them, and judgment was given to **them, even** the souls of those who have been beheaded because of the testimony of Jesus, and because of the word of God.

What is the conclusion? The ones who sat upon the thrones and the ones for whom judgment was given are the souls who had been beheaded because of their testimony, not some other group besides the souls of the martyrs.

2. Judgment Given on Their Behalf. In several versions the translators give their interpretation rather than a translation. For instance they interpret this verse to say that those on the thrones were given authority to judge. Literally the verse says, "and judgment was given to (or *for*) them."[3] The souls are the same souls that were under the altar crying out for God's judgment on their persecutors (6:9-11). They were told to wait for the appropriate time. That time has now come and God has given them the judgment for which they cried. This judgment is not by them, but on their behalf. This interpretation is also in harmony with the parallel passage in Dan. 7:22.

3. First Downtrodden, Then Enthroned. What do the souls represent? Did John see literal souls? Were they only those who had literally been beheaded? Did this group exclude the souls of those who were hanged or crucified or pierced through with swords or shot with arrows or guns, or were killed by starvation or some other means? Do you see the problem with a literal interpretation?

What John saw under the altar was a symbol of the life's blood of the martyrs. The word for *soul*[4] is often translated *life* in the New Testament. It

---

[3] καὶ κρίμα ἐδόθη αὐτοῖς *(kai krima edothe autois)*—literally "and judgment was given *to* (or *for*) *them.*" The dative case of the pronoun αὐτοῖς means either *to* or *for* them.

[4] ψυχή *(psuche)* is the word for *soul* but is often translated *life*, as in Matt. 2:20, "...those who sought the young Child's life are dead." Of twelve passages in Matthew where the word *life* is used, nine of them use the word ψυχή, while three use the word ζωή, (pr. *dzoe-ay*). Most references in John's gospel use the word ζωή because John's constant theme is eternal life. On the other hand, when he talks about the life of the body he always uses ψυχή. These all refer to giving one's life or else loving one's life and losing it. Jesus uses this word when He talks about laying down His life for us (See John 18:11,15,17; 12:25; 13:37-38). Most New Testament writers use ζωή for spiritual life while they use ψυχή for the life of the body.

is as if the martyrs had poured out their life's blood in sacrifice at the base of the altar. This is a symbolic picture of the church under persecution. Many were giving their lives in order to remain faithful to Christ and give their testimony.

The church in Rev. 20 is no longer under persecution but is in a position of power, reigning with Christ over the kingdom of the world. These are those "...who had not worshiped the beast or his image, and had not received his mark on their foreheads or on their hands." These souls are the body of believers who had not been deceived by the False Prophet nor yielded to the pressure to worship the Beast and to accept the mark of the Beast.

4. The Function of Christians During the Millennium. The function of Christians as priests of God will have a special meaning in the millennial reign. As priests of God they will mediate the gospel of Christ to a willing and receptive world rather than to a skeptical and hostile world. They will no doubt lead thousands of those who had been adamantly opposed to Christianity to see the truth concerning Jesus Christ, and to accept the salvation of their souls in Christ.

The millennial reign will be a time when the saints of God will be the major influence in the world. They will reign by virtue of their influence, and not by might of arms nor political power of any kind. Many kings, presidents and prime ministers, parliaments, congresses, and governing boards will be converted to Christ, and in this way the reign of Christ will extend into the political realm, but remember that it is by the power of the word of God rather than by the power of political organizations that we will reign with Christ.

I believe that during this period the nation of Israel will turn to Christ as the Messiah. In Rom. 11 all but the remnant of believers in Christ have been broken off of the olive tree of Israel. Believing Gentiles were grafted in to become part of God's true Israel. Paul says in Rom. 11:25, "...blindness in part has happened to Israel until the fullness of the Gentiles has come in." During the millennium the deceiver will no longer be around to keep the Jews in blindness. Paul said that if they don't continue in unbelief they can be grafted back into their own tree.

When Jesus was about to return to the Father He told His disciples that He would be with them (and us) to the end of the world (age). So we live with Him now, and in the millennium we will reign with Him. Neither requires His physical presence, since He is with us in the person of the Holy Spirit. The sword coming out of His mouth, is the word of God. It is by this sword that the saints will conquer and reign. Righteousness will not be the exception, but the rule, during this period of time. Sin will not have been totally eradicated, so while righteousness will reign, there will still be need for the blood of Christ to keep cleansing us from sin.

B. The Reign of the Resurrected Church for 1000 Years (Verse 4)

"And they lived and reigned with Christ for a thousand years." This is the millennial reign of the saints. As they suffered with Christ during the tribulation they had to undergo persecution by the kingdom of the world which was under Satan's control. In the Millennium they will not only live with Christ but also reign with Him over the very nations that formerly persecuted them. Just as Christ does not have to be with us in person for us to live with Him, so also Christ does not have to be present in person in order for those during the millennium to reign with Him. Christ promised to be with us until the end of the age (Matt. 18:20). He went back to the Father and sent His Holy Spirit to dwell with and in us (John 14:15-23). By this means both the Father and the Son are with us—i.e., in the person of the Holy Spirit.

1. The First Resurrection—Literal or Figurative? (verse 5). The martyrs under the altar are exalted to thrones. This is called *the first resurrection,* indicating that there is to be a second. It is impossible to understand what he is talking about until we have some idea of who these souls represent. When we see the nature of this first resurrection we will have a better idea of the nature of the second.

First, the text does not speak of a bodily resurrection. John did not see bodies; he saw souls. He saw the same souls that were pictured under the altar in chapter 6. That was a symbolic picture of the church under persecution, when souls were being sacrificed due to their faithfulness to Christ. Those souls were representative of the persecuted and downtrodden cause of Christ. The souls on the thrones represent the same cause of Christ, with the same testimony. Only now, instead of being downtrodden and persecuted, the cause of Christ is enthroned.

The same thing is represented with different symbolism in chapter 11. There the two witnesses are killed at the end of the 1260 days, then after three and a half days they are raised from the dead. This corresponds to the first resurrection in chapter 20. These witnesses ascend up to the heavens in a cloud so that all the world can see them. Great fear falls upon the city of the world. They quickly learn to fear God. There is a change in the response of the world. A tenth of the city of the world is destroyed, and the other nine-tenths are afraid and give glory to God. Unprecedented! Those who formerly rejected God and worshiped the beast and his image now worship God. Those who formerly persecuted the saints now give glory and praise to the same God which the saints worship. This corresponds to the beginning of the 1000 year reign in Rev. 20.

The resurrected souls represent the cause of Christ, the body of Christ, the saints of God, who are exalted in this world in a reversal of fortunes. Before, they were persecuted, downtrodden, and rejected in the world. The two witnesses were persecuted, and then killed in that great city of the world where Jesus was crucified. But they don't stay dead; they come back to life. In chapter 11 the witnesses are exalted to the clouds. In chapter 20 the witnesses are exalted to thrones. These are different symbols with the same meaning. Whether the witnesses are represented as souls of witnesses under the altar or witnesses in sackcloth, the message is the same—the cause of Christ is downtrodden and persecuted. Whether they are presented as souls of witnesses on thrones or witnesses ascending in a cloud the message is the same—i.e., the cause of Christ is revived, exalted and triumphant.

2. Not The Process of Becoming a Christian. An interpretation that has been set forth is that the first resurrection is the spiritual resurrection that takes place at the new birth—i.e., when one dies to sin and is raised to walk in a new life in Christ (Rom. 6:3-4; Col. 2:12: Eph. 2:4-6). Years ago I held this view until I realized that it simply did not fit the context of Rev. 20. One decisive element in that context is found in verse 4. The souls that are raised to thrones are those who had been beheaded for their witness to Jesus, indicating that they were already followers of Christ at the time of their death. How could a symbol that is obviously drawn from the death of persecuted

Christians be symbolic of the rising to new life of sinners? In this picture, they were already Christians before their death. Since this is so, this resurrection cannot be speaking of their becoming Christians.

3. The Blessings of Partaking in the First Resurrection (Verse 6) Three blessings await those who have part in the first resurrection. These are: 1) they will not be touched by the second death; 2) they will have the honor of being priests of God and Christ, and 3) they shall reign with Him a thousand years. But if these souls are symbols, how can that affect us? Symbols represent a reality. The souls are symbols of the body of Christ. If you are part of the body of Christ when it is raised and exalted in the millennial reign, then you will have part in that reign, and be subject to the blessings of those who have part in the first resurrection.

The second death is explained for us in the latter part of this chapter and the first part of chapter 21. It has been mentioned before, in the letters written to the seven churches of Asia, but we await the explanation later on. It is enough to know that those who are a part of the millennial reign, the triumphant church of Jesus Christ, need have no fear of the second death.

C. THE SECOND RESURRECTION

The Rest Do Not Come to Life Until After the 1000 Years (Verse 5). Now we are in a position to see what the second resurrection is. The Devil, the Beast, and the False Prophet, who persecuted the body of Christ, have gone into the lowest region of Hades, called *the bottomless pit* or *the abyss*, as if they had died. In Hades the dead await the resurrection. These persecutors (the Dragon, the Beast and the False Prophet) are destined to come out of the abyss at the end of the thousand years. Just as the cause of Christ is resurrected at the beginning of the thousand years, so the cause of Satan is to be resurrected at the end of the thousand years. "But after these things he must be released for a little while" (Verse 3b). "...the rest of the dead did not live again until the thousand years were finished." At the end of the 1000 years Satan, along with the Beast and the False Prophet will ascend from the abyss and appear on the earth again.

D. WHEN ARE THE BODIES OF THE DEAD LITERALLY RAISED?

1. Christ the Firstfruits. The literal resurrection of the bodies of the dead comes later in this chapter. The resurrection of Christ from the tomb was the first resurrection. Afterwards, they that are His will be raised at His coming I Cor. 15:20-23 says:

> **But now Christ is risen from the dead,** *and* has become the firstfruits of those who have fallen asleep. For since by man *came* death, by Man also *came* the resurrection of the dead. For as in Adam all die, even so in Christ all shall be made alive. But each one in his own order: **Christ the firstfruits, afterward those who** *are* **Christ's at His coming.**

2. The Wicked and Righteous Raised at the Same Time. In John 5:28-29 Jesus tells us:

> Do not marvel at this; for **the hour is coming** in which **all who are in the graves will hear His voice and come forth**—those who have done good, to the resurrection of life, and those who have done evil, to the resurrection of condemnation.

Those who have done good and those who have done evil will all be raised in the same hour—the good to eternal life, the evil to everlasting condemnation. There is not 1000 years between the resurrection of the righteous and the resurrection of the wicked. The idea that the bodies of the righteous will be raised in the first resurrection and the bodies of the wicked in the second is not a biblical idea. That is taking the symbolism of Rev. 20 and trying to interpret it literally. Paul wrote in 1 Thess. 4:15-17 to explain to Christians what awaits them. He says:

> For this we say to you by the word of the Lord, that we who are alive *and* remain until the coming of the Lord will by no means precede those who are asleep. For the Lord Himself will descend from heaven with a shout, with the voice of an archangel, and with the trumpet of God. And the dead in Christ will rise first. Then we who are alive *and* remain shall be caught up together with them in the clouds to meet the Lord in the air. And thus we shall always be with the Lord.

Some have mistakenly interpreted this passage to mean that the dead in Christ will rise first, and then the dead out of Christ will rise a thousand years later. That is neither what it says, nor what it implies. The word *first* is not in relation to the dead out of Christ, but to the living in Christ. The question is who will go first, the living or the dead? Paul assures them that living Christians have no advantage over dead ones, because **first** the dead in Christ will rise, and **then** the living in Christ will join them to meet the Lord in the air. The resurrection of the wicked dead is not even considered in this passage.

Paul throws more light on this in 1 Cor. 15:51-52 where he writes:

> Behold, I tell you a mystery: We shall not all sleep, but we shall all be changed—in a moment, in the twinkling of an eye, at the last trumpet. For the trumpet will sound, and the dead will be raised incorruptible, and we shall be changed.

Those who are living at the return of Christ, at the last trumpet, will not have to undergo death. The dead will be raised with spiritual bodies (1 Cor. 15:44), and those living will be changed to be like them. Again, Paul is speaking only about those in Christ. He is not speaking about the wicked, either living or dead.

According to I Cor. 15:22-26, Christ gives the kingdom back to the Father at the resurrection of the saints. This will happen when he has conquered the last enemy, death. The time of the conquest of death is at the resurrection of the saints, according to verses 51-54. This is when death and Hades are cast into the lake of fire (Rev. 20:11-15). This comes at the end of the thousand years, not at its beginning.

For further study on the Millennium go to *Appendix H*.

SCENE 3: SATAN'S RELEASE AND THE FINAL BATTLE
(Read 20:7-10)

The millennium is over. The seal is removed from the Dragon's prison, the door of the bottomless pit is unlocked, and the Dragon emerges. He goes throughout the world, and once again nations are deceived and recruited into Satan's army. They are gathered to make war on the camp of the saints, the beloved city (New Jerusalem). Their numbers are so great that they are like the sands of the sea.

A leader of this army emerges. His name is Gog, and his empire is Magog. The nations follow in hordes as they surround the camp of the saints, the beloved city. Before they are able to strike a blow fire comes out of the sky and consumes them. Then the Dragon, together with the Beast of persecution and the False Prophet of deceit, are thrown into the lake of fire and brimstone. There they are to be tormented forever. They will never again be a threat to the people of god.

A. *NATIONS ARE GATHERED TO DO BATTLE WITH THE SAINTS (Verse 8)*

When Satan is released from prison he "will go out to deceive the nations which are in the four corners of the earth." This is the work of the False Prophet. The nations who are deceived gather to do battle with the camp of the saints. This is the work of the Beast. Their armies are so numerous that they are said to be like the sand of the sea in numbers. They surround the camp of the saints and the beloved city. This is a form of expression called *parallelism;* the beloved city is the camp of the saints. That city is the counterpart of Babylon the Harlot, who has been destroyed. It is the city elsewhere called *the New Jerusalem* which is composed of the saints of God. She is the body of Christ, the church of our Lord. For 42 months that city was trampled under foot according to chapter 11. Chapter 13 pictures this as the Beast and False Prophet persecuting and killing the servants of God. Now there is a renewed attempt to trample the beloved city under foot. That attempt is destined to fail.

This is a renewal of Satan's attempt to persecute the saints of God. Persecution is personified as the Beast with seven heads and ten horns. So the Beast of persecution, as well as the False Prophet of deceit, comes up from the abyss along with Satan. This is the fulfillment of the statement in 17:8, 11. The Dragon, the Beast, and the False Prophet once again are together in their opposition to the servants of God. This is the scene spoken of in the sixth bowl of wrath in 16:12-16. The nations are gathered by evil spirits like frogs which come out of the mouths of the Dragon, the Beast, and the False Prophet. The place of their gathering is called *Armageddon.*

B. FOUR PICTURES OF THIS FINAL BATTLE

In 16:12-16 three evil spirits, appearing like frogs, go out of the mouths of the Dragon, the Beast, and the False Prophet to gather the nations for the final battle. They gather at Armageddon. In 17:12-14 the kingdoms led by the Beast make war upon the Lamb in the final battle. In 19:11-21 the kings and their armies gather with the Beast to make war on the King of kings and His army, as they come on white horses. These are all references to the same battle—i.e. the battle of the great day of God Almighty. Here in 20:7-10 we have the final picture of that same battle. Lets look at these pictures more closely.

1. Picture One is Found in Act Three. In 16:12-16 the sixth bowl of wrath is poured out. Satan, the Beast and False Prophet prepare for the final battle (Armageddon) by gathering the kings of the earth and their armies at Armageddon. The battle is not described here. This battle takes place when Christ returns with His angelic army as in 19:11-21. The description of the battle is that of total destruction of the forces of evil, the Beast, False Prophet, and the kings and peoples of the earth.

2. Picture Two is Found in Act Four. The angel tells John in 17:8, 11-14 that the Beast was about to come up out of the abyss and then go into perdition. The ten horns give their authority to the Beast who is identified as an eighth head. After he comes up out of the abyss this Beast, as an eighth, together with the horns, will make war with the Lamb and be overcome by Him.

3. Picture Three is Found in Act Five. Christ comes with His angels on white horses in chapter 19:17-21. The nations, directed by the Beast and False Prophet, are arrayed together to make war with the rider on the white horse and His army. The Beast and the False Prophet are quickly taken by the King of kings, and they are cast into the lake of fire and brimstone. The kings and their armies (all of mankind who are in opposition to Christ) are slain and left for the vultures.

4. Picture Four is found in Act Six. Here in 20:7-10 we see Satan himself revealed as the one directing the opposition to Christ and the saints, but the Beast and the False Prophet are there also. They are not presented by name but by their function—i.e., the nations are being deceived and the saints are being warred upon. Once again the battle is painted as very short. Fire comes down from God out of heaven and devours the opposing kingdoms. The devil is cast into the lake of fire and brimstone along with the Beast and False Prophet.

I get the impression that Satan's forces do not get very far, in fact they don't get anywhere. The forces of Satan no sooner gather for battle than the battle is all over for them. All we have read concerning this battle seems to speak of a very, very brief period of time. As soon as the kings of the nations gather their armies at Armageddon we are told, "It is done!" (16:17). The Beast comes up out of the abyss and goes into perdition (17:8). The Harlot is destroyed in one hour (18:10). As soon as Christ arrives on His white horse the Beast and False Prophet are taken and cast into the lake of fire (chapter 19:19-21). As soon as the armies of the nations surround the camp of the saints fire comes down and destroys them, and the Dragon, Beast and False Prophet are cast into the lake of fire (20:9-10). How long does it take for Christ to win this battle? How long does it take Him to speak a word?

C. THE IDENTITY OF THE EIGHTH HEAD

The persecuting power which emerges in chapter 20 is called *Gog and Magog*. Gog is the king and Magog is the territory. This king and his country are spoken of in more detail in Ezekiel chapters 28 and 29. I believe them to refer to that territory known as Russia. Although I cannot be certain, I see the seventh head as the Communist Empire, headed by the Kremlin in Russia. The eighth is a return of the seventh after the millennium. Although the eighth may be in a different form than Communism, the same territory is involved as with the seventh. A thorough examination of this subject can be found in *Appendix I: Gog and Magog*.

D. SATAN, THE BEAST, AND FALSE PROPHET CAST INTO THE LAKE OF FIRE

An exact translation of verse 10 is, "And the devil, who deceived them, was cast into the lake of fire and brimstone **where also the beast and the false prophet**." There is a false impression given by many translations of verse 19. Virtually all translations add to the text the words *are, were,* or *had been thrown*. The NKJV and Young's add *are* in italics. Most translations use italics to indicate the insertion of a word not in the original Greek text.

However, most translations which use this convention do not use it in this verse. Darby's translation puts *are* in brackets to indicate that it was not in the original. ASV and KJV insert *are* without italics. NRSV and ISV insert *were* without italics. Worst of all, NIV inserts *had been thrown* without italics or any other indication that it was inserted by the translators.[5]

The original simply says, "where also the beast and the false prophet." Without the *are* or *were* or *had been thrown,* there is an entirely different connotation. This, of course, is poor English but it is good Greek. There has to be something added to make sense in English, but the obvious meaning is that the devil was cast into the lake of fire and brimstone along with the beast and false prophet. Thus they all three were cast into the lake of fire at the same time. As most translations put it by their added words, the impression is left that the Beast and the False Prophet were already in the lake of fire, from a previous episode in chapter 19, which is viewed as a different battle, perhaps occurring before the 1000 year reign, when in fact it is another picture of the same battle.

"And they will be tormented day and night forever and ever." The fate of the Dragon (Satan) is that he is to be tormented day and night forever. The same is said of the Beast and False Prophet. However, remember that the Beast and False Prophet are personifications of Persecution and Deceit. They are embodied in persecuting governments and false religions which change over the years, but in saying they are cast into the lake of fire, it is not the kings and their subjects or people involved with false religious organizations that are relegated to the fire at this point, but the principles of persecution and deceit. All mankind must await the final judgment which follows immediately. What is the significance of representing the Beast and False Prophet as being cast into the eternal fires of hell? The point is, they are totally destroyed, and will rear their heads no more forever. Their destruction is everlasting. The people of God will be forever safe from both persecution and deceit, as well as from the Satan himself.

---

[5]The NIV does not use this convention, making it impossible to tell from the reading that something has been added. To make matters worse, the NIV says, "where the beast and the false prophet **had been thrown**." This implies that the beast and false prophet were already there, interpreting the battle in chapter 19 as a different battle from the one in chapter 20. It would help if **had been thrown** had been italicized so we would know these words were added by the translators.

In the battle as described in 19:19-21, as well as here in 20:9, all the wicked are represented as being killed. In 19 they are represented as killed with the sword of the mouth of the rider on the white horse. In 20 they are represented as devoured by fire coming down out of heaven. The point is, before the final resurrection there are none of the wicked left living on earth. On the other hand, since the righteous who are living at that time are not destroyed in this battle, they remain until the judgment scene and are changed to be like the resurrected saints.

SCENE 4: THE GREAT WHITE THRONE JUDGMENT
(Read 20:11-15)

John sees a great white throne upon which the judge of all sits. From His face, i.e., by His command, heaven and earth flee away. No more place is found for the first heaven and earth which are man's present habitation. It completely ceases to exist.

John sees the dead, small and great standing before the great white throne.[6] They are all raised. From wherever their bodies are, on land or sea, Death gives up their bodies and Hades gives up their souls. Souls and bodies, reunited, stand before the judge of all.

John sees books opened from which the people are to be judged. He also sees the book of life opened. From these books all the dead are judged according to the things they have done.

Death and Hades are destroyed since they will never again have any occupants. To picture this John sees them being cast into the lake of fire. Everyone whose names are not found in the book of life are cast into the lake of fire. This is called *the second death.*

A. *THOSE ALIVE AFTER THE FINAL BATTLE*

1 Cor. 15:51-52 tells us that there would be some of the saints remaining alive to the coming of the Lord. They will not die but will be changed (see also 1 Thess. 4:15-17). The rest of mankind, those not among the saints, will all undergo death. Those who have not already died will meet death in the

---

[6]The *Majority Text* says "standing before the throne" instead of "standing before God."

final battle. In Rev. 19:17-18, the birds were invited to feast on the dead bodies. This includes the flesh of **all people**, free and slave, small and great. Verse 21 tells us they are killed by the sword which comes out of the mouth of Christ—i.e., by the word of God. This is also shown in the bowls of God's wrath. When they are poured out (chapter 16) all those who dwell on earth are killed. The only ones left alive until the resurrection will be followers of Christ. These will be changed to be like the resurrected saints. In the resurrection all the dead will be raised, both the righteous and the wicked, to stand before the judgment throne.

B. THE NATURE OF THE RESURRECTION

Although all will be raised, the saints have the promise of being raised incorruptible and immortal (1 Cor. 15:50-55). In verse 50-54 we are given a description of the resurrected body of the saints:

> Now this I say, brethren, that **flesh and blood cannot inherit the kingdom of God; nor does corruption inherit incorruption.** Behold, I tell you a mystery: We shall not all sleep, but we shall all be changed — in a moment, in the twinkling of an eye, at the last trumpet. For the trumpet will sound, and **the dead will be raised incorruptible, and we shall be changed.** For this corruptible must put on incorruption, and this mortal *must* put on immortality. So when this corruptible has put on incorruption, and this mortal has put on immortality, then shall be brought to pass the saying that is written: *"Death is swallowed up in victory."*

The wicked have no such promise. Apparently, the resurrection of the wicked will be a resurrection of their corruptible and mortal bodies which will then be cast into the lake of fire where they undergo the second death. Gal. 6:8 puts it this way, "For he who sows to the flesh will of the flesh reap **corruption**, but he who sows to the Spirit will of the Spirit reap everlasting life."

C. THE THRONE OF JUDGMENT (Verse 11)

The great white throne is the throne of judgment. It is mentioned in Matt. 25:31, "When the Son of Man comes in His glory, and all the holy angels with Him, then He will sit on the throne of His glory" (Read the whole story of the final judgment in Matt. 25:31-46). This tells us that the one sitting on the throne to judge the nations is God the Son. Acts 17:31 tells us that it is the risen Christ who will judge the world, "because He has appointed a day on which He will judge the world in righteousness by the Man whom He has ordained. He has given assurance of this to all by raising Him from the dead." (See also Acts 10:42).

D. ALL THE DEAD RAISED TO STAND BEFORE THE THRONE *(Verses 12-13)*

Where are the dead? Some are on land, some are in the sea. The bodies of all except the most recently dead will have turned to dust, or gone up in smoke. Some will have been digested by sharks and other marine life while others will have been absorbed by plant life or eaten by wild beasts. But God knows where they all are, and He knows how to bring them all together again. Wherever the bodies are, the souls await the resurrection in Hades, the abode of the dead. "And I saw the dead, greats and small, standing before the throne...."(NRSV)[7] "The sea gave up the dead who were in it, and Death and Hades delivered up the dead who were in them." This is the resurrection of the dead, including the small and great, the slave and free, the good and bad. All will stand before the great white throne.

Matt. 25:32 puts it this way, "All the nations will be gathered before Him, and He will separate them one from another, as a shepherd divides his sheep from the goats." The separation between them is not on the basis of whether they are great or small, or whether they are slave or free, but on the basis of righteousness or unrighteousness as God measures these things. The righteous are the sheep on the right hand, the wicked are the goats on the left. All will be there, both righteous and wicked. Paul writes to Christians in 2 Cor. 5:10, "For we must all appear before the judgment seat of Christ, that each one may receive the things *done* in the body, according to what he has done, whether good or bad." Also he says in Rom. 14:12, "So then each of us shall give account of himself to God."

---

[7]NKJV has "before God." Both the *Majority Text* and the *Nestle/UBS Text* have "before the throne."

E. *THE BASIS OF THE JUDGMENT (Verses 12b and 13b)*

There is going to be a set of books there. One is the Book of Life. What are the others? We cannot say for certain, but we can get a pretty good idea. First, since the dead are to be judged according to their works, one volume must be the record of their deeds. Second, the dead are to be judged by the things written in the books.

The saints of God are made up of two groups of people. The first group is those whose deeds are to be judged by the volume we call *the Old Testament* which contains the law of God. These are those who lived before the cross of Christ. A special category of these is the Israelites, who also have the Law given by Moses, found in Exodus through Deuteronomy. The law of God, however, was around from the beginning and applies to all men. The law of Moses (also called *the law of God*) was given much later, but only to the Israelites. In it was incorporated all the previous law of God, plus things added specifically for the Israelites.

The second group is those who live this side of the cross. They will be judged by the law of God as it is applied in the volume we call *the New Testament*. This applies to all who live this side of the cross. But overriding the judgment of both these groups is the grace of God which has been offered to all men through Jesus Christ.

Christ's death as payment for sin is both retro-active and pro-active. Those both before and after the cross can only be saved by this gift of grace which is received through faith by following the light that has been revealed to us. Those who trusted in God before the cross and lived by faith according to the word of God given to them are the righteous saints of the Old Testament era. Those who trust in Jesus Christ, the Son of God, and live by that faith according to the word of God given them are the righteous saints of the New Testament era. Although the volumes by which each group will be judged differ somewhat in their requirements, no one will be found righteous on the basis of his own goodness. Only those to whom Christ has imputed His own righteousness may stand before the Throne with confidence, for they alone will be saved. These are the ones whose names are in the Book of Life.

According to verse 13b each man is to be judged according to his works. The judgment scene in Matt. 25:31-46 describes the deeds by which we are judged. Verses 34-36 say:

Then the King will say to those on His right hand, "Come, you blessed of My Father, inherit the kingdom prepared for you from the foundation of the world: for I was hungry and you gave Me food; I was thirsty and you gave Me drink; I was a stranger and you took Me in; I *was* naked and you clothed Me; I was sick and you visited Me; I was in prison and you came to Me." Then the righteous will answer Him, saying, "Lord, when did we see You hungry and feed *You*, or thirsty and give *You* drink? When did we see You a stranger and take *You* in, or naked and clothe *You*? Or when did we see You sick, or in prison, and come to You?" And the King will answer and say to them, "Assuredly, I say to you, inasmuch as you did *it* to one of the least of these My brethren, you did *it* to Me."

What is being described here? It is the fulfillment of the command, "Love thy neighbor as thyself." Those who allow the Spirit of God to pour out God's love in their hearts will do these things. These are the deeds of love. He that does not love does not know God. The person who turns a deaf ear to the needs of his fellow man does not love, and therefore does not know God.

What is the reward for those who do these things? Verse 34 says, "Then the King will say to those on His right hand, 'Come, you blessed of My Father, inherit the kingdom prepared for you from the foundation of the world....'" On the other hand, for those who do not do these things verse 41 says, "Then He will also say to those on the left hand, 'Depart from Me, you cursed, into the everlasting fire prepared for the devil and his angels....'"

F. THOSE NOT IN THE BOOK OF LIFE CAST INTO LAKE OF FIRE *(Verse 15)*

The last volume is called the Book of Life. This is the volume which contains the name of everyone who will receive salvation and inherit eternal life. Jumping ahead a couple of verses, verse 15 says, "And anyone not found written in the Book of Life was cast into the lake of fire." These are the ones who worshiped the Beast and his image. These are the ones who were not sealed on their foreheads by receiving the Holy Spirit of God to dwell in them. These are the ones who do not exhibit love to their fellow men. These are the ones destined for the everlasting fire prepared for the devil and his angels. They who served Satan and bore his mark will share the lake of fire with him.

G. DEATH AND HADES CAST INTO THE LAKE OF FIRE (Verse 14)

"Then Death and Hades were cast into the lake of fire. This is the second death." We have already seen that the Dragon (Satan), the Beast (Persecution), and the False Prophet (Deceit) were cast into the lake of fire where they are to be tormented day and night forever. Now we see that both Death and Hades are to be thrown into that lake also. What does this mean? We have seen that the Beast and False Prophet are personifications of the abstract principles of persecution and deceit. They have no concrete existence and so cannot literally be thrown into the lake of fire. By this symbolic picture we see the total eradication of both deceit and persecution. The nations and institutions in which they were embodied are composed of human beings who are literally cast into the lake of fire, being among those whose names are not written in the book of life.

Now we see two other personifications being cast into the lake of fire. The first is the rider on the pale horse in chapter six, at the opening of the fourth seal. Death is not a person but a state. The second is Hades, the one who follows the rider on the pale horse receiving the souls of the dead. Hades is also a state—the state of the dead. At the resurrection death is conquered. There will be no more death. In Rev. 21:4 we read, "...there shall be no more death, nor sorrow, nor crying. There shall be no more pain, for the former things have passed away." If there is to be no more death, then there will be no more need for hades. It is emptied when the dead are raised. No one will be left to die and go into hades. These two states, therefore, will cease to exist. This is symbolized by the picture of their being cast into the lake of fire, and thus destroyed.

H. THE SECOND DEATH

The lake of fire is itself the second death. It is appointed unto men to die once according to Heb. 9:27, but after that the judgment. Except for Enoch, Elijah, and those saints living at the return of Christ, all men will have to die the first death. All men will then be raised for judgment, and then those whose names are not written in the book of life will have to die a second time. There will be no resurrection from that death. It will be eternal. God created mankind to live in His presence and have fellowship with Him. When man fell into sin he was separated from God. Through Jesus Christ, God was reconciling men to Himself (2 Cor. 5:18). All those who accept Christ and are reconciled to God will enjoy fellowship with Him throughout eternity. Those who reject that gift, who are not reconciled to God, will remain separated from Him. There will be no resurrection from the second death. It will last throughout eternity.

I don't want to be among that group. Do you? In Act 7, Rev. 21:1 – 22:5, is a beautiful picture of the inheritance of the saints. Now let us see what Act 7, the final act of the Drama, has in store.

Chapter 21

ACT 7: THE ETERNAL CITY OF GOD
Rev. 21:1 - 22:5

We have come to the end of all things on earth, including the end of earth itself. The final judgment is over. The Dragon (Satan), the Beast (Persecution), and the False Prophet (Enticement) have been cast into the lake of fire, from which they will never again emerge. Death and Hades have been cast into the lake of fire. All those who dwell on earth, who have lived as part of Satan's world system, have been raised from the dead, judged from the books, and cast into the lake of fire because their names were not found in the Lamb's book of life. This is the second death.

The dead in Christ have been raised with incorruptible and immortal bodies. The bodies of those left living until the coming of Christ have also been changed into incorruptible and immortal bodies (1 Cor. 15:51-54). They will never decay or see death anymore. Death is swallowed up in victory. These all together rise to meet the Lord in the air (1 Thess. 4:16-17). They will never again be separated from Him. Where are they going? They are taken to heaven from where they will be brought by Christ to the place which He has prepared for them, i.e., the new heaven and earth (John 14:1-3).

At this point in the drama the earth has already passed away, dissolved with fervent heat (2 Pet. 3:10-11). Once before God destroyed the world by drowning all those who dwelt on earth with a great flood. He preserved Noah, his wife, three sons, and their wives—eight people in all—and began again from their descendants to populate the earth. Heaven and earth were not destroyed then, but mankind was destroyed from the face of the earth

(Gen. 6:7; 7:4). He destroyed them with the earth, i.e., with the flood waters of the earth (6:13).

This time, however, not only the world of living things, but heaven and earth, are destroyed. They flee away from the face of the one who created them in the beginning. No place is found for them any more. If Rev. 20:11 is true then the idea that the saints will dwell on this earth for eternity cannot be true. If 2 Pet. 3:10-13 is true, then the new heaven and earth cannot be the old heaven and earth renewed and renovated.

SCENE 1: THE BRIDE DESCENDS TO THE NEW EARTH
(Rev. 21:1-8)

The Action of Scene 1. John sees a new heaven and new earth. The first heaven and earth have passed away in Scene 4 of Act 6 (Rev. 20:11). There was no sea on the new earth, with all the peril it represents.

Then John sees the holy city, New Jerusalem, descending from heaven. This city is the bride of Christ, adorned for her husband. A loud voice declares that God has set up His dwelling place among men, i.e., on the new earth. They are to be His people and He will live among them as their God. The voice continues, telling John that God will wipe all tears from their eyes. There will be no more death, sorrow, crying, or pain. All these things from their former existence have passed away.

God himself addresses John, telling him that He is making all things new. He tells John to write these things because these words can be trusted to be true and faithful.

God announces that it is done. The eternal plan of God has reached its ultimate fulfillment. He identifies Himself again as *the Alpha and Omega, the Beginning and the End.* Then He promises to give the water of life freely to the thirsty. The ones who are to be heirs of all these things are those who have overcome. He will be their God and they His children.

God then gives a warning so that all who read it may strive to overcome. He announces that the lake of fire and brimstone, the second death, awaits the cowardly, unbelievers, murderers, sexually immoral, sorcerers, idolaters, and all liars.

The Divine Drama in Seven Acts

A. *John Sees the New Heaven and New Earth (Read 21:1)*

The new heaven and earth must be what Jesus was talking about in John 14:1-3 when He told His disciples that He was going away to prepare a place for them. Then He said He would come back and take them to that place. Since Jesus was going away to prepare this place, it must not be on this earth. He said He was going to come again after He had gone to prepare the place and take the disciples to be with Him. What will this new heaven and earth be like? We can't know exactly until we get there, but one thing we do know. The present earth is polluted by sin, but the new one will be perfect in righteousness. There is much that is full of beauty about the first heaven and earth, but there is also much that is ugly. The new heaven and earth will have none of the imperfections that were introduced into this world because of sin. It will be filled with beauty and pleasure far beyond anything we can even imagine.

B. *The Bride of Christ Descends to the New Earth (Read 21:2)*

The bride of Christ is pictured here as the holy city, New Jerusalem. This is the Jerusalem above, spoken of in Gal. 4:26. It is also the heavenly Jerusalem mentioned in Heb. 12:22. She is the body of Christ, the assembly of the saints, the church of God. This is the holy city that was to be trodden under the feet of the Gentiles for 42 months (Rev. 11:2). It is the beloved city that was surrounded by the armies of Satan (20:9). It is the city of God in contrast to the city of the world.

The city of God is the New Jerusalem while the city of the world is Babylon the Harlot. **The city of God is a beautiful bride**, espoused and faithful to one husband, while **the city of the world is a prostitute** who gives herself to all the kings and institutions of the world that will have her. **The city of God will continue eternally**, while **the city of the world has been destroyed** at this point in the drama. She has been burnt with fire and will be no more. This bride is the woman who was pursued by the Dragon, but was protected in the wilderness for 1260 days (years). There she was persecuted, threatened, and downtrodden. Here she is victorious and free from any more harassment or persecution. Here she shares in the glory of Christ. Here she is perfect and without flaw. In Rev. 19 we saw the marriage of the Lamb and His bride the first time In Rev. 21 we are given a fuller description of that bride.

C. GOD SETS UP HIS DWELLING WITH HIS PEOPLE *(Read 21:3)*

A voice from heaven tells John that God has set up His dwelling place with His people. He will be with them in person. The Holy Spirit was given to us as a guarantee of this inheritance (Eph. 1:13-14). Although He is with us on earth in the person of the Holy Spirit, in the new earth we will be in the very presence of God and see His face. He will be the God Who is with us, and we will be His people.

Jesus opened the way into the Holy of Holies by His blood, so that we can come into the very presence of God. Now we do this through prayer, and by listening to the promptings of the Holy Spirit in our heart as He guides us by the instructions given us in His written word. But in the new earth we can walk into the very presence of God in person, and converse with Him as a child to his Father. Now we walk by faith, not by sight. Then, with our own eyes, we will see Him in whom we have believed.

D. GOD WIPES AWAY ALL TEARS *(Read 21:4)*

Just think! There will be no more sickness or dying, no more sorrow or sighing, no more pain or crying. All these things belong to the former existence. With the passing away of the first heaven and earth, these things have passed away too. How marvelous it is to have a sense of physical well being and to really feel good. As I grow older those times are fewer and farther between. Aches and pains, weaknesses, shortness of breath have taken over. Many are the loved ones I have seen pass from this life. Many are the tragedies that bring sorrow and crying. Many are the times when our hearts ache, disappointments come, and friends and loved ones abandon and forsake us. To be free of all these sorrows forever more—what a glorious prospect!

E. GOD MAKES EVERYTHING NEW *(Read 21:5)*

Please notice the use of the word *new.* John saw the new heaven and new earth. The bride of Christ is called the New Jerusalem. Now God declares that He is making all things new. If you like new things, this is the place to be. Everything is new, and everything will continue to be renewed throughout eternity, for God is **continually** making all things new.[1]

John recorded the vision of the new heaven and earth, and of the bride of Christ, the holy city New Jerusalem, coming down from God. Then he wrote what the loud voice from heaven said about God's coming to make His dwelling there, and of the blessed death-free, pain-free, and sorrow-free existence of the saints there. This was all delivered by an angel, but now it is God Himself Who speaks to John and tells him to write the words He is saying, because they are guaranteed to be true.

The first thing God said was that He is making all things new. This is a new creation. All the old things have passed out of existence. The things that cause pain, suffering, and death are gone. There will be no more growing old. The old, failing bodies are gone. The new, resurrected bodies will be young and vigorous throughout eternity. No one will ever grow old and die. Death and Hades are no more. Old enmities have passed away. The newness of the relationships are such that there will be everlasting love, peace, and harmony between man and man, and between man and God. The old corrupt society is gone. Nothing evil will be there to defile or cause abominations or lies. On this earth we walk by faith. Doubts often enter in to bring discouragement and despair. On the new earth our hope will be dissolved in the realization of what we have hoped for (Rom. 8:24-25), for we will be in the presence of our Lord and see His face. The sweet fellowship that Adam and Eve had with God in the Garden of Eden will be restored. Not a shred of the old will be left. He makes all things brand new!

F. THE INHERITANCE OF THE SAINTS (Read 21:6-7)

When Jesus died on the cross He said, "It is finished." The redemption of man from sin was finished at the cross. When the giant Angel of Rev. 10 lifted His hand to heaven and swore by God, he said that when the last trumpet sounds the mystery of God, all the things declared by the prophets, would be finished. The things God planned before the foundation of the world which had been kept secret until the time for their accomplishment would be finished. God's work through the Holy Spirit of drawing sinners,

---

[1]The present tense of ποιῶ *(poio' – I make),* is linear, continuous, or repeated action.

and bearing witness with the saints to a dying world would be finished. When the seventh bowl of God's wrath was poured out, the voice said, "It is done!" The wrath reserved for the wicked is be finished. Final judgment is over. The wicked have been consigned to their punishment, and the faithful have gone to their reward. There will never again be cause for the wrath of God to be poured out on anyone.

Now, when the new order has been established in the new heaven and new earth, when God's dwelling and throne are set up there with men, when the eternal blessedness of the saints is realized, once again God says, "It is done!" The redemption of the saints from the earth has been accomplished. All the saved, all His servants, are with Him, and there will be righteousness, joy, and peace forever more.

God identifies Himself as the Alpha and Omega, the Beginning and the End. In the beginning God was there, creating the heavens and the earth. In the end He will be there to bring that heaven and earth to its end, and to create a new heaven and earth wherein dwell righteousness. God was there in the beginning of all things; He will be there at the end. He is the end of all things in the old universe, as well as the beginning of the blessed eternal state of the redeemed in the new.

There in the new earth will be the water of life for the thirsty. God will give it freely. That water is the Holy Spirit, the source of all life (John 7:37-39). In the seven letters to the churches we read repeatedly that "he who overcomes" would be blessed in various ways. That term shows up again in this last act of the drama. "He who overcomes shall inherit all these things, and I will be his God and he shall be My son." Here is the inheritance of the saints—eternal life with the Father and with the Lamb in the new heaven and earth. All the things already mentioned about this blessed state shall be ours if we are among those who overcome. If we come through the trials and tribulations of this life and are faithful unto death we will receive the crown of life. Not only will we inherit the things already mentioned, but there is more to come.

G. THE PUNISHMENT OF THE WICKED (Read 21:8)

Those who do not overcome, but through fear succumb to the pressures of persecution, will share with the unbelievers and the vile and abominable of mankind in the lake of fire. Those who yield to deceptive doctrines, becoming unbelievers or idolaters, will have their part in the lake of fire. Those who fail to resist the allurements of the world, becoming abominable, murderers, fornicators, sorcerers, and liars, will undergo the second death which lasts for eternity.

These are the warning words of God Himself at the conclusion of what He is saying to John. It seems that this return to the scene of 20:11-15 is a bit out of place here in chapter 21. Why bring this up to mar the beautiful picture of the reward of the faithful? Is it not because God is assuring the righteous that such people will have no place among them? He also contrasts the reward of the faithful with the fate of the wicked as a warning to us who are viewing this drama. This is also a means of increasing our appreciation for the things in store for the faithful. We have heaven to gain and hell to shun. We want eternal life, not the second death.

SCENE 2: THE BRIDE, THE NEW JERUSALEM, DESCRIBED
(Read 21:9-21)

The Action of Scene 2. One of the angels with the seven bowls of wrath comes to John and invites him to see the bride of Christ, the wife of the Lamb. The angel carries John to the top of a high mountain where John watches the holy city, New Jerusalem, coming down out of heaven from God. John describes the city as it descends. The glory of God shines from her like the light of a precious jasper stone, clear as crystal. The angel holds a measuring rod with which he measures the city.

The city is laid out square. The city has a very high wall, 12,000 stadia high, and 144 cubits thick. The wall has twelve gates, three on each of the four sides, with an angel at each gate. The names of the twelve tribes of Israel are written on the gates. Each gate is made of a single pearl. The city is 12,000 stadia long, 12,000 stadia wide, and 12,000 stadia high. There are 12 foundations under the city. On them are the names of the twelve apostles. The foundations are made of precious stones. The city and its street are pure, transparent gold.

A. *AN ANGELS SHOWS JOHN THE LAMB'S BRIDE* (Read 21:9-10)

The angel who had poured out one of the bowls of wrath invites John to come and see the bride of Christ. John must have been expecting to see a woman, perhaps with a crown of 12 stars on her head, as he did in 12:1. He probably expected to see her arrayed in linen pure and bright as he did in 19:7-8. Instead he sees a vision of a city—the holy city, New Jerusalem.

Many have thought that the description of this city is a description of heaven; however, what John is seeing is the bride of Christ, not heaven. The bride is the church, the assembly of the saints, the body of Christ. She is the body of the followers of Christ. Collectively they are the woman, the bride of Christ. Individually they are the woman's children, the saints of God. Paul says in Gal. 4:26 that she is our mother. In like manner Rev. 12:17 tells us that those who have the testimony of Jesus are her offspring. As John describes the New Jerusalem, it is not heaven but the redeemed saints that he is describing in a symbolic picture.

John is taken to a high mountain to view the descent of the bride of Christ. What he sees is the great city, New Jerusalem, coming out of heaven from God. This is a symbol of the fulfillment of Jesus' promise in John 14:1-3. Jesus is taking His people to the place He has prepared for them. Babylon the Harlot, the city of the world, is called *the great city,* in previous chapters, but the New Jerusalem is far greater. In John's day Rome was the embodiment of the Harlot. She was called the eternal city. The bride of Christ is truly the eternal city, whereas Babylon the Harlot is destroyed at the end.

The New Jerusalem encompasses everyone in the new heaven and earth. In contrast, the Harlot did not include everyone on earth, but only those "who dwell upon the earth." The multitude of the saints on earth did not belong to that city. They were not part of the world system but were *those who dwell in heaven.* Now we see those who were not at home on earth, the strangers and foreigners to earth, the pilgrims and sojourners, as they descend to their rightful dwelling where they will be at home forevermore. Their citizenship was not on earth but in heaven.

John calls this city, *the holy Jerusalem. Holy*[2] is a word which means *apart* or *separate*. One of the characteristics of God is that He is completely holy. He is separate and apart from His creation. As one theologian put it, "He is wholly other." In 1 Pet. 1:16 Peter quotes these words of God, "Be holy, for I am holy." As God is holy, he wants us also to be holy. With reference to God's people this term is used to mean separation from those things that are impure. Those who have been cleansed of unrighteousness are said to be *sanctified.*[3] Those who have been sanctified are called *saints*—i.e., *holy ones.* These are the ones who make up God's New Jerusalem, the bride of Christ. This is why she is called *the holy Jerusalem.*

The description of the bride given in 19:8 says, "And to her it was granted to be arrayed in fine linen, clean and bright, for the fine linen is the righteous acts of the saints." Righteousness is her clothing. She has been given her righteousness by being cleansed and made pure in the blood of Christ. Rev. 7:14 speaks of those who have been redeemed from the earth in this way, "These are the ones who come out of the great tribulation, and washed their robes and made them white in the blood of the Lamb."

B. THE GLORY OF THE BRIDE, THE HOLY CITY *(Read 21:11)*

The glory of the bride of the Lamb is the glory of God. That is part of our inheritance. We share in the glory of Christ. The glory of this city is like the light reflecting from a jasper[4] stone which is clear as crystal. In the description given in Rev. 4:3 the glory of God on His throne is likened to a jasper and a sardius stone. The bride of Christ shares that glory. She is dazzling and glorious in her beauty.

---

[2] *ἅγιος (hagios). Young's Greek Dictionary* defines this word as, "*sacred* (physically *pure*, morally *blameless* or *religious*, ceremonially *consecrated*):—(most) holy (one, thing), saint." The word derives from *ἅγος (hágos)* which means *full of awe.*

[3] *ἁγιάζω (hagiazo*—pronounce *ha-gi-ad´-zo). Young's Greek Definitions* defines this word as, "to *make holy*, that is, (ceremonially) *purify* or *consecrate*; (mentally) to *venerate:*— hallow, be holy, sanctify."

[4] *ἴασπις (iaspis).* The jasper stone is an opaque precious stone which is found in many colors, but the word is thought by some to refer to an opal or diamond in the scriptures. In this context the fact that it is clear as crystal causes some to think that a diamond is meant. Yet, the gold of this city is also said to be clear as crystal.

C. THE STRUCTURE OF THE HOLY CITY (Read 21:12-14)

When the Israelites camped in the wilderness after the tabernacle was built, three of the 12 tribes were positioned on each side of the tabernacle. Three were in front, three were in the rear, three on the right side, and three on the left side. The symbol of the throne of God, the mercy seat in the tabernacle, was in the very center of the camp. When the tabernacle was taken down and prepared for travel, the order of march was the same. The tribes maintained their positions as they marched through the wilderness. Later in this chapter we learn that the throne of God is in the New Jerusalem. He is in the midst of His people.

The gates of the city are positioned in precisely the same way as the tribes were positioned in the wilderness. On the gates were inscribed the names of the 12 tribes of Israel. Three gates were in the wall on each side of the city. There were 12 in all. An angel was positioned at each gate. The walls of this city are said to be very high. When we notice the dimensions given later we will see just how high. But let us not forget that this is a symbolic picture of the redeemed church of God. It was through Israel that Christ came into the world. The first Christians were believers among the Israelites. All the nations of the world have access to this city through faith, but in a very real sense they have come in through Israel (see Rom. 11:17-18). It is a fitting symbol to represent the 12 tribes of Israel as the twelve gates to the city.

There were 12 foundation stones under the walls. According to the dimensions of the wall given later on, the stones must have been enormous. On these stones are written the names of the 12 apostles of Christ the Lamb. It doesn't say exactly which 12 since there were a total of 14 names given in the New Testament. We can be pretty sure, however, that Judas Iscariot was not one of them since he was replaced because of his betrayal of Jesus and his subsequent death. Matthias was named to replace him. Paul, the 14th, was not one of the 12, but was a special apostle sent to the gentiles. However, he was not appointed until after the death of James by the hand of Herod. So there was never more than 12 at one time. Was Paul's name on one of the foundations? Actually, it is no more necessary to assign specific names to the 12 foundations than it is to name the souls under the altar in Rev. 6:9 who were said to be beheaded because of their testimony. In both instances we are dealing with symbols.

Paul wrote in Eph. 2:20 that we are the ones who have been built on the foundation of the apostles and prophets, and Jesus Christ Himself is the chief cornerstone. The work of the apostles was the foundation work, the beginning of the church. They are the ones who went about establishing congregations throughout the known world. The foundation stone upon which they built the church was Jesus Christ. Jesus told Peter in Matt 16:18, "...on this rock I will build My church...." He referred to the truth that Peter had confessed, that He was the Christ, the Son of God. Paul wrote in 1 Cor. 3:11, "For no other foundation can anyone lay than that which is laid, which is Jesus Christ." By referring to the apostles as the foundation, Paul was not contradicting himself. Jesus, His person and work, is the one foundation, but the work of the apostles was the foundational work in the beginning and spread of the church. They went about laying the foundation through their preaching and teaching. For this reason, their names are written on the foundation stones in this symbol of God's church, the New Jerusalem.

In this holy city the Old Testament types find their fulfillment. God's eternal purpose was laid out for us in the history of His people in the Old Testament. The tabernacle in the wilderness, the temple in Jerusalem, the city of Jerusalem itself, the 12 tribes—all find their fruition in the bride of Christ, the New Jerusalem, the church of our Lord. The symbolism of numbers also comes into play here, for in the book of Revelation the number 12 and its multiples (24 and 144) are symbols of the people of God. There were 12 gates and 12 foundations. Now we will see a further use of this symbolic number as we see the dimensions of the walls.

D. THE MEASUREMENTS OF THE CITY (Read 21:15-17)

The angel measures the length, breadth, and height of the city. Since the walls are the outer perimeter of the city this means the length, breadth, and height of the walls. They are 12,000 furlongs or stadia long, wide, and high. The city is laid out as a square. That means that the floor plan of the city is 144 million square furlongs. How long is this? The furlong is translated from the Greek word for stadia.[5] In a note in the New International Version 12,000 stadia is said to be about 1400 miles, while the New Revised Standard

---

[5] στάδιον (stádion). The word relates to a stadium or race track. Apparently the distance of one lap in the stadium is a stadia or furlong.

Version translated it 1500 miles instead of 12,000 stadia. This translation is unfortunate because it obscures the symbolism involved. The importance of the numbers is not in the actual length, but 12 and 144 are both symbols of the people of God. These numbers are not coincidental. They identify this city, the New Jerusalem, as the people of God.

The width of the wall is measured as 144 cubits. There is that number again. Literally, 144 cubits would be approximately 225 feet. The text does not actually say that this is the thickness of the wall, but that it is the measure of the wall. Since the wall cannot be both 12,000 furlongs high and 144 cubits high at the same time, it must be talking about the measure of the thickness of the wall. The New International Version inserts the word *thick* in the text for this reason. If this were literal, 225 feet would be far to thin for a wall that is at least 1400 miles high. Come to think of it, if this description were literal, this city would cover one third of the continental United States. A literal interpretation brings up some other interesting speculation—i.e., since the city is as high as it is wide and long, does this mean that the risen saints will have the power of upward mobility as well as horizontal? It is beside the point since the city is not a literal structure. It is a symbolic description of the redeemed saints. The numbers of the measurements are intended to identify the city as the people of God. They are God's city, and God will dwell in their midst.

E. THE ADORNMENT OF THE CITY (Read 21:18-21)

The light of the city, the glory of God, is like a jasper, clear as crystal, and the walls are made of jasper. The foundations of the walls, symbolic of the apostles, are each a precious stone. There were 12 in all. These are jasper, sapphire, chalcedony, emerald, sardonyx, sardius, chrysolite, beryl, topaz, chrysoprase, jacinth, and amethyst. What is the significance of these precious stones? Whatever else they may represent, they certainly represent the beauty, splendor, and radiant glory of the bride of Christ. When God gave to Moses the pattern for the tabernacle and all things pertaining to it, one of the requirements was an ephod for the high priest to wear. The breastplate of that ephod was to contain 12 precious stones. On each was written the name of one of the 12 tribes of Israel. While the symbolism is similar, the 12 stones are not all the same as the ones named on the foundations.

The 12 gates, on the other hand, are not said to be adorned with precious stones, but are said to be pearls. Each gate consisted of one pearl. What is the significance of the pearl? The perfect pearl was the most prized possession of merchants of precious stone. Jesus told of a man who sold all that he had in order to buy the one pearl of great price (Matt. 13:45-46). The pearl not only represents beauty but also purity. Perhaps its most significant meaning is the preciousness of God's people in His eyes. The 12 tribes are a figure for the people of God, the followers of the Lamb, and His bride. His people are His pearl of great price for which He paid the ultimate price, His own blood.

The city is made of pure gold, clear as glass. The street of the city also is pure transparent gold. If this were speaking literally, no one would have any privacy in the houses in that city. The walls are transparent jasper, the structures in the city are all transparent gold and the street is transparent gold. The gold signifies the saints who have been refined by fire. Peter wrote in 1 Pet. 1:6-7:

> In this you greatly rejoice, though now for a little while, if need be, you have been grieved by various trials, that the genuineness of your faith, *being* much more precious than gold that perishes, though it is tested by fire, may be found to praise, honor, and glory at the revelation of Jesus Christ....

In 1 Pet. 4:12 he also wrote, "Beloved, do not think it strange concerning the fiery trial which is to try you, as though some strange thing happened to you...." Job said in Job 23:10b, "*When* He has tested me, I shall come forth as gold." Much of Revelation has focused on the trials of God's people under the pressures of persecution, deceit, and enticements of the world. These are all the refining fires that purify us and sanctify us so that we will come forth as gold. The saints of God are the city of God. They themselves are the pure gold, clear as glass, which makes up this city. They have come through the great tribulation and have come forth as gold. They have overcome. They are gold, and the road they travel is gold. There is but one street of gold, not streets of gold as the songs say.

SCENE 3: THE TEMPLE, LIGHT, AND INHABITANTS
(Read 21:22-27)

As John looked for the temple in the city he saw none. There was no need for a temple for God and the Lamb were themselves the temple. There was no sun or moon to shine in this city, for the glory of God and the Lamb provided all the light. The saved of all the nations walk in the light of God's glory as they bring the glory and honor of their nations into it. The glory and honor of the kings of the earth become part of this city. The redeemed go in and out freely, for the gates are never shut by day. There is no night there, but always day. Nothing and no one who defiles, or causes abominations, or falsehood is allowed in this city. Only those whose names are in the Lamb's Book of Life will be there.

A. THE TEMPLE IN THE CITY (Read 21:22)

The angel has just shown John the structure of the holy city with its measurements and adornments. Now he turns his attention to the things inside the city. In Jerusalem it would be natural to look for the temple of God. But what is the purpose of a temple? When people wanted their gods to be present with them they built temples to house them where they could come when they wanted to be in the presence of their god. The temple of the one true and living God served the same purpose. God gave Moses the pattern for the tabernacle in the wilderness and promised to meet with His people in the tabernacle, the tent of meeting. After the Israelites had settled in the land of Canaan and David had conquered Salem, he made this city his own city and called it Jerusalem. Later David gave his son Solomon the pattern by which he would build the temple in Jerusalem. It followed the basic pattern of the tabernacle. When the temple was dedicated God promised to meet with His people in the temple in Jerusalem.

There was one big problem with the people meeting with God in the temple. They had to do so through the mediation of the high priest. No one else was allowed into the holy of holies where the throne of God (the mercy seat) was located. God met with the high priest there once a year to receive the sacrifice of atonement for the sins of all the people of Israel. The way into God's presence had not yet been revealed for the people, yet, when the people prayed toward this place, God promised to hear them. Heb. 9:8 says, "the Holy Spirit indicating this, that the way into the Holiest of All was not yet made manifest while the first tabernacle was still standing."

When Christ died on the cross the veil of the temple which concealed the holy of holies was torn in two from top to bottom. This signified the opening of the way into the presence of God for all His people. Heb. 10:19-20 says, "Therefore, brethren, having boldness to enter the Holiest by the blood of Jesus, by a new and living way which He consecrated for us, through the veil, that is, His flesh...." The temple was a spiritual dwelling place for God. On earth, following the death and resurrection of Christ, this temple was the church, the community of God's people. God took up His dwelling place in the church by means of the presence of His Holy Spirit. In Eph. 2:19-22 Paul, in speaking to the church in Ephesus, explains it like this:

> Now, therefore, you are no longer strangers and foreigners, but fellow citizens with the saints and members of the household of God, having been built on the foundation of the apostles and prophets, Jesus Christ Himself being the chief cornerstone, in whom the whole building, being fitted together, grows into a holy temple in the Lord, in whom you also are being built together for a dwelling place of God in the Spirit.

In Revelation, beginning in chapter 4, heaven itself is described as the temple of God where His dwelling place and His throne are. Again, the purpose of the temple was that God's presence might be sought there. All His saints had the right to approach His throne of grace in prayer, and are encouraged to come before His throne with boldness in order to receive mercy and grace in time of need (Heb. 4:16).

After the people of God are raised and ascend to heaven, they are then brought down to the new heaven and new earth. They are the bride of Christ, the holy city, New Jerusalem. God moves His dwelling and throne there so that He can be in their midst in person. As a result, no temple is needed. God will dwell in their midst and He will be accessible to all, not just to the High Priest who is Jesus the Lamb. Jesus had already offered Himself as the ultimate sacrifice for sin. He has gone before the throne of God with His own blood as the full and final payment for sins. As a result, each of us will have access to the presence of God. He will dwell among us in person, not just symbolically in a tent or building, nor by the presence of His Holy Spirit in the church.

In Eph. 1:13-14 we are told that we, "...were sealed with the Holy Spirit of promise, who is the guarantee of our inheritance until the redemption of the purchased possession...." God gave us His Holy Spirit to dwell with us and in us as a down payment on our inheritance. That inheritance is realized in the new heaven and earth. At the heart of that inheritance is the presence of God Himself with us. So until then He has sent His Holy Spirit to be with us as an assurance of that inheritance. The Lord God Almighty and the Lamb will Themselves be the temple, not some material structure.

In 21:22 we have the first of several verses which put God Almighty and the Lamb together as a unit. Notice that they are the temple (singular) rather than two temples. This singularity or unity of the Godhead is seen also in the next verse.

B. THE LIGHT OF THE CITY (Read 21:23)

Just as there is no need for a temple structure there, so also there is no need for an external source of light such as the sun or moon. The city is lighted by the glory of God and the Lamb. Notice again the singularity of the light. The glory of God illuminates the city. Then it is said that the Lamb is its light. Now which is it? The Glory of God or the Lamb? The angel is not talking about two different lights. They are one and the same light. In fact, Christ the Lamb is the shining forth of the glory of God. Heb. 1:3 speaks of Christ as "...the brightness of His glory and the express image of His person...." The word for *brightness*[6] is a word which means *emanation* or *shining forth*, in the same sense that the rays of the sun are the shining forth of the light of the sun. So once again we see the oneness of the Godhead in this illustration. There is one source of light in the holy city. That source is God and the Lamb.

---

[6] ἀπαύγασμα (*apaúgasma*). *Young's Greek Definitions* says that this means, "*an off flash, that is, effulgence:—brightness.*" When a camera flash goes off, the light which comes from it is an off flash. The effulgence or emanation from the sun is its rays. Its brightness consist of its output of light. So also is the glory of God in the person of Jesus Christ. He is the off flash of God.

C. *THE GLORY OF THE NATIONS WILL BE IN THE CITY (Read 21:24-26)*

The word for *nations* is also translated *Gentiles*[7] in some passages. The Jews considered themselves unique as God's people, so they divided mankind into two groups consisting of the Israelites and the nations (Gentiles). Yet God had promised that the Gentiles as well as the Jews should have part in His Israel. They were to be brought in and made a part of the tame olive tree of Israel (see *Appendix D* on *The Israel of God*). So both Jews and Gentiles would walk in the light of this city.

Verse 26 tells us that the nations and kings of the earth will bring their glory into this city. It is speaking of those nations and kings who have bowed the knee to the Lamb. Their crowns are seen on the head of Jesus in 19:12, and He has become their King and Lord in 19:16. Whatever glory they gained as kings on earth, they now bring into the New Jerusalem, being themselves part of the bride of Christ.

The church of God is composed of people out of every tribe and tongue and people and nation. Whatever honors they obtain on the earth as Christians are to be a part of the glory which God has chosen to display through them. Christ gives His glory to us. It is only right that we should bring our trophies to Him and lay them at His feet, whether these be the crowns of kings, or the victories of His people, or the honors given us. The glory and honor which the righteous bring to God will be part of the splendor and glory with which God glorifies His servants. God will touch, sanctify, and increase the glory of the saints, adding splendor to splendor by His grace.

The gates of this city will be open all the time, because there will be no night there. In our resurrected bodies we will have no need for sleep. We can be busy all the time serving God and one another. This will be our joy and fulfillment. We will never need to feel that we are useless or helpless or worthless. We will be energized constantly by drinking of the water of life which God will give us (21:6). We will get a fuller picture of this water in the next scene.

---

[7] ἔθνος (*ethnos*) is the word for *nation* or *gentile*. In verse 24 the word is in the nominative plural, ἔθνη (*éthnē*), thus *nations* or *gentiles*.

D. *NOTHING THAT DEFILES WILL BE IN THAT CITY (Read 21:27)*

One of the most wonderful things about the new heaven and new earth is that there will be absolutely no sin there: no violence, no immorality, no enmity, no deceit, nothing that defiles, nothing that is abominable, nothing that is false. Those who dwell there have been prepared by the sanctification of the Holy Spirit to be at home in this picture. The work which God is doing to form the image of the Son of God in us will be brought to completion at that time (Phil. 1:6). We will no longer have the pull of the flesh to draw us into sin. We will truly have the mind of Christ, where our thoughts and actions will all be pure and holy. Not only will the fleshly nature be gone, but our adversary the Devil will also be gone. He will no longer whisper into our ears to tempt us to sin. His agents will not be there to deceive or persecute or allure the saints with the enticements of this world. It will be an entirely new world. Those who would bring abomination into it have been consigned to the lake of fire. Only those who are written in the Lamb's Book of Life will be there. What joy it will be never to be afraid again, never to be intimidated again, never to suffer temptations again!

SCENE 4: THE WATER OF LIFE AND TREE OF LIFE
(Read Rev. 22:1-5)

The angel shows John a river which was flowing from the throne of God and the Lamb. It is the river of water of life, clear as crystal. John sees a species of tree called *the tree of life* growing in the middle of the street as well as on both sides of the river of life. These trees produced 12 kinds of fruit and are harvested every month. The leaves of the trees are also harvested as healing herbs for the nations.

There is no more curse. The curse given in the garden is totally removed. The throne of God is in the city, and the servants of God continually serve Him. They are able to see the face of God, whose name is written on their foreheads.

John observes that there is one eternal day. There is no night there, and there is no need for a sun or any lamps because the light is provided by the glory of God. These servants will reign with Christ in the new heaven and earth throughout eternity.

A. THE RIVER OF THE WATER OF LIFE (Read 22:1)

John first made reference to the water of life in John 4:10-14. Jesus tells the woman at the well in Samaria that if she would ask of Him he would give her living water, which she could drink and never thirst again. The second reference is in John 7:37-39 where Jesus gives the invitation to all to come and drink of this water. John makes it clear that Jesus is talking about the Holy Spirit who would be given to those who believe on Him. We have already read in 21:6 that in the new heaven and earth God will give this water to those who thirst.

Now John is shown the river where this water flows. It is clear as crystal, and it is flowing from the throne of God and of the Lamb. Once again we see the unity of the Father and the Son. The water flows from a single throne. It is both the throne of God and of the Lamb.

The symbolism of this scene is drawn from a vision described in Ezek. 47:1-12. Ezekiel sees water coming from the temple to the right of the altar. It flows eastward toward the Dead Sea. It gets deeper as it goes until it so deep that it becomes a great river too deep to stand in. Along its banks grow every kind of fruit tree. These trees bear fruit every month. The leaves of the trees are for medicine. Wherever the river flows things spring to life. When the water reaches the Dead Sea the sea comes alive. Where there were no living fish because of the extreme saltiness of the sea, that sea now teems with fish.

This, of course, is a symbolic picture of the water of life John talks about. In Rev. 22 we see it flowing from the throne of God. This helps us to understand that the water in Ezekiel which flowed under the threshold of the temple was coming from the mercy seat, the symbol of God's throne. Notice the similarity of the two accounts. While the account in Ezekiel is much more detailed, we see the water flowing from the throne of God. We see the tree of life on each side of the river and in the middle of the street bearing its fruit every month, and its leaves are for the healing of the nations. There is one more reference to this water of life in Rev. 22:17 as part of the Postlude. Now let us turn our attention to the tree of life.

B. THE TREE OF LIFE *(Read 22:2)*

After God had created man, He planted a garden in Eden and placed the man there to cultivate it and care for it. In the garden God placed two special trees. These were called *the tree of life*, and *the tree of the knowledge of good and evil*. Man was free to eat of the fruit of the tree of life, which would enable him to live forever, but he was forbidden to eat of the fruit of the tree of knowledge of good and evil. Eve was deceived by the serpent, the embodiment of Satan, and she ate of the forbidden fruit. Adam was drawn into this with her, although Paul says he was not deceived (1 Tim. 2:14). Because of their disobedience they were driven from the garden and from the presence of God so they could no longer eat of the tree of life and live forever.

The tree of life no longer exists on this earth, nor does the paradise called Eden; however, men are still eating of the tree of the knowledge of good and evil by delving into the deep things of Satan. Because of this all men sin and come short of the glory which God intended for them (Rom. 3:23). Because of sin all die, becoming spiritually separated from God. In this we have all followed in the footsteps of our first parent, Adam.

Yet God has planned for the tree of life to be made available again to all those who are cleansed by the blood of the Lamb. That tree, according to Rev. 2:7, is in the midst of the Paradise (garden) of God. Jesus promised the church in Ephesus that if they overcome they will be able to eat of the tree of life in the midst of this garden. The word *paradise* means a *lovely garden*. Fellowship with God in Eden was lost through Adam's sin. Jesus has restored to those who believe in Him the blessed state of dwelling with God in His paradise. The tree of life was lost to man in the beginning. The tree of life will be restored to man in the Garden of God in the new heaven and earth. Jesus gave His life to make this possible. He went back to heaven to prepare a place for us. He is coming again to take us to be with Him forever in the paradise of God where the tree of life and the river of water of life will be readily available to all.

The tree of life is growing in the middle of the street, and on each side of the river of life. It bears twelve different fruits and is fruitful every month. Not only that, its leaves are for the healing of the nations. From the description given, the picture is of a certain variety of tree called the tree of life, which grows all along the river and in the middle of the street. Its fruit—eternal life—is readily available to all. Those from every nation, tribe, and tongue will eat and live. There will be no more sickness, for the leaves provide healing for them.

C. THERE WILL BE NO MORE CURSE, NO MORE SEPARATION (22:3-4)

The principal curse of sin is death. Paul calls death the wages of sin in Rom. 6:23. Because of sin men must undergo the death of the body. Worse still is the spiritual death which is eternal destruction from the face of God. Jesus told his disciples not to fear the one who can kill the body but not the soul. He said we should rather fear Him who is able to destroy both body and soul in hell (Matt. 10:28).

In Gen. 4:17-24 we learn the extent of the curse brought on by sin. Pain was to be the result of childbearing. The husband was to rule over his wife. Man was to earn his bread by heavy labor. Even the earth itself was cursed, bringing forth thorns and thistles, and making sowing and reaping very hard. Man was destined to return to the dust from which he was formed, and he was denied access to the garden and the tree of life. This curse has all been removed in Christ, though not on this earth. Although we can begin to experience some of the benefits of the removal of the curse here and now, we must wait for our new dwelling place, the new heaven and earth in order to realize the full benefit. There the curse is totally removed. There is no more curse.

Redeemed man will experience full fellowship with his Creator, God, and with his Redeemer, Christ, the Lamb of God. The throne of God and the Lamb are there in the New Jerusalem. The redeemed will have the name of God written on their foreheads because they are God's possession, God's inheritance. They will be able to see His face with their own eyes, and they will never be separated from Him again. Just think—eternal fellowship with our Creator and Redeemer. He will be the center and love of our life.

I think it is both interesting and significant that not only does John refer to the throne (singular) of God and the Lamb, but then says **His** (singular) servants shall serve **Him**. Notice that God and the Lamb are here referred to as Him. This is just another indication of the oneness of the Father and the Son.

D. GOD GIVES THE LIGHT, AND THERE WILL BE NO MORE NIGHT 22:5)

This truth has been presented in chapter 21 (Scene 3), and is reiterated here. There will be no night. Here we need the night in which to rest and refresh ourselves. There refreshing comes continually from the Holy Spirit, the water of life. In our earthly existence our outward man is perishing, but our inward man is being renewed day by day (2 Cor. 4:16). According to Titus 3:5 it is the Holy Spirit who renews us in the inner man. In the new heaven and earth it will be the whole man who is continually renewed.

In our new bodies we will have no more need for night in which to sleep. We will walk in an eternal day. There will be no need for the sun or lamps, because the light is provided by the glory of God. This light is so intense that it is unapproachable by mortal men. 1 Tim. 6:16 reveals to us that Jesus, dwells in unapproachable light so that none can see Him. That situation will be changed in the new heaven and earth, for in our resurrected bodies we will be able to look upon His face. The light of His face is all that is needed to lighten the new heaven and new earth.

The drama ends with the statement, "And they shall reign forever and ever." It was said of the Christ in 11:15, "He shall reign forever and ever!" When the millennial reign is over, Christ will move His reign to the new heaven and earth. In 1 Cor. 15:24-26 Paul speaks of the second coming of Christ when the dead in Christ will be raised. He says:

> Then *comes* the end, when He delivers the kingdom to God the Father, when He puts an end to all rule and all authority and power. For He must reign till He has put all enemies under His feet. The last enemy *that* will be destroyed *is* death.

This passage does not mean that there will be an end to Christs reign, but that the kingdom over which He reigns will be delivered to the Father. This happens when He takes the saints with Him to heaven, and then to the new heaven and earth. The kingdom of Christ is composed of the servants of God. This kingdom which is destined to reign for a time over the kingdom of the world. But the kingdom of Christ will continue through eternity in the new heaven and new earth, where the saints will reign with Him forever and ever! **End of the Drama of the Ages.**

Chapter 22

POSTLUDE

THE ANGEL'S FINAL WORDS TO JOHN
(Read Rev. 22:6-21)

After the drama had been played out the angel who revealed these things to John has a few more words of instruction and admonition to give to John, and through him to us. The admonitions given are for us and not just for John. Let us look at these words of instruction and admonition.

Revelation is Trustworthy (Read 22:6). The angel with one of the bowls of wrath, still speaking to John, gives these words to him after showing him the bride of Christ, New Jerusalem. After the drama ends the first thing he tells John is, "These words are faithful and true." Then he reiterates that the Lord had sent His Angel to show His servants the things which would begin to take place shortly. In other words, the things revealed to John by the Angel of the Lord can be counted on to take place.

Urgency of the Message of Revelation (Read 22:7). Christ Himself tells John, "Behold, I am coming quickly! Blessed is he who keeps the words of the prophecy of this book." At the beginning and again here at the end of the book we are admonished to keep the things written in the book. Christ Himself pronounces blessings on those who keep the prophecy of the Revelation. It must be important. There are things to be kept in this book. According to 1:3 blessings are pronounced on the one who reads, the ones who heed, and the ones who keep the words of this book. It might pay to go back and reread the comments in chapter 1 concerning Rev. 1:3.

374

Angels Are Not to Be Worshiped (Read 22:8-9). For the second time John falls down at the angel's feet to worship him. This angel is not the Angel of the Lord, but one of the seven angels who poured out the bowls of wrath. He is the one doing most of the explaining from chapter 17 onward. For the second time the angel rebukes him and tells him not to do that (see 19:10) since, as an angel, he is a servant of God and of the prophets and of those who keep the things written in this book. Worship God.

The Time Was at Hand (Read 22:10-11). The angel tells John not to seal up the prophecy of this book. Why? The time was at hand for these things to begin to take place. When we reach the completion of the things in this book there will be no more time for repentance or change. Each person will remain in the state in which he meets his Maker and Judge. If he is unjust and filthy, he will continue to be unjust and filthy. If he is righteous and holy, he will continue to be righteous and holy. The prophecy of this book is calculated to bring about repentance so that when we reach the final judgment we will be among the righteous. If the message were sealed up, it could not serve this purpose.

A Message from Christ (Read 22:12-15) Will your name be in the Lamb's book of life, or will you be among those sent away by Him, as in Matt. 25:41? "Then He will also say to those on the left hand, 'Depart from Me, you cursed, into the everlasting fire prepared for the devil and his angels.'" Jesus once again claims to be the Alpha and the Omega, the First and the Last, the Beginning and the End.

Those Who Have A Right to the Tree of Life. The angel tells us that those who do His commandments have a right to the tree of life (access to eternal life) and may enter the Holy City (the redeemed church). Excluded from that city are the dogs of humanity, sorcerers, the sexually immoral, murderers, idol worshipers, and those who are liars.

Jesus Speaks Again (Read 22:16). The words of Jesus reiterate that He has sent His Angel to testify these things to John and the churches. As the root and offspring of David He is the Son of Man. As the Bright and Morning Star He is the brightest jewel of heaven, the Son of God. He has certainly been the star of this show. He has appeared as the glorified Christ, as the Lamb that was slain, as the giant Angel of the Lord, as the Man-child, as the Reaper coming on a cloud, as the Rider on a white horse, King of kings

375

and Lord of lords, the Word of God, the Judge of all, and the One whose throne is the throne of God in the New Jerusalem. His co-star, the church, has appeared as the lampstands, the 24 elders, the souls under the altar, the holy place of the temple of God, the holy Jerusalem, the two witnesses (lampstands), the woman with the crown of twelve stars, the 144,000 of Israel, the souls reigning on thrones, and the bride of Christ.

Jesus Invites you to Drink the Water of Life (Read 22:17). An invitation is offered to everyone. The Spirit of God and the Church of God, the bride of Christ, extend the invitation to a thirsty world. All who hear the invitation are urged to say come also—in other words, pass it on. In Matt. 28:18-20 we read Matthew's account of the great commission. After telling His apostles to go teach all nations and baptize them into the name of the Father, Son, and Holy Spirit, He then tells them to teach them to do all that He had commanded them to do. In other words, Christ wanted the apostles to teach their converts to pass it on.

Whoever will is invited to come and drink of the water of life freely. That water, according to John 7:37-39, is the Holy Spirit who is given to all who believe in Him. Peter adds in Acts 5:32 that the Spirit is given to all those who obey him. This is not a contradiction. Those who believe in Him are the ones who obey Him. The Spirit is pictured as the source of life. If we want to partake of eternal life, we must drink of the Spirit of God.

Does this invitation of Christ tug at your heart? Does the Lamb that was slain as the sacrifice for your sin because of His love for you touch a responsive chord in your heart? If so, will you answer the call to come drink of the water of life? Jesus, with His blood, can wash you free of all your sins, no matter how many or how great they are. You, then, can come into the very presence of God. You will be an heir of eternal life and be able to live forever in the new heaven and earth.

A Warning Against Adding to or Taking from This Book (22:18-19). Those who add to the prophecy of this book will suffer the plagues written in this book. Go back and study the plagues of the trumpets in chapters 8 and 9, and particularly the plagues of the bowls of wrath in chapter 16, and see if you want to have them poured out on you. Those who take away from the words of this book will be removed from the book of life and barred from the holy city. Remember that those whose names are not found in the book of life will be cast into the lake of fire. They will have no part in the rewards written in this book. Serious consequences indeed! Each of us ought to give serious consideration to our spiritual condition, and what the final judgment will be like for us. What about you?

The Benediction (Read 22:20-21)The Lord is coming quickly. Let it be so---come Lord Jesus! The Grace of the Lord Jesus Christ be with you all. Amen. **Thus ends the book of Revelation.**

APPENDICES

APPENDIX A

HADES AND HELL

I. HADES (ἅδης)—THE ABODE OF THE DEAD

Hades[1] is the word for the state or abode of the souls of the dead. The word originated from Greek mythology. Hades was the lower region to which the souls of all the dead were conducted across the river Styx. Hades was also the name of the god of the underworld. The New Testament writers adopted the term and adapted it to portray the truth about the souls of the dead. All the verses containing this word are listed below: They are from the New King James Version.

> (Matt. 11:23-24) And you, Capernaum, who are exalted to heaven, will be brought down to **Hades**; for if the mighty works which were done in you had been done in Sodom, it would have remained until this day. But I say to you that it shall be more tolerable for the land of Sodom in the day of judgment than for you.

> (Matt. 16:18) And I also say to you that you are Peter, and on this rock I will build My church, and the gates of **Hades** shall not prevail against it.

> (Luke 10:15) And you, Capernaum, who are exalted to heaven, will be brought down to **Hades**.

---

[1] ἅδης (hades—pronounced. *hah-days*) – *Young's Greek Dictionary* says, "...properly *unseen*, that is, 'Hades' or the place (state) of departed souls: – grave, hell."

(Luke 16:22-23) So it was that the beggar died, and was carried by the angels to Abraham's bosom. The rich man also died and was buried. And being in torments in **Hades**, he lifted up his eyes and saw Abraham afar off, and Lazarus in his bosom.

(Acts 2:27) For You will not leave my soul in **Hades**, Nor will You allow Your Holy One to see corruption.

(Acts 2:31) He, foreseeing this, spoke concerning the resurrection of the Christ, that His soul was not left in **Hades**, nor did His flesh see corruption.

(1 Cor. 15:55) O Death, where is your sting? O **Hades**, where is your victory?

(Rev. 1:18) I *am* He who lives, and was dead, and behold, I am alive forevermore. Amen. And I have the keys of **Hades** and of Death.

(Rev. 6:8a) So I looked, and behold, a pale horse. And the name of him who sat on it was Death, and **Hades** followed with him.

(Rev. 20:13) The sea gave up the dead who were in it, and Death and **Hades** delivered up the dead who were in them. And they were judged, each one according to his works.

(Rev. 20:14) Then Death and **Hades** were cast into the lake of fire. This is the second death.

Please note that the King James Version translates the word *hades* as *hell* in all these verses. Virtually all later translations, including the NKJV use the word *Hades* so as not to confuse it with *hell*. Many people, however, still consider *Hades* as another name for *hell* due to the earlier confusion.

In the Revelation passages hades is closely associated with death. The rider on the pale horse is Death, and Hades follows him. The idea is that when death claims the body Hades claims the soul.

In the New Testament there are passage that might seem to indicate that Hades is hell, such as the story of the rich man and Lazarus in Luke 16:19-31.

382

In verses 22-23 the beggar, Lazarus, died and was carried to Abraham's bosom. The rich man died also, but he was found in torment. The location is called *Hades* which is thought by some to mean *hell*. He was indeed suffering the flames of torment in the hadean world, but it is a mistake to think that hades is only a place of torment. Being the abode of the dead, both were there—the rich man who was in torment, and Lazarus who was in Abraham's bosom being comforted.

Remember that the place of dead souls is the abode of both the wicked and the righteous dead until the resurrection. This does not mean that they are mixed together. On the contrary, there is a great gulf that separates the wicked from the righteous. This story is not entirely literal, because you could hardly expect physical flames or water to affect immaterial souls. It also stretches the imagination a bit to think that the rich man could see Lazarus and Abraham, let alone have a conversation with Abraham across the great gulf. Of course, with God all things are possible. This is probably a figurative picture of the fact that the wicked dead suffer punishment as they await the resurrection.

II. WHERE ARE THE RIGHTEOUS DEAD?

The rich man looked across the great gulf and saw Lazarus comforted in Abraham's bosom. What is called *Abraham's bosom* here is called *Paradise* elsewhere. There are passages which indicate that the righteous dead are in heaven before the throne of God. For instance, in Rev. 15:1-4 John sees the souls of those who were victorious over the beast and his mark standing before God in heaven and praising Him as they await the outpouring of the bowls of wrath which are the last plagues. The resurrection has not yet taken place, and yet they are in heaven. In Luke 23:43 Jesus told the thief on the cross, ". . .today you will be with Me in Paradise."

In 2 Cor. 12:2 Paul spoke of a man he knew who was caught up to the third heaven. The sky where the birds fly is called *heaven*—this is the first heaven. Outer space where the sun, moon, and stars are is also called *heaven*—this is the second heaven. The third level is the heaven where God resides. In verse 4 Paul calls this *Paradise*. It is reasonable to assume that the location of the righteous souls in the hadean world is heaven. Hades, like death, is more of a state than a place.

Appendices

There is one more time that the word *Paradise* is used. In Rev. 2:7b we read, "To him who overcomes I will give to eat from the tree of life, which is in the midst of the Paradise of God." The tree of life is described as being in the new heaven and earth where the resurrected saints will dwell eternally with God and the Lamb. The word *paradise* means *a beautiful garden.* There is no reason to limit the existence of such a garden to the present heaven where God now resides. He is to move to the new heaven and earth according to Rev. 21. God is to take up residence with His people there and dwell with them in person, so that they will see His face.

III. WHAT ABOUT THE WICKED DEAD?

Hades for the unrighteous is different. It still means that they are disembodied souls awaiting the resurrection, but their condition is entirely different. Instead of being comforted they are under punishment. 2 Pet. 2:9 says, "...*then* the Lord knows how to deliver the godly out of temptations and to reserve the unjust under punishment for the day of judgment." Instead of entering into rest, they have no rest day or night.

In contrast, Rev. 14:13 tells us, "'Blessed *are* the dead who die in the Lord from now on. Yes,' says the Spirit, 'that they may rest from their labors, and their works follow them.'"

Instead of being in Paradise in heaven, the wicked dead are in the lower regions of darkness and gloom. In 2 Pet. 2:4 we read that angels who fell are kept in chains, reserved for judgment, being cast down to hell. The word for hell here is *Tartarus* (τάρταρος).[2] It is found only this once in the New Testament. Although translated *Hell* by most translations, some translations, including *Young's Literal Translation of the Bible* uses the word *Tartarus.*

---

[2] ταρταρόω (*tartaro'o*), a form of τάρταρος, *(tar'taros)* defined in Young's Greek Definitions as "(the deepest *abyss* of Hades); to *incarcerate* in eternal torment:—cast down to hell." Thayer defines the word thus: "1) the name of the subterranean region, doleful and dark, regarded by the ancient Greeks as the abode of the wicked dead, where they suffer punishment for their evil deeds; it answers to Gehenna of the Jews, 2) to thrust down to Tartarus, to hold captive in Tartarus." Since this is the region to which the wicked dead as well as evil spirits are consigned prior to judgment, it is not, strictly speaking, the hell which is known as the lake of fire, but that portion of hades assigned to the wicked.

This is thought by scholars to refer to *the lowest region of hades*, the place where the rich man found himself in torment.

The basic meaning of the noun τάρταρος (*tartarus*), given by *Strong's Greek Dictionary*, as well as *The Englishman's Greek Concordance of the New Testament* is **the deepest abyss of Hades.** *Bauer, Arndt and Gingrich* also concurs with this definition. Darby's *New Translation* translates this word with the phrase, ". . .the deepest pit of gloom." In this verse the fallen angels are held in chains awaiting the judgment. The wicked dead share this region with them.

The word *Hades* makes sense in the context of Revelation only as the receptacle of the souls of the dead. It, like death, is a temporary state which will no longer exist after the resurrection and judgment. Rev. 20:14 says that both death and Hades will be cast into the lake of fire. Now, if Hades is itself the lake of fire, how then can Hades be cast into itself?

IV. JESUS' SOUL IN HADES, WHILE HIS BODY IN THE GRAVE

When Jesus died His body was buried. Where did His soul go? Based on the misunderstanding that Hades is hell, the doctrine was developed that when Jesus died He descended into the depths of hell to preach to the souls confined there. If that is the case, why did Jesus tell the thief on the cross, "Today you will be with me in paradise"? This doctrine of the descent of Christ into hell is bolstered by the passage in 1 Peter 3:18-19:

> For Christ also suffered once for sins, the just for the unjust,
> the He might bring us to God, being put to death in the flesh
> but made alive by the Spirit, by whom also He went and
> preached to the spirits in prison.

It is claimed that when Jesus died He went to hell and preached to the spirits imprisoned there who were destroyed in the flood. This misses the point on two counts. First, those spirits are not in hell, but in Hades, howbeit in torment. Second, the time of the preaching is misplaced. What this verse is saying is that the Spirit who raised Christ from the dead, i.e., the Holy Spirit, is the same Spirit who went and preached to those spirits now in prison. But the preaching was done in the days of Noah. The pre-incarnate Christ, in the person of the Holy Spirit, did that preaching through Noah. It was precisely because they did not listen to the preaching that they are now in prison awaiting the resurrection and judgment of the wicked.

In Acts 2:27 Peter quotes from Psalm 16:10, "For You will not leave my soul in Hades, Nor will You allow Your Holy One to see corruption." Then Peter explains in Acts 2:31 that the Psalmist was speaking of the resurrection of Christ. "...he, foreseeing this, spoke concerning the resurrection of the Christ, that His soul was not left in Hades, nor did His flesh see corruption." The resurrection of the dead involves bringing the bodies from the graves and the souls from the hadean world to reunite them. This includes the souls of the righteous in paradise, or Abraham's bosom, where Lazarus is, where also the forgiven thief on the cross is. It also includes the wicked in torment, where the rich man is. All will be raised in the last day (John 5:28-29). When death and Hades are emptied in the resurrection, then there will be no more use for death or Hades. Both will be destroyed. This is portrayed figuratively by their being cast into the lake of fire.

In the Old Testament, *Sheol*, the Hebrew equivalent of *Hades*, is sometimes translated *the pit* and *the grave*. The pit (abyss) is an Old Testament reference to the lower region of Sheol where the souls of the wicked are preserved for the resurrection. Following are all the Old Testament passages where the Hebrew word *sheol* (שׁאוֹל) is translated as *Sheol* in the New King James Version.

> (2 Sam. 22:6) The sorrows of **Sheol** surrounded me; The snares of death confronted me.

> (Job 11:7-8) Can you search out the deep things of God? Can you find out the limits of the Almighty? *They are* higher than heaven—what can you do? Deeper than **Sheol**—what can you know?

> (Job 17:16) *Will* they go down to the gates **of Sheol**? Shall *we have* rest together in the dust?

> (Job 26:6) **Sheol** is naked before Him, And Destruction has no covering.

> (Psalm 16:10) For You will not leave my soul in **Sheol**, Nor will You allow Your Holy One to see corruption.

(Psalm 18:5) The sorrows of **Sheol** surrounded me; The snares of death confronted me.

(Psalm 86:13) For great *is* Your mercy toward me, And You have delivered my soul from the depths of **Sheol**.

(Psalm 116:3) The pains of death surrounded me, And the pangs of **Sheol** laid hold of me; I found trouble and sorrow.

(Prov. 1:12) Let us swallow them alive like **Sheol**, And whole, like those who go down to the Pit.

(Isa. 5:14) Therefore **Sheol** has enlarged itself And opened its mouth beyond measure; Their glory and their multitude and their pomp, And he who is jubilant, shall descend into it.

(Isa. 14:11) Your pomp is brought down to **Sheol**, *And* the sound of your stringed instruments; The maggot is spread under you, And worms cover you.

(Isa. 14:15) Yet you shall be brought down to **Sheol**, To the lowest depths of the Pit.

(Isa. 28:15) Because you have said, "We have made a covenant with death, And with **Sheol** we are in agreement. When the overflowing scourge passes through, It will not come to us, For we have made lies our refuge, And under falsehood we have hidden ourselves."

(Isa. 28:18) Your covenant with death will be annulled, And your agreement with **Sheol** will not stand; When the overflowing scourge passes through, Then you will be trampled down by it.

(Isa. 38:10) I said, "In the prime of my life I shall go to the gates of **Sheol**; I am deprived of the remainder of my years."

(Isa. 38:18) For **Sheol** cannot thank You, Death cannot praise You; Those who go down to **the pit** cannot hope for Your truth.

(Isa. 57:9) You went to the king with ointment, And increased your perfumes; You sent your messengers far off, And *even* descended to **Sheol**.

(Jonah 2:2) And he said: "I cried out to the LORD because of my affliction, And He answered me. Out of the belly of **Sheol** I cried, *And* You heard my voice."

In the Old Testament many versions translate *Sheol* as *the grave* or *the pit*. Some versions also translate it *hell*. Notice in the verses above how many times that Sheol is associated with death (six passages in all). They seem to go together. The parallelism in the above verses even seems to consider them as one. In fact they are very closely related, since as death claims the body, Sheol (Hades) claims the soul. This relation is maintained in the New Testament, especially in Revelation, linking death and Hades.

Notice also that Sheol is related to the grave, which is another way of speaking of death. One verse associates it with resting in the dust, while another speaks of maggots and worms covering a person. These are obvious references to the bodies decaying in the grave.

Psalm 16:10, which is quoted by Peter, is referring to the resurrection of Christ—particularly the fact that His soul was not left in Sheol (hades in Acts 2:27,31), and His body was not left in the grave to decay.

In these verses, sometimes Sheol is paired with the pit (abyss). This is referring to the lower region where the wicked await the resurrection. This is thought to be the abyss into which the Dragon (Satan) is to be cast for 1000 years. This is probably the same as *Tartarus* in the New Testament where the fallen angels are reserved for judgment.

V. THE SOURCE OF THE WORD TRANSLATED *HELL*

Hades does not mean *hell* as we understand that word, although some translations, especially the King James Version, use the word *hell* to translate *Hades*. In fact, *hell* at one time was broad enough in its definition to include

Hades, but now its use for *Hades* is only confusing. Normally *hell* is the word used to translate the word *gehenna*.[3]

There was a valley outside the gates of Jerusalem called *Gehenna*, the Valley of Hinnom. The children of Hinnom had possessed this place which had been used in various ways. In the time of Christ it was a place where refuse was thrown. Fires were kept burning there to consume the constant flow of refuse. This was adopted as the symbol for the place where the wicked, the refuse of mankind, would be cast. It was literally a lake of fire. It serves as a figure for hell.

The passages in the New Testament where *gehenna* (*γέεννα*) is found are as follows:

> (Matt. 5:22b) But whoever says, "You fool!" shall be in danger of **hell fire**.

> (Matt. 5:29) If your right eye causes you to sin, pluck it out and cast *it* from you; for it is more profitable for you that one of your members perish, than for your whole body to be cast into **hell**.

> (Matt. 5:30) And if your right hand causes you to sin, cut it off and cast *it* from you; for it is more profitable for you that one of your members perish, than for your whole body to be cast into **hell**.

> (Matt. 10:28) And do not fear those who kill the body but cannot kill the soul. But rather fear Him who is able to destroy both soul and body in **hell**.

> (Matt. 18:9) And if your eye causes you to sin, pluck it out and cast *it* from you. It is better for you to enter into life with one eye, rather than having two eyes, to be cast into **hell** fire.

---

[3] *γέεννα (géenna) – Young's Greek Dictionary* defines this word as: "Of Hebrew origin ; *valley of* (the sons of) *Hinnom*; *gehenna* (or *Ge-Hinnom*), a valley of Jerusalem, used (figuratively) as a name for the place (or state) of everlasting punishment:—hell." In the NKJV, in 12 out of 13 appearances *hell* is translated from *gehenna.* The 13th is found in 2 Peter 2:4. There it is the word *ταρταρόω* which refers to the part of hades where there is torment. From this we get the word *tartarus.*

(Matt. 23:15) Woe to you, scribes and Pharisees, hypocrites! For you travel land and sea to win one proselyte, and when he is won, you make him twice as much a son of **hell** as yourselves.

(Matt. 23:33) Serpents, brood of vipers! How can you escape the condemnation of **hell**?

(Mark 9:43) If your hand causes you to sin, cut it off. It is better for you to enter into life maimed, rather than having two hands, to go to **hell**, into the fire that shall never be quenched .

(Mark 9:45) And if your foot causes you to sin, cut it off. It is better for you to enter life lame, rather than having two feet, to be cast into **hell**, into the fire that shall never be quenched.

(Mark 9:47) And if your eye causes you to sin, pluck it out. It is better for you to enter the kingdom of God with one eye, rather than having two eyes, to be cast into **hell fire**.

(Luke 12:5) But I will show you whom you should fear: Fear Him who, after He has killed, has power to cast into **hell**; yes, I say to you, fear Him!

(James 3:6) And the tongue *is* a fire, a world of iniquity. The tongue is so set among our members that it defiles the whole body, and sets on fire the course of nature; and it is set on fire by **hell**.

It is interesting that there is only one use of the word outside the first three gospels. Most are in Matthew. In 5 out of the 12 verses fire is associated with hell. Although Revelation does not use the word *hell*, *the lake of fire* (λίμνην τοῦ πυρός) would be its equivalent. Other passages which speak of the destruction of the wicked as *eternal fire* are: Matt:18:8, "If your hand or foot causes you to sin, cut it off and cast it from you. It is better for you to enter into life lame or maimed, rather than having two hands or two feet, to be cast into the **everlasting fire**," and Matt. 25:41, "Then He will also say to those on the left hand, 'Depart from Me, you cursed, into the **everlasting fire** prepared for the devil and his angels.'"

The lake of fire is prepared for the Devil and his angels. Those of mankind who rebel against God and live sinful lives will have to share in this lake of fire with Satan and his angels (Rev. 21:8). In Rev. 2:11, 20:6, 20:14, and 21:8 the lake of fire is called *the second death.*

VI.   SUMMARY

When the soul leaves the body at death it enters a state called *Hades* in the New Testament, and *Sheol* in the Old Testament. The souls of the righteous await the resurrection in the presence of God in Abraham's bosom, or Paradise. The souls of the wicked await the resurrection in Tartarus or the abyss, a place of punishment. They share this place with the angels who fell. Even Satan will be confined there for a period of time prior to the resurrection.

All souls in the hadean world will reunite with their bodies at the resurrection. For the righteous, this will be an immortal and incorruptible body. They will all stand before the judgment seat of God (the Lamb) to receive the things done in the body. The wicked will then be cast into the lake of fire, where Satan will have already been thrown. This is the second death. The righteous will ascend to heaven, where they will be taken by Christ to the new heaven and new earth, wherein righteousness dwells. Nothing unclean or sinful will ever enter there. There will be nothing but peace and joy, and they will serve and worship the Lamb throughout eternity.

APPENDIX B

DAY FOR A YEAR THEORY

There is ample precedent in the Old Testament for interpreting symbolic days as years in prophecy. In their second year in the wilderness the Israelites were sentenced to 40 more years of wandering because of their unfaithfulness and failure to go in and take the land of Canaan which God had already granted them. This made a total of 42 years in the wilderness. The spies of Israel had spied out the land for 40 days. Only Joshua and Caleb brought back the report God wanted. Because the people believed the other ten spies they refused to go in to take the land. As a result, God told them that they would wander **a year for every day** the spies had been in the land until all that generation had died in the wilderness. Numbers 14:34 explains:

> According to the number of the days in which you spied out the land, forty days, for each day you shall bear your guilt one year, *namely* forty years, and you shall know My rejection.

There are two occasions when Ezekiel was told to lie on his side for so many days. In Ezek. 4:4-5, **390 days represented 390 years**, and in verse 6, **40 days represented 40 years**. Verses 4-6 read as follows:

> Lie also on your left side, and lay the iniquity of the house of Israel upon it. *According* to the number of the days that you lie on it, you shall bear their iniquity. For I have laid on you the years of their iniquity, according to the number of the days, three hundred and ninety days; so you shall bear the iniquity of the house of Israel. And when you have completed them, lie again on your right side; then you shall bear the iniquity of the house of Judah forty days. **I have laid on you a day for each year.**

As a final example of numbers being used to signify a day for a year we go to the book of Daniel. 70 weeks of years are represented in Daniel 9:24-27. The seven days of a week were symbolic of seven years. The 70 weeks represented 490 years. Verses 24-25 tell us:

> Seventy weeks are determined For your people and for your holy city, To finish the transgression, To make an end of sins, To make reconciliation for iniquity, To bring in everlasting righteousness, To seal up vision and prophecy, And to anoint the Most Holy.[1]

> Know therefore and understand, *That* from the going forth of **the command   To restore and build Jerusalem** Until Messiah the Prince, *There shall be* seven weeks and sixty-two weeks [i.e., 69 weeks total]; The street shall be built again, and the wall, Even in troublesome times.

The counting of the time was to begin with the decree to restore and build Jerusalem, and was to be completed when the things mentioned in verse 24 were accomplished, i.e., to finish transgression, make an end of sins, make reconciliation for iniquity, bring in everlasting righteousness, seal up vision and prophecy and anoint a Most Holy place. There would be 69 weeks (7 plus 62) until Messiah comes, or is anointed.

The decree to build Jerusalem could not have been speaking of the decree of King Cyrus in 538 B.C. (Ezra 1:1-4) who sent Zerubbabel back with the exiles who would go with him to rebuild the temple in Jerusalem and reestablish the temple worship. First, it was much too early, because the 70 weeks of years would have ended a half century before Jesus was even born. Second, the decree was for the building of the temple, not rebuilding the walls and city of Jerusalem.

The decree of King Artexerxes to Nehemiah in 445 B.C. (Neh. 2:1-8) to complete the job of rebuilding the city and walls would have been too late, since the 69 weeks of years would have ended some 9 years after Jesus began His ministry.

---

[1] קֹדֶשׁ – *qòdesh*, pronounced *ko'-desh* – *Strong's Hebrew Dictionary* defines this as a *sacred* place or thing; rarely abstractly *sanctity*:—consecrated (thing), dedicated (thing), hallowed (thing), holiness. Several versions translate this as *"a most holy place."*

Nine years earlier in 459 B.C. Artexerxes had allowed Ezra to go to Jerusalem with any of the Jews who would go with him. The king sent gifts including much gold for the house of God in Jerusalem (which had already been rebuilt by Zerubbabel) and gave orders that Ezra be given the funds to do whatever God commanded him to do. This is found in Ezra 7. That this included rebuilding Jerusalem's wall can be seen in Ezra 9:9. Ezra says:

> For we *were* slaves. Yet our God did not forsake us in our bondage; but He extended mercy to us in the sight of the kings of Persia, to revive us, to repair the house of our God, to rebuild its ruins, and **to give us a wall in Judah and Jerusalem**.

In this statement Ezra speaks both of the rebuilding of the temple (through Zerubbabel) as well as the rebuilding of the wall. Since the wall was not included in Zerubbabel's commission, and Nehemiah had not yet come on the scene, it has to be God's command given through Ezra. Before Jerusalem could be rebuilt Israel had to be reformed. After this Neh. 1 tells of Nehemiah's returning with more of the exiles to superintend the rebuilding. Ezra's return and the work he did was by God's decree. Artexerxes did not decree the rebuilding of Jerusalem, but allowed Ezra to do whatever the Lord commanded him. Thus, the decree to rebuild the walls and city was by God's decree, not by a decree of one of the kings of Persia.

If the date of the king's decree for Ezra's return be accepted as the beginning date, then it was to him that God gave the command for the rebuilding of the city and wall. Beginning in 457 B.C. and counting 69 weeks of years we come to the year 26 A.D. which is the year that Jesus was baptized in the Jordan and was anointed with the Holy Spirit on the banks of the Jordan. That is when He began His public ministry as the Messiah, the Anointed One. Three and a half years later, in the middle of the 70th week, He was crucified, was buried, and He arose from the dead. Some weeks later, after Jesus had ascended to heaven, the church had its beginning on the day of Pentecost when the Holy Spirit was poured out on all flesh, and the church, the Holy Place, was anointed by that same Holy Spirit that anointed Jesus. So, in the midst of the 70th week the prophecy was fulfilled. All the things mentioned in Daniel 9:24-25 had been fulfilled.

What about the other three and a half years to the end of the 70th week? Think about it. When you say you are going to do something in so many days, you don't mean to say it will not be until the last hour and minute and second of the day that it will be complete. As long as it is complete on the last day, that fulfills the statement. When you say that something will happen in ten hours, you don't mean that it will happen on the 60th minute of the 10th hour. As long as it happens during the tenth hour, the statement is fulfilled. The same is true with weeks or months or years. Remember that the stated period of time is weeks (of years). To say something is going to be completed in 70 weeks does not mean that it must wait until the last day, the last hour, and last minute of the week. **Anytime during the seventieth week will do to fulfill the prophecy.** So when all the requirements of the 70 weeks prophecy were fulfilled in the middle of the 70th week, we need look for nothing more. Daniel goes on from there to speak of some things which were to happen later concerning events surrounding the destruction of Jerusalem, but they are not part of the 70 weeks prophecy.

These examples **show conclusively the use of a day for a year in symbolism.** The only question is whether this is the case with the 1260 days of Revelation. We have already seen that the symbol of three and a half years is associated with periods of tribulation for God's people, and so serves to symbolize the persecution and tribulation which was coming. We have also seen that the only reference to the number 42 is the 42 years the Israelites spent in the wilderness. This is put as 42 months in Revelation, because it corresponds to the three and a half years and 1260 days that the woman who is the symbol of God's people was to spend in the wilderness. Although three and a half and 42 are both numbers associated with periods of suffering and hardship for God's people, the number 1260 is not found in any such connection. Why does John use this number at all?

Since the events spoken of in Revelation 13 involve a time frame, then perhaps we are to see the 1260 days as a clue to that period of time. Since there is ample precedent for interpreting a day as a symbol for a year, then perhaps the 1260 days is to be interpreted as 1260 years. In my opinion this is the case, and so we should look for a period approximating 1260 years as the time when the seven-headed beast in its ten-horn phase is given power to persecute and overcome the saints.

APPENDIX C

THE TEMPLE OF GOD

I. THE TABERNACLE, A FIGURE OF THE HEAVENLY TEMPLE

The temple in heaven is visited many times in the book of Revelation. We are introduced to it in chapters 4-5, and return to it in 6, 7, 8, 11, 14, and 15, with reference to it in 21. The temple in heaven plays such a central role it will pay us to be thoroughly acquainted with the source of its symbolism. In 15:5 it is called *the temple of the tabernacle,* relating it to the portable temple which accompanied the Israelites in their wilderness wanderings. The word *temple* also refers to the sanctuary, or inner shrine, meaning the Holy of Holies as contrasted with the Holy Place. The former is God's sanctuary or throne-room in heaven while the latter is the church both in heaven and on earth. The manifestation of the Holy Place is principally on earth.

A. THE OLD TESTAMENT HOLY OF HOLIES AND ITS FURNITURE

First, there was **the Holy of Holies** (The Most Holy Place) in which a large chest overlaid with gold, called *the ark of the covenant* or *the ark of the testimony,* rested. This ark contained the stone tablets of the ten commandments which were the basis of God's covenant made with the Israelites in the wilderness; a pot of the manna which the Israelites ate in the wilderness; and Aaron's rod which budded as a testimony from God that Aaron was His chosen representative as high priest. On top if this ark was a lid of gold which served as a throne for God. It was called *the mercy seat.* On this throne God's presence was seen not as a form, but as a shining glory—a brilliance resting on the mercy seat—emanating throughout and filling the Holy of Holies. This manifestation of His presence was called in Hebrew the *Shekina.*

On each side of the mercy seat, and formed as one piece with it, were the figures of **cherubim**, a very high rank of angels. Their wings overshadowed the mercy seat. The Holy of Holies was the representation of God's throne room. Only the high priest could enter, and only on one day each year, the day of atonement (Yom Kippur). Heb. 9:7-8 explains that this was symbolic of the fact that the way into the Holiest of All was not yet open (i.e., in the Old Testament era).

God's throne room in heaven is the true Holy of Holies. Jesus Christ entered there to appear before God for us all (Heb. 9:11-12, 23-24). He did not come empty-handed, but as our Great High Priest He entered once for all (not once a year) with His own blood to make atonement for the sins of the world.

B. THE HOLY PLACE AND ITS FURNITURE

Second, in front of the Holy of Holies was **the Holy Place**, separated from the Holy of Holies by a heavy curtain, which barred entrance into the Holy of Holies to all but **the high priest**. But both the high priest and the rest of **the Aaronic priests** would enter into the Holy Place to perform services daily. It would help to read all of Hebrews chapters 8 and 9 to get a fuller picture of the significance of the symbolism of the tabernacle.

The church is referred to as the temple of God in 1 Cor. 3:16-17. This passage is not referring to individual Christians as temples, but to the collective body of Christians, the church, as the temple of God (notice that the pronoun **you**[1] is plural in the original while *temple* is singular). Also in Eph. 2:19-22 Paul speaks of the fact that we (Christians) are being built upon the foundation of the apostles and prophets into a holy temple of the Lord. 1 Pet. 2:5 also tells us that we are being built up a spiritual house as well as a holy priesthood to offer up spiritual sacrifices to God. Just as the people of God make up the New Jerusalem, so also the people of God make up the

---

[1] ἐστε (*este*), 2nd person plural present indicative active verb – *you are*. "...you are the temple of God...." ὑμῖν – *humin'*, 2nd person plural pronoun – *you*. "...the Spirit of God dwells in you...." [1 Cor. 3:16]. Paul is referring to the body of Christ rather than individual Christians, whereas in 1 Cor. 6:19 he speaks of the individual Christian as being a temple of the Holy Spirit since the Holy Spirit dwells in him.

temple of God, namely the Holy Place in which they offer their sacrifices of service and praise.

In the Holy place were three articles of furniture. First, **the golden altar of incense** stood directly in front of the curtain. On this altar bowls of burning **incense** were offered continually as a sacrifice to God. In Rev. 5:8 we learn that this incense was symbolic of **the prayers of the saints**. Second, there was a **seven branched golden lampstand** upon which **seven lamps of fire** were kept burning. This was positioned on the left side of the tabernacle as one entered through the door of the Holy Place. In the temple in Jerusalem there were ten of these lampstands, five on each side. The lampstand is symbolic of **the churches whose task it is to hold up the light of the gospel**. The lamps are **the seven-fold Holy Spirit of God** in His function of revelation. Third, on the right side there was a table called *the table of show bread* or *the table of the bread of the presence*. **Twelve loaves of bread** were placed upon this table daily—one loaf representing each tribe of Israel. These loaves were to be eaten by the priests, and replenished daily. They symbolize our Bread of Life who is Jesus, the bread of the Presence (John 6:32-35).

C. THE OUTER COURT AND ITS FURNITURE

The third part of the tabernacle was **the outer court**. It was enclosed by a fence draped with coverings. Its gate was in the center of the front fence. This court represents **the world**, and is given to the nations. Into this court **all the Israelites could come** with their sacrificial offerings, which the priests would take and offer upon the altar of burnt offering. In this outer court were only **two articles of furniture**.

Upon entering the gate, the first article was **the altar of burnt offering**, square in shape, with steps leading up to it. The fire upon this altar was to be kept burning continually. Upon it the **animal sacrifices** as well as the **grain and wine offerings** were offered. Once a year, on the Day of Atonement, the high priest would take the blood of a bullock and a goat from this altar through the Holy Place into the Holy of Holies to offer upon the mercy seat, first for his own sins, and then for the sins of the people.

This altar represents first and foremost **the sacrifice of Christ** whose blood was taken into the throne room of God as the payment for our sins.

Secondly it represents **the offering of the Christians' living sacrifices,** including the sacrifice of the lives of the martyrs as they are persecuted and killed because of their testimony.

Between the altar and the tabernacle was a wash basin, called *the laver.* The priests had to cleanse themselves with the water kept in this basin before they could enter the tabernacle. When the permanent temple was built in Jerusalem, this basin was replaced by a much larger bronze basin called *the sea,* no doubt, because of its large size.[2] It was approximately 15 feet across from lip to lip, and rested upon twelve figures of oxen. There were ten smaller basins on carts with wheels which were kept five on the left side and five on the right side of the temple. These were filled with water from the bronze sea for the priests to use for their cleansing. This sea is represented in the heavenly scene by a sea of crystal rather than bronze.

Before men enter **the Holy Place (the church)** to serve as **priests of God (Christians)** they must first be cleansed from their sins in the blood of Christ (Tit. 3:4-7; Acts 22:16). The sea is the symbol of **cleansing by the blood of Christ.** It is pictured in 4:6 as a crystal sea.

D. THE PRIESTS WHO SERVED IN THE TABERNACLE/TEMPLE

Fourth, there was **the priesthood,** composed of Aaron and his descendants. They were of the tribe of Levi. The whole of the tribe was assigned tasks of service for the tabernacle, but only Aaron and his descendants were allowed to minister in the tabernacle to offer sacrifices for the people. Aaron, his eldest son, and the eldest descendant of each high priest after him were appointed to serve as **high priests,** each taking his position when his father died.

1. The High Priest. The high priest was symbolic of **Christ, who is the Great High Priest** who entered into the true Holy of Holies, the throne room of God, with his own blood to offer for the sins of all who believe on Him. He did this not once a year, but once for all. Heb. 9:11-12 shows this:

> But Christ came *as* High Priest of the good things to come, with the greater and more perfect tabernacle not made with

---

[2]See 1 Kings 7:23-44. Since so much of the chapter is spent on the sea with its corresponding lavers, they must have been considered very important.

hands, that is, not of this creation. Not with the blood of goats and calves, but with His own blood He entered the Most Holy Place [heaven] once for all, having obtained eternal redemption.

2. The Aaronic priests—foreshadows of Christians. The descendants of Aaron serve as priests in the Holy Place (the church). The priests were divided into **24 courses** (divisions) according to the descendants of the 24 grandsons of Aaron (1 Chron. 24:1-19). Each division took its turn in serving in the temple. Some of the Levites were appointed to be over **the music in the temple**—singers and players on instruments to offer up **the sacrifice of praise** to God. These were the sons of Asaph, Heman and Jeduthun. There were **24 of these sons also**. Those chosen from their descendants totaled 288, or twice 144 (12 times 12). These also cast lots to determine their order of service by their families. Like the priests, there were **24 divisions of the singers and players on instruments** (1 Chron. 25).

In Peter's first letter to the believers, he writes in 2:5:

...you also, as living stones, are being built up a spiritual house, a holy priesthood, to offer up spiritual sacrifices acceptable to God through Jesus Christ.

According to Peter we, **the believers, are the priests in the temple of God**. The Old Testament priests were anointed by a special, unique oil that was used only to anoint the priests. **We are anointed, as was Christ, by the oil of the Holy Spirit.**

II. MEASURING THE TEMPLE
(Rev. 11:1-2 and Ezekiel 40 – 43)

In Rev. 11:1-2 John is given a measuring rod and told to measure the temple, its altar and its worshipers. The symbolism is taken from Ezek. 40 - 43. Ezekiel sees a man measuring every aspect of the temple and hears the measurements announced. In Ezek. 43 God Himself gives the measurements of the altar. Nothing is said there about the man with the measuring rod. The altar must be very important since God Himself gives the measurements. The altar signifies the worship of the priests as they offer sacrifices on the altar. Although the measuring of the temple in Ezekiel's vision is presented as if the man were measuring the temple in Jerusalem, we should remember that the temple had already been destroyed, so it could not refer to a literal measuring of that temple.

Although the measurements of Solomon's temple, given in 1 Kings 6:1-38 and 7:13-51, and 2 Chron. 3:1 – 4:22 correspond to the measurements given by Ezekiel, a great deal more detail is given in Ezekiel. It appears that there are rooms and porches not mentioned in the description of Solomon's temple. It may be that the vision of Ezekiel was prophetic of the temple as rebuilt by Zerubbabel and later expanded and made more ornate by Herod the Great. This is the temple to which Jesus went. Some have suggested that Ezekiel's description was intended as a pattern for the rebuilding of the temple after the return from Babylonian captivity.

If this is the case, then perhaps it is a double prophecy since none of these versions of the temple conform to all the details of Ezekiel's vision. First, in Ezek. 43:7 God says, "Son of man, this is the place of My throne, and the place of the soles of My feet, where I will dwell in the midst of the children of Israel forever." Since this could not apply to any material temple built on this earth, we must understand that He is talking about the temple in heaven.

Another indication is found in the further description of the temple. Aside from the measurements in chapters 40 - 43, the description of the temple continues through chapter 47. In that chapter Ezekiel sees water flowing from under the threshold of the temple. Based on the vision of Rev. 22:1-2, this water is probably coming from the Holy of Holies, from the mercy seat (the throne of God). As the water flows to the east the stream grows in size. It becomes a mighty river in which a man cannot stand, but must swim to keep above water. It is a life-giving river for wherever it flows life springs up. Trees grow on the banks of the river whose leaves do not wither, but are for the healing of the nations. The fruit does not fail, but the trees bear fruit twelve months out of the year. When the river reaches the dead sea that sea comes to life and is no longer dead. There are very many fish and living creatures in the sea.

This river of water that brings life is the Holy Spirit[3] which comes from the throne of God. It is the Holy Spirit who gives life. To partake of the

---

[3] John 7:37-39. Jesus speaks of the rivers of living water. John adds that He is speaking of

Holy Spirit is to drink of the water of life. Compare Ezekiel's vision to the one in Rev. 22:1-2:

> And he showed me a pure river of water of life, clear as crystal, proceeding from the throne of God and of the Lamb. In the middle of its street, and on either side of the river, *was* the tree of life, which bore twelve fruits, each *tree* yielding its fruit every month. The leaves of the tree *were* for the healing of the nations.

In our discussion of the temple in heaven in earlier chapters of Revelation we have seen that the throne of God (mercy seat) is in the holy of holies (heaven itself—Heb. 9:8-12, 23-24), that Christians are the priests who serve God under their great high priest, Jesus Christ. We have also noticed that the Holy Place where the priests enter to serve is the church. It is represented both in heaven, as saints who have died, and on earth, where Christians still living serve at the altar. While it can truly be said that the temple is in heaven (the Holy Place as well as the Holy of Holies), still, those who serve in that temple include Christians who have not yet departed this life on earth. The Christians still living on earth are a part of that heavenly temple. Eph. 2:20-22 says:

> ...having been built on the foundation of the apostles and prophets, Jesus Christ Himself being the chief cornerstone, in whom the whole building, being fitted together, grows into a holy temple in the Lord, in whom you also are being built together for a dwelling place of God in the Spirit.

Paul further writes in 1 Cor. 3:9, 16-17:

> For we are God's fellow workers; you are God's field, *you are* God's building ...Do you not know that you are the temple of God and *that* the Spirit of God dwells in you? If anyone defiles the temple of God, God will destroy him. For the temple of God is holy, which *temple* you are.

1 Cor. 3:16-17 has been used to prove that we are not supposed to abuse our bodies because they are temples of God. That is a misapplication of this

---

the Holy Spirit who would be given to those who believe.

verse since the pronoun *you* is plural[4] and **temple** is singular, indicating that the temple to which Paul refers here is made up of all Christians, each being a stone in that temple. The passage that speaks of our bodies as temples of the Holy Spirit is 1 Cor. 6:19. We should make sure that we use passages in their proper context. The point Paul is making in chapter 3 is that we, collectively, are being built up into God's building, His temple. In verses 10-15 Paul points out that not only are we each part of this building, but that we have a part in building others into it.

When Moses was about to build the tabernacle (the portable temple in the wilderness which preceded the temple in Jerusalem), he was admonished by God to be sure to build everything according to the pattern given him on Mount Sinai (Heb. 8:5; Exod. 25:40). The reason for this is that it was a copy and shadow of the heavenly temple. Each thing in the pattern had meaning for the true tabernacle, built by God and not man. The tabernacle was the first earthly temple of God—a portable structure built to serve during the wilderness wanderings of God's people. The temple built later in Jerusalem was built upon the same basic pattern, with much added to it. The Holy of Holies and the Holy Place were doubled in length and width (quadrupled in area). The temple was built of materials suitable for a permanent structure. It had courts, porches and rooms which the tabernacle did not have.

The temple in Rev. 11 is seen on earth not as the material temple made by human hands, but that part of the heavenly temple that is made up of the Christians living on earth. The Holy Place corresponds to this. This is the church, the temple being built up of living stones. 1 Pet. 2:4-5 tells us:

Coming to Him *as* to a living stone, rejected indeed by men,
but chosen by God *and* precious, you also, as living stones,
are being built up a spiritual house, a holy priesthood, to offer
up spiritual sacrifices acceptable to God through Jesus Christ.

The only measuring rod for this spiritual house must be a spiritual one. The word of God is spoken of both as a sword and a rod. The rod indicated in the context of such verses is a shepherd's rod which is used as a weapon

---

[4]The pronoun *you* in this verse is *ye* in the King James Version. *Ye* is the plural form of the pronoun, *thou* being the singular. The Greek pronoun in both verses is also plural in its forms—i.e., ὑμῖν and ὑμεῖς.

against the enemies of the sheep (see Rev. 19:15), nevertheless, the word of God is a measuring rod by which we measure our conformity to the will of God.

APPENDIX D

THE ISRAEL OF GOD

I. CHILDREN OF ABRAHAM BY FAITH

A number of times in the New Testament we are told that those in Christ are the true children of Abraham by faith. It is not the physical but the spiritual descendants that count. Gal. 3:29 says, "And if you *are* Christ's, then you are Abraham's seed, and heirs according to the promise." Rom. 9:6b-8 states:

> For they *are* not all Israel who *are* of Israel, nor *are they* all children because they are the seed of Abraham; but, *"In Isaac your seed shall be called."* That is, those who *are* the children of the flesh, these *are* not the children of God; but the children of the promise are counted as the seed.

In Gal. 4:21-31 Paul draws an allegory. Hagar was a bondwoman who was the mother of Ishmael, Abraham's first son. In the allegory she represents the old covenant given at Sinai, the covenant of bondage. Ishmael, her son, was born into bondage because his mother was a slave. In the allegory Ishmael represents the Israelites who are the children of the covenant of bondage. On the other hand, Abraham's wife Sarah was the mother of Isaac the child of promise. She was a free woman and represents the new covenant given by Christ, the covenant of freedom. Hagar also represents the present Jerusalem while Sarah is the figure of the Jerusalem which is above, the mother of us all. To apply the allegory, Paul wrote in Gal. 4:28-31:

> Now we, brethren, as Isaac *was*, are children of promise. But, as he who was born according to the flesh then persecuted him who *was* born according to the Spirit, even so it is now. Nevertheless what does the Scripture say? *"Cast out the*

405

bondwoman and her son, for the son of the bondwoman shall not be heir with the son of the freewoman." So then, brethren, we are not children of the bondwoman but of the free.

Paul says, "Cast out the bondwoman [the old covenant] and her son [children of the old covenant], for the son of the bondwoman shall not be heir with the son [Christians] of the freewoman [the new covenant]." The Israel God recognizes is not made up of the children of the old covenant, but the children of the new covenant.

In Gal. 6:15-16 Paul declares:

For in Christ Jesus neither circumcision nor uncircumcision avails anything, but a new creation. And as many as walk according to this rule, peace and mercy *be* upon them, and [or even[1]] upon the Israel of God.

Rom. 2:28-29 makes it plain who are to be considered real Jews:

For he is not a Jew who *is one* outwardly, nor *is* circumcision that which *is* outward in the flesh; but *he is* a Jew who *is one* inwardly; and circumcision *is that* of the heart, in the Spirit, not in the letter; whose praise *is* not from men but from God.

If one says that in this verse Paul is talking about the physical Jews who are circumcised in the heart as well as in the flesh, then he should read verse 26 also, "Therefore, if an uncircumcised man keeps the righteous requirements of the law, will not his uncircumcision be counted as circumcision?"

II. THE DOCTRINE OF THE REMNANT

In the Old Testament prophets, especially Isaiah, there is what theologians call *the doctrine of the remnant of Israel.* These prophecies are

---

[1]The word καί, translated *and* in the NKJV is translated *even* in some translations. The Greek word καί can be translated as *and, also,* or *even.* Since the Israel of God in this verse refers to those who are new creatures in Christ, I prefer the word *even* here.

set in the context of the remnant of Judah and Israel that are brought back from captivity, but there is a deeper meaning to them. Paul refers to the remnant in Rom. 9:27 in these words, "Isaiah also cries out concerning Israel: *'Though the number of the children of Israel be as the sand of the sea, The remnant will be saved.'*" This is a quotation from Isa. 10:22. In verse 29 he also quotes from Isaiah 1:9, "And as Isaiah said before: *'Unless the Lord of Sabaoth had left us a seed* [a remnant], *We would have become like Sodom, And we would have been made like Gomorrah.'*" In verses 23-26 Paul makes it plain that God's people include both Jews and Gentiles. He quotes from Hos. 2:23 and 1:10 to prove his point:

> ...and that He might make known the riches of His glory on the vessels of mercy, which He had prepared beforehand for glory, *even* us whom He called, not of the Jews only, but also of the Gentiles? As He says also in Hosea: "*I will call them My people, who were not My people, And her beloved, who was not beloved. And it shall come to pass in the place where it was said to them, 'You are not My people,' There they shall be called sons of the living God.*"

What is he talking about? Paul delves into this subject more deeply in Rom. 11. In verses 1-2a he says:

> I say then, has God cast away His people? Certainly not! For I also am an Israelite, of the seed of Abraham, of the tribe of Benjamin. God has not cast away His people whom He foreknew.

So he says in verse 5, "Even so then, at this present time there is a remnant according to the election of grace." Obviously Paul leans heavily upon the Old Testament prophets' doctrine of the remnant of Israel to explain who is to be considered God's people. That doctrine, although found scattered throughout the writings of several Old Testament prophets, is found in its fullest in the writings of Isaiah.

III. THE OLIVE TREE OF ISRAEL

Paul claimed to be one of the remnant of Israel which God had not cast off. But he goes on to show that the remnant is only the starting place. He likens Israel to a cultivated olive tree. He then points out that branches were broken off to allow Gentiles to be grafted in as part of the olive tree. Of the natural branches only the remnant remained. Branches from a wild olive tree (Gentiles) are brought and grafted into the cultivated olive tree (Israel). The natural branches were broken off because of their unbelief. The unnatural branches (Gentiles) are grafted in because of their faith in Christ. Natural branches can be grafted back into their own tree if they do not continue in unbelief. The branches that have been grafted in can be broken off if they do not continue in belief. Rom. 11:13-27 reads thus:

> For I speak to you Gentiles; inasmuch as I am an apostle to the Gentiles, I magnify my ministry, if by any means I may provoke to jealousy *those who are* my flesh and save some of them. For if their being cast away is the reconciling of the world, what *will* their acceptance be but life from the dead? For if the firstfruit *is* holy, the lump *is* also holy; and if the root *is* holy, so *are* the branches. And if some of the branches were broken off, and you, being a wild olive tree, were grafted in among them, and with them became a partaker of the root and fatness of the olive tree, do not boast against the branches. But if you do boast, *remember that* you do not support the root, but the root supports you. You will say then, "Branches were broken off that I might be grafted in." Well said. Because of unbelief they were broken off, and you stand by faith. Do not be haughty, but fear. For if God did not spare the natural branches, He may not spare you either. Therefore consider the goodness and severity of God: on those who fell, severity; but toward you, goodness, if you continue in His goodness. Otherwise you also will be cut off. And they also, if they do not continue in unbelief, will be grafted in, for God is able to graft them in again. For if you were cut out of the olive tree which is wild by nature, and were grafted contrary to nature into a cultivated olive tree, how much more will these, who *are* natural *branches*, be grafted into their own olive tree? For I do not desire, brethren, that you should be ignorant of this mystery, lest you should be wise in your own opinion, that blindness in part has

happened to Israel until the fullness of the Gentiles has come in. And so all Israel will be saved, as it is written: *"The Deliverer will come out of Zion, And He will turn away ungodliness from Jacob; For this is My covenant with them, When I take away their sins."*

IV. ONE FLOCK, ONE SHEPHERD—ONE KINGDOM, ONE KING

There are a number of misconceptions about God's Israel. Some think that there are two Israels: **1) physical Israel**, the natural descendants of Abraham through Isaac and Jacob, and **2) spiritual Israel**, the spiritual descendants of Abraham through faith in Christ. As a result of this misconception there are expectations for physical Israel that have already been fulfilled for the true Israel of God, the real heir of the promises. According to Paul's illustration, both the remnant of the Jews and believing Gentiles make up the one tree of Israel. The idea of two Israels is not a biblical idea. The prophets did not see it that way. They envisioned the Gentiles being brought by God to be included in His Israel. In Isa. 56:6-8 the prophet quotes God as saying:

> Also the sons of the foreigner Who join themselves to the LORD, to serve Him, And to love the name of the LORD, to be His servants—Everyone who keeps from defiling the Sabbath, And holds fast My covenant—Even them I will bring to My holy mountain, And make them joyful in My house of prayer. Their burnt offerings and their sacrifices *Will be* accepted on My altar; For My house shall be called a house of prayer **for all nations**." The Lord GOD, who gathers the outcasts [remnant] of Israel, says, "Yet I will gather to him *Others* besides those who are gathered to him."

He also writes in Isa. 14:1, "For the LORD will have mercy on Jacob [Israel], and will still choose Israel, and settle them in their own land. The strangers will be joined with them, and they will cling to the house of Jacob." The passages in Isaiah which speak of the remnant and the strangers or Gentiles being joined together in Israel are far too numerous to be included here. It should be enough to point out that God was going to send His

Messiah to be the shepherd over His people Israel. The Messiah (Christ) said in John 10:14-16:

> I am the good shepherd; and I know My sheep, and am known by My own. As the Father knows Me, even so I know the Father; and I lay down My life for the sheep. And **other sheep I have which are not of this fold**; them also I must bring, and they will hear My voice; and **there will be one flock and one shepherd**.

John understood that other sheep (Gentiles) were to be brought by Christ and joined to the ones He already had (Jews) and they would become one flock under one shepherd. God does not have two sets of chosen people— i.e., Jews and Christians.

He has only one chosen people. He knows them as His Israel, composed of both Jews and Gentiles. When Jesus was about to be born into this world, Gabriel announced concerning Jesus in Luke 1:33, "And He will reign over the house of Jacob [Israel] forever, and of His kingdom there will be no end." The wise men came seeking the one born "king of the Jews." Jesus does not have two kingdoms. The kingdom of Christ is the house of Israel. This is composed of all who believe in Him and submit to His authority as king.

The prophets did not see two sets of people called Israel. There is only one Israel. The Israel of the Old Testament was its beginning. God purged from Israel those who did not follow Him. Isa. 1:24-27 puts it this way:

> Therefore the Lord says, The LORD of hosts, the Mighty One of Israel, "Ah, I will rid Myself of My adversaries, And take vengeance on My enemies. I will turn My hand against you, And thoroughly purge away your dross, And take away all your alloy. I will restore your judges as at the first, And your counselors as at the beginning. Afterward you shall be called the city of righteousness, the faithful city." Zion shall be redeemed with justice, And her penitents with righteousness.

This was the process of pruning or breaking off the branches. Isa. 10:33 expresses the same thing this way, "Behold, the Lord, The LORD of hosts, Will lop off the bough with terror; Those of high stature will be hewn down, And the haughty will be humbled." Again in Isa. 27:11, "When its boughs are withered, they will be broken off; The women come *and* set them on fire."

After this purging process is finished, notice what is left according to Isa. 17:6-7:

> "Yet gleaning grapes will be left in it, Like the shaking of an olive tree, Two *or* three olives at the top of the uppermost bough, Four *or* five in its most fruitful branches," Says the LORD God of Israel. In that day a man will look to his Maker, And his eyes will have respect for the Holy One of Israel.

These gleanings of the grapes after harvest, or these few olives left after the tree is shaken, are the remnant of Israel. Just as God began afresh after the flood with Noah and his family, so God begins anew with the remnant of Israel to whom he adds the believing Gentiles. These are those who look to their Maker and respect the Holy One of Israel (Jesus the Christ).

V. THE METAMORPHOSIS OF ISRAEL

At this point Israel undergoes a metamorphosis. Like the caterpillar which becomes a beautiful butterfly, God's Israel throws off its old covenant shell and becomes the church of the living God. An illustration of this kind of metamorphosis is the body of those resurrected at the last day. In 1 Cor. 15:35-38 Paul writes concerning the resurrection and the nature of the body that rises from the grave:

> But someone will say, "How are the dead raised up? And with what body do they come?" Foolish one, what you sow is not made alive unless it dies. And what you sow, you do not sow that body that shall be, but mere grain—perhaps wheat or some other *grain*. But God gives it a body as He pleases, and to each seed its own body.

Paul's point is that the body that is buried is like a seed. The body that rises from the grave will have undergone a metamorphosis. It will be changed. This does not mean that the resurrected person is not the same person, but that changes have taken place in his body so that what was mortal

411

(subject to death) will be immortal, and what was corruptible (subject to decay) will be incorruptible. Verses 42-44 explains:

> So also is the resurrection of the dead. The body is sown in corruption, it is raised in incorruption. It is sown in dishonor, it is raised in glory. It is sown in weakness, it is raised in power. It is sown a natural body, it is raised a spiritual body. There is a natural body, and there is a spiritual body.

Some have the idea that in the resurrection we will be given an entirely different body that has no connection with the old body that dies and is buried. That is not the case. The body that goes into the grave is likened to a seed—i.e., a grain of wheat for instance. The stalk and ear of grain that comes up arises from the seed that was planted. There is a connection. So also there is a connection between the old body and the new one. There is continuity. The body that springs forth from the seed will have undergone a metamorphosis from a physical to a spiritual body, like the caterpillar that becomes a butterfly. The butterfly comes from the caterpillar.

Even so, the Israel of God that arose from the seed (the remnant) is not a different Israel, but one that has gone through a metamorphosis. The caterpillar has become a butterfly. While there is the connection between the new and the old, changes have taken place. God began with the seed, the stump of the remnant of Israel from which those who did not believe in Christ were broken off, and He added to this remnant the believers from among the Gentiles. This olive tree of Israel, revived and changed, consists only of those who are in Christ, those who continue in faith. Israel has been changed from a physical body to a spiritual one.

Even though Paul was the special apostle to the Gentiles, he always went to the Jews first and then to the Gentiles. In Rom. 1:16 he wrote, "For I am not ashamed of the gospel of Christ, for it is the power of God to salvation for everyone who believes, for the Jew first and also for the Greek." God's new, transformed Israel is built upon the stump, the remnant of Israel. It is to these that believers from among the Gentiles are added. In Isa. 6:13b the prophet writes, "So the holy seed *shall be* its stump." The context of this statement is the purging of Israel leaving only the seed or stump—i.e., the remnant (see verses 11-13). Isaiah writes in Isa. 14:1:

For the LORD will have mercy on Jacob, and will still choose Israel, and settle them in their own land. The strangers will be joined with them, and they will cling to the house of Jacob.

Paul wrote in Eph. 2:11-19 (notice the highlighted phrases):

Therefore remember that you, **once Gentiles in the flesh—** who are called Uncircumcision by what is called the Circumcision made in the flesh by hands—that at that time you were **without Christ,** being **aliens from the commonwealth of Israel** and **strangers from the covenants of promise,** having no hope and without God in the world. But now **in Christ Jesus you who once were far off have been brought near by the blood of Christ.** For He Himself is our peace, who has **made both one,** and has broken down the middle wall of separation, having abolished in His flesh the enmity, *that is,* the law of commandments *contained* in ordinances, so as to create in Himself one new man *from* the two, *thus* making peace, and **that He might reconcile them both to God in one body through the cross,** thereby putting to death the enmity. And He came and preached peace to you who were afar off and to those who were near. For **through Him we both have access by one Spirit to the Father.** Now, therefore, you are **no longer strangers and foreigners, but fellow citizens** with the saints and members of the household of God....

Paul could hardly make it clearer. The Gentiles who are in Christ are no longer far off, no longer strangers and foreigners, no longer without Christ, no longer aliens or strangers to the covenants of promise. Now they are fellow citizens and members of God's household. The two, Jews and Gentiles, have been made into one new man, reconciled to God in the one body of Christ. Now they stand on equal footing before God, both having access by the one Spirit to God.

Remember that the tree of Israel, as represented in Rom. 11, is composed of both believing Jews and believing Gentiles. In fact, it is composed only of believers. The branches that are broken off are cast off from Israel. They are no longer part of Israel. They no longer have a place in the tree unless they become believers. But Paul makes it clear that those physical Jews can be grafted back into the tree if they do not continue in unbelief.

As a result the whole tree of Israel will be saved. That is why Paul says, "so [thus or in this way] all Israel will be saved." He could not mean all physical Jews, because many of them had been broken off, and had already died without having come back to God. He surely could not have meant all of the future physical descendants of Israel, for there is no hint that they would all believe. In fact, between the time Paul wrote and now when I am writing this, most of the Jews have died in unbelief and are not saved.

I believe that there is coming a time in which the descendants of physical Israel will have their eyes opened and come to Christ en-masse. Otherwise I do not understand Paul's statement in Rom. 11:25:

> For I do not desire, brethren, that you should be ignorant of
> this mystery, lest you should be wise in you own opinion, that
> blindness in part has happened to Israel until the fullness of
> the Gentiles has come in.

James wrote a letter and addressed it to "the twelve tribes of Israel." In James 1:1 he says, "James, a bondservant of God and of the Lord Jesus Christ, To the twelve tribes which are scattered abroad: Greetings." In this letter he wrote nothing that would be considered specifically for Jewish people. It is generally understood that this was a figurative way of addressing Christians throughout the world. As a result, this is considered a general epistle written to all Christians.

In the same way, in Rev. 7 the 12 tribes of Israel are probably to be understood as a figure for Christians, those who are new creatures in Christ, the Israel of God. This agrees with the explanation John gives that these are "the servants of God." The 12 tribes of Israel are the servants of God—all the servants of God, and only the servants of God.

APPENDIX E

THE PLAN OF SALVATION

Before the creation of the world God had devised the plan of salvation. He knew that man, given freedom of choice, would ultimately choose the wrong path. By going against God's will all men fall into sin. In Rom. 3:23 Paul said, ". . .for all have sinned and fall short of the glory of God." Paul also tells us that the wages of sin is death (Rom. 6:23). Eternal life, on the other hand, comes as a free gift of God's grace, unearned by any meritorious works on man's part. But the gift of salvation, offered by God, must be accepted by men. God will not force salvation on anyone.

What is that plan of salvation by which all men have the opportunity to receive eternal life? It is composed of two parts. The first part is God's gift of grace which provided the payment for our sins so that we might receive eternal life. The second part is the conditions upon which it is offered to men. Three times in the book of Acts men asked a similar question—"Men *and* brethren, what shall we do?" (Acts 2:37), "What shall I do, Lord?" (Acts 22:10; 9:6), and "Sirs, what must I do to be saved?" (Acts 16:30) The answer to this question reveals the second part of the plan of salvation.

I. GOD'S GRACE OFFER

God loved us and sent His Son to be our Savior. This plan is called **the divine mystery**. It was kept secret from the foundation of the world, but is now revealed through His holy apostles and prophets.[1]

---

[1]See the treatment of this subject in chapter 10 (concerning Rev. 10:7) under the heading, *II. B. The Finish of the Mystery—God's Eternal Plan.*

The plan includes God's coming to be with us (*Emanuel—God with us*), being begotten as a human by the power of the Holy Spirit rather than being begotten by a man. He was the Son of Man because He came into this world through the human birth process, possessing a human body with all its nature. He was the Son of God because He was begotten by the Spirit of God. In Luke 1:35 we read, "And the angel answered and said to her, '*The* Holy Spirit will come upon you, and the power of the Highest will overshadow you; therefore, also, that Holy One who is to be born will be called the Son of God.'" Although He had no earthly father, He was fully human. Heb. 2:14 says;

> Inasmuch then as the children have partaken of flesh and blood, He Himself likewise shared in the same, that through death He might destroy him who had the power of death, that is, the devil.

The plan includes the death of Christ as a payment and sacrifice for all men. Indeed, this is the heart of the plan, without which there can be no salvation. 1 John 2:2 informs us, "And He Himself is the propitiation for our sins, and not for ours only but also for the whole world." This means He took our debt of sin and paid for it on the cross. Heb. 10:10 says, "By that will we have been sanctified through the offering of the body of Jesus Christ once for all."

The plan also includes the resurrection of Christ. If Christ had not risen we would still be in our sins. 1 Cor. 15:3-4 states:

> For I delivered to you first of all that which I also received: that Christ died for our sins according to the Scriptures, and that He was buried, and that He rose again the third day according to the Scriptures.

Paul says in verse 14, "And if Christ is not risen, then our preaching *is* empty and your faith *is* also empty." Verse 17 goes on to state, "And if Christ *is* not risen, your faith *is* futile; you are still in your sins!" The resurrection is central to the gospel. Some churches preach a gospel that is devoid of the resurrection. Without the divine/human person of Christ, His death for sin and His resurrection there is no basis for salvation. These are essentials without which we cannot be a true church of Jesus Christ.

Add to this the ascension of Christ to the right hand of God where He ever lives to make intercession for us, and His sending the Holy Spirit as the means for God and Christ to live in us, so we can be reconciled to God, and so He can write His law in our hearts to transform our lives. If we don't have the Spirit of Christ, we do not belong to Him (Rom. 8:9).

Further, one day Jesus is coming back to judge the living and the dead. Those who are dead in Christ will rise incorruptible, and those in Christ who are still living will be changed (1 Cor. 15:51-53). These shall enter into eternal life. The wicked will be judged and condemned to everlasting destruction. While the details of our belief concerning these last things may not be quite so important and vital, the previous things mentioned will determine those who are Christ's and those who are not. The measuring stick of the word of God on these matters must be applied.

God's part in the plan is called *grace*. The grace of God which brought salvation is not just a way of thinking or feeling. It required action on God's part to provide the basis of salvation through the giving of His Son, the sending of His Holy Spirit, and all that goes with this. The grace of God is manifest in the working of God. Without His working there would be no grace. God's grace system provided a way for us to be reconciled with God and receive eternal life with Him, even though we don't deserve it. He provided this means of salvation because of His great love for us.

Some churches are teaching that salvation is only a matter of what we do. Salvation comes through our own efforts—through being good, through law keeping, through meriting salvation by our own good works. This is another gospel[2] and does not meet the measurements applied by the divine measuring rod.

---

[2]Paul condemned those who preach a gospel of salvation by the merit of law-keeping in Gal. 1:6-9. He calls it *another gospel*, and says that those who preach another gospel would be cut off. In Gal. 5:4 he said, "You have become estranged from Christ, you who attempt to be justified by law; you have fallen from grace."

II. MAN'S FAITH RESPONSE

A. THINGS REQUIRED OF MAN FOR SALVATION

Let us not fool ourselves. There is something required of men in order to be saved and become members of the body of Christ. It is not that we have a means of earning our salvation. There is no way that our works could ever merit God's favor. His grace is unmerited. However there are some conditions laid down in God's plan. These come under the heading of faith. Without faith no man can come to God. There are several items that make up this faith system. Let's take a look at these:

First: God's plan calls for us to believe the truth about Jesus Christ. Heb. 11:6 says, "But without faith *it is* impossible to please *Him*, for he who comes to God must believe that He is, and He is a rewarder of those who diligently seek Him." Jesus said in John 8:24, "Therefore I said to you that you will die in your sins; for if you do not believe that I am *He*, you will die in your sins." Jesus is asking us to believe in Him as the divine one—the I AM.[3]

We have been commanded to believe. I should point out that we need help in believing. This help is given by God. John 6:44-45 says:

> No one can come to Me unless the Father who sent Me draws him; and I will raise him up at the last day. It is written in the prophets, "And they shall all be taught by God." Therefore everyone who has heard and learned from the Father comes to Me.

We must be willing to take the first step toward Christ, like the father of the child who was possessed by a deaf and dumb spirit which caused him repeatedly to fall into the fire. In Mark 9:24 the child's father said, "Lord, I believe; help my unbelief!" This help, too, is by the grace of God, but even

---

[3] In Exod. 3:14, when God revealed Himself to Moses at the burning bush, it says, "And God said to Moses, 'I AM WHO I AM' And He said, 'Thus you shall say to the children of Israel, "I AM has sent me to you."'" In John 8:24 "I am *He*" is literally "I, I am" *(ἐγώ εἰμι)* or "I am the I am." This title for God indicates that He is the uncreated, self-existent being. Unlike all other beings, He exists in and of Himself. Jesus tells us in this verse that we must believe that He is this self-existent one or we will die in our sins.

so, a response is required on our part. We must not get the idea that by obeying the command to believe we have somehow earned our salvation. In John 6:28-29 Jesus was asked what work the Father would have them do. "Then they said to Him, 'What shall we do, that we may work the works of God?' Jesus answered and said to them, 'This is the work of God, that you believe in Him whom He sent.'" We do not put God under obligation to us by our obeying this or any other command. Obeying the command to believe is, nevertheless, a necessary thing. If we don't we will perish.

There are those who contend that believing the truth about Jesus is all that is required and that we are saved by faith when we have accepted as true the facts about Christ. This is not supported in scripture. Believing the facts is only the beginning of faith. James tells us that the demons do this much, but they are not saved (James 2:18-19). God's word has a great deal more to say about what is required.

Second: we are told that we must confess this belief. In Matt 10:32 Jesus said, "Therefore whoever confesses Me before men, him I will also confess before My Father who is in heaven." John attests to the need for confession of faith in 1 John 4:15, "Whoever confesses that Jesus is the Son of God, God abides in him, and he in God." In Rom. 10:9-10 Paul writes:

> ...if you confess with your mouth the Lord Jesus and believe
> in your heart that God has raised Him from the dead, you will
> be saved. For with the heart one believes unto righteousness,
> and with the mouth confession is made unto salvation.

We are all commanded to confess our faith in the truth about Christ. Does this mean we somehow earn our salvation by obeying this command? Of course not. Even though this is an outward thing that we do with our mouth, it is a condition of faith, required of all of us. Having done this, the salvation we receive is only by the grace of God. He has a right to require any condition He wants in order for us to become recipients of His grace. While this is true, it is also true that every condition He has given plays a vital role in the plan. His commands are not arbitrary. The fact that we have to do something does not make our salvation any less by grace. Every requirement He has given is meaningful, and relates directly to the payment He has made for us.

419

Third: Jesus tells us that repentance of sins is a must. Jesus said that without repenting we will perish (Luke 13:3, 5). When He gave the great commission in Luke 24:46-48 He said in verse 47, "...that repentance and remission of sins should be preached in His name to all nations, beginning at Jerusalem." Peter first proclaimed the gospel message on the day of Pentecost following Jesus' resurrection and ascension. In response to the question in Acts 2:37, "What shall we do?" Acts 2:38 says, "Then Peter said to them, 'Repent, and let every one of you be baptized in the name of Jesus Christ for the remission of sins; and you shall receive the gift of the Holy Spirit.'"

We cannot be saved without believing the truth about Jesus Christ. We cannot be saved without confessing that faith before men. We cannot be saved without repenting of our sins. Christ came to save us from our sins, not in them. All these things make up the faith system. These things are all faith responding to Christ. But is that all? There is at least one more item that comes under the heading of the faith by which we are saved. What is it?

Fourth: We are told that obedience is required of those who want to be saved. Heb. 5:8-9 reads as follows:

> ...though He was a Son, yet He learned obedience by the things which He suffered. And having been perfected, He became the author of eternal salvation to all who obey Him....

Notice that He does not first give eternal salvation and then expect obedience. He gives eternal salvation to those who first obey Him. In Matt. 7:21-23 Jesus has a great deal to say about the necessity of obedience:

> "Not everyone who says to Me, 'Lord, Lord,' shall enter the kingdom of heaven, but he who does the will of My Father in heaven. Many will say to Me in that day, "Lord, Lord, have we not prophesied in Your name, cast out demons in Your name, and done many wonders in Your name?" And then I will declare to them, 'I never knew you; depart from Me, you who practice lawlessness!'"

B. *THE NECESSITY OF OBEDIENCE*

Obedience is not only necessary after one enters the kingdom. One cannot even enter the kingdom without obedience. This is made clear by the passages above. The one who does not obey is practicing lawlessness. There are those who teach that there is nothing required of the one who is saved (except to believe that Jesus is the Son of God). To these there is no command that the Christian must obey except the command to believe. To require anything more, they say, would be legalism. They seem to think that obedience to any command is an effort to earn one's salvation. These ignore plain statements of scripture which do not fit into that way of thinking. This viewpoint is called *antinomianism*. The word carries the idea of being against law-keeping. Such people want Jesus as their Savior, but not as their Lord.

There are also many who accept the idea that obedience to Christ is important, but only after one is saved, and not as a condition to be saved. These fail to realize that one cannot be saved without obeying those commands which are conditions of salvation. We have already noticed three commands that are identified as absolutely essential to salvation. These are: to believe the truth about Jesus; to confess one's faith in Jesus; and to repent of sins. Fail to obey any of these commands and you will fail to receive forgiveness and all of the other benefits of accepting Christ. But is that all the obedience that is required to become a Christian? No, there is one more thing. I speak of baptism. Churches have moved heaven and earth to remove baptism from the place given it in scripture, and have instead placed it after one is saved. Take a look at Mark 16:15-16:

> And He said to them, "Go into all the world and preach the gospel to every creature. He who believes and is baptized will be saved; but he who does not believe will be condemned."

Some grab hold of the second clause of the second sentence which says, "but he who does not believe will be condemned" in order to nullify the first clause which says "He who believes and is baptized will be saved." They argue, "But it doesn't say, 'He who does not believe and is not baptized will be condemned.'" Of course it doesn't say that. After all, what is necessary to be condemned? Disbelieving is all that is required. You don't have to not be baptized. I baptized a lady in southern California who confessed that she believed Jesus to be the Son of God. Later she told me that she did not believe that Jesus was God in the flesh, the divine one who is "God with us," the one who died for our sins. She could not accept the idea of God's being willing to do that for us. She did not believe. This was all that was necessary for her to be lost. She did not have to be unbaptized. But we are not concerned with what is necessary to be condemned. We want to know what is necessary to be saved. Jesus said that two of the things necessary are believing and being baptized.

C. INFANT BAPTISM?

There are some who practice baptizing infants before they are capable of believing. The infant certainly is not obeying, for he/she is submitted for baptism without consulting him/her at all. The infant has no say in the matter. Those who teach and practice this turn Mark 16:16 around. To them it means, "He that is baptized shall be saved, and then he will believe when he gets old enough." The infant is incapable of believing or confessing his belief. He is incapable of repenting. He is incapable of obeying in any way.

D. BAPTISM AFTER SALVATION?

On the other hand there are others who turn this verse around in the other direction. They say, "He that believes shall be saved, and then afterwards he should be baptized if it is convenient." Do you see the problem?

Let's look at it in chart form:

1. BELIEF   +   BAPTISM   =   SALVATION
2. BAPTISM   =   SALVATION then   BELIEF later
3. BELIEF   =   SALVATION then   BAPTISM maybe

Which of these views do you think agrees with Mark 16:16?

E. "FOR" OR "BECAUSE OF" REMISSION OF SIN

Acts 2:38 says, "Then Peter said to them, 'Repent, and let every one of you be baptized in the name of Jesus Christ for the remission of sins; and you shall receive the gift of the Holy Spirit.'" This was in response to the question in verse 37, "Men and brethren, what shall we do?"

Is the scripture unclear? Many who are not satisfied with what the scripture says have gone to great lengths to make it mean something else. Some have said that the word *for* means *because of*, thus baptism is because of the remission of sins. These have failed to notice that this would also mean that repentance is because of the remission of sins in the same verse. This will not do. The New Testament has a great deal to say on the subject of baptism, and is very consistent on this subject. We only need to accept it for what it says and not try to mold it to popular viewpoints.

There is one verse to which those who teach this idea use to prove that εἰς (*eis*) can mean *because of*. It is found in Matt. 12:41 which says, "The men of Nineveh will rise up in the judgment with this generation and condemn it, because they repented **at** the preaching of Jonah; and indeed a greater than Jonah *is* here." The word *at* in this verse is the word *eis*, the same word found in Acts 2:38 translated *for*. Does it mean *because of* in this verse? The basic meaning of *eis*, according to the Greek lexicons is *into* or *unto*. It makes perfect sense to say that Nineveh repented **into** the preaching of Jonah, in the same way that one who hears the gospel of Christ and responds to it enters into that teaching. There is really no precedent for translating this word *because of*. In Matt. 13:21 it is the word διά (*dia—through*) which is translated *because of*. This is also the case in Matt. 13:58. In Matt. 18:7 it is the word ἀπῴ (*apo—from*) There are a few other words translated *because of*, but never *eis*.

F. Benefits Attributed to Baptism in the Scripture

Add to the above passages the following: Acts 22:16—**Sins are washed away** in baptism. Can one be saved without having his sins washed away? Rom. 6:3-4—We are **baptized into Christ and baptized into His death.** Can we be saved without being in Christ or without His death? 1 Cor. 12:13—We are **baptized into the body of Christ.** Can we be saved outside the body of Christ? Gal. 3:27—We are baptized into Christ, and **put on Christ in baptism;** Col. 2:12—Being **raised with Christ** takes place in baptism;

423

1 Pet. 3:21—**Baptism saves us** because it is an appeal of our conscience to God. How does baptism save us? Certainly not by washing dirt off our bodies (1 Pet. 3:21). The water isn't magical, and the act itself is not some magical ritual which results in salvation. If it were, the sacrifice of Christ would have been unnecessary. Do we earn salvation by being baptized? Certainly not. Through obedience in baptism we are making an appeal to God for cleansing.

G. *NAAMAN'S EXAMPLE OF OBEDIENCE, AND ITS RESULTS*

Consider the example of Naaman the leper in 2 Kings 5:1-14. Naaman was told by Elisha, the prophet of God, to dip in the Jordan river seven times and he would be healed of his leprosy. When Naaman dipped in the Jordan seven times he was healed. He was not healed by the water, nor was he healed by the dipping. If the water healed him then the number of times he dipped would not have mattered as long as he stayed under long enough. If the act of dipping healed him, then he would have been one-seventh healed after the first dip, two-sevenths healed after the second dip, etc. The fact is, however, that if he had stopped after the sixth time, he would not have been healed at all, because God had promised to heal him when he obeyed God's command to dip seven times. When he dipped the seventh time he came up healed of his leprosy. He was not healed before this.

Did Naaman heal himself? Did he earn it? Of course not. His healing was totally by the grace of God. But God gave Naaman a condition for receiving the healing—obedience. At first Naaman had been angry because Elisha did not tell him to do some great thing in order to be worthy of the healing. He was well aware that there was no merit in dipping in water, but when he obeyed, God healed him by His grace.

Naaman dipped himself. He, himself, did the work of dipping, but God did the work of healing. Naaman was healed by the grace of God. Baptism in the New Testament is in the passive voice. The one being baptized is dipped by someone else. There are some who have translated Acts 2:38, "baptize yourself." They do so because they say the word in the Greek is either middle or passive. This is true of the present tense of this verb. The context must decide which. They chose the middle which is reflexive—i.e., you do something to yourself. But this will not work, because when the Bible speaks of someone having been baptized in the past tense, as in Rom. 6:3-4, the voice is passive, not active or middle.

H. A PASSIVE RESPONSE

Baptism is passive to the one being baptized. He does not do the work, but yields himself into the hands of the one who baptizes him. The work is done by the one doing the baptizing. Acts 8:38 is an example of this: "And both Philip and the eunuch went down into the water, and he baptized him." Since the one being baptized is not doing the work, how can we say that this is **works** salvation? If it is necessary to obey the command to confess (an active verb), why is it not necessary to obey the command to be baptized (a passive verb)?

I. FAITH IN ACTION

Baptism is very meaningful for several reasons. First, it is part of the faith system by which we are saved. Faith cannot save without obedience, because without obedience it is a dead faith (James 2:14-26). According to James 2:21-23 obedience is a necessary part of faith. James illustrates this by pointing to Abraham's obedience in offering his son Isaac as a sacrifice:

> Was not Abraham our father justified by works when he offered Isaac his son on the altar? Do you see that faith was working together with his works, and by works faith was made perfect? And the Scripture was fulfilled which says, *"Abraham believed God, and it was accounted to him for righteousness."* And he was called the friend of God.

When was the scripture fulfilled that said, "Abraham believed God, and it was accounted to him for righteousness"? According to this passage it was when he obeyed God's command. James calls Abraham's obedience *works.* There is a difference between working to earn merit for salvation and simply obeying God. Both are called works. Works of obedience do not earn salvation, but they are part of faith—of trusting God, as Abraham did when he obeyed God's command. Such works are a matter of yielding to God's will and putting trust in Him. Baptism does no good unless it is done as a matter of trust in Christ. When it is done as an expression of trust, then it is not a work of merit but faith in action.

425

Baptism is an expression of faith not only because it is yielding to the will of the one we trust, but also because of its deep meaning. Martin Luther, in his *Treatise on Baptism* speaks of it as drowning the old man so that a new creature arises from the water. Baptism, according to Paul in Rom. 6:3-5, is a picture of the death, burial, and resurrection of Christ. It pictures dying to sin, being buried in a grave of water, and rising to a new life in Christ, just as Christ died, was buried, and rose again. When a person is baptized he is reenacting the object of his faith—i.e., the death, burial, and resurrection of Christ. He is also expressing his own change and commitment—i.e., his own death to sin, his burial of the old man, and his rising as a new creature in Christ. It is important that the action of burial, the meaning of the word *baptism*, be retained by burying the candidate in the water. Baptism is not only an expression of faith in Christ, it is also an expression of repentance—putting the sinful man to death, as it were. Baptism is also an active and visible means of confessing ones faith in Christ, for in the act he portrays the death, burial, and resurrection of Christ.

One no more promotes justification by works when he teaches the necessity of obeying the command to be baptized than when he teaches the necessity of obeying the command to confess with the mouth that Jesus is Lord. Have people made a legalistic thing out of baptism by teaching that the action itself is what saves? No doubt some have. I have known very few such people. This is "legalism." It is not legalism, however, to insist that God means what He says, and that He requires obedience of all who would be saved. It is not legalism to point out that Jesus is the author of salvation to those who obey him. If it is, then the writer of Hebrews was a legalist. Any attempt to separate faith from obedience is an attempt to change the word of God.

Man's response to God's plan of salvation is called *faith*. Under this heading he must meet these conditions: 1. He must believe the truth about Jesus the Christ, God's Son. 2. He must confess that faith by word of mouth. 3. He must repent of his sins, determining in his heart to live as Christ would have him. 4. He must also yield to Christ's command to be baptized. This whole process belongs under the heading of **faith**. When one has done these things then it can be said that he has believed. Acts 16:30-34 says:

And he brought them out and said, "Sirs, what must I do to be saved?" So they said, "**Believe** on the Lord Jesus Christ, and you will be saved, you and your household." Then they spoke the word of the Lord to him and to all who were in his house. And he took them the same hour of the night and washed *their* stripes. And immediately he and all his family were baptized. Now when he had brought them into his house, he set food before them; and he rejoiced, **having believed in God** with all his household.

At what point does this passage say that the jailer and his household had believed? It was after they had been baptized. James 2:21-23 (quoted above) teaches us the same truth. At what point does it say that Abraham believed God? It was after he had obeyed God's command to offer Isaac as a sacrifice. In other words **it took the obeying to fulfill the believing**. "By works faith was made perfect." The word *perfect* means *full* or *complete*. His faith was incomplete before his obedience, but was completed by his obedience. We do injustice to God's word when we bypass obedience in the plan of salvation. We also do an injustice to the people we seek to bring to Christ when we fail to teach them that their faith is completed in the act of baptism.

III. Both Parts of God's Plan Are Essential

There are churches which no longer teach the details of God's part in the plan of salvation. To some it matters not what you believe or do. According to them, God's grace will save you, not because of what God did, but merely because of His gracious feelings toward mankind. There are churches which have also changed man's part in the plan. Some do not require faith. Some have glossed over repentance. Many have set aside baptism as a part of that plan. How do you measure up? Do you meet the standards of God's measuring rod when it comes to the teaching of your church on the plan of God?

There are times when God overlooked requirements set by His law, such as the law of circumcision (set aside during the 40 years of wandering in the wilderness—Joshua 5:2-6), or the feast of tabernacles (not observed during the Babylonian captivity—Neh. 8:14-18). He did so because of special circumstances. There are many well meaning people who have come to

Christ without knowing the purpose and place of baptism. I believe the Lord deals with them according to what they are capable of knowing, not what they cannot know; but God is able to make up His own mind concerning these people, and will deal with them accordingly, regardless of what I believe. On the other hand, I believe that if a man knows the teaching of the scripture on the subject of baptism but simply will not obey, he is in rebellion against the will of God. I believe the Lord will hold him accountable for his rebellion against His command.

We who are preachers of the gospel need to make sure that we preach the whole truth on this subject, so that men will not be left in ignorance. Will the Lord not require it at our hands if we do not? Do we really believe the Lord doesn't mean what He said on this subject? It is not up to us to decide whom the Lord will accept, and whom He will not. That is His prerogative. It is our job to preach and teach what He has revealed, then leave the judging up to Him. We need to consider seriously lest we be measured by God's measuring rod and found wanting.

APPENDIX F

EXPLANATION OF THE SEVEN-HEADED BEAST

I. THE SEVEN-HEADED BEAST IN REV. 17

In Rev. 17:9-11 John writes:

> Here is the mind which has wisdom: The seven heads are
> seven mountains on which the woman sits. There are also
> seven kings. Five have fallen, one is, *and* the other has not
> yet come. And when he comes, he must continue a short time.
> The beast that was, and is not, is himself also the eighth, and
> is of the seven, and is going to perdition.

The seven heads are seven mountains. These mountains serve a dual
purpose. They help to identify the woman who sits on them—the city of
Rome was situated on seven hills. They also symbolize the fact that the
seven heads are governments or kingdoms. *Mountain* is a frequent Old
Testament symbol for *government* or *kingdom*. As an example, in Isa. 2:1-3a
God reveals through Isaiah this truth concerning the region of Judah and the
city of Jerusalem:

> The word that Isaiah the son of Amoz saw concerning Judah
> and Jerusalem. Now it shall come to pass in the latter days
> *that* the mountain of the LORD's house shall be established on
> the top of the mountains, and shall be exalted above the hills;
> and all nations shall flow to it. Many people shall come and
> say, "Come, and let us go up to the mountain of the LORD, to
> the house of the God of Jacob."

The Lord's spiritual kingdom was to be established in Jerusalem, and it
was to be the highest of the mountains (governments). It would be on the top

of them.[1] Isaiah is not speaking of literal mountains because Mount Zion upon which Jerusalem is built is hardly the highest of the mountains. This is a prophecy concerning the kingdom and government of God which was to be established as the chief of all governments. It was certainly to be higher than these seven heads which are called seven mountains.

The seven heads are also said to be kings. *King* is metonymy for *kingdom*. *Metonymy* is a figure of speech that puts a part for the whole, or the container for the contents. "Drink the cup," we say. We do not mean drink the container, but what is in it. We speak of ordering a plate when we mean the food on the plate and of a sumptuous table when we mean the food on the table. That is metonymy. When we count cattle we say there are so many head. by this we mean the whole cow. As noted in *Appendix G*, Daniel used *King* to mean *kingdom* in Daniel chapters 2, 7, and 8.

Five heads (kingdoms) are fallen, one is (in John's time), and one is yet to come. The sixth head or kingdom is the Beast of John's day, the Roman Empire. In Daniel's visions the beast with the ten horns was the symbol of the Roman Empire. The beast in chapter 13 is the ten-horn phase of the sixth head, which was still in the future from John's day.

Some say these seven heads are seven emperors of the Roman Empire. Others say they are seven successive forms of government of the Roman Empire. Daniel's prophecy shows that they are to be understood as separate empires. Since the angel in 17:10 points to five that are fallen, one existing, and one coming, then we understand that seven specific kingdoms are chosen as representative of all the persecuting governments of the world, in the same way that the seven churches of Asia are chosen to represent the whole church, and each congregation can find itself among those seven churches. So also every human government that opposes God's people can be found among these seven heads.

There seems to be no reference to the seventh head in the progress of the drama, except here in Revelation chapter 17. However, we can use some clues given in the book to determine just where it fits in. In 13:5 we are told

---

[1]The word used for *on the top of* is ראשׁ (*ro'sh*) which is defined by *Brown, Driver and Briggs Hebrew Lexicon* as *head, top, chief,* etc. The NIV translates this as "chief among the mountains," while the NRSV translates it as "the highest of the mountains."

that the existing head, the ten horn phase of the sixth head, the revived Roman empire, was to continue for 42 months. That implies that after the 42 months the seventh head would come into power.

In 11:3,7, in the preview of the drama, we are told that the two witnesses were to prophesy in sackcloth for 1260 days (42 months—the period of the ten horns), and when they had finished their testimony they were to be killed by the beast which is to come up out of the abyss. Notice that this is after the 42 months, after the time of the ten horn phase of the sixth head. That means that it must be the seventh head that kills the witnesses who very shortly come back to life. This is an important clue, taken together with the information of chapter 17:10. There we are told that the seventh head would only last a short time. The angel showed John a vision of the beast with a woman clothed in purple and scarlet riding on his heads. He explains to John in 17:8 that the beast was, and is not, and will come up out of the abyss and go into perdition. 17:11 says that this beast is an eighth, and is of the seven.

The fact that the 11th chapter identifies the killer of the witnesses as the beast which is coming up out of the abyss is also an important clue. 7:11 tells us that the beast which was and is not (i.e., is in the abyss) is an eighth and is of the seven. This is an important clue. Each of the previous heads is an empire which arose outside of the ones before. The eighth does not. He is of the seven. He is only counted as an eighth because he has ceased as a persecuting empire, and then comes up out of the abyss to renew his efforts of persecution. The beast that goes into the abyss is therefore the one which comes out of the abyss. The seventh goes into the abyss and then comes out as an eighth.

17:8 tells us that the Beast will come out of the abyss and go into perdition. According to verses 12-17, the Beast has some things to do before he goes into perdition. He is to make war with, and be overcome by, Christ the Lamb. Immediately, then, he goes into perdition (see 19:11-21). But he is also to be used by God to destroy Babylon the Harlot and burn her with fire. This must, of necessity, be before he goes into perdition. Chapter 18 is an account of this destruction. The time element for this destruction is not a matter of months or years, but one day according to 18:8, or one hour according to 18:10, 17, 19. Although this event is given last in chapter 17, it must be before the war on the Lamb, because he has no time after that to

Appendices

destroy the Harlot. He is immediately cast into the lake of fire (perdition). Chapter 18 details the destruction of the Harlot which was to be accomplished by the beast. Chapter 19:11-21 tells of the beast's being cast into the lake of fire (perdition).

17:8 tells us that when the beast comes up out of the abyss the unsaved of earth will marvel because the beast was and is not, and yet is. This is a wonder to the world, as if the beast that went into the abyss has been resurrected from the dead. The time frame for this resurrection is seen in 20:7-10. After Satan and the Beast come out of the abyss, the nations are gathered together to attack the camp of the saints and New Jerusalem, but the people of those nations are defeated, killed, and will be raised as individuals to be judged at the great white throne judgment. The Dragon, Beast and False Prophet are cast into the lake of fire.

We also get a clue in 20:7-10 as to which kingdom is represented by the eighth head. This kingdom would also be the seventh since the eighth is a revival of the seventh. This is treated at some length in Act Six on Rev. 20.

The following chart may help to visualize the beast with seven heads:

Five Heads Are Fallen

1) Egypt   (1st rib in the bear's mouth in Daniel 7)

2) Assyria   (2nd rib in the bear's mouth in Daniel 7)

3) Babylonia   (3rd rib in the bear's mouth, The lion of Daniel 7)

4) Medo-Persia   (The bear devouring the 3 ribs in Daniel 7)

5) Greece   (The leopard in Daniel 7)

One Head Existed in John's Day

6) Rome (the 10-horned beast in Daniel 7) which fell and was revived in the ten-horn stage

One is to Come

7) This is called Magog in its revived eighth head state.

The Beast Himself is an Eighth, One of the Seven

8) This is a revival of the seventh head, Magog, with Gog as its king.

If the above chart is accurate (I believe that it is) then the sixth head is the Roman Empire, and the seventh and eight heads are the land of Magog, headed by its king, Gog.

II. THE TEN HORNS OF THE SIXTH HEAD

How does Rev. 17 interpret the ten horns? "The ten horns which you saw are ten kings who have received no kingdom as yet, but they receive authority for one hour as kings with the beast" (Rev.17:12). These are ten kings (kingdoms) which had not arisen in John's day, but which arise out of the beast later (See Dan. 7:24). Some say these are the ten kings following the emperor Domitian who died in 96 A.D. Yet it is more likely, from the precedent set in Dan. 8:22, that the horns refer to kingdoms. Remember that *King* is metonymy for *kingdom*. These are the kingdoms that were to arise from the Roman Empire in the future from John's day. Some present day interpreters say that the ten horns are ten present day European kingdoms which will unite in the European Economic Alliance. Although such an alliance has formed, and is growing, I see these kingdoms as later stages of the empires which sprang from Rome. They can, however, still do damage in persecuting Christians.

The number ten is used in symbolism for an indefinite number (some), a few, a short time, etc. There is no need to identify exactly ten kingdoms which arose out of the Roman Empire. Yet there are certain criteria that probably should be followed in identifying them: 1) They are persecuting kingdoms—i.e., they partake of the nature of their parent (13:4-7); 2) They arise from the territory of the old Roman Empire, involving all the Near East, south eastern Europe, northern Africa, most of western Europe, and the British Isles. This does not mean that their conquests would be limited to that territory, however. They might even expand their borders to the New World but they are still kingdoms which arose out of Rome. Some look upon these horns as the territories of fallen Rome which developed into kingdoms, such as France, Germany, Switzerland, Austria, England, Spain, Italy, Greece, Egypt, Palestine, etc.

I lean toward the idea that they represent the empires which developed among these nations. Many such empires can be named: the Western Roman Empire, the Eastern or Byzantine Empire, the Mohammedan (Saracen)

Empire, The Carolingian (Frankish) Empire under Charlemagne, the Holy Roman Empire under the Germans, the Hapsburg Empire, the Turkish (Ottoman) Empire, the British Empire, the Spanish Empire, the French Empire (under Napoleon), the Italian Empire, the Third Reich (Germany under Hitler). These may not be all, but those named total twelve. Which are the ten horns? They would include the ones that were unified under the influence of the False Prophet, and that have been involved in persecuting those who worship God according to their understanding of scripture.

They do not need to number exactly ten in order to fit the symbolism. Is the British Empire to be included? Some of the American colonies arose because people left England to escape just such persecution. What about America? She is, after all, an extension of Britain to the New World. If America ever gets to the place of being a principle persecutor of God's people, to that extent it will be part of the Beast. As I write this, efforts have been made to put down the church, Christianity, and belief in the God of the Bible. Some have been imprisoned and otherwise persecuted because of their faith. There are strong forces at work to counter the move in that direction. The United States has become polarized along these lines, and Satan's forces are doing all they can to discredit the people of God, and to vilify those powerful enough to make a difference. The battle ground is found in all public institutions, particularly in government institutions, educational institutions, the media, the entertainment industry, and in every area which can wield a strong influence on the thinking of people. Christians, there have been more people martyred for the cause of Christ in the last century than in all the centuries since the cross put together. The battle is raging in this world right now as never before. We have been asleep, and many of us don't care. As long as our little acre seems secure we want to ignore the rest; but we can bury our heads in the sand only so long. We shall surely come to know the meaning of Paul's statement in 2 Timothy 3:12, "Yes, and all who desire to live godly in Christ Jesus will suffer persecution."

III. THE TEN HORNS UNDER THE EIGHTH HEAD

We have seen that the ten horns on the sixth head were in power in chapter 13. The horns constituted the Beast at that time. But in chapter 17 there are indications that the ten horns have a different relationship to the

Beast which comes up out of the abyss. The horns there are not seen as arising out of the Beast, but kingdoms which give their power and authority to the Beast, and receive authority with the Beast for a brief time (17:12-13). God orchestrates this alliance, for He is the one who puts it into their hearts to give their kingdoms to the Beast (17:17).

These have two functions—to bring destruction to Babylon the Harlot, and to make war with the Lamb (17:14, 16). In destroying the Harlot they, with the Beast, are carrying out God's will, although inadvertently. In making war with the Lamb they are doing the will of Satan, but with the Beast they will be overcome by the Lamb and destroyed. Their relationship with the Beast is that of an alliance rather than one of arising from the Beast. This relationship is said to last for one hour, which is the time it takes to destroy the Harlot (18:10, 17, 19).

These horns are probably the kingdoms mentioned in 19:19-20, and in 20:7-9). In Ezek. 38 - 39 certain nations are named as the allies of Gog and Magog. These are probably to be understood as some of the ten horns who give their power and authority to the Beast. Among these are Persia, Libya, Ethiopia, Gomer, and Togarmah. These are situated in the regions formerly held by the Roman Empire, and thus might be characterized as among the ten horns arising from Rome. In the 17th chapter they give their power and authority to the eighth head which is the resurrected seventh head.

Magog is the territory of the seventh/eighth head, and is composed of Rosh (Russ), Meshech (Moschoi), and Tubal, around the northern part of the Caspian Sea. This is part of the former Soviet Union. This is a clue to the possible identity of the seventh head, which is revived as the eighth.

APPENDIX G

HOW DANIEL'S VISIONS RELATE TO REVELATION

I. DANIEL'S VISION OF FOUR Beasts (Dan. 7:3-7)

And four great beasts came up from the sea, each different from the other. The first *was* like a lion ...another beast, a second, like a bear ...another, like a leopard ...a fourth beast ...had ten horns.

These four beasts, like the seven-headed beast of Revelation, came up out of the sea. Daniel describes them as a lion, a bear, a leopard, and a ten-horned beast. Daniel begins where he is, with the lion (Babylonian Empire) and goes forward through the bear (Medo-Persian Empire), the leopard (Grecian Empire), and the ten-horned beast (the Roman Empire).

John, on the other hand, sees them in reverse order since he is prophesying during the fourth beast, the ten-horned beast of Rome. So he looks backward from there and sees the leopard, the bear, and the lion as part of the description of the seven-headed beast.

The angel in Daniel explains that the four beasts are four kings (verse 17). Then he says that the fourth beast is a fourth **kingdom** (Verse 23). The fourth beast, one of four kings, is a fourth kingdom. Which is it—king or kingdom? A king and his kingdom are so closely related that often one is put for the other. This is a figure of speech called *metonymy*. *King* equals *kingdom*. Read Daniel 2:37-40; 7:17,23; 8:20-22 for examples of this use of *king* for *kingdom*. This is important because it will help us understand the explanation of the ten-horned beast in chapter 17.

II. NEBUCHADNEZZAR'S VISION OF THE GREAT IMAGE
(Dan. 2:31-45)

Nebuchadnezzar was king of Babylon in Daniel's early years in captivity. Nebuchadnezzar's vision of the great image in Dan. 2:31-45 corresponds to that of the four beasts of Dan. 7. The two visions represent the same thing. Verses 31-33 are as follows:

> You, O king, were watching; and behold, a great image! This great image, whose splendor was excellent, stood before you; and its form *was* awesome. This image's head *was* of fine gold, its chest and arms of silver, its belly and thighs of bronze, its legs of iron, its feet partly of iron and partly of clay.

Here the four kingdoms are represented as different parts of a great image. In verses 38b-40a Daniel says to King Nebuchadnezzar:

> ...you *are* this **head of gold**. But after you shall arise **another kingdom** inferior to yours; then another, **a third kingdom of bronze**, which shall rule over all the earth. And **the fourth kingdom** shall be as strong as iron....

The head (the lion of Daniel 7) is identified as Nebuchadnezzar (Babylonia) and the other three parts of the image as three succeeding kingdoms. It is easy enough to identify these kingdoms from history (Dan. 2:37-40). The second (chest and two arms) is the Medo-Persian Empire represented by the bear in chapter 7 and the ram in chapter 8. The third (belly and thighs) is the Grecian Empire, the empire of Alexander the Great, represented by the leopard in chapter 7 and the he-goat in chapter 8. The fourth kingdom (legs and feet with ten toes) is the Roman Empire, the same as the ten-horned beast in chapter 7.

III. THE BEASTS OF DANIEL 7 AND THE BEAST OF REVELATION

As said before, the beast in Revelation is the symbol of persecution, embodied in persecuting governments of the world. Just as seven churches in chapters 1 - 3 were chosen to represent all the churches, so there are seven persecuting governments which are chosen to represent all the persecuting governments.

An important difference between the beast in Revelation and the four beasts of Daniel is this: Daniel's prophecy presents four beasts, each representing one specific kingdom which was involved in persecuting the people of God. On the other hand Revelation presents one beast with seven heads as the symbol of all persecuting powers (*seven* is the symbol for *complete* or *all*). Each head represents one specific world power engaged in persecuting God's people, while the seven heads, taken together, represent all persecuting powers. Any governmental power which lets itself become involved in oppressing the people of God becomes an agent of Satan, and thus a manifestation of the beast. The beast, as a symbol of persecution embodied in political powers, goes beyond just the seven specific kingdoms.

IV. THE DIFFERENT TIME FRAMES COVERED BY THE BEAST

The first five heads in Revelation were five political world powers which functioned in their respective times prior to the Roman Empire. There is also more than one time frame envisioned in Revelation. For instance, 1) the time during the 1260 days—i.e., the period when the crowns are on the 10 horns (Rev. 13); 2) a short time following the 1260 days—i.e., the short period of the seventh head; and 3) the time after the beast and the dragon come up out of the abyss, during the final battle which ends with the final judgment. This beast is then called an eighth kingdom. Rev. 13 is concerned with the 1260 days of the ten-horned beast, but in Rev. 17 John sees the beast who is to come up out of the abyss as an eighth.

V. HOW DOES DANIEL INTERPRET HORNS?

A horn is a symbol of power. A horn can be the power of a person, or an organization, or a government, etc. Daniel can help us understand the meaning of horns. In Dan. 7:24 the ten horns on the fourth beast are said to be ten kings. We have already seen that Daniel uses *kings* and *kingdoms* interchangeably. He uses the king to stand for his kingdom by a figure of speech called *metonymy*. This view is strengthened when we see how Daniel interprets horns in chapter 8.

Daniel is given a vision of two beasts In Dan. 8—a ram and a male goat. In Dan. 8:20-22 an angel explains the vision. The two beasts correspond to the bear and leopard of chapter 7. These are identified as the Medo-Persian and the Grecian Empires (8:20-21). The ram's two horns represent the kingdoms of Media and Persia. Just as the bear of chap. 7 has one side higher than the other, so the ram of chapter 8 has one horn higher than the other. This was to indicate that in the combined Medo-Persian empire Persia was higher than Media—i.e., Persia was the controlling power. Consequently, in history the empire was often called simply the Persian Empire.

The goat's four horns of chapter 8 are interpreted as kingdoms arising out of the Grecian Empire. This gives us a precedent for understanding the meaning of the horns in Revelation. The ten horns on the fourth beast in Daniel 7 and the ten horns on the seven-headed beast are both representations of the same thing—the powers that arose out of the breaking up of the Roman Empire. More specifically, they are persecuting powers that arose from within the Roman Empire. Dan. 7:24 says, "The ten horns *are* ten kings *Who* shall arise from this kingdom [the fourth beast]." The fourth beast of Daniel is the sixth head of the beast of Revelation. Since in Daniel 7 the ten horns are all on the fourth beast, then we can reasonably assume that the ten horns of Rev. 13 are all on the sixth head which corresponds to the fourth beast..

In Daniel's discussion of the four beasts, when the bear comes along he has three ribs in his mouth. Dan. 7:5, "And suddenly another beast, a second, like a bear. It was raised up on one side, and had three ribs in its mouth between its teeth. And they said to it, 'Arise, devour much flesh.'"

VI. THE THREE RIBS IN THE BEAR'S MOUTH

What is the significance of the three ribs? The four beasts began with the Babylonian Empire in Daniel's own time, and looked forward to coming empires. Although preceding empires are not presented as beasts in Daniel's vision, it does give us a hint of former kingdoms. Since the bear, representing Medo-Persia, is only the second beast, why are there three ribs in his mouth? Could it be that there were two other persecuting powers before Babylonia? That is, in fact, the case. There were two world powers prior to Babylonia. The first was the Egyptian Empire which persecuted God's people, the Children of Israel, by enslaving them for hundreds of years; and the second was the Assyrian Empire which conquered the northern Kingdom of Israel and all the cities of the southern Kingdom of Judah except for Jerusalem. Assyria deported the people of the northern kingdom to other nations, and settled people from other nations in the territory of Israel.

Both of these empires were engaged in persecuting the people of God, and so they would have a place as part of the beast of Revelation. The three ribs, given in reverse order then, would indicate Babylonia, Assyria and Egypt. The fact that they are in the bear's mouth indicates that he has devoured them. The five empires which persecuted the people of God and had fallen before John's day include Egypt, Assyria, Babylonia, Medo-Persia, and Greece. The one existing in John's day is the fourth beast with ten horns, which is Rome. The beast of Revelation chapter 13 is Rome revived with the ten horn kingdoms in power.

APPENDIX H

THE MILLENNIUM

There are certain facts concerning the millennium that are revealed in Rev. 20 that should help us in understanding just what the millennium is.

I. THE BEGINNING

The millennium has its beginning with the resurrection of the cause of Christ, symbolized as the souls of martyred witnesses. I understand this resurrection to be symbolic rather than literal for the following reasons: The martyrs are first introduced in chap. 6 at the opening of the fifth seal. They are part of a vision of the altar. The horses and horsemen of the first four visions are symbols of certain principles pertaining to the fortunes of the church—i.e., victory, bloodshed, starvation and death. It would be strange if the fifth vision were suddenly to be understood literally, especially since that would mean that John literally saw invisible souls, and they were literally beneath a literal altar in heaven.

A. A SYMBOLIC PICTURE

The picture, taken as a whole, is a symbolic picture of the saints as they are persecuted in this world and slain because of their proclamation of the word of God. The souls under the altar are not literally the souls of specific individuals, such as Peter, Paul, and Polycarp, men who were martyred for their faith, but the souls are a symbolic representation of the saints as a body, i.e., the church, and the persecution that they undergo in this world.

Surely no one assumes that the altar is literal, especially since it no longer existed at the time, having been destroyed in the destruction of Jerusalem by the Romans in A.D. 70. If the altar is figurative, then the souls under the altar

441

must be figurative also. They are as blood spilled under the altar in the offering of sacrifices. The picture is of the sacrificial suffering of the saints, the body of Christ under persecution, seemingly defeated and dead.

In Rev. twenty John sees the resurrection of these souls in victory to live and reign with Christ 1000 years. Notice that he sees souls, not bodies. It is symbolic souls, not literal bodies, that are raised. The meaning here, as in chapter six, is also symbolic. As the souls in chapter six symbolically represent the persecuted cause of Christ, the suffering community of the saints, so the resurrected souls represent the victorious cause of Christ, the conquest of Satan's world for the saints, over which they reign with Christ upon thrones.

B. THE LITERAL RESURRECTION

Jesus speaks of the literal resurrection of the saints as concurrent with the resurrection of the wicked. John 5:28-29 makes this clear:

> **The hour** is coming in which **all who are in the graves** will hear His voice and come forth—**those who have done good** to the resurrection of life, and **those who have done evil** to the resurrection of condemnation.

In this verse John says that the righteous and the wicked are to be raised in the same hour. If Rev. 20 were speaking of this same resurrection, then the two passages would be contradictory, because in Rev. 20 there would be 1000 years between the resurrection of the saints and that of the sinners.

Since the literal resurrection is to include both saints and sinners, then Rev. 20 must be speaking figuratively not literally. John is drawing a symbolic picture of something that is going to happen—i.e., the cause of Christ is to be resurrected in this world and reign victorious for an extended period of time, after which the forces of sin will again reassert themselves (the second resurrection), but to no avail. After this the literal resurrection will take place in which all men, good and evil, will come forth to be judged and receive the rewards or punishments for their works.

The resurrection of Rev. 20:4-5 is the beginning of the millennial reign, whereas the resurrection at the coming of Christ is after the end of the reign on earth. Then the kingdom will be turned back to God (1 Cor. 15:20ff).

II. THE TRIUMPH OF THE SAINTS IN THIS WORLD

The resurrection of Rev. 20 marks the triumph of the saints over the kingdom of the world, thus making the kingdom (dominion) of the world the kingdom (dominion) of our Lord and of His Christ (Rev. 11:15). According to Rev. 20 that triumph is to occur in some dramatic way—i.e., suddenly, rapidly—reversing the prevailing order of things. The Dragon, along with the Beast and the False Prophet, are taken and consigned to the abyss. The saints are suddenly in charge.

A. VICTORY OVER THE BEAST AND FALSE PROPHET

I conclude that the Beast and False Prophet are included in this exile to the abyss for two reasons:

1) Although Rev. 20:1-7 does not mention them by name, it does mention their functions which cease with the consignment of the Dragon to the abyss. Persecution of the saints is the work of the Beast (13:7), and deception is the function of the False Prophet (13:14); The Devil (Dragon) does his work of deceiving and persecuting through these two—the Beast and the False Prophet.

2) Rev. 11:7 and 17:8 both speak of the Beast as one who is to come up out of the abyss. In order to come out of the abyss he must first go into it. It makes sense that he goes into the abyss with Satan, since that is the point at which his work of persecution ceases for 1000 years. We will notice his coming out of it later.

B. JUDGMENT ON BEHALF OF THE SAINTS

Dan. 7:22, 27 represents the nations as being controlled and governed by the saints during this time. World dominion (the kingdom of the world) has suddenly become the dominion of the saints. In the process judgment is given on behalf of the saints against the kingdoms which formerly held dominion and used their power to persecute the saints. Rev. 20:4 says, literally, that judgment is given to (or for) them.

Many modern translations erroneously leave the impression that judgment was given into their hands—i.e., that the responsibility and power to judge was given them. The phrase in the original could mean that, but its most logical meaning is that here is the answer to the cry for judgment and vengeance of the martyred souls of 6:10. This also harmonizes with the vision of Daniel 7, especially in verses 22-27 in which judgment is given on behalf of the saints. That judgment, given on behalf of the saints, is the cause of Satan's confinement in the abyss along with his deceit and persecution (the False Prophet and the Beast).

C. THE SEVENTH HEAD CONFINED TO THE ABYSS

The Beast with the seven heads, which represents world dominion by persecuting powers, is consigned to the pit. This occurs after the brief reign of the seventh head, according to Rev. 17:10-11. The Beast of Rev. 17 is the power which is to come up out of the abyss and go into perdition according to verse 8. The time frame of the vision of chapter 17 is after the confinement of the Beast to the abyss. "The beast that you saw was and is not,"--i.e., he is, at that point, in the abyss. But the vision also looks forward to the future when the Beast "is to come." In John's vision the time is almost here. He is about to come up out of the abyss and go into perdition. This Beast—i.e., the one which comes up out of the abyss, is an eighth kingdom (verse 11), but is "of the seven"—i.e., one of the kingdoms represented by the seven heads. In Rev. 20:7-8, the persecuting power that arises when the dragon comes up out of the abyss is called "Gog and Magog" (see *Appendix I: Gog and Magog*).

The parallel between Daniel's vision in chapter 7 with that of John in Rev. 12 - 20 is too striking to be accidental. John is seeing in greater detail what Daniel saw. Even the time of the persecution and subjugation of the saints is the same—i.e., a time, two times, and a half time, or three and a half years (Dan. 7:25, Rev. 12:14). This period is also represented in Rev. 11:2,3; 12:6; 13:5 as 42 months (three and a half times 12 months) and 1260 days (42 times 30 days). In Daniel and Revelation the period of persecution culminates with the overcoming of the saints prior to their victory. A striking reversal is seen when the dominion is taken from the Beast and given to the saints (Dan. 7:21-22, 26-27; Rev. 11:7, 11-15; 13:7; 20:4). Since Daniel and Revelation are speaking of the same thing, one helps us to understand the other.

D. *GOG AND MAGOG, THE EIGHTH POWER, USED TO IDENTIFY THE SEVENTH*

Gog and Magog, the power which is reestablished when the Dragon comes up out of the abyss after the reign of righteousness (Rev. 20:7-9), is a revival of the seventh persecuting power (Rev. 17:8, 11). This agrees with the fact that in Rev. 11:7 it is the Beast which comes up out of the abyss which kills the witnesses prior to their resurrection and reign. Notice that it does not say "when he comes up out of the abyss" or "after he comes up out of the abyss." It only says "the beast which comes up out of the abyss." In other words, the beast which kills the saints in Rev. 11:7 is the same beast which comes up out of the abyss in Rev. 17:8, 11. It must be the seventh head phase which is referred to in chap. 11—the short-lived head of chapter 17—which is to make a last ditch effort as the eighth following the millennium of chapter 20. For identification of Magog go to *Appendix I.*

It is interesting to note that after only seventy years (a short while compared to the other persecuting empires) most of the communist empire crumbled. It is also interesting to note that this empire and the ideologies associated with it have had more to do with causing Christianity and the Bible to be considered dead issues than any other world power. It is those who have allied themselves with her philosophies and taught them in our universities and schools, and in our communications media, who have brought things to a state in which, from the world's viewpoint, the witnesses are dead. The sixth head of Rome and its offshoots (the 10 horns) have chalked up a remarkable record of waging war upon the saints (Dan. 7:21; Rev. 13:7), but the power and influence of Christianity remained alive and active through it all.

It takes the seventh head, which I believe to be world communism, (socialism is its social and economic ideology), together with the work of its ally, the False Prophet who fostered secular humanism, to bring the world to a state where it considers Christ's body and God's word dead—no longer relevant to living in this world. Let's face it! That is how the world as a whole views the church and the Bible. But it is also interesting to note that there are thousands, perhaps millions, out of every people, nation, tribe and language, who will not give up on the dead corpses. They will not let them be buried.

Now the time is ripe for the first resurrection in which the corpses of these two witnesses will stand upon their feet and, very much alive, be exalted to the heavens in the sight of all people as their cry for judgment is answered, and they receive the dominion of this world (Rev. 11:7-15), while deceit and persecution will be curtailed as though thrown into the abyss. Once again the church, together with the word (the two witnesses), will bear testimony to the world, only now the world's ears will be attuned to hear. Perhaps the unbelieving body of the Jews will come to accept their Messiah since the false prophet will no longer be blinding their eyes.

III. THE END OF THE MILLENNIUM

I don't think we have seen the last of the communist empire—or at least of the power that was expressed as communism. The eighth power, the revival of the seventh head, is to come up out of the abyss to resume its war on the saints with a vengeance (Rev. 20:7-9). This time, however, he won't get very far, for that battle will be over almost before it begins. According to Rev. 11:17-18 events are to take place in this order: First the reign of the saints, then the raging of the nations, and finally the rewarding of the saints and destroying the destroyers. For details of the final battle see Rev. 16:12-16; 19:11-21; 20:7-10.

A. THE SECOND RESURRECTION

The millennial reign will end at the resurrection of Satan's forces followed by the coming of Jesus Christ. The resurrection of the Dragon, the Beast, and the False Prophet will be the second resurrection spoken of in Rev. 20:4-6. "But the rest of the dead did not live again until the thousand years were finished." At the first resurrection there will be a reversal of roles—i.e., the Beast and the False Prophet will no longer persecute and deceive. Satan will, in effect, be exiled from this world in the abyss, understood to be the lowest region of Hades, while the saints will be sitting on thrones, reigning.

But, just as the saints' cause was resurrected, so also at the end of the thousand years the cause of the Beast and False Prophet will be resurrected, coming forth from the hadean world to renew their assault on the saints. Just as the subjugated saints—i.e., the martyred souls under the altar (6:9-11)—

are to be raised to thrones (20:4-6), so also the subjugated forces of evil are to be raised and come to the forefront once more (20:7-9). This, like the first resurrection, is a figurative one. The works of Satan will be very much dead for an extended period of time, but they will come back to life as he, with the Beast and False Prophet, emerge from the abyss.

B. THE FINAL FORM OF THE BEAST

The revival of the persecuting forces of Gog and Magog (20:8) is a return of the Beast in its final form. This is a resurrection of one of the seven heads (17:8, 11). Magog, the eighth power who is of the seven, must be **the seventh head** since the first six have been identified as Egypt, Assyria, Babylonia, Persia, Greece and Rome (i.e., all the persecuting powers that have held world dominion), none of which can be identified with Magog.

C. THE DESTRUCTION OF THE DRAGON, BEAST, AND FALSE PROPHET

The Dragon's success in restoring the beasts of persecution and deceit is short lived. The eighth form of the Beast is even shorter in duration than the seventh, for he barely comes up out of the abyss when he is finally and forever defeated and cast into the lake of fire at the second coming of Christ (Rev. 19:11-21, esp. verses. 19-20; 20:9-10). They undergo a second death, or destruction (20:14). Those who were part of the first resurrection (the people of God) will not be hurt by the second death. They are raised to eternal life (John 5;28-29).

At that time the resurrected forces of Satan do not succeed in overthrowing the saints. In fact, they get no farther than surrounding the camp of the saints. Fire comes down and consumes the nations who are the forces of Satan. The millennial reign is then absorbed into the larger reign of eternity. Although the reign on earth comes to a conclusion at Christ's coming (I Cor. 15:21-28), the kingdom goes up to God where the throne is occupied by God and the Lamb forever and ever (Rev. 22:3-5; Dan. 7:14,18,27).

APPENDIX I

GOG AND MAGOG

I. THE IDENTITY OF THE BEAST WHO IS AN EIGHTH
(Read Rev. 20:7-10)

The leader of the nations who gather for the final battle is called *Gog and Magog*. Gog is the king and Magog is the territory. Here, then, is the eighth head who is of the seven. The Beast of persecution is here embodied in the land called *Magog* and the king called *Gog*. The nations who give their authority to Gog and Magog, are the ten horns spoken of in chapter 17.

Ezek. 38 - 39 is a prophecy concerning the final battle. In 38:1-3 Gog is the Prince of Rosh, Meshech, and Tubal in the land of Magog. Among the nations allied with Gog and Magog are Persia, Ethiopia (Cush), Libya (Put), Gomer, and Togarmah. Most of these are ancient names of nations and lands, used here to identify the territories that will be allied with Magog against Christ and His church in the final battle. They are some of the nations which make up the ten horns which give their authority to the Beast. Ezekiel pictures them as being drawn by God into battle as though He puts hooks in their jaws and leads them and their armies, fully arrayed, into the battle. The following excerpts from chapter 38 correspond with the final battle of Revelation 19:11-21 and 20:7-10: The verse numbers are indicated.

> [8]After many days you will be visited. In the latter years you will come into the land of those brought back from the sword *and* gathered from many people on the mountains of Israel, which had long been desolate; they were brought out of the nations, and now all of them dwell safely.

According to Rev. 20 this will be at the very end. The war is against those who have been brought out of every tribe and tongue and people and

448

nation to become servants of God. They will have been dwelling in safety for a period called *1000 years* when the forces of Gog and Magog come against them.

> [9]You will ascend, coming like a storm, covering the land like a cloud, you and all your troops and many peoples with you.

The Beast ascends from the abyss (Gog and Magog), then the nations and kings will be deceived into allying themselves with him, and with them he will surround the camp of the saints.

> [12]...to stretch out your hand against the waste places *that are again* inhabited, and against a people gathered from the nations....

He is to make war with the people of God who have been called out of every nation, tribe, tongue and people, but he will not prevail. The Lamb will overcome him.

> [13]Sheba, Dedan, the merchants of Tarshish, and all their young lions will say to you, "Have you come to take plunder? Have you gathered your army to take booty, to carry away silver and gold, to take away livestock and goods, to take great plunder?"

The kings and merchants and all who are made rich by Babylon the Harlot will stand afar off and wail at the destruction of the Harlot, which will be accomplished by Gog and Magog, the beast of the eighth head, just prior to his battle with the Lamb.

> [15]Then you will come from your place out of the far north, you and many peoples with you, all of them riding on horses, a great company and a mighty army.

The locale of Magog is in the far north, encompassing Rosh, Meshech, and Tubal.

> [16]You will come up against My people Israel like a cloud, to cover the land. It will be in the latter days that I will bring you against My land, so that the nations may know Me, when I am hallowed in you, O Gog, before their eyes.

The camp of the saints will be surrounded just prior to the end of the world.

> [18]"And it will come to pass at the same time, when Gog comes against the land of Israel," says the Lord GOD, "*that My fury will show in My face.*"

God will bring a quick end to the armies of the nations.

> [19]For in My jealousy *and* in the fire of My wrath I have spoken: "Surely in that day there shall be a great earthquake in the land of Israel...."

See Rev. 16:18 for the great earthquake which occurs at the end.

> [22]And I will bring him to judgment with pestilence and bloodshed; I will rain down on him, on his troops, and on the many peoples who are with him, flooding rain, great hailstones, fire, and brimstone.

Pestilence and bloodshed are seen in the seven bowls of wrath, great hailstones in the judgment on the Harlot, and fire and brimstone in Rev. 20:9-10. The passage speaks of God's people as Israel. Remember that God's Israel includes all those who are children of Abraham through faith. They are the children of God. If you haven't already done so, I suggest that you read *Appendix D* on *The Israel of God*.

Ezekiel 39 continues with the battle which brings destruction to Gog and Magog. In verses 1-6 we read:

> [1]And you, son of man, prophesy against Gog, and say, "Thus says the Lord GOD: 'Behold, I *am* against you, O Gog, the prince of Rosh, Meshech, and Tubal; [2]and I will turn you around and lead you on, bringing you up from the far north, and bring you against the mountains of Israel. [3]Then I will knock the bow out of your left hand, and cause the arrows to fall out of your right hand. [4]You shall fall upon the mountains of Israel, you and all your troops and the peoples who *are* with you; **I will give you to birds of prey** of every sort and to the beasts of the field to be devoured. [5]You shall fall on the open field; for I have spoken,' says the Lord GOD.

⁶'And **I will send fire on Magog** and on those who live in security in the coastlands. Then they shall know that I *am* the LORD.'"

In this quotation we see a correspondence with the description given of the battle in Rev. 19. The dead bodies are said to be food for the birds of prey. In Rev. 20 fire is sent by God to destroy the armies of Magog.

The location from which Gog and Magog comes is from the far north. The prophecy is written to Israelites who were at that time in Babylonian captivity. If you go directly north either from Israel or Babylonia you will end up around the Caspian Sea and regions north of there. This is the territory which was the heart of the former USSR. Many scholars agree that Magog is to be associated with the lands north of the Black and/or Caspian Seas.

What is the identification of this Beast who is the eighth head? Magog¹ seems to incorporate three nations, namely: Rosh², Meshech³ and Tubal. All

---

¹In the footnote on Ezek. 38:2 the NRSV *Harper Study Bible* states: "Magog is headed up by Gog. That nation, along with Meshech and Tubal, are descendants of the sons of Japheth (Gen. 10:2). They have been identified with the Russians, Scythians, Goths, and Cretans, but such identifications are not certain."

²*The International Standard Bible Encyclopedia* (Eerdmans, Grand Rapids, 1957) Vol. IV, pp. 2623-4 states, concerning the name *Rosh*: "This name occurs in the prophecies against Gog in Ezk 38:2,3 and 39:1, where AV [i.e., KJV] has "Gog, the land of Magog, the **chief** prince of Meshech and Tubal.' This tr is due to *ro'sh* being the common Heb word for "head" or "chief' {cf the Gr variant and the Vulg), and is regarded as incorrect, that of the RV, 'Gog, of the land of Magog, the prince of Rosh, Meshech and Tubal,' being preferred. The identity of Rosh is not without its difficulties. Gesenius [Heb. scholar] regarded it as indicating the Russians, who are mentioned in Byzantine writers of the 10ᵗʰ cent. under the name of ῾Ρῶς, *Rhos*. He adds that they are also noticed by Ibn Fossian (same period), under the name of *Rus*, as a people dwelling on the river Rha (Volga)."

³Meshech and Tubal are usually mentioned together in the O. T. Both are sons of Japheth. Meshech is thought to have been located somewhere near Armenia, in the territory of what was recently the USSR. *ISBE*, Vol. V, p3027 says, "...They are most probably the Τιβαρηνοί, *Tibarenoi*, and Μόσχοι, *Moschoi*, first mentioned in Herod. iii.94 as belonging to the 19ᵗʰ satrapy of Darius, and again (vii.78) as furnishing a contingent to the host of Xerxes. Equally obvious is their identity with the Tabali and Muski of the Assyr monuments, where the latter is mentioned as early as Tiglath-Pileser I, and the former under Shalmaneser II...."

of these are generally identified as bordering the Caspian sea. *Rosh* has been mistranslated in the King James Version because it was mistaken for the Hebrew word for *head* or *chief.* That version, as well as a few others, reads," Chief prince of Meshech and Tubal." Many have identified Rosh with Russia, while others think it is a corruption of the name of a southerly district of Persia, which does not agree with its location given in Ezekiel. Since the three are given as part of the territory of Magog it is likely that they are all northern countries in what was to become the territory of the USSR under the control of Moscow. There seems to be a correspondence between the term *Rosh* and the name *Russia,* especially in its more ancient forms. The similarity between the Greek name for Meshech (Moschoi) and Moscow may also be more than coincidental. We should mention, however, that the identities and locations of these three territories are in dispute.

Of those countries associated with Magog as allies, three are easily identified. They are Persia, Ethiopia and Libya. Persia is in the Near East, known formerly as Elam, and today as Iran. Ethiopia and Libya are both on the African continent, one south of Egypt and the other west of Egypt. Gomer and Togarmah are not so easily identified. Gomer is thought to have been a tribe of barbaric Aryans originally located in what we know as southern Russia, but in the seventh century B. C migrated to Cappadocia in Asia Minor.[4] Togarmah is thought to be Armenia. It is probably true that Magog with its three nations are identified with Russia, while the five allies mentioned are situated both in Asia and Africa.

Magog, then, is made up of Rosh, Meshech, and Tubal. The allies that are named are Persia, Ethiopia, Libya, Gomer, and Togarmah.

---

[4]*ISBE*, Vol. II, p1276. The first article on GOMER states, "The name evidently designates the people called Gimirrâ by the Assyrians, Kimmerians by the Greeks. They were a barbaric horde of Aryans who in the 7th cent. B.C. left their abode in what is now Southern Russia and poured through the Caucasus into Western Asia, causing serious trouble to the Assyrians and other nations. One division moved eastward toward Media, another westward, where they conquered Cappadocia and made it their special abode.... The Armenian name for Cappadocia, Gamir, has come from this people."

II. THE IDENTITY OF THE SEVENTH HEAD?

The information given above also helps us identify the seventh head, since the eighth is of the seven. Magog was no part of the first six heads since it was outside the territories conquered by them. It must, therefore, be the seventh and eighth. The seventh head was to continue a short time. This is not talking about the kingdom itself, but the kingdom in its role as a persecutor of God's people. Communist Russia was an avowed enemy of God and the worshipers of God, both Jews and Christians. Many more Christians lost their lives during the short reign (approximately 70 - 75 years) of Communist Russia than in the first three centuries of the church's existence.

World communism, led by Moscow, has had a profound effect upon the world. Its false philosophy, which was followed with the fervor of a religion, was secular humanism. The theory of evolution served as a basis for its atheism as well as for the existential philosophy, secular humanism, socialist economic theory, and communist political theory. These philosophies captured the hearts of the academic and social world, and turned untold millions away from faith in God and His Son Jesus. The territory of the Communist empire spread to two-thirds of the world's surface. There are still nations which are governed by Communism although Russia itself, and all its satellites, have abandoned Communism.

Russia's Communist Empire meets all the logical criteria for one of the heads of the beast: 1) it arose outside the territory of the previous empires, as did each head in order; 2) as each in turn incorporated much of the territory of its predecessor, so did the USSR; 3) like each previous head, the Communist Empire became larger than all its predecessors; 4) like all the others, it became a world power; and 5) it was engaged in persecuting God's people, an avowed enemy of God and Christians.

I would presume too much to say that this is without a doubt the seventh and eighth heads, although it seems to me to be the logical candidate for the job as well as being located in the right region. The first six are more easily identified, and with greater certainty.

To say that the eighth head is the seventh returning after 1000 years in the abyss does not necessarily mean that it will return in the same form. In other words, it may or may not be a revival of the communist political system. The only necessary characteristic of the eighth head is the location of the country involved, and its overt opposition to God, His word, and His people. Almost certainly there will be a revival of the godless philosophies and teachings which drove communism, whether it be communism itself, or of some other godless ideology. Communism was set against the materialism of the world. Since the eighth head destroys the Harlot who personifies worldly materialism, perhaps at least that aspect of Communism will be renewed.

The False Prophet has truly been at work in this world. If world communism is indeed the seventh head, we can point to the fact that the false philosophies and the false science it espoused are the very ones that have caught the imagination of the world as a whole, and which the world as a whole has accepted as true. Through these they have declared both the Bible and Christianity, and even faith as a whole, to be dead issues. This allows them to live as if there is no God to whom they must give an account.

The idea that truth is relative and that morals are relative is a very popular view which allows men to justify themselves in anything they want to do. The false teachings of secular humanism, which exalts man to the position of god, have gone a long way toward destroying the influence of the church and the word of God. In the world as a whole these two witnesses are considered dead, and the world rejoices over the fact. But the witnesses will not stay dead. They will rise again, and we will see the kingdom of the world become the kingdom of our Lord and of His Christ. It is a matter of opinion as to whether Christianity is as dead as it will ever be, or if we may already be seeing signs of stirring to renewed life. I favor the latter view.

III. The Seventh Head Emerges As an Eighth Power

With the revival of the witnesses the Beast as the seventh head will go into the Abyss—i.e., the Beast will no longer be operative in this world, using nations to fight against the saints. The binding of Satan, an act of God, is what brings this about. The Beast will emerge as an eighth power following the reign of righteousness and will attempt to renew his war against the saints. Satan, who will go into the abyss, along with the Beast and False Prophet, will also emerge along with the Beast and False Prophet. In fact, if

Satan is in the abyss so that his activities are curtailed, the Beast and False Prophet are necessarily there also, because their works of persecution and deceit are the activities of Satan.

When the Beast comes up from the abyss God will put it into the mind of the Beast and the kingdoms which give their authority to the Beast to destroy the Scarlet Woman, the Harlot, the great city known as Sodom, Egypt, Babylon the Great, and Rome. In doing this they will be carrying out God's purposes rather than Satan's (Rev. 17:16-17).

Then they will focus their attention on fulfilling Satan's purpose of destroying God's people. They will vainly attempt to overthrow the Lamb (17:14). Then the end will come quickly. As soon as the armies march from Armageddon and surround the camp of the saints, fire comes from heaven and consumes the kings and armies of the nations. Then the Devil, the Beast and False Prophet are all taken and cast into the lake of fire.

TABLES

BIBLIOGRAPHY

Bibles

Unless otherwise noted all quotations in this book are from the New King James Version. Following are all Bibles referenced or quoted in this work.

The Holy Bible, New Kings James Version (NKJV), Thomas Nelson, Inc., 1982

New Revised Standard Version Bible (NRSV), Division of Christian Education of the National Council of the Churches of Christ in the United States of America, 1989.

The Holy Bible, New International Version (NIV), International Bible Society, 1984

The Holy Bible, American Standard Version (ASV), Electronic Edition STEP Files, Parsons Technology, Inc., Cedar Rapids, IA, 1998.

The Holy Bible, Darby's New Translation, Electronic Edition STEP Files, Parsons Technology, Inc., Cedar Rapids, IA, 1998.

The Holy Bible, International Standard Version, The Learn Foundation, Santa Ana, CA., 1999.

The Holy Bible, King James Version (KJV or AV), Electronic Edition STEP Files, Parsons Technology, Inc., Cedar Rapids, IA,1998.

Young's Literal Translation of the Bible, Electronic Edition STEP Files, Parsons Technology, Inc., Cedar Rapids, IA, 1998.

Hebrew and Greek Texts of the Bible

The Hebrew Bible, Massoretic Text, Hebrew Publishing Co., New York.

The Greek New Testament According to the Majority Text, 2nd Ed., Ed. Zane C. Hodges and Arthur L. Farstad, Thomas Nelson Inc., Nashville, 1985.

The Greek New Testament, Ed. Kurt Aland, et. al. In cooperation with the Institute for New Testament Textual Research, 2nd Ed., United Bible Societies, 1968.

Concordances

Strong's Exhaustive Concordance of the Bible, James Strong, S.T.D., LL.D., Abingdon Press, Nashville, 1986. Electronic Edition Step Files in *Quick Verse*, 1998, allowed easy access to all works using Strong's key words. It was especially useful in accessing the Hebrew and Greek definitions.

Analytical Concordance to the Bible, Robert Young, LL.D., Riverside Book and Bible House, Iowa Falls, IA. This work allows for the identification of the various Greek and Hebrew words translated with a single word or its cognate in the King James Version.

Hebrew and Greek Lexicons

Gesenius' Hebrew and Chaldee Lexicon to the Old Testament Scriptures, Translated with additions and corrections from the works of Dr. William Gesenius by Samuel Prideaux Tregelles, LL.D., Wm. B. Eerdmans Publishing Company, Grand Rapids, MI, 1846.

Brown-Driver-Briggs' Hebrew Definitions, Electronic Edition STEP Files, Parsons Technology, Inc., 1999. This work made it easy to access the Hebrew words.

James Strong, *Strong's Hebrew and Greek Dictionaries*, Electronic Edition STEP Files,1998, Parsons Technology, Inc., Cedar Rapids, Iowa, provided easy access to lexical definitions in both Hebrew and Greek. This work is keyed to *Strong's Exhaustive Concordance* numbering system, making it easy to access the word definitions in the original languages.

Thayer's Greek-English Lexicon of the New Testament, From Grimm's Wilke's *Clavis Novi Testamenti*, translated, revised, and enlarged by Joseph Henry Thayer, D.D., Baker Book House, Grand Rapids, MI, 1977. This was prepared from the edition published by T. and T. Clark, 1901. This lexicon was considered the foremost dictionary of New Testament Greek until the translation of Walter Bauer's work by Arndt and Gingrich. A work entitled *Thayer's Greek Definitions* is also published in Electronic Editions STEP Files,1999, Parson's Technology.

A Greek-English Lexicon of the New Testament and Other Early Christian Literature, A translation and adaptation of Walter Bauer's *Griechish-Deutsches Wortenbuch* by William F. Arndt and F. Wilbur Gingrich, 4th Revised and Augmented Edition, The University of Chicago Press,1952. Although I, as well as many Greek scholars, prefer Thayer's Lexicon, this work has replaced it as the foremost lexicon of New Testament Greek in the eyes of the majority of scholars.

George V. Wigram, *The Analaytical Greek Lexicon of the New Testament*, Hendrickson Publishers, Peabody, Massachusetts, 1983. This volume enables the student, with an introduction to the Greek language, to locate the tense, mood, voice, and person of verbs and the case and number of nouns and pronouns with ease.

Archeological Studies on Video

Ray Vander Laan, *That the World May Know,* Volume Five, *Faith Lessons on the Early Church,* Focus on the Family, 1999, Dist. By Zondervan Pub. House. The two cassettes in this volume present ancient archeological sites in the time of the writing of Revelation. They contain valuable insights into the history, geography, and conditions in the cities of Ephesus, Pergamum, Sardis, and Laodicea.

Other Reference Works

W. Hendriksen, Th. D., *More Than Conquerors—An Interpretation of the Book of Revelation*, Baker Book House, Grand Rapids, 1959. This is a presentation of the "philosophy of history" view of Revelation. I am particularly indebted to this commentary for insights into the interpretation of the visions of the seven seals and seven trumpets.

461

H. A. Ironside, *Lectures on the Book of Revelation,* Loizeaux Brothers, Inc., Bible Truth Depot, New York, 1932. This is a definitive commentary, supporting the "futurist" view of Revelation, particularly that of dispensational premillennialism.

Josephus—The Complete Works, Translated by William Whiston, A.M., Thomas Nelson Pubishers, 1998. This incorporates an autobiography, *The Life of Falvius Josephus,* His two main works, *The Antiquities of the Jews,* and *The Wars of the Jews,* and two lesser works, *Flavius Josephus Against Apion*, and *An Extract of Josephus*'s *Discourse to the Greeks Concerning Hades*. The most helpful sections were from *The Wars of the Jews,* Books 4-7, dealing with the siege of Jerusalem and the destruction of the city and the temple in A.D. 70.

The Rev. Alexander Hislop, *The Two Babylons,* Loizeaux Brothers, Neptune, N.J., 2nd American Ed. 1959. This volume provides insight into the development of the pagan religions, tracing their origins back to the origin of Babylon.

NRSV Harper Study Bible, Expanded and Updated—Study helps written by Harold Lindsell, PhD, Ed. Verlyn D. Verbrugge, Ph.D. The annotations in this volume have been extremely helpful in researching historical data.

A. T. Robertson, A.M., D.D., LL.D., Litt.D., W. Hersey Davis, A.M., Th.D., D.D., *A New Short Grammar of the Greek New Testament*, Harper & Brothers, 1933. This volume is my source for the Koine Greek numerals, as well as the use of Greek tenses.

H. E. Dana, Th.D., and Julius R. Mantey, Th.D., D.D., *A Manual Grammar of the Greek New Testament,* The MacMillan Company, 1948. This volume was used as a source of the use of tenses.

James Orr, M.A., D.D., Gen. Ed., *The International Standard Bible Encyclopaedia,* Wm. B. Eerdmans Pub. Co., Grand Rapids, MI, 1957. This volume is an excellent source of Biblical definitions and historical information

INDEX

-Numerals-

-A-

-B-

-C-

-S-

-T-

-V-

-W-

-Z-

Printed in the United States
57670LVS00005BA/16-42

9 781597 814751